GODS, GACHUPINES
AND
GRINGOS

A People's History of Mexico

RICHARD GRABMAN

Gods, Gachupines and Gringos
copyright ©**2008** Richard Grabman
edited by David W. Bodwell
published by

Editorial Mazatlán

David W. Bodwell, Editor and Publisher

calzada Camarón Sábalo No. 610
centro comercial Plaza Galerías, Local No. 11
fracc. El Dorado C.P. 82110
Mazatlán, Sinaloa, México
Tel: (+52 *or* 011-52 *from the U.S and Canada*) (669) 916-7899
email: mazbook@yahoo.com

U.S. office:
6919 Montgomery Blvd. NE
Albuquerque, NM 87109
Ph: (505) 349-0425

Book Design: 1106 Design
Cover and Interior Art: Joaquín Ramón Herrera / XOLAGRAFIK
Maps: Dennis Slack
Typeset in Utopia by 1106 Design

Library of Congress Control Number: 2008925693

Publisher's Cataloging-in-Publication data

Grabman, Richard.
    Gods, gachupines and gringos : a people's history of Mexico / by Richard
Grabman.
    p. cm.
    Includes index and bibliographical references.
    ISBN 978-0-9816637-0-8
1. Mexico—History. 2. Indians of Mexico. 3. Mexico—History—Wars of
Independence, 1810–1821. 4. Mexican War, 1846–1848. 5. Mexico—History—
Revolution, 1910–1920. 6. Villa, Pancho, 1878–1923. 7. United States. Army—
History—Punitive Expedition into Mexico, 1916. 8. Education—Mexico. 9.
Spain—History. I. Title.

F1226 .G78 2008
972.21 —dd22   2008925693

First Edition
10 9 8 7 6 5 4 3 2 1

Printed in the United States of America

Table of Contents

Quetzalcóatl and chaos

The Good, the Bad and the Ugly

A not-so-clean break: The Revolution, part 1

Total War: The Revolution, part 2

Introduction

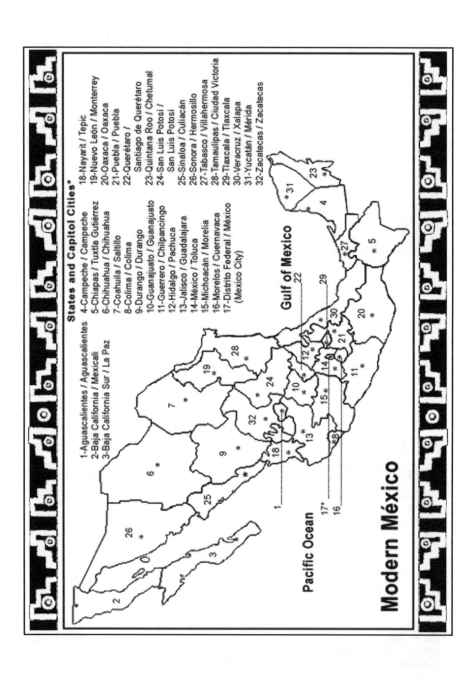

Modern México

States and Capitol Cities*

1-Aguascalientes / Aguascalientes
2-Baja California / Mexicali
3-Baja California Sur / La Paz
4-Campeche / Campeche
5-Chiapas / Tuxtla Gutiérrez
6-Chihuahua / Chihuahua
7-Coahuila / Saltillo
8-Colima / Colima
9-Durango / Durango
10-Guanajuato / Guanajuato
11-Guerrero / Chilpancingo
12-Hidalgo / Pachuca
13-Jalisco / Guadalajara
14-México / Toluca
15-Michoacán / Morelia
16-Morelos / Cuernavaca
17-Distrito Federal / México
   (Mexico City)
18-Nayarit / Tepic
19-Nuevo León / Monterrey
20-Oaxaca / Oaxaca
21-Puebla / Puebla
22-Querétaro /
   Santiago de Querétaro
23-Quintana Roo / Chetumal
24-San Luis Potosí /
   San Luis Potosí
25-Sinaloa / Culiacán
26-Sonora / Hermosillo
27-Tabasco / Villahermosa
28-Tamaulipas / Ciudad Victoria
29-Tlaxcala / Tlaxcala
30-Veracruz / Xalapa
31-Yucatán / Mérida
32-Zacatecas / Zacatecas

Gulf of Mexico

Pacific Ocean

¡Hay Pozole!

Pozole. A filling hominy and pork or chicken soup of pre-Hispanic origin. Pozole is such a popular soup that you'll see temporary signs posted at restaurants announcing hay pozole meaning "there's pozole today". Table condiments, typically served in little bowls, are oregano, chopped white onions, sliced radish, and shredded cabbage or lettuce. From each condiment bowl, diners hand-pinch the seasonings, since spoons for this are seldom provided.
Marita Adair. The Hungry Traveler: Mexico. Kansas City:
Andrews McMeel Publishing, 1997

GRADE SCHOOL HISTORIES of the United States used to describe the country as a melting pot. The idea of one people created from several different immigrant cultures suggested that the United States was unique. Of course it is. But the United States is not the only unique culture in the Americas. México has a much, much older culture—or cultures—including not only natives but immigrants from several different cultures.

Though schoolbooks in the United States now talk about multiculturalism—the idea that different groups in the United States kept or developed different customs—Mexican multiculturalism goes back several thousand years. The "mother country", Spain, is a particularly rich multicultural country. Andulusians, Basques, Catalans, Castilians and Gypsies have extremely different customs, and in some cases, languages. People often describe México as a mixture of "Indian" and Spanish culture. Today in México, there are over one hundred fifty indigenous groups, each with their own customs and language.

Mexicans are not only Indian and/or Spanish: Italian, German, French and Irish immigrants were all important in México, and that's only speaking of Europeans. Chinese immigrants started arriving in the 1580s and have had a profound impact on Mexican customs. The Philippines were once part of México and left their mark on the "mother country", México. Recent immigration from Japan and Korea is changing Mexican culture in still other ways. African slaves, West Indians, South Americans, Arabs and Eastern Europeans all made their mark.[1] There have even been immigrants from the United States.

If the United States is a melting pot as we once believed, or a "stew" with a mixture of ingredients more or less all cooked to the same consistency, as the multiculturalists tell us, México is pozole. México and the Mexicans are nearly unknown, even by their next-door neighbor, and, except superficially, so is their cuisine—even by knowledgeable neighbors. Pozole may be one of the most popular items on a Mexican menu, but it's very rare to find it in a "Mexican" restaurant outside of México.

It has meat and vegetables floating in broth; it is served in a bowl; it is eaten with a spoon. While the recipe varies from chef

---

[1] Russian Jews and Arabs both settled in Mexico City's old Merced area in the 1940s. Today it's considered a dangerous slum, but adventurous diners flock to the Merced for its unique Russian/Jewish/Arab/Mexican cuisine. Vicente Fox y Quesada, the former president, has German (by way of the U.S.) and Basque ancestors. Lázaro Cárdenas del Rio, the icon of the Mexican left and the president in the 1930s, was of Spanish and Huasteca ancestry. His son has an Aztec name, Cuauhtémoc Cárdenas. Cuauhtémoc's son Lázaro married Mayra Coffigny Pedroso, an Afro-Cuban woman. Their son, the scion of the Cárdenas dynasty, has Spanish, indigenous and African ancestry.

to chef, it includes ingredients on the side you can take or leave as you like. But it is not soup—it's served in Mexican restaurants AFTER the soup and the "dry soup" – *sopa seca* – usually a pasta course. That alone makes it a main course. Normally, it includes European introduced meats, like pork or chicken, and often European vegetables—though the main ingredients are indigenous *maíz* – corn – (or maize, as it is sometimes called) – and chiles, of course. There are some odd ingredients—lettuce or cabbage, radishes, onions, cilantro—floating on top. Is it a salad with soup underneath, or meat, vegetables, salsa and salad all in the same bowl? It is…whatever it is. Like Mexican culture, it's a unique thing, all its own.

Mexican history is sometimes as confusing to outsiders as Mexican cuisine; even sophisticated visitors often misunderstand what they see or hear or read. In a country where the past is very much part of the present—whether the corn and chiles in pozole, or the lingering resentment over the American (let alone Cortés') invasions—the misunderstandings are costly. In 2003, when the United States invaded Iraq, the U.S. government expected its neighbor and friendly ally, México (at the time, a member of the United Nations Security Council), to back the invasion. When México refused—for reasons going back ten, thirty-five, sixty, one hundred fifty and five hundred years—both countries experienced serious problems. The arguments weren't just raised by professors and professional historians. Mexicans don't consider five hundred years that long a time, nor do they consider history as something belonging only in a classroom. Whether one is trying to do business or just visiting the country, you will find Mexicans think about and react based on their history; more often than most people.

Intended for foreigners, some early readers questioned my use of *Gringos* in the title. They are under the impression that the word is an insult, which it can be, if modified by one of the plethora of Mexican swear words. Like other facets of Mexican history, the people of the United States have attempted to put their own "spin" on something they either don't understand or want to explain in their own terms. Despite the most popular story, gringo has nothing to do with the Mexican-American War or the Pershing Expedition. In that story, U.S. soldiers, wearing green uniforms were told by Mexican countrymen, "Green...go". Alas, even amateur historians need to check their facts: U.S. Army uniforms were blue in 1848, and brown in 1916.

Gringo is not a pejorative at all and dates back to medieval Spain. It is a corruption of *griego* – Greek. During the Spanish *Reconquista* – the war between the Christian northerners and the Islamic Moors – Byzantine Christians, many of whom settled in Spain after the fall of Constantinople in 1453, were generically referred to as *grecos* – Greeks – and were allies of the Western, Christian Spaniards (the most Spanish of all Spanish artists, El Greco, was born Doménicos Theotokópoulos. He could have easily been known to us as El Gringo.) Gringos are outsiders; foreigners who may have some odd customs and practices (in Chile, a gringo is a Portuguese-speaking Brazilian), but they are not necessarily *invasores* – invaders – as United States citizens are sometimes called.[2] Throughout this book I have used gringo as it is used in México—any non-Spanish-speaking foreigner. In México, I refer to myself as gringo without hesitation. I used gringo throughout this book in the neutral sense of any foreigner.

Gachupín, which is pejorative, has a specific meaning. Originally a Náhuatl word referring to the spur on a fighting cock—by analogy, applied to the spurs a horseman wears—it became a rude term for the Spanish overlords: originally the only people who could ride

---

[2] In México, "gringos" are not exclusively from the United States. British, Germans, Scandinavians, Australians and even Canadians, are gringos. French-Canadians are also "gringos", despite the efforts of a few "culturally correct" people to claim that Québec is part of "Latinoamerica". After all, Québec, like Haiti, speaks French, which is a language based on Latin, and like the Spanish and Portuguese speaking countries, it is primarily Roman Catholic. But it is not a country, and Québecois remain gringos. "Hispanic" (*hispánico* in Spanish) means Spanish to a Latino. Where Canadians often take pains to learn to say *¡No soy gringo, soy canadiense!*, Mexican visitors in the United States learn to carefully say, "I am not Hispanic, I'm Mexican". In both cases, the speaker is likely to be met with an indifferent shrug.

a horse, and who wore spurs. It is still used to mean an overbearing, foreign, Spanish-speaking twit, especially a Spaniard, and I use it in that sense.

It's a shame, in some ways, that I have to explain two simple words, let alone write an entire history of a country about which we should know more. Mexicans are known for their extreme good manners and are sometimes loathe to contradict even basic misunderstandings for fear of showing bad manners. We gringos are often forgiven our lapses in manners, but if we live in México, we learn to at least say *por favor* and *gracias* and to say a proper *bendición* – "grace" – before digging into our bowl of pozole.

...la Bendición de la mesa

I NEVER INTENDED A MOVABLE feast of pozole, but I ended up adding bits and pieces to what was originally a quick 'n easy guide to Mexican history for students and business travelers when I sat down and banged out a draft back in Houston over the summer of 2001.

At the time, I was a technical writer. After Y2K, the market for tech writers had more or less collapsed...besides, I had written "Press any key to continue" more times than was good for me. Living in a Mexican-American and Mexican immigrant neighborhood, I had a serious fixation on the culture, and—during the days when tech writers made very good money—could think of nothing better to spend it on than cheap flights and bus trips back and forth to México.

A friend of mine was along on one trip to Mexico City, where he asked if the Templo Mayor was an Inca temple. On the same trip, I overheard two American tourists looking at the Palacio Nacional and speculating about which balcony was used by Eva Perón. The Incas, who had a mighty civilization in their own right, and Ms. Perón are both fascinating subjects and worth reading about, but neither has much to do with México...or come from anywhere near México.

Mexicans take their history very seriously, and these kinds of faux pas could scotch a business deal or ruin a grade point average. So I began obsessing over the Mexican history of México, undoubtedly to the amusement of Steve Leger, John Kirsch, David Lamaroux, Dan Goldberg, Willie Luna and others who had to put up with my odd compulsions.

Having moved to México in August 2001, ostensibly to finish the book, I took a job teaching English in a Cuernavaca school while looking for something saner than teaching junior high school kids. I was in Cuernavaca during the 9/11 attacks, which, we are told, "changed everything". One thing it changed was the direction of this book.

U.S. and Mexican media reports on the follow-up (and subsequent invasions of Afghanistan and Iraq) were wildly at odds with each other—often for historical reasons. The impact of foreign events—and foreigners—on México was added to the mix. Just living in México, mostly in Mexico City, I learned more and more—most of it true.

I am grateful, in an odd way, to both Mel Gibson and a Naucalpan con man claiming to be an Australian attorney working for the Mexican government while regaling me with history—true and false—in a futile attempt to sell me a "discount" plane ticket. Chris Jones' versions of Mexican history in general and Gibson's of Mayan history in particular, spurred me to carefully fact-check my research.

Sorting out the nuggets of truth from his lies uncovered some of the more colorful bits and pieces that are floating around this pozole of a book. Dr. Enrique Krauze and the late José Manuel Nava generously shared their vast knowledge of Mexican history and culture, as did waitresses, neighbors, fellow passengers on buses, tour guides, road signs, newspapers, TV reporters, street vendors, soldiers and taxi drivers. It seems as if everyone I met in México added more ingredients. Señor Salvador of Saltillo, taxi driver José Mondragón and the nice Zapatista lady I met in Oaxaca stand out among the many, many chance encounters with people whose names I often never learned, but who contributed key ingredients to this book.

Among my English students, Ing. Rafael Morfín and Lic. Octavio Contreras were the best at contributing useful information. Other English teachers, among them Victoria Martínez, Araceli García García and Mari Inés Lozado made suggestions, as did Elaine Prince. Gordon Jardine provided employment as long as possible. Eva Perra (*más o menos* a collie, but she was, like her namesake, a charming blonde of uncertain parentage from the streets of a Latin American city) and Itzaccihuatl the poodle kept me company.

The book itself was neglected, though I started writing regularly on Mexican and foreign affairs for my website. My editor and publisher David Bodwell, stubborn as a mule and with the patience of a burro, pushed, pleaded and prodded me to finish the book. Living in an isolated corner of west Texas, I appreciated correspondence with Dr. Ted Vincent of Florida; Glenn Williford of Chihuahua; Linda Keelan of Boulder, Colorado; Delbert Gilbow in far-west Texas; John Todd Jr. in Veracruz; and Scott Parks in Jalisco about various matters that had been overlooked or needed revision. Lee Strong, the former editor of the Rochester (New York) *Catholic Courier* gave his imprimatur to my reading of recent Church history.

I also discovered that we gringos can be rather prickly about "our" México. The moderator of a message board dealing with the Mexican Revolution was incensed that I don't see Pancho Villa as the beginning and end of that important (and confusing) era. An Ohio doctor querulously complained about my attitude towards certain European royals, and a distant descendant of Ulysses S. Grant registered a mild complaint about a joke in a footnote. I removed the joke, but for the others, what can I say but that I like a lot of salsa in my pozole, which may not be to everyone's taste.

Finishing the book while in the Texas-México borderlands, I have been fortunate to have access to the Alpine Public Library, where Anitra Clausen has been particularly helpful. The El Paso Community College and University of Texas online resources have been invaluable. Thanks are also due to Robert Halpern, publisher of the Marfa, Texas *Big Bend Sentinel*; Allyson Santucci and her staff and customers at La Trattoria Cafe (providing a literary atmosphere and decent coffee); José Aguayo (formerly with the *Mexico City Times*) and Los Pocolocos, all from Alpine, Texas. Mary Grabman of Burlington, North Carolina did what moms do best and provided encouragement and preliminary critical reading.

With Mexican history, as with Mexican cuisine, it's sometimes best not to inquire about the actual ingredients too closely. It's the end product that counts. If I'm a little heavy on the salsa or the rambling anecdotes, at least I can present something colorful and palatable.

¡Buen provecho!

Pre-Conquest

Pre-Conquest Mesoamerica

Sites mentioned and the modern state they are in.

1-Aguascalientes (Aguascalientes)
2-San Lorenzo (Tabasco)
3-La Venta (Tabasco)
4-Monte Albán (Oaxaca)
5-El Tajín (Veracruz)
6-Cholula (Puebla)
7-Xochicalco (Morelos)
8-Cancún (Quintana Roo)
9-Chichén Itzá (Yucatán)
10-Tula (Hidalgo)
11-Tlaxcala (Tlaxcala)
12-Isthmus of Tehuantepec

Valle de México
(greater Mexico City, includes Distrito Federal and parts of the Estado de México)

Teotihuacán (Estado de México)
Chapultepec (D.F.)
Culhuacán (D.F.)
Tenochtitlán (D.F.)
Xochimilco (D.F.)
Toluca (Estado de México)
Texcoco (Estado de México)
Tacuba (D.F.)
Tlatelolco (D.F.)

Gulf of Mexico

Pacific Ocean

Mayans

Olmecs

Totonacs

Mixtecs / Zapotecs

Toltecs / Aztecs

Valle de México

Ten thousand years (more or less) in a few paragraphs...

ONE CHARGE ALWAYS MADE against the Spanish conquistadors was that they burned the Aztec records and tried to wipe out all traces of the older civilization. People forget that the Aztecs did exactly the same thing when they took control of central México ninety years earlier. The surviving records of previous cultures suggest that every new ruler destroyed the defeated people's historical records and monuments. The Aztecs were recent arrivals in an ancient country themselves. Much of what is known about the civilizations and nations that existed before the Aztec conquest is based on pure guesswork. Many of the older nations still existed (the Aztecs expected obedience but only had interest in local cultures when they threatened Aztec rule), but their own customs and records were either destroyed or mixed with those of the later Aztec and Spanish conquerors. What's left is guesswork.

A good example is the Totonac *Voladores* – flyers. These people still perform a ritual going back at least six hundred years, though no one is quite sure what the ritual originally meant. The voladores climb a twelve-meter (thirty-nine foot) pole with a platform at the top. The leader plays a drum and a flute. Four other men tie themselves to long ropes wrapped tightly around the top of the pole, push off and slowly spin to the ground. The best guess is that they once worshipped the sun and are honoring the four compass directions. Why, or what the worship signified, is long forgotten. The ritual only survived because the early Christian missionaries thought it was a harmless sporting event, and the Totonacs, upon becoming Christians, turned the ritual into one honoring the Virgin Mary.

Furthermore, while people always knew there were ancient cultures throughout México, archaeology only became a serious science in the late 1800s, and many ancient records had been destroyed by the time scientists came upon them. Scientific discovery of the pre-Aztec world ran backwards; the older the civilization, the later scientists were in finding any traces of it. Many civilizations were only discovered by complete accident. Workers laying a new water main in Aguascalientes stumbled across a completely unknown civilization in 2001.

One of the most important early Mayan sites was only "discovered" (the local Mayans knew it was there all along) during World War II. The discoverer had a slight problem—he had deserted from the United States Army during wartime and faced arrest (and possible execution) if the gringo authorities discovered his hiding place.

What little is known about the Olmec civilization is largely guesswork. Stones are the only things that survive more than a few years in the highly acidic jungle soil, so what the Olmecs thought, what they ate, how they lived, even what they looked like is based on the few monuments that have been found by oil exploration crews...or stumbled upon accidentally.

As best we know, early México's history goes something like this. Ancient humans living in Siberia arrived in Alaska sometime during the ice age, and these people slowly spread throughout the Americas. In México the ancient nomads found a place to settle between 40,000 BCE and 5,000 BCE. The tropical mountains supported a rich plant and animal life—people could stay in one place and get enough to eat. At lower altitudes, México is tropical;

wild fruit, fish and tropical meat animals like tapir and iguana are abundant. The higher altitudes are temperate. In the volcanic lakes around modern Mexico City there was a rich supply of fish and shellfish, there were birds as well and larger animals like deer. Furthermore, there was a wonderful plant with edible seeds. Corn grew wild, and an ancient genius discovered that throwing the seeds in the ground meant the plant would grow where you wanted it. Another genius discovered you could dry the seeds to throw in the ground later, and still another genius discovered that the seeds could be put in the fire to taste better and yet another genius discovered that soaking the seeds in lime water softened the hulls, making it suitable for making tastier foods like tacos, tamales and tortillas. With agriculture, people were able to settle in communities.

Although the discovery of agriculture happened slightly later in ancient America[3] than in the Middle East (where wheat was the plant that made settlement possible) or China (where rice filled the same role), the result was the same. A dependable food supply changed the way humans lived. People could think about something other than where their next meal was coming from. They had something to defend, and the man who controlled more food was rich, the man with no food, poor. No one person could do everything necessary to supply all the food, so people began to live in groups. Once they started living together, people discovered the advantages of dividing up work. When they learned to cook, someone had to make utensils. Corn and beans (and later chiles, tomatoes and other crops) weren't the only food, and somebody had to hunt while others grew corn and still others guarded the cornfields and defended food from marauding nomads. Agricultural settlements made other changes necessary. You had to have some way of knowing when you needed to put the seeds in the ground and how many seeds you had. You needed a way to keep records—a

---

[3] 7000–1500 BCE

writing and a number system—and keep track of the change of seasons—a calendar—and somebody had to be in charge.

While human civilizations started the same way everywhere, there were a few differences in México. Other ancient peoples had sheep, goats, pigs, horses, camels, reindeer, yaks or water buffalo. Outside of the Andes in South America, where there are *llamas* – a small relative of the camel – there are no American animals suitable for domestication. The horses in America were tiny animals (a little bigger than a modern cat) and had died out before humans settled in any large numbers. The wild horses and cattle of America are descended from herds brought by the Spanish and other European immigrants. The closest American relatives to the animals domesticated in other cultures are the bison – American buffalo – and bighorn sheep. Both were too wild to be captured and tamed. The only domestic animals in México before the Spaniards arrived were small dogs, turkeys and ducks.

There's a common myth that the ancient Mexicans never learned to use the wheel. They had wheels, but with no animals big enough to pull a cart the only use people had for wheels was to make children's toys. They could have built human-powered carts, but the mountainous terrain made it more practical to simply carry things than to pull them.

At some point, civilizations as complex as any elsewhere in the world flourished in México, but we know very little about their development. By 1000 BCE, archaeologists speculate there were probably one hundred thousand people in México, but the number is simply an educated guess, and open to revision as more information becomes available.

Or maybe they came from Mars...

THE OLMECS, THE EARLIEST PEOPLE we know enough about to even make guesses, had a long history, stretching from 1500 BCE to 400 BCE. They had calendars and a written language, but little is known about their language, and not enough is known yet about these people. Some Olmec sculptures show people whom 19th-century writers decided looked like Africans. So, based on just a handful of sculptures, these writers came up with complex theories of African settlement in eastern México. That many people in modern eastern México have some African ancestry made the theory seem plausible. These writers either forgot, or didn't know, that African slaves and West Indian immigrants (Cubans, Dominicans, Haitians and others) had made African ancestry common in this part of México.

Later archaeologists discovered a handful of Olmec sculptures that showed people wearing helmets of some kind. They look something like 1920s football helmets, but more than one commentator decided they were space helmets, and that the Olmecs came from another planet. What these outer-space enthusiasts would make of later Olmec findings—sculptures showing hunchbacks, half jaguar-half human figures, men with beards and what look like old ladies—would be interesting to hear. Perhaps the Olmecs worshipped dwarfs. Or maybe they had a dwarf who was a leader. Did they believe in wer-jaguars? Who knows?[4]

The Olmecs were an American people, and the African and outer-space theories are now seen as naïve explanations by early Europeans who couldn't fathom that the Americas could have ancient cultures too. By 1200 BCE they had cities (at San Lorenzo and La Venta, both in Tabasco State) that included the oldest pyramids we know of in the Americas. These early pyramids were earthen mounds and little is known about them. The idea that the pyramids were somehow connected to volcano worship (or that the people built volcano-shaped mounds to hold their gods) makes as much sense as any other theory.

Sometime about 315 BCE, La Venta was purposely vandalized. Whoever wrecked the place went to a lot of work. The only way some of the giant heads could have been smashed together was using cranes to lift one and swing it against the other...or so it appears.

Whatever brought down the Olmec cities—drought, invaders, disease, volcanic eruption—they had spread their culture throughout southern México by the time La Venta was destroyed. Other early peoples, those from Monte Albán (ruins), outside Oaxaca, and the Zapotec people of our own time, who live in the same area, have similar art. Because Monte Albán's development overlaps that of the Olmecs, the obvious conclusion is that Monte Albán was either an Olmec colony or was influenced by the Olmecs. More is known about the Monte Albán people—we have gold and stone jewelry and funeral ornaments from Monte Albán—but they too are a mystery to us. The Zapotecs are well known; surviving as a unique culture up to the present time.

It would be as much a mistake to assume modern Zapotec culture is the same as Olmec culture as it would be to assume people

---

[4] A sculpture that apparently shows two men having oral sex has led to long scholarly articles "proving" that gay men were part of ancient American society...or that this was a taboo activity. For all we know, maybe there were ancient porn shops.

in today's Cairo are the same as the ancient Egyptians, or that Saddam Hussein acted the same way Nebuchadnezzar would. Still, the Zapotecs are the only link with a now unknowable past.

The Olmecs were coastal people, living in cities. The Zapotecs are mountaineers, living in villages. They are fiercely independent (even the Aztecs were somewhat afraid of them). When the Spaniards first tried to collect taxes from the Zapotecs, one source says they ate the taxmen, then asked the Spaniards to send fat bureaucrats the next time! An unusual aspect of the Zapotecs is that some of them have a matriarchal culture—you inherit your name and property from your mother, and women are the economic and political leaders.[5]

---

[5] A lot of nonsense has been written by casual visitors to Oaxaca about the "gay friendly" Zapotecs. There's no reason a matriarchy can't be sexist. Zapotec men are often shy and unassuming and the women often aggressive. It wasn't so long ago that women who wanted a business career in the United States or Europe wore masculine clothing. Zapotec men wanting to compete against the "female chauvinist" Zapotecs have to be tough enough to wear a dress.

The rise and fall and rise and fall...

D URING THE CLASSICAL ERA (200 BCE–1000 CE), several different central Mexican cultures came and went. These different city-states had much in common. Their leaders all promoted order and strict regimentation. Because these were large and growing communities, farming was important. Guessing the seasons wasn't good enough for large-scale agriculture, so exact calendars were required. It was during this time that the Mayans (and others) invented the "0" – zero – for calculations—long before it was known in India—much, much earlier than the zero reached Europe. These cultures were all centered on cities (as México is today), they all worshipped Quetzalcóatl as the chief god and they were all fanatical "basketball" fans.

Each Mexican culture seems to have had its own version of *ulama* – the ancient Mesoamerican form of basketball. Having discovered rubber, they found a good use for it: a seven or eight inch solid rubber ball had to be bounced off a player's hip through a ring on the wall. Not an easy task.

Depending on the people and their customs, this was a pretty serious sport. Some teams sacrificed the losing coach. At least one city had a rule that IF someone made a basket, the spectators had to strip naked and the winning team got to keep everybody's clothes. Ulama is still played, under kinder, gentler rules (no one gets sacrificed to the gods, though players often limp away badly bruised), in a few places in México today.

Teotihuacán, the most important of the classical cities, had a population of around one hundred thousand at its height. It appears to have been the capital of some kind of empire but fell to barbarians (or was abandoned) around 750 CE. It had three satellite cities (which could have been provincial capitals): El Tajin in Veracruz State (the ruins include an especially impressive ulama court), Cholula in Puebla (where Cortés massacred the local population) and Xochicalco in Morelos State. Xochicalco was an unusual city in that it showed Mayan influence and was fortified.

The Mayans

THE MAYA PEOPLES—speaking over thirty different languages, following different customs and living in different environments (highlands and tropical jungles)—until very recently, were considered peripheral to Mexican history. One of the better known Mexican histories in English devotes barely a paragraph to the Mayan civilization.

México has been more or less synonymous with the Náhuatl-speaking, or Náhuatl-dominated, peoples north of the Isthmus of Tehuantepec. The Maya territories stretch from Honduras to parts of Tabasco (south of the Isthmus) and include the Yucatán peninsula. Until the late 19th century, the connection between the present-day Mayas and the culture that built temple cities wasn't clear (early researchers speculated the temples had been built by Welsh or Chinese visitors...or the "lost tribes of Israel"). The Mayan peoples in México (Mexican control over most Mayan territory ended soon after independence when the Central American states seceded) only merited Mexican attention when they rebelled—which they did regularly: Yucatecas staged violent uprisings and almost succeeding in taking over the peninsula in 1847 and 1860. Chiapas witnessed Tzeltal uprisings in 1712 and 1868. Recently, there has been a well-known Maya resistance movement, the

Ejército Zapatista de Liberación Nacional (*EZLN*) – Zapatista Army of National Liberation – occupying large parts of Chiapas since 1994. Several Maya groups within México did not even recognize the authority of the state until the 1920s; the Lacandón—who are forest dwellers—not doing so until the 1970s.

It was only with the Mexican Revolution of the early 20th century and with the recent spectacular growth of tourism on the Yucatán peninsula (Quintana Roo—whose largest city is Cancún—has only been a state since 1974) that Mayan political and economic needs and aspirations were recognized.

It was the Maya that absorbed the first contact with the Europeans. Christopher Columbus mentioned meeting a "merchant of the province of Maia" in the Gulf of Honduras in 1502. It was Yucateca Mayan gold objects that first fired Cortés' interest in México, and it was Maya who fought the first battles against the Spanish invaders.

The ancestors of today's Maya—who probably all spoke the same language—lived for the most part in small villages governed by hereditary elders and practiced slash-and-burn agriculture.[6]

These farming communities apparently traded jade and salt with the Olmecs and eventually came under Olmec influence after 1000 BCE. Absorbing ideas from other cultures (very possibly including the Chinese[7]), the Maya were building temples and had a complex political system under the rule of kings by around 300 BCE.

The early Maya cities were not cities in our sense of the word but more shopping malls with a palace and temple complex. The king and his retainers might live in the city, but the people themselves

---

[6] Jungle soil, even in the highlands, is not rich enough to support long-term farming; by slashing down forests and burning the brush, farmers are able to create enough soil to grow crops for a few seasons before they need to abandon their fields and start the process over in another forested area.

[7] Recent scholars point out that the Chinese were capable of sailing across the Pacific. Both the Chinese and Maya used the exact same mathematical calculations for astronomical calculations, and certain later cultural features of the Maya are strikingly similar to those of the Chinese.

continued to live in outlying villages. The world's first suburban commuters, the Maya only came into these cities to worship, trade and shop (maybe to pay their taxes—we still know very little about the ancient Maya).

The small Maya kingdoms gradually came under the control—economic or direct—of more northern peoples. Teotihuacán, just outside Mexico City, was the center of an "empire" that included the Maya region—something the Aztecs were never able to accomplish.

Although the Maya had been building pyramids since about 1 CE; after 350 CE, architectural monument building accelerated. The cities grew, eventually becoming places to live as well as shop. Mayan culture reached its zenith from about 400 CE through 900 CE. The Mayan Classical Period was one of high sophistication, shown not only by their unique art (the Mayans were one of the few peoples who depicted people's individual features) but also by their advanced literary culture. We are only now beginning to decipher their texts, only a handful of which survived the Conquest.

How widespread Mayan literacy was is a matter of conjecture. We know children were educated and boys lived apart from their families in some kind of boarding school, but whether this included all boys, or only the sons of the elite is unknown, as is just what they were taught.

The Mayan economy was based on trade and agriculture—cacao, cotton, salt and jade were the main exports. Like the Chinese, the Mexicans (both the Náhuatl-speaking northerners and the Maya) buried their dead with a small jade chip in their mouths.

Mayan cities sprang up, often under Náhuatl rulers (Chichén Itzá's *Castillo* – castle – a very late Maya construction, commemorates a Toltec conqueror, Kukulkan – the Maya version of Quetzalcóatl). People actually lived in the cities, and the culture flourished...then collapsed about 900 CE.

Why? Internal dissention or a rebellion against foreign influences is unlikely. The Maya did—and still do—absorb outside ideas. A more likely culprit was environmental collapse. Most likely, the population had outgrown the amount of food that could be produced by slash-and-burn agriculture, and starvation led to political and economic collapse.

While a few small Maya kingdoms and vastly reduced cities continued to exist as late as the 1600s, the people themselves went back to their roots as village-dwelling farmers, and for the most part, remain so today.

Having always absorbed other cultural influences, but on their own terms, Mayans have maintained their identity as a unique people. Separated culturally (until recently politically, also) from the mainstream Mexican culture, the Maya are more likely to be Protestants in a Catholic country, or to practice their own religion with or without Christian influence. One large Maya community's religion includes shamans who guard statues of Christian saints and worship Jesus – the Sun God – and Mary – the Moon. The three hundred or so Lacandón are Fundamentalist Christians, at least in theory.

With many Maya now forced to work outside their own communities, Mayans regularly commute (for years at a time) to jobs as far away as North Carolina. In the last few years, entire Mayan communities have also emigrated outside their traditional homelands, settling in Puebla and Zacatecas States, and in Mexico City.

The Invasion of the Sons of Bitches

THE MEXICAN DARK AGES (750 CE–1000 CE) were slightly later than the European Dark Ages (476 CE–1000 CE), but they were much the same. Barbarian invasions swept down from the north, and as in Europe, people retreated behind fortified walls and put themselves under the power of local warlords. The barbarians more or less adapted the civilized customs of their new homes and fell to other, less civilized barbarians, who eventually learned to behave and were, in turn, overthrown.

In Europe, the barbarians had been Germans and Vikings, although people had more colorful names for them. The Náhuatl-speaking Mexicans called their invaders *Chichimecas* – literally, "sons of bitches". During the post-classical era, Mesoamerican civilizations tended to be militaristic states depending on tribute from subject peoples: just the same as early France, England and other European states. The meanest sons of bitches around were the Mexica, the people we know as the Aztecs.[8] According to their own legends, they had wandered in the desert for a number of years,

---

[8] The Mexica never called themselves Aztecs. The people came to be known as "Aztecs" because of a mistaken translation by a French scholar. Since the city, country and its citizens are already named for the Mexicas, calling this particular group the Aztecs makes things simpler.

following a hummingbird. The hummingbird had told them of a promised land—an island where they would find an eagle sitting on a nopal cactus eating a snake. Early Christian missionaries were fascinated by the legend—it had too many parallels to the story of the Jews wandering in the desert, following a "pillar of smoke by day and fire by night". More than one Catholic writer concluded the Aztecs were the lost tribe of Israel.[9]

After 1100 CE, Aztecs began arriving in central México, and like the Germans in the late Roman Empire, hired themselves out as mercenaries. Where the Germans looked to Rome for clues as to how to become a civilized people, and the Romans to the Greeks, the Aztecs looked to the Toltecs. To the Aztecs, Tula (destroyed in 1168 CE), the capital of the Toltecs, was their Rome and their Athens. By 1250 CE, the half-civilized mercenaries were settled around Chapultepec (in present-day Mexico City). In 1300 CE, they were enslaved by Culhuacán (yet another city-state in the area) but collectively earned their freedom, not by building pyramids (though they probably did their share of that), but—again like the Jews—by escaping across a body of water to the promised land—Tenochtitlán. More practically, they were rewarded for destroying Xochimilco (bringing back the Xochimilcans' ears as proof). Keeping up their reputation as sons of bitches, the Aztecs destroyed Culhaucán in 1325 CE. They slowly acquired control of other communities; only by about 1460 CE did they control most of modern México.

The Aztecs were never an empire in the way Europeans use the term, but the image has stuck. They were a powerful city-state with rulers chosen from one large family (the same way the Saudi Arabian leadership is selected), but they were never the majority. It's simply because they were the power when Cortés arrived that we think all indigenous Mexicans are Aztecs. As with the later Europeans, they adopted the older culture as much as they affected

---

[9] In the 17th century, a German writer came to the same conclusion about the Incas, based on the fact that both Incas and Jews were circumcised. Mormonism was founded on the belief that indigenous Americans were the lost tribes of Israel.

it. Their power was more like a modern superpower's—they used a combination of diplomatic effort, economic dominance and military threat to maintain control.

Rewriting history was part of the control strategy. Rather than dirty, nomadic barbarians, they made themselves the heirs of Toluca...and Toluca the lost city of all learning and elegance.

Toluca was probably not quite as learned and elegant as the Aztec stories said—everyday life was probably much the same as it was in Tenochtitlán—and whomever it was that the Tolucans looked to as their founding fathers probably had day-to-day lives much the same. Things change, but in México daily life did—and still does in many ways—follow the same patterns.

The Aztecs

ALTHOUGH THE NATIVE PEOPLES lacked some of the technology of the Europeans they were by no means primitive. Because they believed that the main purpose of war was to take captives, their war technology was limited to spears and obsidian swords. Obsidian is volcanic rock; easy to obtain, it took the place of glass for things like mirrors. They had the tools and know-how to work metals (and they mined metals) but used most metals for ornaments and artwork rather than tools. Not having coins didn't mean there wasn't a complex economic system. Cacao beans (drinking chocolate was for the very rich—sort of like lighting a cigar with a one-hundred-dollar bill), feathers and even flowers were currency.[10] They had a complex market system. While men dominated business, women ran the markets. Then, as now, shops selling similar goods would be on the same street. Today in Mexico City, businesses along a single street still specialize in one product: a street for office supplies, another for self-service copies and camera equipment, another for eyewear and optical

---

[10] The concept of currency that represented goods and services, without any particular value in itself, didn't gain much acceptance elsewhere until the 1930s. As far as I know, John Maynard Keynes never studied the Aztec economy, though Keynes and the Aztecs had the same monetary policy.

examinations, and yet another street for wedding dresses. *Calle* Miguel Schultz has funeral parlors.

Women had more rights than in Europe. Women did not need their husband's approval (or anyone else's) to either go into business or to go to court. The legal system was harsh by our standards but included some modern features. For minor offenses, the Aztec judges sentenced criminals to the street-cleaning brigade rather than jail time, a sort of early work-release program. Public intoxication was an extremely serious crime, although first offenders generally got work release.

Indigenous Americans may have a genetic inability to handle alcohol, and alcoholism is still a serious problem among their descendants. The Aztecs either recognized this or feared that Tezcatlipoca would take advantage of drunks. Tezcatlipoca didn't seem to bother the old—grandparents could get as drunk as they wanted, at any time they wanted, with impunity. For everyone else, public intoxication was an extremely serious crime. A second offense merited the death penalty. First offenders were lucky to get off paying a fine and working on the street-cleaning crew. Aztec justice was somewhat balanced, ruling class offenders were punished much more harshly than ordinary people were. If a judge was found guilty of taking bribes; he was tortured and then executed.

When the Spaniards arrived, Tenochtitlán, the original Mexico City, was larger and better organized than any European city. When the Aztecs had fled their captors in 1325, Tenochtitlán was a barren island in the middle of Lake Texcoco. It provided protection, and the Aztecs could survive by selling island products to the mainland. Their warriors hired out as mercenaries and quickly became a power in the region.

The upper-class rulers liked to claim their ancestors toughened up by living on snakes and cactus. They didn't give enough credit to their inventive farmers who developed a unique way of growing crops on a barren island. *Chinapas* – giant rafts filled with soil – were built on the lake to grow corn, beans, chiles and vegetables. People in the cities generally ate well, even though meat was a luxury. They did have turkey, duck and fish (ducks were raised in pens along the lakeshore, and the Aztec farmers built dikes for fish farms). Dogs were also eaten, along with venison, game birds, iguanas and other wildlife. A special dessert was made from insect eggs skimmed off the lake surface and mixed with honey…add bees to the short list of domestic animals. A few chinapas still exist, though on a depleted lake, in Xochimilco.

Farmers, like other city residents, were organized into *calpulli* – a sort of village within the city. Some of these farmers were technically slaves, but they owned most of the crops they raised (land rent and taxes were paid to the calpulli in produce) and could pass on the right to grow crops to their children. Farmers' children, like all children, attended public schools, and everyone paid taxes to the calpulli to support the teachers and school buildings. Even though all boys, including farmers' sons, were expected to be warriors, they received a thorough education. Schools stressed mathematics and history (as they still do in México), as well as animal and plant identification and, of course, military training for the boys and home economics for the girls (the Aztecs did not have complete sexual equality, but no one in the world did at that time). At ten, a boy's head was shaved and he wasn't allowed to grow his hair long until he had taken a captive in battle. When a warrior's hair started to grow out, he was "date bait" to the calpulli girls.

Upper class boys were sent to boarding schools where they received additional training as officers, administrators and priests. Soon after the Conquest, when some Spanish hoped to rule the country through the existing elite, these schools continued with a change in management (Catholic priests took over from Huitzilopochtli's priests), and new religion classes, Spanish and Latin were added to the curriculum.

Medical and dental care was well above European standards.[11] Mexican doctors had a better knowledge of the human body

---

[11] Modern medicine was set back several hundred years when the Escorial Palace Library burned down in the 1600s. Felipe II (Philip II, "Bloody Mary's" widower, and the enemy of Elizabeth I for English history buffs) sent his personal physician to México. He consulted with the surviving Aztec doctors, but the research on anesthetics, birth control and pharmaceuticals was still in manuscript form when it was destroyed in the fire.

(perhaps learned from Mexican chefs) than the Europeans had. The Aztecs had a wider range of pharmaceuticals (mostly from herbs), effective birth control methods[12] and skilled surgeons. Since there were anesthetics available (mostly hallucinogenic mushrooms and narcotic herbs), and doctors understood the importance of cleanliness (they didn't know about germs—no one did until the 19th century), Mexican surgical patients generally lived. European patients normally died. Aztec dentistry was far enough advanced to include orthodontics.

By 1375, the Aztecs were secure enough to improve their image. No longer wanting to be known as barbarian mercenaries and ex-slaves, they invented a Tolteca ancestry for their king,[13] Acamapichtli, and began to acquire some mainland property, starting with what is now Chapultepec Park (the Aztecs wanted control of the natural springs). Through royal marriages and trade treaties they became allied with two cities on either side of the lake, Texcoco, famed for its intellectual life, and Tacuba. These two cities became allies of Tenochtitlán and formed the original Aztec empire. They maintained some independence throughout the Aztec era, though eventually it became independence in name only. The last independent king of Texcoco, Nezahualpilli, cursed the Aztecs for destroying his city's independence and predicted their downfall.

The Aztecs very slowly expanded their empire though both trade and conquest. A favorite excuse for conquest was to claim the targeted city's officials had abused Aztec merchants and made them wear ladies clothing.[14] From 1428 to 1440 Izcoatl expanded

---

[12] The "pill"—which revolutionized sexual relations in the 1960s—is a synthetic chemical version of an herbal recipe learned from traditional Huasteca healers.

[13] "King" and "Emperor" were European terms. The Tlatoani was selected by the leaders of the main family. Being polygamists, the leader would have several sons by different mothers, and when it was necessary to chose a new leader, they were the candidates. The present-day Saudi royal family is the parallel here. Tlatoanis had a religious role as chief priest and war leader, making them something like a Roman emperor.

[14] Though the Zapotecs, who DO make merchants wear women's clothing, never were completely under Aztec control.

the empire, though it was still just the area around today's Mexico City (the Aztecs really didn't expand into most of modern México until the 1460s).

Izcoatl's reign also marks the debut of Tlacaélel, the evil genius of the Aztecs. Not only was he the power behind the throne, he completely rewrote history to justify Aztec control and changed the religion to justify Aztec power.

Tlacaélel consulted all the history books and papers he could find. He rewrote the story, changing the Aztecs from wandering desert nomads into the descendants of the Toltecs. Then he had the sources destroyed.[15] Rewriting history was easy. Changing the people's beliefs was trickier...but much more important to Tlacaélel. Like his contemporaries in Spain, Ferdinand and Isabella, Tlacaélel recognized the value of one religion tied to the state. If all subjects had the same religion, and the religion was tied to the government, then Tlacaélel, who controlled the government, could control the people. Ferdinand and Isabella recognized this in Spain and forced the Jews and Moslems to convert or flee the country; though for several generations there were "secret" Jews and Moslems in Spain.

Ferdinand and Isabella wanted to enforce loyalty to their crown. Tlacaélel's purposes were slightly different. He couldn't eliminate the other gods or the other people, but he could eliminate their ability to revolt. Subjects without warriors were no threat to Aztec control. Huitzilopochtli, the sun god, had been a hummingbird—nothing particularly scary about him—but Tlacaélel wanted to scare people into submission, so Huitzilopochtli became a god who lived on human hearts. Every town in the empire had to have it's own Huitzilopochtli "church". There was a huge demand for human sacrifices. Captured enemies were the obvious sacrifices. When captured enemies started to run out, the Aztecs had to refine the

---

[15] Tlacaélel missed a few. There was nothing in the official histories about bearded strangers coming from the east. A private scholar in Xochimilco named Quilaztli had his own library and was called in for consultation when Moctezuma couldn't decide if the invaders were just barbarians or returning gods.

practice and took warriors as tax payment. Sacrificing the warriors to Huitzilopochtli kept the subject peoples from rebelling—they simply lacked the soldiers.

Tlacaélel played down the other gods, especially Quetzalcóatl and Tezcatlipoca, both of whom were still remembered and would play a pivotal role in the downfall of the empire. Quetzalcóatl (Plumed Serpent) and Tezcatlipoca (Smoking Mirror) were deadly enemies. There were several different beliefs about these two gods. Some people believed Quetzalcóatl had been driven out of México by Tezcatlipoca but would someday return from the east (which the Spaniards did). According to some, Quetzalcóatl had a beard (as did several of the Spaniards). Still others believed that Quetzalcóatl had a virgin mother (and the Spaniards believed in a god with a virgin mother). Still others believed, perhaps pessimistically, that Tezcatlipoca, the god of all created things, would get bored with the Aztecs and destroy them. Tezcatlipoca was that kind of god.

When Moctezuma's ambassadors were returning from their first meeting with Cortés, they met Tezcatlipoca disguised as a drunken old man. He told the ambassadors to pass on a message to Moctezuma, the Aztec empire was about to collapse and there was nothing to do but accept it.

The Aztecs began running out of enemies to conquer (maybe people stopped making merchants wear ladies underwear), and there weren't enough criminals and slaves available for Huitzilopochtli's daily meals, so Tlacaélel invented a new "sport", the Flower War. Smaller towns were given a choice: fight a Flower War or be destroyed completely. The object of these fake wars wasn't to kill each other but to take captives. The losing team (which only once was the Aztec team, and only when the opponents refused to play fair) lost its best warriors this way, so was in no condition to rebel. Their leaders would be rewarded secretly and hustled out of Tenochtitlán in the middle of the night.

To get the people to accept this sort of religion required changing the educational system. Religion was added to the curriculum, and the lesson was drummed in that a warrior's death was every man's duty. Boys were taught to capture, rather than kill, the enemy. When the real enemy showed up a few years later, most warriors didn't know how to deal with them.

Human sacrifice had always been part of the local religion, but Tlacaélel made it central to the belief system. There's no nice way to say it, but after a captive's heart was ripped out, they were eaten. How much cannibalism went on in the days before Tlacaélel is unknown, probably some, but not nearly as much.

Most people accepted cannibalism. Bernal Díaz, in his memoirs of the Conquest, talked about the Aztecs taunting their Spanish enemies, giving detailed recipes for Spaniard tamales. Tlaloc, the rain god, also required human sacrifice. Crying babies were his favorite. Parents, understandably, were reluctant to offer up their children. To keep the parents from hiding their children the Aztecs began keeping detailed birth records—children born on unlucky days or at unlucky hours were destined for Tlaloc.

Tlacaélel lived to be nearly one hundred, only dying in 1492.[16] Kings came and went, but Tlacaélel stayed. Moctezuma I ruled from 1440 to 1469. He added to the empire and rebuilt the city. His half-brother, Nezahuacóyotl – Hungry Coyote – of Texcoco, combined ruling with careers as an artist and engineer. Among Nezahuacóyotl's accomplishments was a dike across Lake Texcoco to control the water and salinity level and a design to secure a water and drainage system for Tenochtitlán. Interest in his poetry is still strong, and Náhuatl is still a living language, partly because of his literary accomplishments. He also was a philosopher, who speculated on the nature of one god.

---

[16] 1492 was a fateful year for the future Hispanic world. Spain only came into existence as a country in January, when the Castilians captured Granada, the last Islamic kingdom. One of the first things the new Castilian rulers did was to order the conversion or expulsion of all Jews and Moslems. In October, Columbus reached the Americas. The first Spanish language grammar was published and Castilian became the language we call Spanish. At the time several romance languages were spoken on the Iberian peninsula (besides Basque, which is a different language family), most of which have since disappeared.

Axayacatl (1469–1481), who expanded the empire aggressively, died at the age of thirty and was succeeded by his teenaged son, Tizoc. Tizoc proved something of a disappointment and was probably poisoned by Tlacaélel in 1486.

Tlacaélel's finest moment came during the new king's coronation. Possibly as many as eighty thousand people were sacrificed to Huitzilopochtli to honor Ahuízotl (1486–1503) and also to inaugurate the new temple to Huitzilopochtli. This is the Templo Mayor, which was torn down by the Spaniards to supply building material for the Cathedral and National Palace.

Ahuízotl's death was extremely odd—he was dedicating a new plumbing system for the palace when something went wrong (or maybe one of the royal plumbers had had a child sacrificed to Tlaloc, or maybe Tezcatlipoca was feeling frisky that day). Ahuízotl meant to ceremoniously fill his bathtub, but instead the palace flooded. Trying to swim out of the Imperial bathroom, he hit his head on a roof beam and spent the last three years of his life in a coma.

With Tlacaélel finally dying of old age, and the emperor in an irreversible coma, things began to fall apart. Tenochtitlán had grown to the point where it consumed more than it created. It faced the same problem Mexico City has always faced—too many people want to live in the Capital—food, water, goods and services (and in our day, electrical power) have to come from the outside. Then, as now, it required more tax assistance than its citizens could raise. This did not go over well with the businessmen of Tlaltelolco, who rebelled in 1473. The ruler of this businessmen's suburb also complained that Tenochtitlán was only waging war to acquire captives for sacrifice. Its leaders complained about taxes (as Mexico City suburbanites still do) and preferred live customers to dead warriors.

A causeway connected Tenochtitlán to Tlaltelolco. The Tlaltelolcans cut the causeway. The Aztecs dumped construction trash along the causeway until they built up a solid land bridge between the two cities; then they marched in and took control.

Minorities like the Otomi people felt discriminated against by the Aztecs and never accepted the Aztec religion or customs. The Otomi were tolerated because they were hard working but disliked, mostly because of their fashion sense—or lack of it—they didn't wear clothes. Aztec fathers would tell their daughters, "You're dressed like an Otomi," if she showed too much skin on her way out to cruise young warriors.

The Totonac people (in modern Veracruz State) had only recently been brought under Aztec rule. They were reluctant subjects, and at best, they thought of the Aztecs as uptight and dour. The Aztecs thought the Totonacs were frivolous and of questionable morals. People in Mexico City and Veracruz still think of each other in these terms. Tlaxcala, a small independent kingdom surrounded by the empire, maintained an armed truce with the Aztecs. In 1504, the uneasy truce between the Tlaxcalans and the Aztecs turned into a real war when the Tlaxcalans changed the rules and used an invitation to a Flower War to launch a real one.

The Zapotecs in the west (mostly in modern Oaxaca) never were conquered, although the Aztecs controlled their business centers. The Zapotecs (never quite conquered by the Spanish either and who would later produce México's greatest leader, Benito Juárez) kept an informal alliance with their traditional enemies the Mixtecs so both could resist Aztec control. They would ignore imperial commands when they could and sometimes simply ate visiting bureaucrats. The Tarascans (in modern Morelia State) were in a "cold war" with the Aztecs. They had only avoided Aztec control because they had superior weaponry (copper spears and arrowheads), which they kept as a closely guarded secret from their adversaries, just as the U.S. had tried to keep nuclear secrets from the Soviets during the 1950s.

This was not a good time for an insecure ruler, but Moctezuma II, who had spent most of his career as a religious scholar, was finally selected as emperor. Moctezuma closed the upper class schools to anyone who wasn't born to the upper class (there seems to have been a scholarship program of some kind and some way of recruiting the best and brightest commoners into the ruling class).

Moctezuma effectively cut the people off from their ruler. He was no longer seen in public and to even look at him became a capital crime. From then on, the only people who came near the emperor were the born nobility. Furthermore, if the Church was part of the State, and the emperor was head of the Church, then Moctezuma must be Huitzilopochtli in the flesh! Not even Tlacaélel would have gone that far.

The emperor did not need to be a god to know that things were going badly in the empire, and the god-emperor was also receiving other disturbing messages. Nezahualpilli, the last independent king of Texcoco (son of the poet-king, Nezahuacóyotl), cursed the Aztec empire when he died and predicted the Aztecs' doom. A trunk of strange clothing appeared on the Caribbean shore. People began reporting odd events, two-headed babies and weird visions. One story said that a magic bird appeared with a mirror attached to its head. In the mirror Moctezuma saw a vision of invaders riding deer and carrying burning sticks. The magic bird flew away.

Moctezuma, at his wit's end, sent for magicians. When the magicians told him that he was being invaded from the southeast coast, he had the magicians thrown in jail. Besides having some advance knowledge of the Spaniards, the magicians had an even better trick—they all vanished from the jail one night, never to be seen again. The emperor put out an all-points bulletin for bad dreams. Anyone having a nightmare was supposed to report to the police. A surprising number of people did. Some of these people found their nightmares were mild compared to what happened to them. If Moctezuma found the nightmares too frightening he had the dreamer fed to the jaguars at the zoo.[17]

Finally, a peasant from the coast (he made an impression on the people who met him; they didn't remember his name but remembered the man had no ears and no thumbs) showed up

---

[17] Moctezuma's zoo was the largest in the world at the time. Besides the jaguars and other animals, it included an aquarium, complete with live sharks.

with the amazing news of ships landing on the east coast. After considering the matter, Moctezuma decided either Quetzalcóatl had returned to claim the world, or some totally unimaginable people had appeared. Modern writers have pointed out that the news would be as bizarre to the Aztecs as being told the aliens had landed would be to us. It would take some getting used to.

Alien Nation

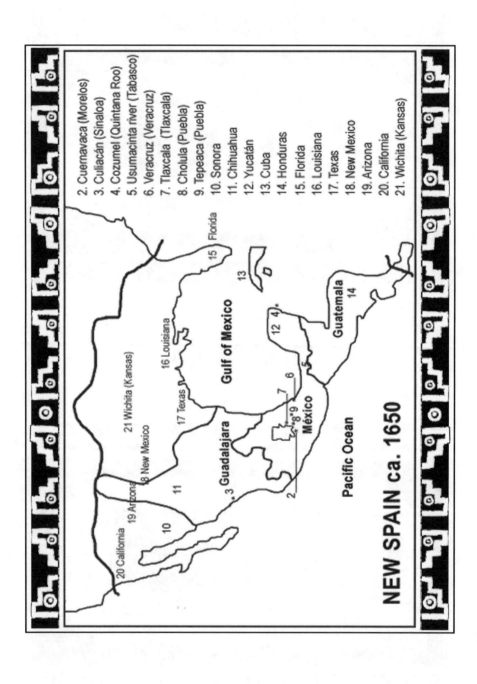

NEW SPAIN ca. 1650

2. Cuernavaca (Morelos)
3. Culiacán (Sinaloa)
4. Cozumel (Quintana Roo)
5. Usumacinta river (Tabasco)
6. Veracruz (Veracruz)
7. Tlaxcala (Tlaxcala)
8. Cholula (Puebla)
9. Tepeaca (Puebla)
10. Sonora
11. Chihuahua
12. Yucatán
13. Cuba
14. Honduras
15. Florida
16. Louisiana
17. Texas
18. New Mexico
19. Arizona
20. California
21. Wichita (Kansas)

20 California
19 Arizona
10
11
21 Wichita (Kansas)
8 New Mexico
17 Texas
16 Louisiana
15 Florida
3 Guadalajara
2
México
8 9 7
6
5
Gulf of Mexico
13
12 4
Guatemala
14
Pacific Ocean

Just another barbarian tribe

T HE SPANISH, LIKE THE AZTECS, were newcomers in
a land of old civilizations. The Spanish peninsula
had seen Celto-Iberians replaced with Romans who were eventually
replaced by Goths and Moors. The Moors, an Islamic people, had
shared the country with Jews and the older Roman people, who
were Christians. About the same time the Aztecs were beginning to
appear in central México, northern barbarians had begun invading
and conquering down the Spanish peninsula. Like the Aztecs, they
adopted much from the older cultures, using royal marriages and
conquest to expand their territory and religion to bind the people
to the state. In Spain this meant a crusade against the Moors. Part
holy war, part land conquest, the northern European barbarians
believed that conquering other people and converting them to
their religion was moral and proper.

Like the Aztecs, the Spaniards were a warrior society and being
a warrior was the highest calling in life. Unlike the Aztecs, they
thought any other work was beneath a warrior's dignity. With the
Aztecs, farmers, tradesmen, workers and businessmen were also
warriors. For the Spaniards, the only roles for a warrior were as a
landowner or ruler. Both the Aztecs and the Spaniards rewarded

their warriors by giving them control of the land and people they had conquered.

In January 1492, the Spanish barbarians ran out of people to conquer. The last Moorish territory fell to the Spaniards, and there was nothing left to do but convert Moors and Jews to Christianity. Those who refused to convert were expelled from the country. Fortunately for these unemployed warriors Columbus opened up an entirely new world to convert and conquer when he landed in what he called the "Indies".

Restless Knights

T HE WHOLE POINT OF BEING A Spanish knight was
to obtain land and win converts to the Catholic
religion. As Cortés was to tell his men during their war against the
Aztecs, "The principal reason for the war is to preach the faith of
Jesus Christ, even though at the same time it brings us honor and
profit."

If there was nothing to conquer, working for the government
was the only other option. Columbus and the settlement of what he
called the Indies saved Cortés from his bureaucratic fate. Hernán
Cortés (1485–1547) started out to be a lawyer. As very minor nobility, his family expected their son to take a respectable job (which
meant the Church, the military or the government). Hernán was
sent to law school but was too much of a party animal and playboy
to finish his training. He never became a lawyer, but he learned
more than enough law to serve him in the future.

At loose ends and not particularly interested in becoming a
government clerk, Hernán decided to try his luck in Cuba. He might
have ended up as a forgotten colonial administrator if he had been
a little more respectable. As it was, he had a lucky break…literally.
He was sneaking out of his girlfriend's house and fell off the balcony,
broke his leg and spent the next six months in traction. When he

was finally able to take a boat to Cuba there was a new governor on the island: a distant cousin who found Hernán a decent job. Not that Cortés was going to clean up his act, however. When he seduced the governor's sister-in-law, he was forced to marry her.

Cortés wasn't making a fortune as a colonial administrator and began paying attention to the stories he was hearing about the land to the west. The settlement in Panama hadn't found much wealth, but Juan de Grijalva had explored the Yucatán (which he thought was an island) and the Gulf coast. While the Mayan people Grijalva met were not rich, they had rich neighbors somewhere—they had plenty of gold trinkets.

With Grijalva's second expedition overdue to return to Cuba, Cortés sold the Cuban authorities on a search and rescue mission and recruited a few veterans of Grijalva's first exploration: Bernal Díaz del Castillo, Francisco de Montejo, Cristobal de Olid and Pedro de Alvarado among them. He managed to recruit nearly half the Spanish men in Cuba before the government realized this wasn't just a search and rescue mission. A search and rescue mission doesn't normally include thirty crossbow men, twelve archibuses (a sort of 16th-century cross between a bazooka and a shotgun), fourteen cannons, sixteen war-horses and a pack of attack dogs—big dogs were used as weapons in the 16th century and even wore armor. They managed to also find Melchor, the Mayan translator.

No one had bothered to learn Melchor's real name. He was an elderly, cross-eyed Mayan, out minding his own business, fishing off the Yucatán a few years earlier when a wandering Spanish explorer decided he needed a translator and kidnapped the old man. Melchor was baptized and forced to learn Spanish. He probably had never had much to say to begin with and was even less talkative after his kidnapping, but he was the only person around who could speak any Spanish and any Mayan. The crew also included women—cooks, maids and the Estrada sisters. The sisters' parents were dead, and their brother didn't want to leave them alone. Or maybe they were just adventurous—when the fighting got fierce, María de Estrada turned out to be a better soldier than most professionals. For good measure, Cortés recruited two priests, a doctor and a team of lawyers.

The Spaniards had inherited Roman and Jewish traditions that required written legal authority for any action. When the Pope had given the king of Spain the right to conquer and convert people, the Spanish had devised an official document explaining their right to take possession of the land and to convert any inhabitants to Christianity. Furthermore, if the inhabitants refused to convert they were in violation of the Pope's orders, and the Spanish could attack them. The lawyers read out the document, in Spanish, of course; a language the people hearing it wouldn't understand even if they knew who the Pope, the king of Spain or the Christians were.[18]

Grijalva's ships sailed into sight of Cuba, so the Governor sent Cortés a letter calling off the search and rescue operation. Cortés claimed he never received the letter, but that excuse wouldn't buy him the time he needed to organize his expedition. He would have to leave immediately. He didn't have time to buy all the supplies he needed, so turned pirate, seized a shipload of food being sent to Panama and sailed west. The governor was not pleased.

---

[18] Bartolomé de las Casas, who would become a defender of the indigenous people, said he didn't know whether to laugh or cry the first time he saw a lawyer read out the rules.

Heaven helps those who help themselves

CORTÉS HAD INCREDIBLE LUCK off Cozumel. His ships were separated, and Pedro de Alvarado had arrived first. Alvarado, who turned out to be one of the greediest of the conquistadors, was stealing turkeys from the local villages when Cortés arrived. More importantly for Cortés, his crew had found two Spaniards. They were the last survivors of a shipwreck eight years earlier—the others had been sacrificed and eaten. Gonzalo Guerrero, a sailor, had married the local chief's daughter. He had three children (these little Guerreros are probably the first modern Mexicans, *mestizos* – mixed bloods – part European and part indigenous), a responsible job as an advisor to his father-in-law and no intention of becoming a common sailor again.

The other Spaniard, Gerónimo de Aguilar, was a priest and carpenter. It was his carpentry skills that kept him alive; they made him a valuable slave. Father Aguilar was more than happy to be rescued. Slavery was bad and the human sacrifice worse,[19] but what terrified Father Aguilar were women. As a priest, he had taken a vow of celibacy and the indigenous people simply couldn't comprehend a healthy young man refusing to take a wife. Eight years

---

[19] When she learned of her son's shipwreck and his probable fate, Aguilar's mother became a vegetarian.

of temptation was enough. He considered his rescuers Godsent. He spoke fluent Mayan and was more talkative than Melchor.

Father Aguilar preached a sermon in Mayan, pouring out eight years of built-up frustration and anger. Though the people had treated their visitors kindly and fed them, the Spaniards insulted their hosts, destroyed the local temple and sailed north. Landing at the mouth of the Usumacinta River (near modern Frontera, Tabasco), they found much warier Mayans—they had evacuated their women and children and cautiously approached the Spaniards, sprinkling incense. The Spaniards thought it was a compliment, but the truth is that Europeans didn't bathe, and the indigenous people were extremely clean. The Spaniards smelled terrible, but the Mayans were much too polite to say anything about it.[20]

These extremely polite people fed the Spaniards a turkey dinner and then nicely told them to go home, otherwise, regrettably, they would have to kill them. The smelly Spaniards asked to visit the Mayans' houses. The Mayans, still polite, suggested the Spaniards had missed something in the translation. Cortés trotted out his lawyers, read the official document and turned his cannons against the Mayan stone clubs and obsidian swords. It was only a test to see if cannons, horses and war-dogs were effective weapons. The cannons scared people as much as killed them. Horses were unknown in the Americas, and the only dogs were small animals (ancestors of today's *Xoloitzcuintle* – Mexican Hairless – or its off-shoot, the Chihuahua) that were used for guard dogs, food and for pets. Melchor, the grumpy old cross-eyed fisherman, took this as his cue to exit history.

As part of their peace negotiations, the Mayans gave the Spaniards a valuable slave girl. Malinali, called Doña Marina by the Spaniards and La Malinche by Mexicans today, came from

---

[20] Americans, north and south, in general bathe daily—one of the few indigenous customs adopted throughout the hemisphere. In Mexico City, the custom is so well engrained that "bath houses" are just that—places to clean up when there's no water at home. This confuses some gay visitors, for whom a "bath house" has a different purpose, though such institutions also exist.

minor Aztec nobility. During a political power struggle, her mother had disposed of her by selling her as a slave. La Malinche was an intelligent woman who spoke both Náhuatl and Mayan (until she learned Spanish, she would translate Náhuatl into Mayan, and Father Aguilar would translate into Spanish). She knew the customs and practices of the upper class Aztecs, and she wanted revenge on her family. Given her pivotal role in the conquest and the destruction of the indigenous people that followed, Malinche is the great villainess of Mexican history. Artists often show her as beautiful but bend all their artistic skill to paint her as incarnate evil.

After stopping at San Juan de Ulúa (Grijalva had been there the year before), Cortés landed at Veracruz[21] on Good Friday, 22 April 1519. Proving that he hadn't wasted his time in law school all those years ago, he remembered that Spanish cities could govern themselves. At any rate, a city did not have to answer to the governor of Cuba…and it just so happened the lawyers that had tagged along had a draft city charter on hand. Everyone was still on the beach, and no shelters had gone up yet, but the new city council's first act was to appoint Cortés commander of the city militia.

Because it was Easter weekend, a solemn religious holiday (and it took the lawyers a few days to draft a city charter), the City of Veracruz didn't meet with their partying neighbors,[22] the Totonacs of Cempola, for a few days. The Totonacs were under Aztec rule but had been thinking about rebellion for some time. They recognized the Spaniards were a potential ally against the insufferably uptight Aztecs—and the Spaniards had superior weapons.

---

[21] Not today's Veracruz, but Chalchihuecan, slightly north of the port city.

[22] Veracruz' reputation as a party town predates the conquest!

An offer that can't be refused

THE SPANIARDS COULDN'T PRONOUNCE the Totonac leader's name. Bernal Díaz' memoirs call him the Fat Chief. The Fat Chief had other visitors, too. Moctezuma, still unsure what the alien invaders were—gods or humans—sent a special agent. The agent carried the sort of food Quetzalcóatl liked, as well as the kind of clothes he would wear. The agent traveled with artists who had instructions to return with pictures of the strangers. If these foreigners turned out to be enemies and ate him, Moctezuma promised the agent his family would be well provided for.

Cortés played his part perfectly. After demonstrating their superior weapons, the Spaniards met the Aztec agent. La Malinche may have whispered something in Father Aguilar's ear, and Father Aguilar may have said something to Cortés—he ate the right food and wore the right clothes but said something odd—he said his men suffered from a rare heart condition and they required heavy doses of gold. Moctezuma's agent thought that didn't sound like the gods, and he also noticed that the Spaniards partied like the Totonacs. Aztec gods would never do that.

When Aztec tax collectors showed up, the Spaniards tied them up and abused them. The Fat Chief decided that if the Spaniards weren't gods, they were the new power. The Spaniards were allowed to turn the temple into a church, and candles were introduced to México.

The first serious battle between the Spaniards and the indigenous people happened at Tlaxcala. The Tlaxcalans, like other indigenous people, thought in terms of capturing the enemy, not killing him; their weapons were designed to wound, not kill. They also thought that staying out of your enemy's range was dishonorable. The Spaniards had other ideas, and their cannons decided the battle. Most of the Tlaxcalan warriors were Otomis, the people all Aztecs thought were stupid. The Otomis weren't at all stupid. After the battle, they offered to pay for the horses that had been killed. Not out of any sense of remorse, but never having seen horses and not knowing about them, they wanted to dissect the dead animals and figure out the weaknesses of the Spanish secret weapon. Cortés had the horses secretly buried.

The horses proved invaluable; fifty years later, when Bernal Díaz was writing his memoir, he could remember what each horse looked like; its name and even its personality, but the soldiers were all a blur. The Spaniards pillaged the local villages, though Díaz claimed Totonacs did most of the slaughter. Despite the battle, the Tlaxcalans also wanted the Spaniards as allies—especially after they had just witnessed the effectiveness of Spanish weapons.

The Tlaxcalans were independent from the Aztecs. Sort of like Switzerland, they were several small independent nations united for self-defense against the superpower. The two sides reached an agreement. The Tlaxcalans would become Spanish allies, but they wanted to maintain their independence and their own way of life.[23] Cortés wanted to force the Tlaxcalans to convert, but one of the priests, Father Olmos, was a practical man. He suggested holding off on any conversions. However, Father Olmos did convert the slave girls the Spanish received during the peace negotiations. Adultery was a sin to the Christians (many of the Spaniards, like

---

[23] They did, more or less. Tlaxcala remained independent of the viceroy throughout the colonial period.

Cortés, had neglected or abandoned wives back in Cuba), but somehow the priest decided that adultery with Christians was less sinful than adultery with pagans. For reasons having to do with Spanish law, Olmos also wanted the children, who he realistically expected would be born about nine months later, to have Catholic mothers.[24]

Cholula was the first target of the Tlaxcalan-Spanish alliance. Sitting on the Aztec side of the border between the two nations, the Tlaxcalans were particularly anxious to destroy the town. They looted the city for two days while the Spaniards massacred the people. This was as much to frighten the Aztecs as anything. There was talk of mass conversions, but Father Olmos recognized that the survivors weren't likely to become good Christians under those circumstances, so he was satisfied with adding a statue of the Virgin Mary in the temple.

With the Spaniards closing in on Tenochtitlán, Moctezuma tried one last time to buy the invaders off. An Aztec witness remembered that the Spaniards "seized on the gold like monkeys" and "starved and lusted for it like pigs". The bribes weren't a good idea; they only made the Spaniards hungrier for more gold, and they advanced on the city.

---

[24] There was also a religious reason. Father Olmos, a well-educated clergy-man, faced a unusual theological problem. Catholic doctrine held that "virtuous pagans"—good people who never had the chance to be exposed to Christianity—could go to Heaven, even if they were never baptized. Thomas Aquinas, who codified Catholic doctrine in the 13th century, was talking about Greek and Roman philosophers who were unbaptized for the simple reason that they lived before Christ was born. Jews and Muslims, having been exposed to Christians, had no excuse not to be baptized, and Isabella's forced conversions were seen as ethical. But, in the Americas, people had not been exposed to Christianity and could—presumably—go to Heaven. However, Cortés and company had exposed these particular women to Christian teaching. If they died unbaptized (and many could be expected to die during childbirth) they would be doomed to Hell. God – or the gods – only know what would have happened had they not been baptized: Aztec beliefs held that mothers who died in childbirth were judged like warriors or sacrificial victims who died an honorable death and were rewarded in the afterlife.

We're not in Ávila anymore

THE SPANIARDS HAD NEVER SEEN anything like Tenochtitlán. It was larger than any city in Europe, and may have been the largest city in the world at the time (as Mexico City is today—depending on just who and what is being counted). It was cleaner and better organized than anything the Europeans knew: a city of canals, palaces, pyramids and running water. The Spaniards were at a loss to describe what they saw. A few sailors who had been to Italy, compared it to Venice, but most, like Bernal Díaz, took their descriptions from fairy tales and romance novels.

At the entrance to the main causeway, Moctezuma met with Cortés on 8 November 1519. Through La Malinche, Cortés made a polite speech, adding the lie that the Spanish king (who still knew nothing about this expedition) had sent Cortés to establish friendly relations. He added, for good measure, that the Spaniards intended to set up a buffer state between Tlaxcala and the Aztecs. They exchanged gifts, and the emperor (who really had no choice) welcomed the foreigners into his city. The Spaniards fired off their guns (whether to impress the Aztecs or out of celebration, no one knows, but it was the start of the Mexican custom of setting off explosives at celebrations) and marched into the city.

The Spaniards were housed in Axayacatl's old palace (presumably, the plumbing problem had been fixed). "My house is your house," is a standard greeting, both in Náhuatl and Spanish, but the Spaniards took the emperor at his word and began pocketing souvenirs—not just the trinkets laying around on end tables but everything from wall carvings to plumbing fixtures; anything that looked like it had gold or jewels in it. During their hunt for valuables, they ran across a secret room piled with still more treasures. They were happy with the new find until it started to dawn on them that inviting them into the city also meant they were prisoners of the Aztecs.

The Empire strikes back

CORTÉS DECIDED TO MAKE the emperor HIS prisoner instead. He kidnapped Moctezuma. A sword at his back, the emperor bluffed his way past his own guards by telling them Huitzilopochtli requested he move in with the Spaniards. While the emperor attempted to run the country from his captivity (he even became friendly with some of the Spaniards), it was obvious to everyone that he was not really in charge. The ruling class considered a new emperor, but as long as Moctezuma was alive they were stuck with him. Cortés, interrogating the emperor about the sources of his gold, discovered something that would prove even more valuable—the tax records. From the records the Spaniards would learn where gold and silver mines were located, as well as the best farmland and the source of other valuables like vanilla, chocolate, rubber, cotton fields, gems and furs.

Cacama, Moctezuma's nephew and king of Texcoco, had enough of his uncle's puppet regime. However, before he could act, the Spaniards kidnapped him. Pedro de Alvarado, the turkey thief and Cortés' second-in-command, took Cacama with him when he went to collect the ransom in gold. Wanting more, Alvarado tied up the king and started torturing him with hot pokers until his people came up with even more gold, but de Alvarado kept the king prisoner.

Cortés, realizing that Moctezuma was losing credibility as a ruler, came up with alternatives: while lawyers drew up a legal document for the emperor (who could neither read nor understand Spanish) recognizing the Spanish king as his ruler, the conquistadors planned an escape. Martin López was put in charge of the boat building operation.

Having stolen gold from everywhere they could think of, including the zoo—gold wasn't particularly valuable to the Aztecs except as an easy-to-work, pretty metal and it kept the parrots happy in the bird house—the Spaniards turned to the temples. Remembering that they were supposed to convert the Aztecs, they marched into the main temple and started smashing up the local gods. Moctezuma, trying to avoid a complete disaster, suggested that the Christians share the temple with Tlaloc and Huitzilopochtli. Cortés' luck held. There were pilgrims in town praying for rain the day the Spaniards installed their religious statues, and it started to rain.

Moctezuma lost any remaining support he had among the ruling class when he ordered his priests to clear out of the temple. The priests hauled out their gods and hid them. For the next sixty years Spanish priests would be terrified by the thought that those gods were still out there somewhere, and worse, that someone would bring them out of hiding and undo all their conversions.

Cortés was nominally in charge of a very rich empire, but he was still in trouble with the governor of Cuba: there was that little piracy incident to clear up. He had already dispatched lawyers and documents to Spain to justify his actions, along with a careful accounting of—and the payment on—the "King's fifth": the twenty-percent tax on any precious metals or treasure found in Spanish territory. The last thing Cortés wanted was a tax problem on top of that little piracy charge. He also sent money to buy more supplies, gifts and bribes for officials, souvenirs of México and five Totonacs. The ship stopped in Cuba, but nobody could keep that much wealth a secret, so the Governor sent one thousand soldiers under Pánfilo de Narváez to take over the expedition and hang Cortés.

By the time the ship arrived in Spain, there was a new king. Carlos, a twenty-year-old Belgian (his mother had become queen of Spain by a second marriage), barely understood Spanish. He did understand gold, jewels and adding new kingdoms (and, as if king of Spain and Flanders—mostly in modern Belgium—wasn't enough, he was also elected the German Emperor[25]). The news that his kingdom included a town called Veracruz, and that the Justice of the Peace in Veracruz had just added another kingdom the size of Spain, didn't quite sink in with the young king, but he gave Cortés the legal authority needed and turned the matter over to the bureaucratic monks who ran the Indies for him.

Carlos did, however, realize that the Totonacs were probably as unhappy in Spain as he was (he preferred his northern homeland, never was comfortable with the language and spent as little time in the country as he could). He personally bought them warm clothing in the latest style (Spain was much colder than Veracruz). He also made sure the Totonacs were well treated, given Spanish lessons and eventually returned (though they never made it closer to home than Cuba).

---

[25] As Holy Roman Emperor, he was Charles V (or Karl V). It gets confusing, because the next king of Spain named Carlos is Carlos II.

Resistance...and non-resistance

IT COULD TAKE AS LONG AS six months for a ship to reach México from Spain. Cortés still thought he was an outlaw and had to face de Narváez' army in Veracruz. Taking half his men (leaving de Alvarado in charge), he marched back to Veracruz with as much treasure as he could. The treasure convinced most of de Narváez' soldiers to change sides. There was a short battle (de Narváez lost an eye in the surprise night attack, and the Fat Chief was stabbed in the confusion—being so fat probably saved his life, since nothing vital was hit). Bribery and threats were the recruiting tools. Even de Narváez was convinced to change sides. With a thousand more soldiers and fresh horses and weapons, Cortés returned to Tenochtitlán.

De Narváez didn't realize it, but his forces brought the weapon that actually conquered the Americas. Smallpox was unknown in the Americas, and people had never developed a resistance to the disease. There was an epidemic in Cuba when de Narváez sailed, but Europeans were used to the disease (they usually survived it), so no one thought anything about it. The indigenous Cubans would be entirely wiped out within a few years. Within a hundred years, the former Aztec empire would have only a million people (that includes immigrants from Europe). In 1520 the population was somewhere from nine to twenty-five million. México wouldn't recover until the 20th century.

The disease spread throughout the Americas wiping out entire civilizations. The Amazon river basin, lined with cities, would be inhabited only by small bands of hunter-gatherers within two hundred years. Agricultural settlements in modern northern Chihuahua and west Texas collapsed, the former farmers eventually being displaced by marauding Apaches and Comanches. By the time the English arrived in North America, there were very few indigenous people to block their way. Squanto, who hosted the first Thanksgiving for the New England colonists in 1621, would die a few months later from smallpox. Smallpox was only the first European disease to reach the Americas—every boatload of Europeans brought more diseases—and the indigenous peoples never recovered. As late as the 1920s, new epidemics were reaching the Inupiat – Eskimos – in northern Alaska.

Back in Tenochtitlán, the Aztecs had lost all patience with de Alvarado. They stopped sending food, and the servants either went on strike or were told to stop coming by. The one Spaniard who was brave enough to go shopping claimed he overheard people talking about a sacrifice to be celebrated with Spaniard tamales flavored with wild onions. This news unnerved the Spaniards. De Alvarado, thinking a dose of terrorism might convince the people to leave him alone, mounted an attack during a religious celebration. When the massacre started, the warriors ran home for their weapons, and the Spaniards were fortunate to get back to the palace alive. For some reason, they murdered Cacama and several other prisoners. Moctezuma, who still thought he could avoid disaster, went to the roof of the palace and somehow convinced the people to stop the attack.

Cortés and his reinforcements arrived on 24 June. While they were able to reach Ahuízotl's palace without incident, there wasn't enough food for the new men, let alone for the people already there. Cortés convinced, or ordered, Moctezuma to get the markets open. Moctezuma sent his brother, Cuitláhuac, to open the markets. Cuitláhuac and his teenage cousin, Cuauhtémoc, took over the empire and began organizing an anti-Spanish resistance. The warriors gathered in front of the palace.

Moctezuma was sent up to the roof to address the crowd once more. It had worked the first time...but not the second. A well-aimed rock ended Moctezuma's speech...and Moctezuma. There weren't any lawyers around when Cortés claimed the emperor had given him the empire. The people who were there claimed the emperor only begged the Spaniards not to rape his daughters or kill his sons (some of these children would later marry into the Spanish nobility and one of the daughters would father a Cortés[26]).

With the Aztecs ready to slaughter them, Cortés planned to return to Veracruz, gather what men were there and return. The Spaniards retreated at midnight, 30 June 1520—the *Noche Triste* – Night of Sorrow. Moving quietly (they had wrapped the horses' hooves in rags), they nearly reached the causeway before they were discovered. The traditional story is that a woman sitting in the latrine raised the alarm.

The Aztecs adopted a Spanish tactic—they weren't out to take prisoners, but to kill the invaders. They also adopted some Spanish weapons, especially the long lances that were effective at stabbing men out of the range of Aztec swords. Not all of the six hundred Spaniards and one thousand Tlaxcalans who died on the causeway were killed by the arrows fired from canoes or lances. Most were either knocked into the canal by panicky troops behind them or were pulled in. Weighted down with gold, the Spaniards drowned. The two hundred Spaniards who had somehow been left behind in the palace would end up as sacrifices to Huitzilopochtli.

The survivors of the Noche Triste included Martin López, the boat builder. Told that López was still alive, Cortés only said, "Let's

---

[26] The colonial government, and the Republic of México continued to pay a pension to Moctezuma's heirs. The several hundred European aristocrats (mostly with Italian or Spanish titles) descended from the Aztec nobility filed a claim in Spanish courts in 2004 trying to recover back pension payments from the time México stopped payments in the 1930s.

go, we have what we need." The four hundred survivors had to fight their way from Tacuba back to Tlaxcala. Desperately short of fighting men, María de Estrada proved her value as a soldier. She grabbed a lance and killed several Aztec warriors in close combat.

When the Spaniards reached Tlaxcala, they found their old allies would remain with them...for a price. In addition to guaranteeing their independence, they wanted guarantees that they wouldn't be paying taxes to the Spanish king. Furthermore, they wanted another Aztec city, Tepeaca. Using the dubious argument that Moctezuma had given the Aztec empire to King Carlos, the Tepeacans were conquered and treated as rebels—their citizens were branded, shipped to Cuba and sold as slaves.

Pillaging towns and enslaving "rebels" as they went, the Spaniards returned to Tenochtitlán. This time they would attack the city from the water (which is why Cortés was relieved that Martin López had survived) or starve it into surrender. Smallpox had already started the job—Cuitláhuac, the new emperor, was already dead—but young Cuauhtémoc was prepared to fight on. The Spaniards arrived in Texcoco where López' half-built boats were docked and where he could build new ones. As the Spaniards marched in they saw the last of Texcoco's citizens canoeing towards Tenochtitlán. After looting the city and burning the city archives, the Spaniards began their conquest of the cities along the shore. A few simply gave up, agreed to convert to Christianity and survived. Others were destroyed, and their people enslaved. In Tenochtitlán, food ran out, and people were dying of smallpox. Cactus, snakes, bugs and eventually grass were all that was left to eat. Surprisingly enough, the Aztecs didn't seem to have considered eating the dead—being eaten was a warrior's fate, not a normal way of supplementing their diet. Cortés, while he waited for López to finish his boats, sent a letter to King Carlos. He informed the king he was now governor of New Spain and requested that the king send Christian missionaries. Along with the letter, he sent back what treasure he'd saved from the Noche Triste. Gold had this magic property of making any legal irregularity clear itself up.

By the end of April 1521, López' boats were patrolling the lake. On 23 May, the Spaniards captured Chapultepec (today's park) and cut Tenochtitlán's water supply. With no clean water source, dysentery broke out in the city. Still, Cuauhtémoc refused to surrender. From the boats, the Spaniards began to bombard the city, eventually fighting their way across the causeways. They destroyed the city block by block, using the rubble to fill in canals between streets and give the horses room to maneuver. The Aztecs slowly retreated to Tlaltelolco. On 21 August 1521, with the largest city in the world in ruins and most of the population dead or dying, Cuauhtémoc finally surrendered.

The Conquest and the Conquistadors

CORTÉS HAD GREAT SKILL as a commander, but administering an empire and balancing the political infighting among the conquistadors and between them and the royal administration was another matter. Most of the gold had been spent, was at the bottom of the lake or had already been sent to Spain. The soldiers who originally sailed with Cortés thought they deserved more than those who had come with de Narváez, or those who had come with a few later missions. Martin López had paid the ships' carpenters out of his own pocket. The indigenous allies had their expectations, but most of the empire wasn't under Spanish control, and the Spaniards needed the old Aztec bureaucrats to run the system.

At first, things went about as well, or better than could be expected. Living just outside the city (today's Coyoacán), Cortés put the people to work rebuilding the Capital, renamed *Ciudad de México* – Mexico City. Under the Aztecs, people had always paid part of their taxes in labor. People were used to paying rent and taxes through their local city "kings", so Cortés settled up with some of the less patient conquistadors by giving them the rents and produce of various cities. In other places local rulers were left in place to keep the taxes coming in.

The conquistadors couldn't resist abusing their residents. They expected cities that had lost half or more of its people to smallpox and other diseases to pay the same amount it did before the epidemic, and they expected the same amount of free labor. Where there were gold mines, indigenous people were worked until they dropped. The workers needed to be fed, but on top of everything else there were less farmers to raise the crops. The farmers who survived the plagues couldn't plant their corn if they were off working on building a new house for the new overlord or digging in the mines.

The Spaniards didn't want the feathers, cacao beans or seashells some people paid in taxes; they wanted gold or produce. Where conquistadors couldn't directly oversee tax collection, they would leave the former Aztec administrators in place with their names changed to Christian ones, making them dependent on the local Spanish landowner for their independence. Some Aztec administrators made themselves rich by overcharging the citizens and pocketing the overcharges before they were sent in with the city's taxes.

Still other conquistadors couldn't settle into civilian life and were still anxious to go conquering. Pedro de Alvarado, the turkey and gold thief, ended up as Captain-General of Guatemala. He was killed fighting his way out of an attack on another looting expedition when his horse fell on him. In one of the weirder moments of the conquest, de Alvarado's widow seized the government but was killed when an earthquake triggered a flood that drowned the entire Guatemalan administration.

Pánfilo de Narváez, Cortés' one-eyed rival, was killed during an expedition in Florida. Most of the expedition's survivors were killed in a shipwreck off the coast of Louisiana. Two men, Álvar Núñez Cabeza de Vaca and Esteban the Slave, eventually made it back to México. They wandered across Texas, New Mexico, Arizona and Sonora before stumbling into Culiacán (in present-day Sinoloa State) in 1536. The two had a wild story about seeing *Cibola* – the Seven Cities of Gold. They may have seen the mica-flecked adobe walls of a Zuñi pueblo in bad light, or maybe they were hallucinating. Having sometimes been slaves and sometimes medicine men during their wanderings, it's hard not to think that they may have been just stoned on peyote.

Francisco Coronado, the Governor of Nuevo Galicia (including modern Jalisco, Nayarit and Sinoloa), believed the stories told by Cabeza de Vaca enough to abandon his post in Culiacan and wander as far north as *Quivira* – present-day Wichita, Kansas. Despite his later reputation as a discoverer and conquistador, the truth is that Coronado was hopelessly lost, and other than killing a lot of harmless Pueblo Indians while bumbling around what is now New Mexico he accomplished very little. He lost some horses along the way, which may have revolutionized the cultures of the region's nomads: the Sioux, Crow and Cheyenne, among others.

Martin López finally sued Cortés for his unpaid boatbuilding, as did several others for debts owing. López died a poor man. Father de Aguilar died soon after he returned to Spain where he had entered an religious community. The sailor shipwrecked with de Aguilar, Gonzalo Guerrero, who "went native" and fathered the first mestizos, died a hero to the Maya. He was killed in 1536 while commanding a fleet of his adopted people's war canoes that were trying to fend off a Spanish attack.

Cortés settled down to run his vast landholdings and imported new crops like olives and grapes but couldn't stay out of trouble. Soon after his wife arrived from Cuba, she died of what looked like strangulation.[27] On two different occasions, judges sent from Cuba to look into the affairs in New Spain suddenly died. Partly to avoid the lawsuits, partly to avoid murder investigations and partly out of habit, Cortés launched an expedition into Honduras. Cristobal de Olid had gone on a conquest without Cortés' permission, much as Cortés had gone to México without the governor of

---

[27] Cortés' mother-in-law filed a lawsuit over her daughter's death. It took another one hundred years to settle the suit. The Cortés family had to pay the mother-in-law's family, by which time all the original parties, and the original lawyers and judges were long dead.

Cuba's permission. There was no gold there, and the expedition was a disaster. De Olid had already been executed by the time Cortés arrived. Cuauhtémoc, who had been dragged along because the Spaniards thought the young ex-emperor might know where more gold was hidden, rebelled again and was hanged. In Mexico City, rumors circulated that Cortés was dead, and the Spaniards fought among themselves for control of the government. The royal authorities finally decided to regularize the government and sent administrators.

About the only positive thing one can say about Nuño de Guzmán, the administrator sent by Spain to take over for Cortés, was that de Guzmán was zealous. When the Tarascans fell behind in their tax payments, de Guzmán tied their king to a horse, dragged him through town and burned him alive. That was only the beginning of his campaign against the Tarascans. When Archbishop de Zumárraga threatened to complain to the king, de Guzmán stopped the archbishop's mail and had him tailed by spies. To make sure the archbishop couldn't slip out a message, all clergymen were strip-searched before they could board a ship out of the country. The archbishop finally smuggled a message out, hidden in a monk's rectum. The monk was unhappy in the New World and would do anything to get back home.

Carlos was not quite sure what to do. He couldn't admit that replacing Cortés was a mistake, and he couldn't offend the archbishop. De Guzmán was sent off on an exploration, while a temporary administrator took over. The indigenous people told de Guzmán there was an island of rich women somewhere in the Sonoran desert. It made some sense; Mexico City was an island, but the women were an interesting addition. It also kept de Guzmán out of the way until Carlos called him back to Spain in 1530 to make a full report and face the king's wrath. Carlos' punishment was perhaps the best way to deal with a sadist like de Guzmán—the king made him wait…and wait…and wait, the rest of his life. Francisco de Montejo, who had been one of the first Cubans to join Cortés, was put in charge of the Yucatán. The Mayans rebelled in 1527, but de Montejo was not particularly worried. The Mayans weren't nearly as powerful as the Aztecs. After nine years of fighting he gave up, turning the task over to, confusingly enough, Francisco de Montejo and Francisco de Montejo (his son and his nephew). After several more years of fighting, the two Franciscos claimed they had the Yucatán more or less under control by 1547, then the first of another series of Mayan revolts (still flaring up today) broke out.

Bernal Díaz was paid with land and indigenous workers in Guatemala. He became a respectable but talkative old man and the local mayor. In his memoirs Díaz exaggerated some stories, and he sometimes got things wrong, but *The True History of the Discovery and Conquest of México* is a classic adventure story, as well as the best source for the Spanish viewpoint of the conquest.

La Malinche had a son by Cortés and outlived two more conquistador husbands. A not-well-planned plot was hatched a few years later to overthrow the viceroy and make her son, Martín Cortés, king of México. The plotters were executed, and Martín was thrown out of the colony. No Cortés ever lived in México after that.

Cortés was given the title Marquis of Oaxaca and was the second-richest Spaniard (after the king), but he never completely settled down. Even fighting his in-laws in the courts didn't completely fill his time. He explored along the Pacific coast (the Europeans still believed China was close by). He also apparently did a lot of reading. Searching for a shortcut to China, he named one new land California, after an island in a popular fantasy novel of the time. Back in Spain to clear up some of his legal problems, he died in 1547. His remains were returned to México in 1556 and eventually buried in the Hospital de Jesús in Mexico City. In 1836, Lucas Alamán y Escalada, then a hospital administrator and later a pro-Spanish historian and Foreign Minister under Santa Ana, hid Cortés' bones during an anti-Spanish riot. Alamán sent a letter to the Spanish embassy telling them where Cortés' remains were hidden. The letter was misfiled and not discovered until 1946, and Cortés was finally buried in the wall next to the altar of the hospital's chapel.

Diego Rivera's mural in the National Palace gave Cortés his Mexican image—malignant, sickly, hollow-eyed and fanatical. There are no streets or towns named for Cortés in México. The only statue of him in the Republic is in a Cuernavaca hotel lobby, commissioned by a United States citizen, not a Mexican.

The Reign of Spain

20 *

* 23

* 9

* 5

* 10
* 26

* 32

* 14

3

* 8

24

*15

* 16

27

*25

Gulf of Mexico

35

13 *

31

Pacific Ocean

* 30

* 6

* 17

18

7

12

* 21

34

* 11

4

* 22

* 28

* 2

* 19

1

33

29

New Spain ca. 1786

1-Acapulco
2-Chiapas area
3-Galvez Town
4-Lerma
5-Los Ángeles
6-Mexico City
7-Mount Orizaba
8-San Antonio
9-San Francisco
10-Santa Fé
11-Tarascan area
12-Veracruz
13-Zacatecas

Political Subdivisions of New Spain

14-Arizpe
15-Coahuila
16-Durango
17-Guadalajara
18-Guanajuato
19-Guatemala
20-Louisiana
21-Mérida
22-México
23-Nuevo California
24-Viejo California

25-Nuevo León
26-Nuevo México
27-Nuevo Santander
28-Oaxaca
29-Puebla
30-San Luis Potosí
31-Veracruz
32-Texas
33-Tlaxcala
34-Valladolid
35-Zacatecas

Carlos wants you...

WHERE TLACAÉLEL HAD USED the Huitzilopochtli cult to control the various peoples under Aztec rule, the Vikings and Goths who conquered Castile used Christianity. Their centuries of Castilian conquest in the rest of Spain brought large Jewish and Muslim communities under Christian control. In 1492, with the last Muslim territory under her control, Isabella decreed that all subjects who did not become Christians had to leave the country. There has been speculation that Columbus may have been looking for someplace to settle these people when he began his voyage later that year. There were no Protestants anywhere in Europe yet, so Christian meant the Catholic Church.

The Catholic Church is sometimes said to be the world's oldest multinational. It is also the world's oldest government contractor. From headquarters in Rome, bishops, the Pope's regional managers, oversaw parish priests. In addition, there were subsidiaries – called "orders" – within the Church—Franciscans, Augustinians, Dominicans and others—with specialized tasks like teaching or preaching. While only men, and single men at that, could be priests, monks or friars (a type of monk); women could become nuns within any of their own orders. Monks and nuns were at a disadvantage in that they took vows of poverty and their personal assets passed to their order, which became very wealthy organizations in their own right. However, becoming a monk or nun offered the best chance at a decent education, and in Spain, monks were often more or less subcontracted to the government as judges and administrators by the various orders.

With entire communities of recent converts common in Spain, the ruling class reserved higher ranks in the Church and throughout society to descendants of Catholics. A Muslim or Jewish grandfather could keep you from becoming a bishop or a judge. When the need for administrators in the Americas outran the supply available in Spain (people with good jobs or the prospect of one in Spain had no reason to risk their lives on a dangerous sea voyage), *conversos* – Jews and Muslims, mostly Jews, who had converted to Christianity – from families with a tradition of scholarship or public service under the former Muslim rulers found a use for their skills and learning. The best of the early administrators in New Spain—especially the Church leaders—were conversos.[28]

The early colonies, like Cuba, had been relatively easy to control. The people either died from the new diseases or were turned into slaves. The native Cubans were completely wiped out, but there weren't that many to begin with. Cortés' conquest had added a country larger than Spain, but one neither Muslim nor Jewish nor Catholic, to the kingdom. It was at least as complex a society as Spain, and Cortés had no illusions of ruling it through military superiority alone. He recognized that he would need the local rulers, but he needed local rulers loyal to Spain. That meant making good Catholics out of the Aztecs, Tlaxcalans and other peoples of México. It's not at all surprising that Cortés asked Carlos for missionaries before he even completed the conquest. Carlos, surprisingly, chose Franciscan monks to complete the conquest.

---

[28] A surprisingly large number of the early Spanish settlers in the Americas were conversos. DNA evidence shows that most of the New Mexico "Spanish" (descended from settlers during the colonial era, and who do NOT consider themselves "Mexican-Americans") are genetically Jews.

The Franciscans were not an obvious choice; trained as preachers and admired for their lives of voluntary poverty, they might be willing to take on the hardships of life in a new country, but they weren't particularly known for diplomacy, administrative skills or scholarship.

Carlos was not only the king of Spain; he was also Holy Roman Emperor, ruling most of what is now Germany, Switzerland, Liechtenstein, Luxembourg, the Czech Republic, Austria, Slovenia, Belgium, Netherlands and parts of modern France, Poland and Italy—he could chose whomever he wanted.

One connection was a brilliant Belgian monk, Peter of Ghent. Peter, called Pedro de Gante in Spanish, was a genius when it came to organization. He recognized that a special kind of monk was needed in New Spain. Religious conviction was not enough. The missionaries would have to learn new languages, live in an alien culture and develop effective "marketing strategies" for working with that culture. If that weren't enough, these monks, gentle as their reputation might be, would have to hold their own against greedy conquistadors and (supposedly reformed) cannibals. Finally, they had to be physically fit.

The first twelve "Super-Monks" (naturally, they were called the Apostles) astounded both the Spaniards and the indigenous people by walking from Veracruz to Mexico City—barefoot. To preach to the indigenous people, they set about learning the local languages and peoples. De Gante himself took over the former Aztec upper-class school. Because the Náhuatl language was written in hieroglyphics, more as cue cards for memory than as a readable text, de Gante used roman script (the same letters used by Latin, English and Spanish) to translate Náhuatl into something the missionaries could understand. This also made it easier for the students to study Náhuatl, Spanish and Latin. Latin was the Church's international language and the language of all European scholarship and diplomacy at the time. The young nobles were being trained as European-style leaders. Left unsaid was that the indigenous students, no matter how brilliant, would not be given leadership posts in a Spain that didn't even grant equal rights to men with one Jewish grandparent. At best, they could aspire to a local administrative post or maybe a job as a behind-the-scenes administrative assistant.

Cortés had some experience in converting people—but conversions at sword point had not been particularly effective, besides, there were too many people to convert. In Spain, missionaries had been familiar with Jewish and Muslim beliefs and had some idea of what objections people might raise to changing their practices. With the Mexicans, they were working with too many unknowns to be effective. De Gante assigned the task of studying Aztec religion to a converso scholar, Bernardino de Sahagún. In the process, de Sahagún developed an entirely new science, anthropology. Many of the processes he first devised—especially collecting oral histories—are still used today. The students from the Nobles School became field researchers and collected oral histories. They set out to interview the old nobility about their religious beliefs and morals, but those old men and women talked about everything. De Sahagún's students wrote it all down—religious services, children's lullabies, family recipes. Everything went into traditional Náhuatl "comic books", with the new Náhuatl roman script and Spanish translations in the margins.

The converso scholar came to admire the Aztec culture (though he disapproved of their gods and cannibalism, of course), their ethical system and their scientific skill. De Sahagún has been criticized in our day for neglecting to interview the ordinary people and for pushing his beliefs on his interviewees, but he was a missionary, and the ordinary people were probably too busy farming and trying to survive after the Conquest to talk to curious students. In the process though, he preserved what little we know of the Aztecs' history and beliefs. Most monks and conquerors destroyed Aztec records and libraries. They claimed the hieroglyphic writing was a sign of devil worship. More practically, they destroyed things like land records to obliterate any legal claim to property. Villa, Zapata and the other later revolutionaries followed this tradition four hundred years later, taking care to destroy landlords' financial records. De Sahagún's students performed one other service: writing a history of the conquest from the indigenous point of view.

Conversions went faster than anyone anticipated. De Sahagún was perhaps the father of market research as well as the father of anthropology. Thanks to de Sahagún and others like him, the missionaries tailored their preaching to local beliefs. They stressed common features. For ordinary people, sometimes this was enough. Both religions featured sacrifice (though the Christians had an edge with the ordinary people, since their sacrifice didn't mean losing any relatives). Both had the same ideas of sin and the forgiveness of sin (but confessing sins took a different form: Catholics told their sins to the priest who assigned a penance; the Aztecs wrote their sins out, gave them to the Goddess of Garbage and then devised their own public penance). Finally, the Spaniards were the new rulers, and the people had always taken the new ruler's gods.

The mass conversions (at one point, the Apostles were baptizing up to a thousand people a day) turned the supermonks into supermen. While the religious life involves spiritual exercises it tends to neglect the body, and the European monasteries, stressing austerity, tended to offer a very poor diet to their residents.

One thing that surprised early commentators (and even modern ones) on México was the excellent state of people's teeth. In Europe, people's teeth tended to rot by the time they were in their twenties, but in México, even elderly people often had good teeth, indicating they had a healthy diet. The missionary monks, living among their new charges, were supposed to eat what was available, and they were walking from village to village, up and down mountains, carrying heavy religious statues. Carrying heavy weights at a high altitude (where the body is forced to work harder to obtain oxygen) and eating a healthy balanced diet is still the basis of body-building. The first archbishop faced a budget crisis, not having planned to replace the robes of skinny pious scholars for "athletic fit" robes for his pumped-up, broad-shouldered, muscular Christians. In recent years, Lerma (between Mexico City and Toluca) has gained a world-wide reputation among professional body builders as one of the best places to train, precisely because of it's altitude.

The several conversos among the early Church leaders in México had another important effect. Jews and Muslims have common beliefs with Christians, but conversions in Spain had caused bloody wars, mass exterminations and lingering resentment—even among the conversos who had joined the orders of the Church. Converso missionaries were more likely to overlook variations from strict Catholic practices as long as people adopted the main points. Fortunately for the new Catholics in México, the first archbishop had come to México with two strikes against him: he was from a converso family, and he was also a Basque—an ethnic minority with customs and a language very different from other Spaniards. In Spain, he might have been a minor bishop or perhaps a royal administrator. In México, his power was second only to the Pope.

In most of the Catholic world, the Pope appoints archbishops and bishops. In Spain, the king, rather than the Pope, appointed them. México was too far away for even that, so the archbishop could appoint his own bishops. Juan de Zumárraga, chosen for his administrative skills, was handed one of the most powerful jobs in the Church. Far from Spain and even further from the Pope in Rome, de Zumárraga could accept dancing in front of his churches and Náhuatl hymns inside. If the incense in the churches wasn't exactly the same as the incense in Europe, at least there was incense. Flowers had often been used for currency, and people liked looking at the floral displays in the churches. For de Zumárraga, the important thing was that they came to church. If some Christian saints were suspiciously similar to local gods, it could be conveniently overlooked.[29]

---

[29] Until the 17th century, the Church supported co-opting local customs if they could be given a Catholic overlay. A good example is the Christmas tree, which originally had to do with a German winter ceremony honoring their own gods but was "Christianized". Christmas itself was put in the middle of winter to conform with a Roman holiday featuring merrymaking and gift giving. However, the Church had not done any mass conversions since the Vikings and Slavs several hundred years earlier, or the Jews and Muslims in Spain. At any rate, the previous convert groups were Europeans and already familiar with the European way of doing things.

New World Order

N EW SPAIN WAS TOO LARGE and too complex to rule
through the informal methods that were used
in the early years. The king couldn't depend on ships showing
up every now and again with treasures or discovering a problem
when bishops found novel ways to send messages. The Council of
the Indies had worked for a time—a few monks managed most of
North and South America out of a house in Seville, but it was just
too much to expect a few monks—even the outstanding monks
of the early years—to handle. Carlos—king of Spain and the Low
Countries (Belgium and Holland) and Holy Roman Emperor to
boot—just couldn't be bothered every time an old conquistador
claimed he was still owed some money and the local judge couldn't
make a final decision.

It sometimes took a year to send messages back and forth. Like
in any of his other kingdoms, Carlos needed someone to run day
to day government activities: judges, regional governors, military
leaders, tax collectors, customs inspectors, road commission-
ers and clerks. The solution was to appoint a Viceroy – assistant
king – *virrey* in Spanish. The king and the monks in Seville might
still send out instructions, but it was up to the viceroy to put them
into action. Carlos was intelligent enough to understand his limits

and the problems involved in sending instructions that might make no sense by the time they arrived. If necessary, the viceroy could ignore the instructions. With time, royal instructions ended with the phase, "...or do whatever you think best."

The only limit on the viceroy and not on the king was that the viceroy had to answer to the *Audiencia* at the end of his term. The Audiencia was a high court, sort of a royal grand jury; it investigated irregularities in the viceroy's accounts and made suggestions for improvement.

Vasco de Quiroga, who arrived as Audiencia judge in 1530, would have a lasting impact far beyond colonial administration. De Quiroga, who was past sixty (an old man for his time) was something of a pioneer—the first foreigner who came to México to retire but found a new and meaningful second career in his adopted country. Among many other things in the 16th century, monasteries were assisted living centers. Even peasants often invested a small sum with their local monastery over their lifetime to pay for their care when they got too old to work. De Quiroga, who had a good pension as a senior bureaucrat, planned to invest in a new Mexican monastery that would take care of him the rest of his life when he finished up this last assignment.

De Quiroga found two things in his Audiencia that bothered him deeply. Pedro de Guzmán's abuse of the local indigenous peoples, especially the Tarascans, and the huge number of minor criminal cases where the defendant was drunk. De Quiroga was one of the first people to recognize alcoholism as a disease. His money for the monastery went to open the world's first alcoholism rehab center, Hospital de San Cosme y San Damián in Mexico City.

His concern for the Tarascans led to a whole new career. Having himself ordained as a priest (like other Spanish judges, he was nominally a monk), he pulled strings to have himself appointed Bishop to the Tarascans. After a lifetime as a careful bureaucrat, the old man wanted a challenge and was open to radical ideas. Seizing on the new bestseller from England, Thomas More's *Utopia*, he reformed Tarascan society and in the process developed legal concepts that México would still find useful in the 21st century.

More, like de Quiroga, a royal bureaucrat (More was Henry VIII of England's personal attorney), envisioned a Christian communist state. In *Utopia*, the village, under the direction of priests, would be the basic unit of an egalitarian community of workers. Each village would specialize in producing a single product needed throughout the larger community, and all would help grow food. Under Tata Vasco (de Quiroga's Purépecha name), the Tarascans turned their villages into just such communes. Villagers worked six hours a day producing goods like pottery or tools or musical instruments; pooled their funds to buy food and supplies and shared the profits. Like any Communist society, they spent a lot of time in meetings. These consciousness-raising sessions, besides being religious sermons, included the latest ideas in self-government, information on new European crops and discussions of de Quiroga's particular contribution to the community—contracts. Having spent his life as a bureaucrat and lawyer, he knew how to write good contracts that would stand up—in some cases they stood up for centuries.

De Quiroga's actual birth date is unknown, but he lived to be at least ninety-five. Although the communes didn't long survive him, the Tarascan communities still specialize in single products. Rural communities throughout México adopted some of de Quiroga's ideas, creating the legal basis for *ejidos* – a type of commune – and farmers' cooperatives. It's no accident that Lázaro Cárdenas, the 20th-century president who is most associated with bringing the rural indigenous communities into the Mexican "Revolutionary family", was governor of the modern Tarascan State of Michoacán. Although never an official saint, Quiroga's image is venerated in churches throughout Tarascan territory.

In addition to oversight by the Audiencia, the viceroy had to share power with the archbishop. Not only could the Mexican archbishop appoint his own bishops, but the Spanish Church had an unusual legal right: clergymen could only be tried for crimes in their own courts. Clerical courts not only tried religious crimes, but any crime involving the clergy: robbery, murder and, in one famous case, selling uninspected beef. The archbishop insisted his butcher shop was Church property and off-limits to the viceroy's health inspector. The viceroy insisted all butcher shops had to be inspected. The archbishop threatened the viceroy with the hellfire; the viceroy threatened the archbishop with cannon fire. The archbishop called on good Christians to ignore the viceroy, and a mob looted and burned his palace. Health code violations involving clergymen stayed in the clerical courts.

To further tie the Church to the state, Spain also had the Inquisition. Spain was only completely united in 1492. In a world where loyalty to the king meant loyalty to the king's religion, and in a country where there were many new Catholics, enforcing belief was a serious matter. The Inquisition was a religious loyalty court with its own police and prisons. It investigated charges of heresy (having beliefs other than the approved Catholic ones). The archbishop of Mexico City was given his own Inquisition. Archbishop de Zumárraga normally ignored local variations from strict Catholic practice, especially when they involved indigenous converts. His first Inquisition case only strengthened his conviction to tread cautiously in indigenous practices.

The case was a mess. An Inquisition agent reported that a well-respected Aztec nobleman was secretly practicing the old religion. Worse yet, the nobleman was a graduate of Pedro de Gante's school. Conservative clergymen, who resented the un-Spanish characteristics of some native practices, saw the Inquisition as a way to purge these native elements. Other Spaniards adopted the attitude that if the natives were educated they would take advantage of their new rulers. Still others realized how few Spaniards there were…and how many Aztecs. It hadn't been all that long ago that the Aztecs had threatened to cook up Spaniards and serve them in tamales. What haunted all the Spaniards was the possibility of a plot to overthrow their rule.

The nobleman freely confessed but took an unusual line of defense. He had been forced to convert against his will. He had paid attention in his religion classes: if, as Catholics asserted, man had free choice, he couldn't be forced to become Catholic.

More ominously, the nobleman added that if people could turn Christian overnight, they could just as quickly turn cannibal. While de Zumárraga allowed the nobleman to be executed, he made indigenous heretics off-limits to the Inquisition. Indigenous people were to be treated as religious children, just as the Law of the Indies treated them as legal children.

The Mexican Inquisition (and the Inquisition in other colonies) was never as ferocious as it was in Spain. For one thing, it had too large a territory to handle (after 1565, the Inquisition in Mexico City had to hear cases from the Philippines) and too small a staff to ever look at more than the most egregious offenses. Jews practiced their religion more or less openly in México until the 1600s and seldom were persecuted after that. In some ways, the religious courts acted as a brake on abusive government officials. The reputation for cruelty of the Inquisition—and the Spanish in general—is largely due to one of its more outstanding judges, Bartolomé de las Casas.

De las Casas wrote a classic of Spanish literature and America's first exposé, *A Short Account of the Destruction of the Indies*. De las Casas had arrived in Cuba in 1502, just ten years after Columbus first came to the Americas. In his 1552 book, he related the horrors of the Spanish exploitation of the native Cubans in gory detail. Besides being an early investigative reporter, he was probably the first actuary. De las Casas came to México in 1525, as the new bishop of Chiapas. He studied death records to determine what happened to people forced to labor against their will. Not surprisingly, he found that they died. Although he shared many of the assumptions of his time (he thought the indigenous habit of a daily bath might be responsible for the high indigenous death rate and preached continually on the dangers of bathing), he noted that people from the tropics sent into the colder highlands, or highlanders sent to the tropics, died sooner than others. A one-man Civil Liberties Union, crossing the Atlantic, even when he was over ninety, to lobby the Pope (a personal friend) for better treatment of the indigenous peoples, he also suggested that African slaves be imported to work in the tropics.

As inquisitor and bishop, de las Casas took an unusual tack when fighting Spanish abuse of the natives. Having convinced the Pope and the King that indigenous people had rights, he prosecuted a Spanish landowner for the heresy of abusing the natives. To make his point, he had the offending landowner burned at the stake.

Because of his support of slavery (which he later regretted), his role as an inquisitor and his shocking insistence that even pagans had rights and couldn't be forced to convert, de las Casas was never made a saint by the Roman Catholic Church, though—as a civil rights pioneer—he is a saint in the Anglican and Lutheran Churches. He is also considered the father of liberation theology, the mostly Latin American movement within the Catholic Church to define the Church's role as defender of the poor and downtrodden. Liberation theology has only been around since the 1960s, but several Chiapas bishops over the centuries have been outspoken defenders of the indigenous community. In the 1990s, the Bishop of Chiapas openly sided with the Zapatista guerrilla movement. After being forced to resign, his conservative successor attacked foreign multinational corporations for their exploitation of poor farmers.

Under the Law of the Indies, indigenous people were treated as children. Children (in this case, the indigenous people) were seen and not heard, and in some ways this unfortunate Spanish attitude preserved indigenous culture. Legally, they were ignored except when they came into conflict with Spaniards. Their religious practices blended Christian and the old ways, but they were left alone. Viceroy de Velasco finally outlawed the practice of having indigenous slaves in 1550.

Viceroy de Velasco also ended the labor obligations Cortés used to rebuild Mexico City. Under the old system, entire communities were drafted as unpaid construction workers, which meant their fields were neglected. The labor obligations were replaced with the *reparimento*, which meant that every indigenous man had to contribute forty-five days' labor a year to public works. Reparimentos were only supposed to be six-hour workdays, but often lasted twice that long. The workers were supposed to be paid a set wage, but people regularly "forgot" to pay, or were late, or misplaced the pay records, or any number of excuses. The Spaniards may have thought the indigenous workers were children, but these children hired lawyers and went to court. This system lingered on into the middle 1600s, when it finally was abandoned in all but the mining regions. What finally killed the reparimento was simple economics. With fewer people after the epidemics, labor was expensive. High wage workers found any excuse they could to avoid reparimentos.

Despite abuses, reparimento workers often threw themselves into projects that interested them. Indigenous laborers, under indigenous architects and builders invented new building styles and techniques for churches, palaces and public buildings. Early churches often feature Aztec gods peeking out of the stonework, or indigenous saints and angels.

Although technically free, the indigenous people continued to lose power. Most were peons—not slaves—but hopelessly mired in debt (and likely to be killed or punished if they left their landlord's employment), and that debt was passed on to their children and grew larger with each generation.

Imported African slaves had no protectors like Las Casas or the Law of the Indies, but they did have a few rights. Oddly, as property, the state said slaves could not be tortured or executed by the Inquisition. The Church, recognizing the humanity of slaves, said they had a few basic rights. Slaves could keep money they earned on their own, and they could marry whomever they wanted. Married slaves could not be kept away from their families. Indigenous men were more in contact with Europeans, and more died from the new diseases than women. With a shortage of available men, indigenous women often married African slaves. Their children were free. The free wife often sold the slave husband's work in the marketplace, sometimes earning enough to buy the husband out of bondage.

The Spanish were continually haunted by fears that the indigenous people might rebel, which they occasionally did. Even more frightening was the prospect that the slaves might do so. The first slaves (besides those with early expeditions and personal servants) had arrived in 1537. There were slave revolts around Mexico City throughout the 1540s. In the 1560s and 70s, runaway slaves joined Chichimecas in raiding parties around Zacatecas. In 1570, the most successful slave revolt started when Gabonese slave, Gaspar Yanga, led several hundred runaways into the wilderness near Mount Orizaba (in modern Veracruz State). Living from raids on local Spaniards and from trade with other mountain communities, the slave stronghold grew as more and more runaways joined Yanga. Unable to defeat the runaways for thirty-nine years, the Spanish authorities finally recognized Yanga's community as a self-governing commune and granted all those arriving before 1608 status as free persons. While San Lorenzo de los Negros is no longer ethnically Afro-Mexican, it is still a thriving community.

The Saints come marching in

ARCHBISHOP DE ZUMÁRRAGA HAD REFRAINED from forcing the people to conform to strict Spanish religious practices. The indigenous people had enjoyed singing and dancing in their old religion, and Catholic hymns were a great hit with the people. Both European and Mexican musical instruments and rhythms enriched church services. The missionaries were less comfortable with the dancing, but as long as it didn't have too obvious a relation to the old gods the people were free to dance in front of the church. In the 21st century, they still do.

The Náhuatl-speaking people had always believed that their dead relatives were all around them. They would leave offerings for them (though the Huastecs sometimes complained about dead relatives who partied all night and drank too much pulque and got rowdy). The Christians had a religious holiday to pray for the recently dead. The people combined the two and visit cemeteries and leave party food on their dead relative's graves, on *el día de los muertos* – the Day of the Dead – 2 November.

Even when Tlacaélel imposed the Huitzilopochtli religion throughout the Aztec empire, every town still had its own local festival and parties. They still do, although the local festival and party honors a Christian saint. Every village had its local god, and they still revere their local saint and will defend that saint. In a Tlapan indigenous neighborhood in Mexico City, a thief was beaten to death when he attempted to steal the local saint's statue. Mexico City's mayor was quoted as saying, "With the traditions of the people, with their beliefs, it's best not to get involved." This wasn't in 1601 or 1701, but in July 2001.

Popocatépetl, the volcano, was a Náhuatl god, but today Saint Gregory guards the volcano. Or maybe he lives there. Local people still bring the saint food and gifts to remind him to ask God to send the rain and good weather the farmers need for a good crop. When the volcano erupted in December 2000, one local man suggested that Saint Gregory was hungry…and maybe a few tortillas would solve the problem.

The Spanish farmers and settlers introduced domestic animals and new crops. Horses and large dogs had come with Cortés. Within a few years, the Spaniards introduced *burros* – donkeys – sheep, goats, cattle and pigs. Although pigs are particularly destructive to the environment (They root up the soil. Cuba was completely forested in 1492. Within twenty years pigs had destroyed the forests and they have never grown back.), the monks felt pigs were a success in America. Despite their respect for Aztec aristocratic values, they could never reconcile civilized people with cannibals. The monks tried everything to convince the upper class Aztecs to give it up, but nothing would do…until the monks tried pork. The Aztecs thought it tasted just like human. That was enough to convince some that the new religion wasn't so bad. Lower class people could keep a pig or two and eat like the upper class on special occasions.

Sheep and goats are also environmentally destructive, but with epidemics leaving large areas of the country depopulated, the animals were allowed to breed and roam free. Cattle created serious problems. Cows would wander into farmer's fields and eat their corn. As soon as there were courts, there were lawsuits between indigenous farmers and Spanish cattlemen. The cattlemen became an important special interest group in New Spain, with their own full-time lobbyists and lawyers in the Capital to look out for their interests. Naturally, the cattlemen usually won their case.

Beef was impossible to export in the days before refrigeration. Low-paid cowboys drove the cattle to the nearest market, where beef was incredibly cheap. The only exportable cattle product was leather. The indigenous people had always made their own leather goods (they used deerskins, mostly) and quickly developed entire communities of skilled leatherworkers. Milk was not transportable, either, but the Spanish brought cheesemaking along with them, and cheese became an integral part of Mexican cuisine.

Horses could carry much more than a human porter could, but in the first years, they were still extremely expensive to import. Burros were smaller, but strong, patient and able to survive in deserts where horses can't. Mules, a cross between a horse and a burro, are the size of a horse and tough like a burro. Mule drivers were the independent truckers of New Spain with their own subculture and lifestyle. They attracted a fair share of outlaws and misfits, one of whom charmed the Pope.

This particular mule driver was unusual in another way—not just a Spaniard and presumably too high class for a rough job like this—but "he" was a she. Back in Spain, Catalina de Erauso had been growing up to be a future juvenile delinquent. Her family, hoping to straighten her out, placed her in a convent. Catalina was a very bad nun. She disguised herself as a man and set out for Peru. As a man, she was a swashbuckler and a "hired sword". Arrested for murder, the judges didn't quite know what to do when they found the defendant was not only a woman, but a nun. Even a bad nun was supposed to be tried in clerical courts. The Peruvians shipped her back to Spain. The Spanish judges couldn't decide what to do either, so they turned her over to the Pope. The Pope found her adventures much more interesting than the legal case, and gave her special permission to live as a man, but on one condition—she could not go back to Peru or resume her career as a "hitwoman".

She became a mule driver in México about 1645 and fought at least one duel when a gentleman took exception to Catalina's attentions to his wife. She died in 1651. A novel, based on Catalina's "true story", said to be the first printed in the Americas, was printed in Mexico City in 1653.

Mexican exports included the native plant products: chocolate, vanilla, rubber, sisal and henequen. These last two were rope-making fibers. Most cotton was used locally. Corn, tomatoes and chiles conquered the world, but once the seeds reached Europe there was no longer a market for those products. Tropical fruits were another export.

Imported plants started arriving from the day Cortés stepped ashore. Burdocks and other weeds were in the horses' feedbags. The first wheat farmer in America was neither European nor indigenous, but a freed African slave named Juan Garrido. Cortés imported Spanish fruits and the European vegetables now used in Mexican cuisine—carrots, onions, garlic and peas—soon followed. México is mostly in the tropics but has high mountains that are cooler (some have snow). Nearly any type of plant can be grown somewhere in México. Rice is grown on the Gulf coast.

Haciendas produced nopal cactus for *nopales* – prickly pear cactus pads used as a tasty food, their fruit – *tunas* – and for *cochinal* – cochineal – from an insect that lived on the nopal cactus. They also produced another purely Mexican crop, *agave* – a large relative of the yucca, also called maguey. Sisal, a fiber used for rope making comes from one variety, henequen, another rope-making fiber, comes from another variety and yet another variety is used for *aguamiel* – agave juice – which can be fermented into *pulque*.

Monks in the Jalisco village of Tequila began distilling pulque, creating another uniquely Mexican product. Agave was cheap to grow but required large amounts of land. It didn't sell for much, so agave haciendas paid very little, providing their workers with barely enough to eat and not much else. The owners, however, got incredibly rich off pulque, especially once the strict Aztec laws against drunkenness were gone. The indigenous people, without enough to eat and often with their communities destroyed, could still afford to get drunk. And did! People noted the serious alcoholism problem, but as long as it only affected indigenous people not much was done about it. People only seemed to notice when alcoholism turned to crime.

Brother, can you spare two bits?

THE SMALL AMOUNTS OF GOLD and silver Cortés found were nothing compared to the discoveries in the 17th century. Ironically, the fabulous wealth of the Mexican mines bankrupted Spain. The Guanajuato mines alone produced more gold and silver than had ever existed in Europe before. The two metals were the currency of the time, but no one had ever faced a situation where there was just too much money available. The rich bought imported goods, and Spanish industries languished. Spanish farmers couldn't compete with lower priced foreign products and abandoned their land. The only way the upper class could spend their money at home was to buy land, throwing still more farmers out of work, creating an army of tramps and beggars. Some sailed for México (the government rounded up still more, put them on ships and dumped some of them in México to get rid of them). More than a few ruined aristocrats—and a few con men—tried to convince indigenous people to support them, simply because they were Spaniards. If that didn't work, they could always become thieves or take up highway robbery. México became a dangerous country. Most of the farmers, though, married into local families, producing the modern Mexican, a person with both indigenous and European ancestors—the mestizo.

Spain, dependent on the Mexican (later, the Peruvian) mines, became poorer and poorer. More and more of its wealth was paid in interest to creditors in England, Holland and the rest of Europe, and less and less stayed in the country. Even Hungarians got rich from the Mexican silver mines. Mercury was essential to silver production, and Hungary was the main source for mercury. Everybody got rich except the Spanish.

Spain attempted to gain control of the economy through bureaucratic regulations. Partly to control the flow of money into Spain and partly because the country was too poor to afford regular naval patrols, only one commercial fleet a year sailed to and from México. To keep Spanish industries from collapsing, Mexicans were forbidden to open competitive businesses. Silk worms were a particular concern, since Spain had a thriving silk industry, but the early colonials—like their 21st-century descendants—found a source for cheaper, though illegal, Chinese imports.

Miguel López de Legazpi and Andrés de Urdaneta (a retired sailor turned monk, who was along as a chaplain, but took over as pilot when most of the crew died of scurvy) discovered a route to Manila in 1565, giving Spain a backdoor to China. The Philippines were added to the Spanish Empire, and Franciscans were again called on to convert the native peoples. Successful in the Philippines, the monks had a harder time in Japan, although Japanese monks were studying and working in Cuernavaca by 1600.[30] The Philippines remained a part of México until 1814, and a Spanish colony until 1898 when the United States gained possession. Much as the Mexicans had adapted Spanish customs to their own culture, the Filipinos adapted Mexican ones. There was less Filipino influence in México, but monks were not the only Filipino immigrants, and Filipino ancestry is common, especially around Acapulco. The close ties between the two cultures became important during

---

[30] The frescos in the Cuernavaca cathedral were supposedly the work of Japanese monks and indigenous Mexican artisans. However, most Japanese influence in México dates from immigration after the Second World War.

the Second World War when Japan invaded the Philippines and México joined the Allies to fight the Japanese.

As with the European trade, where trade was limited to one fleet a year from Veracruz, the Spanish limited trade with Manila to one Pacific port, Acapulco. Chinese silk, traded in Manila for Mexican silver, unloaded at Acapulco and carted to Mexico City—with new taxes at each step—was still better quality than Spanish silk...and more fashionable, too. The lively silk smuggling business convinced enterprising Mexican farmers to try growing their own silkworms. Mexican silk production worried Spanish authorities throughout the colonial period. Before he turned complete rebel, Miguel Hidalgo defied the authorities in minor ways, raising silkworms being one. What finally stopped the Mexican silk industry was a tiny wasp that preyed on silkworms.

Another insect proved more valuable. Cactus and agave grow everywhere. Cacti are eaten as nopales and tunas, used for fiber and fed to animals. Even the parasites have value. Cochineal is produced from the bodies of flies that live on cactus. It was the best source of red dye before artificial dyes were invented in the late 1800s. It was the ONLY source for the shade of red the British army used for their coats. The cochineal haciendas couldn't pay much more than food (and not enough of that), so kept their workers as slaves in all but name.

During the American Revolution, México supplied both the red for the British redcoats and the dollars that paid George Washington's troops. The first American dollars were simply silver Mexican or Spanish eight *reales* – later known as a *peso* – coins, commonly called Spanish dollars. The symbol on the eight real coin shows a banner wrapped around a pillar, which may be the reason the dollar and peso both use "$" as a symbol. Since coins smaller than a dollar weren't common, it became common to cut these pieces of eight into one-eighths, called bits, equal to one Mexican or Spanish real. Although the peso and the dollar have long been divided into one-hundredths, and cutting up coins now makes them worthless, in the United States two-eighths—a fourth—of a dollar (twenty-five cents) is still called "two bits".

Despite serious defects, Mexico City was the cultural, business and government center of México. Mexico City sits in a bowl in the mountains with nowhere for water to drain naturally. Flooding was a continuous problem. The Spanish ideas of a city did not include canals and more were filled in every year. The lakefront was continually filled in. Nezahuacóyotl's engineering projects had been forgotten or abandoned. In 1607 the viceroy authorized a drainage ditch that was never finished. Taxpayers complained about the costs, and landowners complained about the big ditch running through their neighborhood. A flood in 1629 left most of the city underwater for three years. Priests conducted "float by" services from church towers. People who could moved out. The rest shifted as best they could, living on their roofs, or adding a second story to their houses (and hoping the ground floor didn't collapse) and traveling by canoe.

Nearly every institution that mattered was—and still is—in Mexico City. The government and the Church were headquartered there. The only university (founded in 1543) in North America until Harvard was founded a hundred years later and all the decent schools were in Mexico City. Owners of Zacatecas mines, Veracruz shippers and rural hacienda owners preferred La Capital, and all businesses were headquartered there. Nearly all artists and intellectuals also lived in the city.

The greatest of México's colonial intellectuals produced mystical and erotic poetry, feminist tracts and philosophical studies. If that wasn't enough, she defended scientific education in a religious age. This was an unusual combination of talents, especially for a nun. Juana Inés María del Carmen Martínez de Zaragoza Gaxiola de Asbaje y Ramírez de Santillana Odonoju was a child prodigy. Born in 1651, she could read and write by the time she was three. The only place for a prodigy like Juana was Mexico City, so she was sent there to live with relatives. She was a talented writer and musician by the time she was a teenager and was a beauty on top of everything else. The viceroy's wife heard about this amazing country girl and moved her into the palace. The girl could hold her own with scholars and fended off would-be boyfriends with witty verses. Some of her most erotic poetry was addressed to the viceroy's wife, which some people take to mean she was a lesbian. She may have been, but the only career paths for respectable women were as wives or nuns.

Since a housewife wouldn't be able to pursue intellectual interests, she joined the Carmelite nuns, taking the religious name Sor (Sister) Juana Inés de la Cruz. The Carmelites practiced strict discipline with no personal comforts: they would only sleep for an hour or two on cold floors between religious services and never eat hot meals. Sometimes they whipped themselves as a religious practice. This nearly killed Juana, and the viceroy's wife rescued her once again, sending her to the Jeronomytes, whom the Carmelites probably considered slackers. The Jeronomyte convents were more women's residential hotels with religious obligations. Juana collected books, wrote and, shocking the entire Mexican clergy, wrote theology and defended science studies and women's education in general. When the viceroy and his wife returned to Spain, Juana lost her powerful defenders. Visitors dropped off and the Jeronomyte superiors were suspicious of the radical nun. Cut off from her friends, she either became depressed or developed serious religious ideas. She gave up her studies, put away her papers and books, moved into an isolated room in the convent and took up the Carmelite practices. In her own blood, she wrote out religious vows, signing them, "Juana, the worst of all." Two years later, at age forty-three, she died in a cholera epidemic, one of the major intellectuals and writers of the 17th century.[31]

The Church attracted all kinds of people. For some, it was a way to get an education. José María Teclo Morelos y Pavón y Pérez, the guerrilla leader during the War of Independence, was a cowboy who wanted to study literature. The priesthood was the only way a poor man could get a decent education. As the only source of education, people wanting certain careers joined the Church, or became clergymen as a way to join the bureaucracy. Women like

---

[31] Sor Juana is probably the only pre-Independence woman (other than the Virgin of Guadalupe) whose name you see on street signs. Her portrait is on the 200-peso note. Fittingly, the convent where she lived is now a university named for her.

Juana Inés joined convents because they didn't want to marry, or couldn't afford a dowry, or they wanted a job—nuns ran hospitals, farms, schools and factories. Men joined the Church for the same sort of reasons, or because they had no particular talents and wanted a relatively easy, respectable lifestyle...of course, some people joined the clergy out of religious conviction.

The Catholic Church ended up as the largest landowner and richest single organization in México. There were no banks, so the Church was also the biggest lender in the colony. Besides church buildings, schools, monasteries and convents, they owned everything from haciendas to apartment houses in Mexico City, ships, mines and factories. They even owned the largest pawnshop in the world, the Monte de Piedad (still in business, although the government took it over in the 1850s).

While respectable people could join the clergy, less respectable ones found other opportunities. Mule driving or banditry appealed to some. Prostitution was common, although Archbishop Aguilar y Seixas did his best to stamp it out in the late 1690s.

A wealthy Spaniard, repenting of his wicked past, had left his house to the archbishop to be used as a home for reformed prostitutes. The archbishop assigned three young priests to fill the *Belem*. Preaching sermons around Mexico City advertising the new facility didn't bring in any customers, but it amused the prostitutes (and a lot of others) in the congregation. When sermons failed to bring the Belem clients, the priests turned to kidnapping. Prostitutes fought back—one priest, who was handsome and well built, was a special target. Called to a deathbed confession by a dying madam, the "dying" woman jumped naked from the bed, bolted the door and began to strip the priest. He jumped out the window.

What started as a refuge ended as a prison. Some of the women went insane from mistreatment, and the Belem became a dumping ground for all kinds of inconvenient women: prostitutes, delinquents, criminals and the insane. One of the three priests would also go insane, and end up in a similarly squalid facility.

The new kings on the block

CLERGYMEN AND PROSTITUTES WERE NOT the only ones going crazy. The Hapsburgs, the Spanish royal family, had married their cousins and close relations for centuries. It seems as if every inheritable problem possible showed up in Carlos II. Carlos the Bewitched had serious physical abnormalities that made his mental and emotional problems worse. In addition to facial deformities and a hunchback, as a child he was thought to be profoundly retarded and was not toilet trained (or even bathed) until he was a teenager. He was probably not retarded, but the early neglect made him profoundly depressive. He was suicidal and incapable of ruling the country. Until Carlos died in 1700 at age thirty-four, the bureaucracy kept the country from entirely collapsing.

Dying was probably the only useful thing Carlos II ever did, but it created a problem...or an opportunity. He had no children,[32] so the Spanish government could shop around for a better royal

---

[32] Carlos was not completely incapable. His first wife, whom he apparently loved and who loved him, died suddenly after a ten year marriage. There were rumors she was poisoned because she was barren. She probably died of appendicitis. His second wife, who was young and slender when she was married off to Carlos for political reasons, was so disgusted by the king that she developed a serious eating disorder and died of extreme obesity.

family. The Hapsburgs objected, and there was war for the next twelve years, but the more forward thinking, reformist Bourbon family took over the kingdom. The idea of doing without a king never crossed their minds in 1700.

The Bourbons had made France a superpower, reformed the bureaucracy and modernized the economy. Spain was a basket case. Philip, the new French-born king, had to start somewhere. Spain had ignored México for years, depending on the one fleet a year, as much out of habit as out of a lack of better ideas. México's silver was still coming into Seville but went straight out again to pay interest on a hundred and fifty years' worth of overdue bills. Opening the port at Cádiz, with better facilities and space for more ships to dock, was an improvement. By 1740, the old, one fleet a year system was abandoned. Pirates might still be a problem (a French pirate took the entire population of Veracruz hostage in 1683), but it was better to lose a few ships as long as there was regular trade.

The Hapsburgs had rewarded loyal subjects with business monopolies in México. The Bourbons broke up most of these monopolies, then sold new ones, saving a few to keep the cash coming in. New ports were built, shippers could sell some products wherever they could find a market within the Spanish-ruled territories and industries were allowed to set up in the colonies.

In Spain, the army and navy were modernized. With officers no longer automatically chosen from the old knightly families, the armed services attracted upwardly mobile middle-class people. Uniforms became fashionable. Beyond a few soldiers guarding ports and acting as the viceroy's guards, there hadn't been a regular army in México until 1763. In México, the army was also a new opportunity for the people who now called themselves *criollos* – Spaniards bred and born in México.

The Bourbons, like the Hapsburgs, had reserved the top jobs for *peninsulares* – people born in Spain. The Spanish had a long history of reserving certain jobs for the right people. In the Americas, with its diverse European (including conversos), African and indigenous peoples, the bureaucrats went to absurd lengths to distinguish between racial backgrounds. A person with two indigenous, one African and one European grandparent would have a different classification than someone with one indigenous, one African and two European grandparents, for example.

In a mixed culture like México, this required a lot of odd classifications. A person with one African grandparent and three indigenous ones was a *zambo*, but if European grandparents were in the mix, the person was a *mulatto*. If you had two indigenous and two African grandparents, you were a *chino*. A person with kinky curly hair is still called *chino* by Mexicans. Confusingly enough, you were also a *chino* if you were of Chinese descent (there were Chinese living in Mexico City by 1600). Filipinos were *negro*.

Mexicans simply ignored these distinctions. Most people were poor farmers or general laborers, where racial classifications didn't matter for the most part. For professions limited to people of entirely European ancestry, such as medicine, qualified people simply changed their family records. Sometimes bribery was involved, and sometimes the people who were supposed to enforce the restrictions simply went along with the deception. If a town needed a doctor and an indigenous doctor was available, then a European could usually be found to claim the new doctor was his cousin.

The only restriction that couldn't be ignored was the one between Spaniards born in Spain and Spaniards born in México. For the Mexican-born criollos, even those who had maintained pure Spanish ancestry, that difference mattered. More and more, the criollos saw their interests conflicting with the Spanish-born gachupines. Criollos became aware that the attitude they held towards the mestizos and the attitude the mestizos held towards the indigenous people was the same attitude the Spanish-born rulers had towards all Mexican-born people. The Spanish even suggested just being born in México made you a little stupid and lazy.

The north had been more or less forgotten since Coronado had returned from his travels, reporting nothing more interesting than "shaggy cows" (it was as close as he could get to describing the bison). The semi-independent Tlaxcalans had established a few colonies as far north as San Antonio, Texas, but the area was basically unexplored territory. To encourage settlement in the north, Bourbon viceroys set up military posts in neglected communities in the north or founded entirely new towns. A few became sizable cities, like San Francisco, Los Angeles, San Antonio and Santa Fé. Missionaries were sent out to pacify the indigenous people (especially in California, where a string of towns still have "Mission" in their name). Under the Bourbons, military government became the rule, rather than the exception, throughout the colony.

Cops and Robbers

To oversee the military and bureaucratic changes, Spain sent a royal inspector-general with the new army. Inspector de Gálvez, later appointed viceroy,[33] with an army to back him, was a roving police chief, bureaucratic reformer and tax auditor rolled into one. He reorganized the government, replaced department heads and changed the tax rates. He hanged corrupt officials, bandits and pirates. De Gálvez would be completely unknown outside México if it weren't for the pirate he never caught.

Jean Lafitte was a leading social and business leader in New Orleans (Louisiana). Though he was an elegant and proper businessman, it was best not to inquire too closely about him. The "cousin" who lived with him was no cousin, and exactly how Lafitte acquired hard-to-find luxury items was best attributed to his outstanding business skills. Lafitte's elegant manners and refined tastes didn't keep him from his real business as a pirate captain.

Louisiana, which had been under Spanish control, was ceded to France in 1803. The French Navy was more efficient than the Spanish one and ruthless in hunting down pirates. Lafitte, like a modern businessman, simply moved his facilities "off-shore", out of

---

[33] Only briefly. His brother was also viceroy, which can be confusing even to specialists in this area of scholarship.

the reach of pesky regulators. Northern México was little patrolled, and even de Gálvez' reformed army didn't patrol the uninhabited north coast. North of Matagorda Bay (Texas), Lafitte found an uninhabited island with a hidden harbor. Ruling over French and American pirates, escaped convicts, British naval deserters and runaway slaves, the respectable New Orleans businessman ran a pirate kingdom. He and his New Orleans "cousin" lived openly as a gay couple, built a luxury home and threw elegant dinner parties for their crew and rare visitors.

The new United States acquired New Orleans in 1803. Lafitte was the first to realize that Texas ports were an ideal location for doing business in both the United States and México. Lafitte's stolen goods sold well, both in New Orleans and in Veracruz. Inspector de Gálvez was a humorless man, who would not have appreciated the joke, but the homosexual pirate had an odd sense of humor. The one corner of México the inspector ignored was where Galvez Town would quickly become Galveston, Texas.

While de Gálvez reformed the bureaucracy and security apparatus, Viceroy Bucarelli worked to improve life in the Capital. After having the first streetlights in the Americas installed in Mexico City, he turned his attention to the blocked streets, especially around the markets.

De Gálvez was an outstanding policeman, but Bucarelli deserves the credit (or blame) for one of the most important innovations in modern urban life. To keep the streets clear on market days, Bucarelli wrote the world's first traffic code. When no one observed the rules, the viceroy founded the world's first traffic police. Mexico City's residents soon began their unending feud with the *tamarindos* – the traffic cops. After stepping in a pile of horse manure while waiting for his coach after a night at the theater, Bucarelli introduced two new urban innovations: the loading zone and the no parking zone. He didn't want the horses standing in front of the theater.

When the world's first traffic code and world's first traffic cops still didn't keep things moving on market days, Bucarelli invented the world's first public transit system, with mule-drawn buses to bring the shoppers and merchants to the markets and back home again.[34]

New viceroys replaced the clergymen in the civil service with soldiers, businessmen, lawyers and "injun" fighters. For a short time, late in the Bourbon era and before the Louisiana Purchase, French Louisiana (all the land drained by the Mississippi and Missouri Rivers) was ceded to Spain.[35] The area was almost completely unknown and México's Bourbon rulers were desperate to find even marginally qualified administrators. Daniel Boone, the famous American frontiersman, had gone bankrupt in Kentucky (besides which, it was too settled for his tastes) and he once again moved west into the forests. He was only semi-literate in English and ignorant of both the Spanish language and Spanish law, but very few inhabitants in the area were any better qualified. Boone knew the frontier and was a shrewd judge of character. He was more than qualified to serve as *Synic* – more-or-less Justice of the Peace – for the Spanish territory that now included most of Missouri and Iowa.

Boone was not even a Catholic. The Bourbon government took a different attitude towards the Church than the Hapsburgs. The Mexican Inquisition lost nearly all its power in a single afternoon. Viceroy de Croix purposely picked a fight with the Inquisitor and was called to the fearsome religious court. The viceroy answered his summons but casually mentioned the artillery regiment just outside the door. After de Croix called the Inquisition's bluff, it limited itself to cases involving the clergy. Symbolic of the Bourbon reforms, the Inquisition moved to smaller quarters, their old palace becoming the *Protomedica* – the first medical society in the Americas. The old torture chamber was used for anatomy classes.

---

[34] Predictably, today's Avenida Bucarelli has daily traffic jams.

[35] When Napoleon Bonaparte made his kid brother, Joseph, King of Spain, he had already lined up a buyer—the United States—for the area that both Spain and France had found too large and sparsely inhabited to effectively administer. Napoleon needed the money, his brother needed the job.

By no means was the Church on the decline. The Metropolitan Cathedral facing the viceroy's palace was enlarged and rebuilt. Finished just before Independence, it is one of the largest churches in the world. With some Mexicans becoming wealthy, newer and more opulent churches replaced earlier functional but bland buildings. If anything, taking the clergymen out of the bureaucracy made the Church wealthier. Its well-trained accountants, lawyers and managers could concentrate on Church properties and Church businesses, and they could develop entirely new businesses. There were enough rich people in Mexico City to create a need for a form of trust fund. To take care of relatives, wealthy families would endow a small chapel inside a larger church. The trust fund was invested, and the relative was paid a salary for maintaining the chapel out of the investment interest. In reality, the relative seldom even visited the chapel he supposedly cared for—the normal practice was to hire a servant, who often handled several of these chapels. Of course, the Church made a healthy return from management fees.[36]

The Society of Jesus – the Jesuits – was one of the most successful clerical entrepreneurs. Besides schools, churches and seminaries, the society managed tracts of urban real estate and had over ten million pesos worth of farms and haciendas. Unfortunately, the Jesuits in Spain had been involved in plots against the king in 1766 and were ordered to leave all Spanish territory. This caused riots in some parts of México, where the Jesuits were seen as relatively good landowners. Religious orders were the biggest slumlords in Mexico City, but they were often popular with the poor, because they would overlook unpaid rents and were less likely to evict their tenants.

---

[36] To handle the legal problems created after the Second World War when foreigners began investing in Mexican vacation properties in the "exclusion zone", i.e., beachfront properties, the colonial church's *fideicomisos* – trusts – were dusted off and given new life as a way to allow non-Mexicans to legally hold title to their investment and to pass on the property to their heirs.

There were two unintended results from expelling the Jesuits. In exile, the Mexican Jesuits wrote pro-Mexican, anti-Spanish propaganda and the first histories of their country from the Mexican people's point of view. Smuggled back into México, these tracts and books allowed educated people to be able to see themselves, not as Spaniards living in the Americas, but for the first time, as Mexicans who lived in culture very different from Spain. The other unintended consequence was that the forced sale of Jesuit property revealed how much of México's land and wealth was in Church hands.

The Bourbons successfully controlled an increasingly complex society for over one hundred years...but there was a larger world outside. When the Bourbons lost control, the many Méxicos—Inspector de Gálvez' professional army, the wealthy and independent Church, the businessmen, the criollos, the gachupines, the mestizos and the indigenous peoples—violently collided. Huitzilopochtli, Tezcatlipoca and Quetzalcóatl were set to continue their ancient feud.

Independence

Cities and Towns

a-Acapulco
b-Brownsville
  Matamoros
c-Chilpancingo
d-Cuernavaca
  Cuatla

e-Guadalajara
f-Guanajuato
g-Mexico City
  Ecatepec
  Guadalupe Hidalgo
h-Monterrey
  Saltillo

i-Nautla
j-Nayarit area
k-Pachuca
l-Puebla
m-Querétero
n-San Jacinto
o-San Luis Potosí
p-San Miguel
  Dolores

q-Tampico
r-Tenango
s-Valladolid
t-Veracruz
u-Zacatecas

1
* Santa Fe
13
* The Alamo
n*
18
4
5
2
b*
h
*12
7
20
23
o
*
ů *17
9 *e 8
Gulf of Mexico
16
6
11 *
k*
g*
d*
c
*
i
21 19
22
10
*
m
14
3
a*
Pacific Ocean

México
after Independence - 1824
States and Territories

1-Alta California	7-Durango	13-Nuevo México	19-Tabasco
2-Baja California	8-Guanajuato	14-Oaxaca	20-Tamaulipas
3-Chiapas	9-Jalisco	15-Puebla	21-Veracruz
4-Chihuahua	10-México	16-Querétero	22-Yucatán
5-Coahuila & Texas	11-Michoacán	17-San Luis Potosí	23-Zacatecas
6-Colima	12-Nuevo León	18-Sonora & Sinaloa	

Who's in charge anyway?

CARLOS I GAVE MÉXICO a Spanish government and instituted effective rule. Carlos II was an incompetent, but the bureaucracy was able to survive. Carlos III reorganized México, sending both Viceroy Bucarelli and Inspector de Gálvez to reorganize the colony. The colony would not survive Carlos IV. His first viceroy, Count Revillagigedo was honest and effective. Carlos IV would never do that again.

Carlos IV was an incredibly stupid man; some have suggested he was brain damaged. He spent his time playing with toys and let the queen do what she wanted. The queen's favorite toy was Manuel Godoy. Godoy was young, handsome, ambitious and smart enough to pay attention to the lonely, plain-looking queen. He was running the Spanish government by the time he was twenty-five. The only credentials Godoy required for government office or for a military commission was the ability to pay. Viceroys, *Intendentes*[37] and generals sent to the colonies had paid good money for their posts, and they expected to get a return on their investment.

---

[37] The Bourbon reforms had combined a number of military and civilian positions. Intendentes were regional governors and commanded local garrison troops.

de Gálvez and Bucarelli's work was falling apart. The colony was still rich but mismanaged, and Godoy's appointees were stealing the tax money.

Spain itself was still rich enough to throw its weight around in political affairs. Godoy's government backed the new United States with ships and money during the American Revolution. Helping an American colony break away from Europe seemed like a good idea at the time. Having made one enemy out of England, Godoy then created another in France.

The French Revolution overthrew the king's cousin, Louis XVI, and then executed him. Godoy sent the badly officered and indifferently soldiered Spanish army to attack France. Aside from wasting men and money, Godoy made himself a serious enemy: the French general, Napoleón Bonaparte. When Emperor Napoleón marched into Spain in 1808, the Spanish army was no match for the French. The king, queen and Godoy were whisked off to France, and the king was forced to abdicate, turning the throne over to Napoleón's brother.

No one in México was going to miss Carlos, the queen or her boy toy (he was pushing forty and a little old for that particular job anyway), but it created an interesting problem. Who was in charge? Who did the viceroy work for? The most powerful resistance group, in Seville, wrote a constitution giving Spain a parliament and limiting the king's power. They had a fairly good claim to be the legitimate government. The *Junta* wrote a constitution, proclaimed Carlos' son Ferdinand a constitutional monarch, set up a parliament (a new idea at the time) and gave orders to the colonial administrators. Other resistance groups claimed Ferdinand was an absolute monarch, or that Carlos was still king. The viceroy in Mexico City had paid good money in order to steal Mexican tax revenue. He didn't expect to answer to either a Frenchman or a parliament. The Mexico City Council (mostly criollo) and the viceroy's staff (mostly gachupines) fought each other; for and against the Seville government and for and against the viceroy. The only thing they could agree on was that they should continue to run México, and that Ferdinand was probably the king.

With this much confusion, other people considered a novel alternative solution. Run México themselves. The United States had thrown out their colonial rulers; France had thrown out their kings; and Haiti (the Hispañola of the early colonialists) had taken the French and American Revolutions one step further—there the slaves overthrew the masters. Haiti haunted the criollos and the gachupines. They did the math—there were about three million indigenous people, one million African slaves and only one hundred fifty thousand criollos and gachupines. No one wanted to think what would happen if the slaves, indigenous peoples and peons in México revolted. As time went on, Napoleón Bonaparte, the general who made himself emperor, ending the chaos of the French Revolution and bringing the middle class into the ruling class, looked better all the time.

¡Mueran los gachupines!

I T WASN'T ONLY IN MEXICO CITY that people were discussing ways to overthrow the government. The Querétaro Literary Society wasn't reading the latest novels or discussing poetry—they were discussing things the Inquisition or viceroy forbade, like the American "Declaration of Independence", military manuals and French and American revolutionary propaganda. They discussed the best type of government for an independent México, and how they might achieve their ends. They planned an army uprising for October 1810. Don Ignacio Allende and Juan de Aldama, both army officers, were in charge of the plans. The pair had been passed over for promotion both for being honest and for being criollos. The two knew officers throughout the army (criollo, honest, or both) who were willing to act.

Miguel Hidalgo y Costilla, a priest from the nearby town of Dolores (modern Dolores Hidalgo), had been a popular professor of religion before he was sent to administer a poor, indigenous community. He had friends throughout the clergy. Like the officers, Hidalgo was criollo, not a gachupín. He could not expect a high position in the Church, although his talents would have qualified him to be at least a bishop. Hidalgo had been in some trouble with his Spanish-born bishop (he apparently threw wild parties for his students, liked gambling and had fathered children). Sent to Dolores, more or less as punishment, Hidalgo, like Las Casas and Vasco de Quiroga, dedicated himself to his people. A skinny, bald-headed old man with piercing green eyes, he could command an audience; he was an eloquent defender of the poor against the rich and powerful. He could preach; he could open businesses to employ local people (always something of a rebel, Hidalgo openly grew wine grapes and raised silkworms—both forbidden economic activities). He started a shoe factory that is still in business today but was helpless to stop Spanish officials from abusing the poor.

The Literary Society's less than literary activities were an open secret. Everyone from the viceroy to the local army commander knew what was going on during the literary gatherings. When the local police chief was ordered to arrest Allende and Aldama, he wasn't sure what to do. He thought it was a plot to trap him. After all, he and his wife were both members of the Literary Society. Not quite trusting his wife and hoping to keep the arrest orders a secret, he locked her in her bedroom. Josefa Ortiz de Domínguez was a stout lady if later portraits are any indication, but she wasn't the typical indolent criollo lady of her time. According to some stories she broke out her window, tied sheets together and mounted a mule to ride off to warn the plotters. More likely, she sent her maid to warn Allende. Allende and Aldama rode over to Dolores to warn Hidalgo. It was 15 September 1810.

Hidalgo stuck a pistol in his belt, rang the church bell in the middle of the night and preached a sermon. Very few of his parishioners could read or write, and a professorial lecture on the American "Declaration of Independence", or Thomas Paine's *Rights of Man* wouldn't mean very much. These people had not argued over the best form of government for an independent México, but they understood Spanish oppression.

Hidalgo hadn't taught rhetoric for nothing. He gave the sermon of his life. It began with a three hundred-year history of the people's abuse by the Spanish. Warming up, he accused the Spanish of plotting to turn the Church over to French atheists.

Historians have never agreed on exactly what Hidalgo told the people that night, but he worked the crowd into a frenzy and turned the congregation into an army by the time he delivered his *Grito de Dolores* – Shout (or Cry) of Dolores[38] – "*¡Viva el rey! ¡Viva México! ¡Mueran los gachupines!*" – "Long live the king, long live México, kill the Spaniards!" Killing the Spaniards is exactly what Hidalgo's parishioners set out to do. This wasn't the professional army Allende and Aldama expected, but it would have to do. Instead of soldiers they had farmers, workers and miners. Instead of rifles, they had sharpened farm tools, pitchforks, clubs and axes. For a general, they had a rabble-rousing, pistol-packing ex-professor priest, but they were winning, and the army was growing. At San Miguel (now San Miguel de Allende), the regular troops joined the rebellion, but they couldn't stop the people from slaughtering the hated Spaniards and looting the city. Allende thought this was no way to run a rebellion. Hidalgo said that people who had been abused and gone hungry for generations needed to get the hatred out of their system. Besides, Hidalgo pointed out, it was the only army he had.

Hidalgo's army numbered over twelve thousand by the time they reached Guanajuato. Thanks to the silver mines, it was the richest city in the world at the time. The Spanish Intendente refused to surrender and herded the Spanish civilians into the *alhóndiga* – a combination fortress and public grain warehouse. The Intendente was killed almost immediately by one of Allende's soldiers. While the Spanish soldiers argued over who was in command, a miner known only as *El Pípila* – Tom Turkey[39] – ran up to the front gate and set it on fire. Hidalgo's army poured in, and *¡mueran los gachupines!* is what they did. After slaughtering the men, women and children in the alhóndiga, they sacked the city. Anyone who looked like they might be a Spaniard, criollo or gachupín, was killed. Hidalgo and Allende weren't the only ones horrified by the

---

[38] And, in a very apt pun, it also means "cry of pain."

[39] Actually, it's the masculine form of turkey hen, and slang for a prostitute. This humble Mexican hero may have been a male prostitute or a transvestite.

slaughter. A criollo teenager named Lucas Alamán cowered on a near-by rooftop. Alamán, who would later hide Cortés' remains from Mexican nationalists, would spend his life defending Spain's historic role in México, and championing elitist rule. He would be the only intellectual to serve Santa Ana.

Criollos all over México, hearing of the slaughter in Guanajuato, began to back the Spanish. Most were for independence of some kind, but with criollo control. The social revolution, and fear of another Haiti, made them reluctant allies with the Spanish until they could find a better solution. The ordinary people—mestizo, indigenous and poor criollos—joined Hidalgo's forces or rose up on their own. Village priests, like José María Morelos, became generals overnight. An illiterate peasant leader captured Guadalajara; a mineworker took over Saltillo. A monk leading only a small group of farmers captured San Luis Potosí without a fight. Nuevo León and Texas, where there weren't a lot of rich criollos—just poor ones, along with mestizos and indigenes who all despised the gachupines more than they despised each other—joined the revolt.

By October, the *Insurgentes* – insurgents – were in Valladolid (now Morelia in Michoacán State). In the city where he had once been a professor, Hidalgo tried to organize some sort of government for his chaotic revolutionary forces. The military men had only set out to seize the government not start a social revolution. Allende and Aldama gave up on the mob that had joined the uprising and set about organizing their military units. The two military professionals made contact with regular army officers, including Augustín de Iturbide y Arámburu (who wasn't interested). Other insurgent leaders, like Morelos, agreed to coordinate their forces with Hidalgo's. A young lawyer and writer from Mexico City, Andrés Quintana Roo, came to write propaganda and offer his services to the people.

Romantic Revolutionaries

QUINTANA ROO HAD MORE TO OFFER than just his literary skills—he was in touch with the anti-Spanish underground in Mexico City and had a spy in the viceroy's camp. His girlfriend was a rich heiress named María Leona Vicario. It is almost too good a romance story to be true. Andrés, the hero, was a poor, honest, handsome employee of a rich viceregal official with the all too perfect, villainous name of Santiago Pomposo. His ward, María Leona, was a pretty, orphaned heiress to a silver mining fortune. In an era of arranged marriages, she was a valuable commodity; one that could be bartered into high social position, even into the Spanish nobility if she was married off correctly. Leona had no interest in marrying the Spanish officer her uncle had arranged for her, staying true to the overlooked office assistant, Andrés. Leona would politely listen to the Spaniard, but out of love and loyalty to the young lawyer, she joined him in the insurgent underground movement. Leona played the ingénue, asking innocent questions and flirting with the officers and politicians. Love letters to Andrés were risky enough, but she also sent details of the Spanish troop movements and an update on what was going on in the viceroy's palace. When Uncle Pomposo found out what Leona was doing, she remembered the story about the runaway nun who became a mule driver. She was caught trying to sneak out of Mexico City. Leona's disguise didn't fool her uncle, who wasn't sure what to do with her. He locked her up in the Belem, the old prostitutes' refuge turned women's prison.

The women prisoners were as mistreated by the gachupines as any peon could claim to be. The women organized a riot and helped from the outside by the insurgents, staged a mass jailbreak. Leona joined Andrés, and they were married by Father Morelos, the cowboy-priest turned general. Andrés later served in a number of high government positions and had a state named for him. Leona remained a sentimental favorite and a few towns are named in her honor. They did, as far as anyone knows, live happily ever after.

At Valladolid, Hidalgo tried to balance the people's wants with the criollos' expectations. For the criollos, he offered to set up a congress that would govern the country in the king's name. Naturally, the congress would be criollo. He appointed criollo generals and gave them important titles in a nonexistent government. For the people, he offered to return the haciendas to their rightful owners, the people who lived on them. Hidalgo wasn't capable of controlling his army; Allende and Aldama were right; a mob of farmers, craftsmen and miners, no matter how enthusiastic or committed, was no substitute for trained, well-armed soldiers.

Hidalgo's forces moved on Mexico City under the banner of the Virgin of Guadalupe. The Royalists, better trained, better armed, and with artillery, had their own Virgin—the Virgin of Remedios, a blue-eyed, blonde statue, brought to México by Cortés himself—that was dressed up in a general's uniform and paraded before the defenders. While neither side won the Battle of the Two Virgins, Hidalgo's army began to fall apart. The insurgents retreated, losing more and more people, both to hit-and-run battles with the royalists and by the desertion of farmers who simply returned to their villages.

The royalists recaptured Guanajuato and took their revenge for the massacre of the gachupines. General Calleja rounded up every man he could find in the city, lined them up, and had every tenth man hanged. Hidalgo's army, then in Guadalajara, retaliated, marching out Spaniards into the bull-fighting area to have their throats cut by a local butcher. Calleja marched on Guadalajara. Despite Allende and Aldama's trained soldiers, the insurgents were no match for the better-trained, better-armed royalists. The defeated leaders had to flee for their lives.

At Zacatecas, Hidalgo turned over command to Allende. Allende headed for Saltillo, hoping to raise more troops and possibly recruit soldiers in the United States,[40] but the government in Saltillo had already switched back to the royalist side. The leaders were eventually caught. Allende, Aldama and Jiménez, the insurgent miner, were shot. Their heads were chopped off and hung from three corners of the alhóndiga in Guanajuato. As soon as a religious trial could strip Hidalgo of his priestly functions, his head was hung from the fourth corner.

---

[40] Had he succeeded, Jim Bowie and Colonel Travis might not have died at the Alamo, but become Mexican heroes instead.

The first modern guerrilla

JOSÉ MARÍA MORELOS CONTINUED the revolt. Of Spanish, African and indigenous ancestry, the village priest had a very different strategy for fighting the Spanish. An ex-cowboy,[41] he knew how to live off the land and how to survive in the wilderness. Unlike Hidalgo, the former professor, and Allende, the officer, Morelos was a peasant—he didn't have to claim French atheists were taking over the Church. He could frame the arguments for independence in simple terms: the poor and downtrodden deserved better lives. He read widely, especially military histories, and made himself the first modern guerrilla leader.

When Hidalgo made Morelos General of the South, Morelos only had twenty-four men, but his men were armed and trained. Rather than enlist entire villages, he only recruited when he had enough guns and ammunition for his recruits and the time to train them. He recruited men like himself—those who could live for months in the wilderness if they needed to, fight battles, change tactics when necessary and accept discipline.

---

[41] Morelos took up the priesthood not only because he was religiously inclined, but also because it was the only chance a poor man had for a higher education. He wanted to study Spanish grammar. At twenty-five, he was an adult learner, about ten years older than most of his classmates in the seminary.

He was a shrewd judge of character, selecting good officers without any interest in their social background. Vicente Guerrero was a peasant farmer; Maríano Matamoros a village priest; Leonardo and Nicholas Bravo were rich landowners and Félix Fernández was an eccentric hermit and mystic who changed his name to Guadalupe Victoria – Victorious (Virgin of) Guadalupe.

Matamoros and Nicolas Bravo were Morelos' "right and left arms" and invaluable subordinates. Both were resourceful guerrillas, able to command personal loyalties for themselves but unquestioning in their support of Morelos. Matamoros seemed a younger version of Morelos—another peasant-priest turned guerrilla out of love of the people and love of justice. He was almost a son to the guerrilla leader. Bravo was honored for his military prowess and devotion to duty (as an old man, he would lead the final defense of Chapultepec Castle against the United States), but as a criollo landowner, his background was just too different from Morelos for them to ever become *compadres* – literally companions, but figuratively a much closer relationship.[42]

What Morelos thought of Pedro Elías Beán isn't recorded. Born Peter Ellis Bean, he was an early U.S. emigrant to Mexican Texas. Bean had been a horse trader, a horse thief and a mercenary before ending up on Morelos' staff. Involved in an ill-fated attempt to set up a private kingdom in east Texas in 1800, Bean had been shuttled around México, vaguely under arrest but still awaiting trial, until 1810. Finally convicted, he was sent to prison in Acapulco just as Morelos was invading. Using the attack as a diversion for staging a jail break, Bean escaped. Bean brought himself to Morelos' attention because of his knowledge of how to make gunpowder.[43]

---

[42] The bonds between *compadres* are life-long and often closer than those between man and wife. "Soul brother" may be the only good English translation of the term.

[43] Bean apparently learned a number of trades while waiting to be sentenced. Although technically a prisoner under a death sentence, he had a thriving hat-making business in Chihuahua for a few years.

By the end of 1811, Morelos controlled the countryside from Acapulco on the Pacific to the outskirts of Mexico City. The royalists, having neutralized Hidalgo, realized Morelos was the real threat and turned their attention towards his armies. With the full might of the viceroy's army against him, Morelos held on, though everything began to go wrong. His army was trapped at Cuatla, in modern Morelos State.

The rebels fortified Cuatla and settled in for a siege. While they waited for the rainy season, the townspeople and the rebels were reduced to eating bugs, soap and even shoes. They hoped yellow fever would decimate the Spanish down in the swamps while they holed up in their mountain town.[44] Unfortunately, the rains were late in 1812.

The Spanish never expected the guerrillas to hold out, but they did, only evacuating on the first of May 1812. While they were able to evacuate their army and some townspeople, the residents that were captured were shot as rebels.

Retreating into the hills (in modern Guerrero State, named for the peasant officer, Vicente Guerrero), the guerrillas regrouped. Mariano Matamoros was captured at the end of 1813 and shot without going though the formality of a clerical trial. Saying, "My right arm has been cut off," Morelos continued to soldier on, though he'd control less and less territory as time went on.

Desperate for foreign aid (and weapons to continue the fight), Morelos dispatched Peter Bean to the United States. Unlike George Washington, who in the 1770s had three European superpowers (France, England and Spain) to play off against each other and was only at war against one of them, Morelos was—indirectly—at war with all three. Spain was controlled by France. England was

---

[44] The connection wasn't made until much later, but it is mosquitoes, not rain, that carry *vomito*, or yellow fever. Until mosquito control became common, wealthy people in tropical regions moved to dryer and cooler climates during the rainy season, especially if their ancestors were not native to the area. Indigenous peoples in tropical regions are often immune to the generally fatal disease. Mexican (and other) generals in the tropics often factored the rainy season into their defense strategies, much as Russians waited for winter.

at war with Napoleón and supported the juntas seeking to restore Carlos IV or Ferdinand VII. No European government had a reason to undermine Spanish control in the Americas. That left the United States. Bean, managing to avoid capture, made it to Nautla, where he ran into a British naval patrol.

Bean tried to get the English to supply Morelos. They politely declined to get involved but did let slip the interesting news that England and the United States had been at war since 1812. As a matter of fact, they were hunting for American pirates. Jean Lafitte, the New Orleans "businessman" who'd become an American in 1803 when the United States bought Louisiana, was who they were looking for. Maybe Bean didn't understand geopolitics and superpower diplomacy, but he knew enough to stay out of fights he couldn't win. He told the British that as a Mexican, it really wasn't any of his concern...and promptly set off to warn the pirates.

Lafitte happened not to be on this expedition, but the pirate captain was grateful for the warning about the British. After a skirmish (which the pirates lost), Bean and the pirates escaped to New Orleans. Bean never managed to contact the U.S. State Department in Washington, but he did try recruiting pirate crews to join the Mexican Navy (which didn't exist) and joined Lafitte at the Battle of New Orleans. Lafitte became an American hero and almost respectable. Bean eventually returned to Texas and used his service with the insurgents to wrangle a position in the Mexican administration after independence. In 1836, during the Texas War of Independence, he was locked up but, as a friend of Sam Houston, was paroled. He returned to México after Texas' independence and died in Veracruz State shortly before the U.S. invasion.

Even though he was losing territory, Morelos was holding his own in the overall war for the hearts and minds of the people. He was a modern revolutionary in more ways than one. Thanks to Leona Vicario, Andrés Quintana Roo and others, he was in contact with *los guadalupes*, a Mexico City–based insurgent underground composed of intellectuals and others plotting to overthrow the viceroy. Besides money and intelligence, they produced propaganda. In a world without radio or Internet, that meant printed material or word of mouth. Printing was dangerous, given that there weren't many printing presses available, and the viceroy's agents watched every print shop in the city. Literacy was rare—most people depended on friends or the local educated person (usually the village priest) to read them the news.

Despite the obstacles, Los Guadalupes were a successful propaganda unit. They managed to get a few underground papers out (and, thanks to the viceroy's inability to make up his mind whether he supported independence or not, they were sometimes able to openly publish). Though Morelos was always grateful for the help that came from the Capital, when Los Guadalupes managed to smuggle out a printing press and more importantly, a skilled printer. General Morelos received the important new weapon and its technical expert with full military honors. Father Morelos held a *Te Deum* – an elaborate Church ritual – to thank God for special gifts. The highly valued (and guarded) printing press and printer moved with the army, allowing Morelos not only to put out a regular newspaper in rebel territory, but to print legal documents, orders and wage economic warfare against the Spanish by turning out his own paper currency (he also minted coins).

Modern insurgents understand the importance of economic warfare. Mining had come to a halt during Hidalgo's campaign, so the government depended on two main sources of funding: customs revenue and a monopoly on tobacco sales. Morelos may have been a poor peasant, but he was no fool; capture the ports, and you captured customs revenues. Then, without tobacco, the government would be strapped to pay the army. So Morelos and his soldiers attacked tobacco fields and warehouses when they weren't capturing more weapons.

Unpaid soldiers are unhappy soldiers...or hungry soldiers. Hungry and unhappy people join the revolution; they don't fight against it.

By August 1813, he controlled everything from Acapulco in the west to Veracruz on the Gulf, except for Puebla, Veracruz itself and Mexico City. Now it was time for the real revolution to begin. Morelos convened a congress in Chilpancingo, now the state capital of Guerrero State, but then a small village. It was at Chilpancingo that Morelos' brilliance and modernity stood out.

The cowboy-priest and his men were not interested in re-creating a culture of criollos, mestizos and indigenous peoples. Nor did they want a country filled with a few "haves" and many "have-nots". This would be a government of the people; there would be no special rights based on birth—all people in México would be simply citizens. Race basically ceased to exist as a meaningful legal term. All jobs would be open to any qualified man; special courts and privileges for clergy and army officers would be abolished. The Chilpancingo Constitution of 1814 was the first legal document ANYWHERE to proclaim all persons—regardless of race—equal before the law.

Finally, unused haciendas would be seized—half would be sold to pay for the new government, half would be given to landless peasants. During the Mexican Revolution, one hundred years later, this was still a dangerously radical concept.

Although the Congress proposed setting Morelos up as dictator, he refused. The priest's reasons were echoed, one hundred years later, by those of both Emiliano Zapata (who wanted no man to control another) and Pancho Villa (who recognized his skills were military, not diplomatic). Morelos saw himself as too rough and ragged for the job. Although the United States had managed to avoid a strongman, single ruler, the Mexicans saw the American Revolution as one of the haves against the also-haves. They viewed their revolt more in terms of those in France and Haiti, revolts of the have-nots against the haves, both of which ended up under an emperor. Morelos did accept supreme military command, but answered, at his own request, to an executive committee.

What undid Morelos was his personal modesty and political radicalism. The Congress continued to argue over the forms of government, even as their territory disappeared. Once Congress had selected a head of state (or rather a committee), Morelos turned over his power as supreme leader to them in October 1814.

The Executive Committee argued among themselves and fought each other for control, while the radical constitution alarmed even liberal criollos. While they wanted freedom from Spain, they were the educated people and the best people. They were the only people who could rule the new country. The criollos continued to back the Spanish, not even complaining when all criollo hacienda owners were drafted into the army; and if the army needed cannon fodder, the Spanish drafted the workers out of the fields.

Under siege, the executive committee and what was left of Congress retreated from town to town, finally begging Morelos to rescue them from the Spaniards. The Spanish finally captured Morelos near Tenango (in modern Guerrero State) while Nicolas Bravo led the remaining congressmen to safety. The soldier who captured Morelos had fought with the guerrillas before changing sides and recognized the insurgent priest. Asking Morelos what he would have done if the situation were reversed, Morelos told him he was a priest and a general. He would have heard the soldier's confession, as a priest should, then shot him, as a general must.

Once a priest, always a priest...

Sentencing Morelos to be shot as a rebel general was easy, but as a priest, he had to be tried by the clergy. He had the dubious distinction of being the last man ever condemned by the Inquisition in México.[45] Although Catholic priests are not supposed to marry, it was extremely common for country priests to have children. Priests lived in their small country towns for years and were expected to be part of the community—that included having a woman to take care of his house and have his children.

The Mayans had never understood nor completely trusted Cortés' shipwrecked translator, Father Aguilar, given his strange (to them) attitude about women. Attitudes in the country hadn't changed all that much since the 1520s, and country priests weren't expected to wait for years for their ship to come in. Besides, not all priests had the devotion to clerical celibacy the shipwrecked Father Aguilar exhibited. Priests had children, but the Church generally

---

[45] One of the last condemned in Spain would be Hidalgo's and Morelos' former bishop, Manuel Abad y Queipo (who was also a close friend and collaborator with the German explorer Alexander von Humboldt, who had lived in México shortly before the Insurgent revolt). Bishop Abad y Queipo was too liberal for the reactionaries who eventually triumphed in Spain.

ignored the issue, only insisting that the children did not inherit their fathers' names.

Morelos had been a teenaged father and did not start studying to be a priest until he was twenty-five. Morelos' son, Juan Almonte, would play a significant role in later Mexican history, but one less honorable than his father's, by serving the French occupiers as regent until the Emperor Maximilian was installed. The Inquisition used Almonte's existence as evidence that his father was secretly a Protestant; specifically that he was a Lutheran.[46] A more serious charge was rebellion against the Church.

Morelos was a devout and sincere Catholic. The charges hurt. He had gone to the trouble of asking his bishop for permission to join the rebellion as a chaplain, arguing that even rebels need religious instruction and without a priest there would be no one to perform weddings…or funerals for dead rebels, but the Bishop, naturally, turned down the request. Faced with the evidence, Morelos finally broke down and confessed his "mistake". He was defrocked and turned over to the viceroy's courts. In the thinking of the time, Morelos had been rebelling against the world's order, and by extension, against God.

He confessed his role in the revolt and even cooperated with the court. He knew he was doomed and was more concerned with making it right with God than continuing the revolt. Despite his cooperation, he was still seen as a threat by the authorities. Under heavy guard and in a closed carriage to avoid demonstrations by pro-insurgent crowds, he was taken from prison in Mexico City to Ecatepec where he was executed by firing squad on 22 December 1815.

---

[46] Lutheran clergymen can marry and have children. When Protestantism became more a threat to the Spanish Church than the Jews and Muslims, condemning someone as a Protestant was often a way to make an already serious criminal charge stick. If a criminal couldn't be charged in civil courts, he could in religious courts. English pirates captured in Veracruz in the 1570s were burned at the stake as Protestants, not simply beheaded as pirates. The Inquisition, by this time, normally only prosecuted priests for rape, murder or theft, ignoring cases like Morelos'. However, they needed to get a conviction on a clerical charge before they could defrock Morelos and turn him over to the civil authorities.

No one condemned Morelos for his final moment of weakness or his religious beliefs. His revolt was collapsing anyway. Having lost criollo support and unable to get foreign aid, it couldn't have succeeded.

In the 21st century, there has been a movement in México to have the Pope overturn the priest's clerical condemnation on a technicality (his bishop was only a temporary appointment and shouldn't have had jurisdiction in the first place).

If pushing radical concepts of equality was Morelos' mistake, the viceroy's mistake was recruiting the criollos. The viceroy was arming people who wanted their own country. In the short run though, the viceroy's army was winning. Morelos was dead, the Congress gave up, the insurgent printer was captured and the printing press publicly burned, and rebel officers were offered pardons and commissions in the colonial army. More and more rebels simply switched sides but were still convinced they, not the Spanish, should control the country. Vicente Guerrero refused to give up, taking his few men with him into the hills. When the mystic, Guadalupe Victoria, was surrounded, his men agreed to surrender, but Guadalupe Victoria took off his uniform and walked into the forest in his underwear.

Emperor? That'll work

THERE HAD BEEN CIVIL WARS in Spain all this time, and the situation was just as confused. When Napoleón was driven out of Spain, the new king had no choice but to accept the constitution written by the Seville junta. Ferdinand did not believe in constitutional monarchy and threw out the document (and the parliament), starting a civil war in Spain. In 1820, an army, which was supposed to be sent to México to help keep the rebellious colony under control, turned around and overthrew the Ferdinand's government. Ferdinand was a constitutional monarch once again. This new constitution limited the Church's power, and the conservatives in the Mexican clergy began to think maybe those radicals, Hidalgo and Morelos had been on to something. Independence from Spain might not be so bad, if the Church's privileges were maintained.

México wasn't the only colony drifting away from European control. Simón Bolívar had been liberating one Spanish colony after another in South America. José de San Martín was doing the same thing in the cone of South America (Argentina, Chile and Uruguay). In Brazil, the Portuguese royal family had sat out Napoleón's occupation, leaving a prince behind as the new Emperor of Brazil.

Appointing a Mexican emperor was not that bizarre an idea. Brazil, Haiti and France had all opted for monarchy after their revolutions. An obscure army officer, Augustín de Iturbide, realized there were three important groups pushing for independence: criollos and liberals who wanted an independent México; conservatives (especially in the Church) who wanted to preserve their old privileges against the changes in the Spanish constitution; and the guerrillas, who would have to be given something. Iturbide's "Three Guarantees" gave something to everyone—guarantees of special privileges for the Church, guarantees of criollo control of the economy and guarantees of racial equality for the people (the equality of the indigenous people remained mostly theoretical, and it would be generations before anyone considered the concept of economic equality to be important).

De Iturbide loved symbols, and he modeled himself on Napoleón. The French had a tricolored flag representing their three ideals—liberty, equality, brotherhood—so México needed a three color flag—green for independence; white for Church privileges; red for the mixed indigenous and European blood of the people. An alternative explanation, favored at the time by comedians and humorists, was that the down-to-earth Vicente Guerrero and de Iturbide had watermelon for lunch when they met. Guerrero, with peasant humor, looked at the watermelon's green husk, white rind and red fruit, suggested the color combination and just sat back as de Iturbide concocted an explanation.

Worrying about the flag was typical of de Iturbide, but the de Iturbide-Guerrero plan to gain independence with criollo and Church support was the best plan anyone had come up with. There was no real opposition. Spain sent a new viceroy, hoping to reestablish control, but not really expecting to do so. Stuck aboard ship with a small Spanish regiment in Veracruz harbor and facing armed Mexicans (one of whom was a young officer, Antonio López de Santa Ana), the viceregal family was struck with yellow fever. The viceroy first lost his wife, then his children to the then mysterious killer.

De Iturbide, in the meantime, was busily creating the symbols of a new country and creating the right tone for a new empire in the making. The rotting heads of Hidalgo, Allende, Aldama and Jiménez were finally taken down from the alhóndiga in Guanajuato and given a military burial. Gathering up Nicolas Bravo and luring Guadalupe Victoria out of hiding (and finding him a decent suit to wear), the new Mexican government entered Mexico City on 27 September 1821. The grieving viceroy, Juan O'Donoju,[47] was allowed out of Veracruz to see what was supposed to be his palace, now called the Palacio Nacional, surrender and head home.

There was a new Congress left in charge until an emperor could be selected. Some assumed they would be choosing a member of the Spanish royal family. There were even a few supporters of Moctezuma's distant relatives, who had become Spanish nobility. A few others talked about the Hapsburgs, who had plenty of unemployed relatives to select from.

De Iturbide, acting as temporary dictator, thought about his hero. Napoleón Bonaparte had also been a military commander and temporary dictator in France. When the Mexican leader accused some of the congressmen of treason and had them arrested, Nicholas Bravo and Guadalupe Victoria revolted. Bravo was jailed, and Guadalupe Victoria headed back into the woods. Congress' crime was their realization that they couldn't afford to pay the old colonial army with all the Insurgent officers and the criollo draftees already on the army payroll. They had to cut the army down to sixty thousand men.

This might have been acceptable to the *hacendados* – hacienda owners – who had been drafted along with their workers, but for a lot of junior officers and sergeants the army was their only source of income. They had nothing to loose when Iturbide paid them to shout, "*¡Viva Augustín Primero!*" – "Long live Augustín the First!" – and threaten the congressmen. Napoleón Bonaparte had become Emperor of France through a military coup. Augustín Iturbide could do the same.

---

[47] Yes, there were Spanish counts with Irish names. The Protestant English conquest of Ireland from the 1580s through the end of the 17th century forced the Catholic Irish nobles into exile, many eventually marrying into the Spanish nobility.

Augustín de Iturbide was crowned Emperor of México on 21 July 1822. No one seemed to have considered what to do after the coronation...or given much thought to the national treasury. During the wars, mining equipment had broken down and replacement parts were no longer available. Haciendas had been abandoned or destroyed in the fighting. Unpaid soldiers had turned bandit to survive. When Congress questioned whether an emperor who spent his time designing medals and inventing titles for his new dukes was earning his pay, the emperor threw several congressmen in jail and told the rest of them to go home.

The Spanish had not quite completely given up on their old colony. They attempted to maintain control over the new nation's shipping by occupying San Juan de Ulúa, the old fortress in Veracruz harbor, and trying to launch an invasion to retake the port. The attempt failed, but it created more problems for the new country than holding the fort ever did. Put in charge of defending Veracruz and driving out the last remnants of the Spanish Army was a lazy but charming criollo general, Antonio López de Santa Ana (often spelled Santa Anna; even the Mexicans can't decide which is correct.[48])

---

[48] His full name was Antonio de Padua María Severino López de Santa Anna (or Ana) y Pérez de Lebrón. Mexicans (and Spaniards until recently) use both the *apellido paterno* (the father's family name) and the *apellido materno* (the mother's father's family name). Because of the Spanish obsession with bloodlines, people like Santa Ana often had FOUR family names, to show that all four of their great-grandfathers were Catholics, but used a short form (like Santa Ana) for everyday use. Beginning with the Reforma of the 1850s, Mexicans legally received only two family names (a few double names still exist—López Portillo and Orozco y Berra are common ones). By law, even married women keep their birth name, although some women, by social custom, use "de" followed by their husband's *apellido paterno* in place of their *apellido materno* for everything except legal documents. One side benefit is that children born out of wedlock are not identified as such in any way. Lázaro Cárdenas del Río married Amalia Solórzano. Their son, Cuauhtémoc Cárdenas Solórzano married a woman who always calls herself Celeste Betal *de Cárdenas*. Their son is Lázaro Cárdenas Betal, which makes distinguishing between the two Lázaros much easier. Most people are known only by their *apellido paterno* but there are exceptions. Important people with a very common *apellido paterno* like López or García are usually referred to by both names: López Mateos and López Obrador, for example. A very few are best known by their *apellido materno*, like 1930s interim president Abelardo Luján Rodríguez who always gave his name as Abelardo L. Rodríguez.

The government didn't want Augustín, the people didn't want Augustín and the army hadn't been paid. They turned to the newest hero. Santa Ana called for a republic, but he wasn't sure what that meant. Guadalupe Victoria emerged from hiding to explain the concept and to buck up Santa Ana, who started to panic after Imperial loyalists put up a token resistance. The new general was ready to run for the United States border, but the old rebel cheerfully told him it wasn't over until their heads had been chopped off. Besides, the rebellion wasn't going to take very long.

With almost no army, no government and no money, Augustín realized the game was up. He had the congressmen called back to Mexico City—mostly to arrange his pension. He complained about the terms they offered but finally sailed off into exile.

Emperor Augustín came to a tragic or foolish...or maybe heroic end. When the Spanish landed another token invasion force in 1824, Augustín sailed back to México, planning to help drive out the invaders and retake his throne. After all, Napoleón had done the same thing, returning from exile to drive the Bourbons out of Paris and have the army restore him as emperor of the French, but...México was not France. Congress had warned Augustín he would be shot if he returned. He did...and he was.

With de Iturbide gone, México was a Republic. The honest eccentric, Guadalupe Victoria, was president, to much rejoicing. Guadalupe Victoria knew his own limitations. Having no idea who to ask for good advice, he asked everyone. Perhaps he was ahead of his time, or perhaps after living in the woods for so many years, he was just lonely, but he adopted the very modern political technique of asking focus groups for their opinion on government issues. What horrified his advisors (and delighted the populace) was that his focus group was made up of market vendors, delivery men and his fellow shoppers when he emerged from the new Palacio Nacional to buy his own groceries.

Although the reign of Huitzilopochtli was coming to an end, it was not the time for the return of Quetzalcóatl. Reality was about to sink in, and Tezcatlipoca, the god of reality, is a trickster.

The New Republic

At independence, de Iturbide ruled over an empire stretching from Wyoming to Nicaragua. What are today the Central American countries (Guatemala, Belize, El Salvador, Costa Rica and Nicaragua) had been a sort of "vice-viceroyalty" and opted for their independence from Mexico City (partially because the local criollos would not accept the three guarantees that recognized the indigenous peoples as citizens. Costa Rica would not grant their indigenous people citizenship until the late 20th century.) Chiapas, originally part of Guatemala, seceded from the new Central American Republic, its leadership preferring to become part of México.

Post-independence México was a mess. It would average more than one president a year for the next forty years, have four different systems of government, be invaded several times and lose more than half of its territory. While the chaos and violence might suggest that Huitzilopochtli had come to earth, it was more the era of the trickster god, Tezcatlipoca...and the closest thing México has seen to his human incarnation.

After de Iturbide, México was ruled by criollos and the few mestizos who pulled themselves into the upper middle class or had become rich. Guadalupe Victoria served out his term.

The next president, the black farmer turned general, Vicente Guerrero, was convinced by the U.S. ambassador to expel the Spanish, who still made up most of the management and technical workers in the country—a monumental blunder. With no educational resources, México wasn't able to train enough replacements for the gachupines. The upshot was that foreigners gained more and more control of the economy, often financing the overthrow of governments to benefit their own interests.

Even if the Mexicans had been allowed, by the now-departing Spanish, to run their own country and take high-administrative posts, there would have been very few people with any experience in managing a complex enterprise like a large country. Unlike their neighbor to the north, very few people in México had any experience—or tradition—of managing more than their own local affairs. There were intelligent, honest, sophisticated people, but politics and administration had never been something these people had undertaken.

Like the priests who turned general, what you had were gifted amateurs doing the best they could, or people with limited experience trying to apply what they knew about administering their own small farm to the administration of a very large territory. Even without scoundrels like Santa Ana—who would become president eleven times over twenty-two years—México's early attempts at self-governance were bound to be problematic.

Partially as a result of damages during the War of Independence and partially as a result of the stupid decision in 1829 to expel all Spaniards, México became poorer and poorer. The loss of manpower was only the start of the problem—farms and mines had been destroyed, all the rebel armies were combined into the national army and unpaid soldiers became bandits. While the soldiers might go home, many of the officers had unappealing civilian jobs or had no farms to return to. The army ate up most of the national budget.

The army payroll was often several million more than the national budget. By 1850 there were twenty-four thousand officers and only twenty thousand soldiers. Landowners ruined by the insurgency had no other income but their army pay. Criollos wanted the jobs left behind by the Spanish, and even then there were unemployed criollos. The State governments filled their payrolls with more unemployed officers. There were no products to sell and nothing much that could be taxed. Every State, and often every town, had its own import duty, and that meant customs inspectors. There had to be smugglers. Of course, there had to be police to look for smugglers.

Fanny Erskine, a Philadelphia schoolteacher, became Marquesa Calderón de la Barca upon her marriage to a Spanish diplomat. When her husband was appointed Spain's first ambassador to the new Republic, she amused her friends back home in the United States with gossipy letters detailing diplomatic and upper-crust life in the decadent, exotic capital. Her letters were later compiled and published in 1842 as *Life in Mexico*. Fanny, Mrs. Calderón de la Barca, was a sharp-witted observer of a city full of out-of-work generals and colonels who could be seen in full uniform running grocery stores, keeping books or even mending shoes. General Barrera, who made a fortune in smuggling, bought a palace from a departing Spanish nobleman and draped his cigar-smoking wife in diamonds. He was a tailor.

Expelling the Spaniards had created more problems than just filling the civil service. The Spanish who stayed behind in México earlier had been businessmen, engineers, skilled laborers, farm managers and Church administrators. The Spaniards had been the only source of capital outside the Church. The Church, without sufficient administrators, had to abandon schools, hospitals and missions. Already the largest landowner in the country, they were also the main source of financing for the land-rich, but cash-poor hacienda owners. When hacienda owners found they couldn't keep up their mortgage payments, the Church ended up owning even more unproductive farmland that it didn't have the resources to manage. In Mexico City, they were the largest landlord. Furthermore, the empty Church properties gave squatters a roof over the heads...if they weren't filled with garbage. The city had no money for garbage collection, and the poor had nowhere else to shovel it except into empty lots or abandoned buildings. With garbage came more diseases, and epidemics were common, especially in the poor neighborhoods.

With no one to run schools or hospitals, the minimal social services of the era ceased functioning altogether. Rural schools simply disappeared, and the missionary monks, who would protect indigenous people from the local landowner or advise them about filing a lawsuit, went back to Spain.

Mining required mercury, and Spain had been the conduit for the vital ingredient in gold and silver processing. British companies that also had access to mercury bought up the mines but sent the profits home to England. The British were looking for quick profits and quickly abandoned any mines that required investment in major repairs or in new equipment.

While the criollos had some romantic notions about the indigenous people (many families discovered Aztec nobility among their ancestors in those years), no one gave serious thought to including them in ruling the country. Spain had always been governed by the upper class. The criollos saw no reason México should be run differently. At least, under the viceroy, the Church protected the indigenous people from the viceroy, and the Spanish viceroy protected them from the Church. Now there were only the criollos. The criollos had inherited the old Spanish idea that a gentleman is a landowner. Generals and colonels didn't want to be shoemakers or grocers, they wanted to be landowners, even though they didn't have the money to run a farm or meet their other obligations. Not being particularly skilled farmers, they tried to squeeze money out of their haciendas by planting more crops. The only way they could do this was to increase their size of their holdings by taking land from their neighbors any way they could. The indigenous communities never had Spanish land titles and were an easy target. Church lands were a tempting one.

The criollo obsession for land had one benefit for the rest of the nation. With criollos unwilling to take regular jobs, the skilled trades, jobs in businesses and the professions were increasingly managed by mestizos and indigenous people.

There were two broad visions of how to proceed with independence. Conservatives, grouped around Lucas Alamán, wanted to maintain the strong central control, with rulers in Mexico City replacing the rulers in Spain. In Spain, the king had controlled the Church, but the Mexican conservatives only wanted government control of the Church under a conservative government. Liberals, with Lorenzo de Zavala and a Zacatecas doctor, Valentín Gómez Farías, as leaders, wanted the Church controlled by the government, but for a different reason. They saw the immense wealth of the Church as a drag on the economy and wanted the government to sell off the landholdings and invest the funds in large-scale agriculture.

The liberals were for a looser government, with the new States having more power than the central government.[49] The liberals wanted an agricultural and mining nation, with exports supporting the economy and middle-class rulers. The conservatives wanted to develop industries, not so much to strengthen the economy, but to keep foreign products and foreign influences from the United States, France and England from contaminating the Mexican people. Both sides had some success. Conservatives could claim credit for encouraging farm-implement, clothing and other factories; the liberals for expanding existing ports, like San Blas on the Pacific and opening new ones, like Tampico, Sisal and Progresso on the Gulf of México.

Alexander von Humboldt, the Prussian scientist and explorer (at the time, the most famous man in Europe after Napoleón Bonaparte), had lived in México at the start of the War of Independence and was publishing his scientific and economic studies of the Americas at the time of independence. Humboldt's description of the mineral wealth and potential for development of México caught the attention of French, British and American readers. The French, after

---

[49] Conservatives and liberals in the United States had exactly the opposite attitude towards "States rights".

Napoleón's defeat, were in no position to take up foreign adventures, though individual Frenchmen began coming to México in search of wealth. The British and the Americans, sensing an opportunity opening up when the Spanish left, were both interested in exploiting the opportunity. Neither country wanted to directly rule the area (not at the time, anyway), but they did want those markets and resources.

The British, French and American ambassadors were vying with the market ladies of Tepito (then, as now, a rough neighborhood near the National Palace, noted for its lively public markets) for Guadalupe Victoria's attention, and their representatives would continue to try to influence Mexican affairs for the next two centuries.

The first British ambassador, H. G. Ward, sent back long reports on mining operations, the potential for English investors and even helpful hints for would-be English mining experts coming to the country. Ward was delighted to discover that rutabagas and turnips (favorites with the English) grew well around Pachuca, where there was a small colony of British miners already working. Those English miners were indirectly responsible for a local specialty, *pasties* – a meat- and vegetable-filled Cornish pastry popular with the miners. Traveling about in a carriage with armed guards, his sixteen-year-old male secretary, his wife, new baby and nurse, Ward introduced something new to the world…baby bottles.

Rubber was still mostly a local product in the 1820s. Ward's Mexican nurse and Mrs. Ward found feeding the baby in that crowded carriage a challenge, so the nurse made an artificial nipple out of a piece of rubber, filled a bottle with milk and the rest—as they say—was history.

The British ambassador brought back baby bottles from his time in México. The United States ambassador tried for much more, but only returned with a few plants.

The Masons jar México

JOEL ROBERTS POINSETT WOULD BE the first United States ambassador to meddle in Mexican politics, but certainly not the last. Born in 1791 into a wealthy, slave-owning South Carolina family, Poinsett is a major historical figure in México—and in Latin America generally—but practically unknown in his own country. As a young man, he had been educated in a British military academy and traveled widely though Europe and Central Asia (he was the first American citizen to visit what is now Kyrgizia). He spoke English, Spanish, French and Russian fluently and had served as a congressman and senator—all before he began his diplomatic career in Latin America.

At the time the United States was a radical government (nearly every other nation was a monarchy, and a republic of the people—excluding slaves, women and "Indians", of course—was a danger to the civilized world). Diplomats from radical revolutionary nations before and since have been suspected of plotting against their host countries. In Poinsett's case, it was true. He was America's first spymaster, a one-man (he answered only to Secretary of State John Quincy Adams) CIA.

In Buenos Aires (Argentina was still a Spanish colony), he financed several plots to overthrow the government. Run out of

Argentina, he crossed the Andes into Chile (another Spanish colony) where he enjoyed more success. Thanks to Poinsett's plotting, the Chilean revolution started on 4 July 1821 and the Chilean flag is modeled on that of the United States.

As the first United States representative to the new Mexican government, Poinsett found several un-American ideas to fight. de Iturbide was emperor, Poinsett and Adams favored a republic. México was Catholic, and Poinsett was a Protestant representing a secular state, and México would soon outlaw slavery. Poinsett, whose personal fortune rested on slavery, was farsighted enough to realize slavery was doomed in the United States unless the country expanded and more states—where the "peculiar institution" was legal—could be added to the Union.

De Iturbide was the easiest problem to settle. Almost as soon as Poinsett arrived in México, he began making contact with republican plotters like Guerrero and Santa Ana.[50] President Guadalupe Victoria may have listened to everyone, but Poinsett talked to him more than most. Convincing the eccentric president that México needed a navy was easy. Convincing him to appoint an out-of-work United States admiral took some work, but David L. Porter became father of the Mexican Navy.

To further his aims of acquiring Mexican territory for the United States, Poinsett worked through the *Yorkistas* – York Rite Masons. As an international organization, the Masonic lodges were also a counterweight to the other major international organization of the time—the Catholic Church.

He had originally intended the Yorkistas to be a counterweight to the British-backed *Escosistas* – Scottish Rite Masons. The British had two strikes against them—they were used to working with monarchies and the British saw the newly independent Latin American countries as a replacement for the business they lost

---

[50] Like the future CIA, Poinsett recruited and paid future enemies. Manuel Noriega (the Panamanian dictator and drug lord), Osama bin Laden, the Taliban guerrillas in Afghanistan and Saddam Hussein of Iraq were all paid by the CIA at one time in their careers.

in the new United States. The United States was also aggressively trying to make itself the dominant power in the Americas. With Poinsett as leader of one Masonic lodge, where better to find support for expanding gringo influence—including slavery—than through the Yorkistas? The Yorkistas included most important Mexican liberals, such as Vicente Guerrero and Lorenzo de Zavala. The liberals wanted a less centralized government. In return for his—United States'—support, Poinsett wanted a liberal government that would sell Texas.

In 1828, the last great surviving insurgent leader, Vicente Guerrero, was the liberal (and Yorkista) candidate. With some truth, the conservatives could claim Guerrero's Yorkista backing was proof of Masonic and gringo interference. The conservatives distrusted Guerrero and the liberals to begin with, so they ignored their own Escosista Masonic connections and played up the liberals' Yorkista connections as proof of an antichurch conspiracy. The Church and the conservatives had a less radical general as their candidate. State legislatures elected presidents, and the conservatives could bring in enough army troops to threaten enough legislatures to throw the election to their candidate.

Guerrero accepted the results, but the liberal General Santa Ana, who had overthrown de Iturbide, did not. Santa Ana's attempted rebellion was quickly put down (trickster that he was, the general escaped by dressing as a nun and slipping into a convent), but there were enough liberal rebellions in enough states to finally force the Congress to accept Guerrero as president. As a consolation prize to the conservatives, an ultra-conservative, General Anastasio Bustamante, became vice president.

Poinsett was practically a member of the Guerrero cabinet...but he went too far. Hoping to increase United States business influence in México, Poinsett and the Yorkistas pushed Guerrero to expel the remaining Spanish citizens in México. The old gachupines had not been popular. Rich Spaniards had controlled big businesses and banking, but most of México's remaining Spaniards were middle-class people with Mexican wives and families—shopkeepers, blacksmiths, mule-route managers, innkeepers, teachers, priests, doctors and engineers—including mining engineers. Neither México nor the United States had enough engineers to fill the void (nor the money to buy the mines from deported Spaniards), so the British ended up controlling the Mexican mines, just the opposite of what Poinsett intended.

The only way the United States could expand slavery was to expand its territory. The only way to expand was into Mexican territory—specifically Texas. The Yorkistas had always been open to gringo—or other—settlers in Texas. Yorkistas favored a looser federal government anyway, and they saw little harm in having Protestant settlers.

Poinsett went too far again—compromising himself and the Yorkista cause. On no authority but his own, he tried to buy Texas for the United States. Guerrero may have been a Yorkista, an admirer of the United States, a personal friend of Poinsett and he may have taken bribes from Poinsett...but in the end he was a Mexican patriot. In an unusual move for the time, he leaked Poinsett's letters (including veiled threats of United States military action) to the newspapers. It was two more firsts for Joel Poinsett: he was the first United States ambassador attacked by the Mexican press, and the first American spy to have his cover blown by a foreign newspaper.

The Yorkistas still exist and are still a powerful force in Mexican politics. With international connections and pro-United States biases, they are now seen as conservatives and are prominent in conservative parties, despite traditional mistrust by the Church, the other main conservative force. In 2003, when México sat on the United Nations Security Council and was pressured to back the United States invasion of Iraq, nearly every sector of Mexican society opposed the war and Mexican support for the United States. The Yorkistas were the only group to favor supporting the United States. Respected journalists openly speculated on President Fox's Yorkista membership as a factor in the decision México would take in the Security Council. As it turned out, México, staying true to the Juárez Doctrine, voted against the United States.

Poinsett left México disappointed. If he is known at all in the United States, it's not as a world traveler or the first Latin American specialist or even as the United States' first international spy. In December, Mexican gardens bloom with the red and green leafed *flor de noche buena* – Christmas Eve flower. Poinsett first saw the plant gracing a *nacimiento* – Nativity scene – in a Cuernavaca area church. He swiped the plants from the Baby Jesus and brought home...not Texas, but the poinsettia.

Santa Ana-once more with feeling

WHILE COLORFUL FIGURES LIKE DE ITURBIDE, Guadalupe Victoria, Poinsett and Alexander von Humboldt all figured in the early history of independent México, the era is often called "the Age of Santa Ana", after the dominant Mexican leader of the era, Antonio López de Santa Ana.

He was Tezcatlipoca come back to life, sometimes a liberal, sometimes a conservative, always a trickster. Once he even convinced foreign invaders to pay for their own attackers. Like Cortés, he would have incredible luck. When the Texans disgraced him the French made him an accidental hero and returned him to national power.

In 1829 the Spanish tried one last time to retake México. Santa Ana had very little to do with their defeat. He left the Spanish surrounded in Tampico, where yellow fever killed off the invaders. Santa Ana—not the mosquitoes—became the hero of the battle, even though he had stayed home on his ranch outside Veracruz, raising roosters for cockfights and waiting for another interesting plot to turn up. Because of the invasion, Guerrero was given emergency powers as dictator. When he was a little too slow to give up his emergency powers, Santa Ana staged an army uprising against the dictator.

Guerrero's main accomplishment had been to outlaw slavery. The new president, Anastasio Bustamante, only had one major accomplishment. He replaced the dictator with a tyrant…himself. When Guerrero tried to flee the country on an Italian ship, the captain sold the exile to Bustamante, who forced Congress to declare the fleeing president insane and impeach him. Ex-president Guerrero was put in front of a firing squad, where every other enemy of Bustamante would soon be. Lorenzo Zavala, the liberal leader, fled to Texas.

Guess who decided to overthrow the tyrant? This time Santa Ana himself became president. Things started well; there was a civilian vice president for a change, Dr. Valentín Gómez Farías. Dr. Gómez Farías was a *puro* – a pure, uncompromising liberal. Santa Ana soon discovered that plotting to become president was a lot more fun than being president. He left the work to Dr. Gómez Farías and retired to his farm. The civilian doctor made the changes liberals wanted: eliminating the special Church and army courts, cutting down the size of the army, taking education out of Church hands, eliminating the tithe (a tax used to support the Church) and insisting Church leaders stick to religion and stay out of politics. For good measure, Congress decided the government would appoint the Church leaders, taking the Spanish king's old job.

The Church and the army both objected, and they had the money and the weapons to back up their objections. Dr. Gómez Farías was out, and the new conservative dictator was in—who else but General Santa Ana? In 1833 the general overthrew his own government, but that was just a technicality. His first order of business was to replace the constitution with something satisfactory to the conservatives—the states lost most of their power to the federal government in Mexico City.

Santa Ana managed to stay in power either by shifting sides when it was convenient, or because everyone got tired of fighting over whether there should be a conservative or liberal president. Guadalupe Victoria had been an honest man, but he was a simple man who would stop to listen to any market woman who wanted to tell him how to run the country. He also listened to a land developer named Stephen Austin, who had a plan to settle mostly uninhabited Texas. With few Mexican settlers wanting to live in the wilderness, and bands of Comanches roving around through large sections of the territory, Austin was given permission to bring in settlers. In return for cheap land and tax exemptions, Catholics who agreed to become Mexican citizens would be allowed to move to Texas. The requirement to be a Catholic could be somewhat overlooked. The army wasn't going to enforce the rule, and the Inquisition had gone out of business, even in Spain.

Unable to recruit Catholics from Europe, Stephen Austin ignored the slave-holding Protestants from the United States who settled in the otherwise unsaleable territory. Vicente Guerrero had abolished slavery, fulfilling one of Morelos' goals, and this particularly affected the Texas territory. While early settlers had largely accepted this (at least on paper they freed the slaves, turning them into underpaid peons), U.S. born residents had flooded the territory, ignoring the laws, the religious requirements and anything else that differed from things in the United States. Santa Ana's new constitution was the last straw for the liberal de Zavala; he joined with the immigrants when they declared independence from México in 1836.[51] With immigrant leader David Burnett as president, he was elected vice president of the new Republic of Texas.

---

[51] At least that's the Texas version. An alternative Mexican version has de Zavala, another of Poinsett's "assets", planning for Texas independence as early as 1829.

Santa Ana is caught napping...

Santa Ana finally had something more interesting than running the government to keep him occupied. To launch a surprise invasion and put down the rebellion, he organized his army in San Luis Potosí and marched it across the desert in record time. He lost nearly a quarter of his four thousand troops on the desert march but quickly subdued the breakaway province. Santa Ana may have been careless with his troops, but he wasn't a bloodthirsty killer either. He never had political enemies killed, he only forced them to retire, or if they were particularly dangerous, exiled them. His terrible reputation in the United States comes from two small battles. At the Alamo, Texas soldiers and United States mercenaries refused to surrender and were slaughtered. At Goliad, General Urrea captured a gang of invaders—from the United States—who were attempting to march on Matamoros in Tamaulipas State. General Urrea hesitated over what to do with his captives, but they were nothing but pirates under both United States and Mexican law, so Santa Ana ordered them shot.[52]

Assuming most resistance had ended, Santa Ana took his troops back along the Gulf coast. In one of the stupidest military blunders of all time, he failed to post guards while his troops rested at San Jacinto (near what is now the Johnson Space Center in Houston). The Texans had regrouped under Sam Houston and forced Santa Ana to order his army's withdrawal across the Rio Bravo (the river that the United States calls the Rio Grande). Houston, a former governor of Tennessee who had fled to Texas to escape court-ordered alimony and child-support payments, and who would later be president of the Republic of Texas, then governor of the State of Texas, received the credit for liberating the new Republic. Santa Ana, for his part, could only complain that nobody could expect their siesta to turn into such a disaster. José Enrique de la Peña, the Mexican soldier whose diary provides the best Mexican view on the war, points out that had the remaining Mexican Army counterattacked, history would have been very different.

At that time, the border between Texas and the rest of México was the Rio Nueces. Withdrawing below the Rio Bravo would be the excuse used by the United States to invade in 1846. Santa Ana was also forced to sign a secret agreement to accept Texas' independence. Although several Texans wanted to shoot the Mexican president, cooler heads suggested sending him to the United States.

After a reluctant visit to Washington (where President Andrew Jackson gave him a lecture), Santa Ana returned in disgrace to his farm in Veracruz. No longer trusted by either the conservatives or the liberals, he resigned as president, and went back to raising his roosters.

---

[52] José Enrique de la Peña, at the time a thirty-year-old army engineer, despised Santa Ana and defended General Urrea. His diary, translated into English by Carmen Perry as *With Santa Ana in Texas: a Personal Narrative of the Revolution* (Texas A & M Press, 1997), is still considered controversial by Texans, and some have tried to claim it is a forgery, mostly because de la Peña contradicts the accepted stories of the heroic deaths of Jim Bowie and Davie Crockett at the Battle of the Alamo.

...but wakes in time to enjoy French pastries

A FRENCH DOUGHNUT MAKER was responsible for Santa Ana's return. There were some French citizens living in México who claimed they had suffered property damage during the several coups and countercoups since independence. M. Remontel, who ran pastry shop in the Capital, complained that army cadets had locked him in his backroom and did eight hundred–pesos worth of damage.[53] Adding the unpaid doughnuts to other damages to French citizens and adding interest, the French government presented the Mexican government for a bill for six hundred thousand pesos. The Mexican government had no money and no real way to collect taxes. There was a sales tax, which people ignored and avoided by using barter, and an import tax that people got around by smuggling. Cities and states couldn't depend on the government, so raised their own taxes—even charging import fees on goods from the next town. What little money the government had went to pay off loans or to pay the army.

---

[53] The cadets were teenage boys, and they can eat a lot, but eight-hundred of today's pesos will buy two-hundred-sixty-seven extra-large cream-filled doughnuts at my local panadería. The 1838 peso was equal to about two-hundred thousand pesos today. The cadets must have been extremely hungry.

The only way the French could collect their bill was to take over Veracruz and collect the customs taxes themselves. They sent another two hundred thousand peso bill to Mexico City to cover the costs of the invasion. It was too much to expect the Mexican government to swallow, and the Pastry War of 1838 was on.

Santa Ana used the same tactic he had used against the Spanish, bottling up the invaders on the coast and letting his ally, yellow fever, do its work. While inspecting the blockade, a lucky French cannon shot took off the ex-president's left leg. He was no longer the national disgrace who lost Texas; he was the wounded hero of Veracruz.

Finally paying the French their six hundred thousand pesos to go away, México was in worse shape than ever. The army was inefficient and useless for defense, taxes kept going up, and people found new ways to avoid them. In Mexico City, life became even worse for the poor when there was no money for collecting garbage in their neighborhoods. In small towns, the richer and more skilled moved to Mexico City, or at least to the bigger cities.

Ironically, the indigenous villagers were able to preserve their culture because no one could afford to bother them, other than the local hacienda owners who still stole their land. When the big landlords discovered that it was too expensive to keep even underpaid workers on the payroll, they generally left the indigenous villagers alone. With the army weak, and nobody to stop them, Comanches and Apaches raided throughout the north, even traveling nearly a thousand miles south to attack Zacatecas.

It wasn't only warrior tribes and the small villagers that took advantage of the neglect. Criollos were less and less interested in anything outside their immediate concerns, so mestizos and indigenous leaders took over city and state governments and came into their own as businessmen and leaders. If criollos weren't landlords, they were army officers. The upper class avoided politics altogether. One upper-class criollo general, Manuel Mier y Terán, committed suicide when he feared he might be made president. The lawyers, politicians, small farmers, businessmen and laborers selected their own leaders, who tended to be liberals. Benito Juárez, a small-time lawyer in Oaxaca, and a Zapotec who hadn't learned Spanish until he was a teenager, worked his way up from city councilman to mayor to governor during these years. Santa Ana paid no attention to indigenous leaders in distant states. He probably didn't remember, but he had met Governor Juárez on an earlier visit to Oaxaca. The governor was a teenage servant at the time. Santa Ana had come to dine with Juárez' employer and made a remark about "stupid Indians". The stupid Indian servant kept his mouth shut, but he remembered Santa Ana.

Amputations

SANTA ANA, LITERALLY WITHOUT a leg to stand on, was technically president, but he took on the trappings of king with the grand title of His Most Serene Highness. While the garbage piled up in the streets of the Capital, and the hospitals ceased functioning altogether, there was still money for monuments to Santa Ana. The new opera house was named for him, as were other public buildings. In 1842, with great ceremony, his left leg was reburied in an impressive marble tomb. He was emperor in all but name, a situation that suited Lucas Alamán perfectly. Then, Santa Ana was overthrown once again. The monument to his leg was torn down. The leg itself was used for a football during the riots that broke out, before it was added to the piles of uncollected garbage. But Alamán never gave up his conviction that a king was the only solution for México's problems.

Others had come to the same idea, including Morelos' son, Juan Almonte. Alamán died before he could carry out his program, and Almonte had given up on criollo dictators. He hoped a European king would be above politics and give the government a leader who would at least implement some of his father's radical ideas of equality.

After years of coups and countercoups, there was no real government outside of the Capital. Santa Ana was the national leader, but there was no real nation to lead. Every state and locality had its little "Santa Ana". States declared war on each other and seceded from each other with regularity. In Puebla a *colonia* – neighborhood – seceded from the city. On the haciendas, owners ran their farms as little kingdoms, sometimes forming their own armies to keep the peons in line, sometimes borrowing the state or federal army to do the job for them. Indigenous people had their little Santa Anas too. Tomás Mejía united several tribes into a confederation in Nayarit State, where he ruled as absolute dictator. The national government and Mejía's kingdom simply ignored each other. Even after Santa Ana had left the scene, indigenous groups were slow to think of themselves as part of the nation. The people of Xochimilco, a suburb of Mexico City, would fight the later French invasion as an ally of the Republic.

México was falling apart, and the United States was becoming more of a danger than Spain or France had ever been. Alamán was foreign minister at the end of his life. He had been willing to accept Texas independence, if the United States would agree to leave Texas as a buffer state between México and the United States.[54] In the Yucatán, where another breakaway republic had never really gotten off the ground, there was civil war between the indigenous people and the criollos. The criollos were considering joining not only the United States, but also France or even Britain,[55] as long as they could maintain control over the rebellious Mayans. The aging Andrés Quintana Roo, who as a young man had been the

---

[54] When Lucas Alamán made his proposal he may have been thinking of Uruguay, which was also founded to keep the warring parties—Argentina and Brazil—apart. Under Alamán's proposal France would have had naval bases in Texas to keep the U.S. and México from interfering in Texas affairs, as Argentina and Brazil did in Uruguay throughout the 19th century.

[55] South of the Yucatán, the British pirates and timber harvesters had occupied parts of the coast, and the British created a colony called British Honduras. Until the 1990s, when México finally recognized the by then independent British Commonwealth country of Belize, Mexican school maps showed the area as "British occupied Guatemala".

hero in the insurgency love story of Leona Vicario, was called out of retirement to diplomatically resolve the Yucatán revolt. In 1904, Quintana Roo was honored for his effort when part of the Yucatán was named the Territory of Quintana Roo (admitted to *Estados Unidos Mexicanos* – United Mexican States – as the 31st and last state, in 1974).

There would be no diplomatic settlement of the Texas revolt. The United States annexed Texas in 1845. Based on Santa Ana's 1836 troop withdrawal, they insisted that the Rio Bravo (Rio Grande) was the new border. Looking for still more land for their growing population, the United States tried to buy California and the rest of northern México. Texans had painted Santa Ana as a butcher, and anti-Catholic prejudice was growing in the United States, especially when Irish and German Catholic immigrants and refugees poured into the country in the 1840s. Newspapers and books in the United States painted a picture of México as an impediment to U.S. expansion and the Catholic country as a danger to Protestantism.

John Slidell, the United States ambassador, was the wrong person to send to México. Besides an inability to speak Spanish, he was pro-slavery and a rabid anti-Catholic, and he was also ham-handed in his approach to President de Herrera, one of the few honest men to hold the job. De Herrera leaked Slidell's offer to buy Texas to the press, quoted some of the ambassador's less diplomatic language and ordered him out of the country. This was Slidell's real mission: to create an incident that would justify United States action against México. If the United States couldn't buy northern México, they wanted an excuse to take it. Claiming the Rio Grande (Rio Bravo) as the border, the United States sent their army to occupy the region between the Rio Nueces and the Rio Grande.

During early 1846, there was a "Mexican standoff"[56] between the United States troops at Brownsville, Texas and the Mexicans at Matamoros. Almost half the soldiers in the United States Army

---

[56] The phrase, meaning two armed sides staring each other down, comes from this event.

were recent immigrants—often Irish and German Catholics who had served in armies at home before arriving in the United States. With a few exceptions, the United States officers openly expressed anti-Catholic, and especially anti-Irish, prejudices.[57] To the Irish soldiers, recent immigrants from a country where Protestants had driven the Catholics into exile, the United States looked all too much like home. In Ireland, English Protestants had used the army to steal the land from Catholic peasants. Twenty percent of the United States Army would desert to the Mexicans. Most of the deserters simply settled in México and were the founders of the large Mexican-Irish community. Santa Ana, called back to service (he was one of the few generals who had fought United States soldiers), recognized the value of the Irish and other deserters. He gave them their own unit, *El Batallón San Patricio* – the Saint Patrick Battalion – and let them select their own officers. Both sides agreed that the San Patricios were the best soldiers in the war and the fiercest fighters. They couldn't give up. If they were captured by the United States, they were hanged as deserters when they weren't shot outright.

---

[57] President Polk—himself anti-Catholic—did what he could to resolve the problem. When Congress refused to fund Catholic military chaplains, Polk found two priests to accompany the Army as civilians, hiding their expenses from congressional scrutiny by listing the priests' travel expenses under the White House liquor and entertainment budget. Two officers refused to give in to prejudice and were considered decidedly odd by their superiors as a result, but immigrant Catholic soldiers serving under Lieutenant Ulysses S. Grant and Captain Robert E. Lee had the lowest desertion rates in the Army. As opposing generals in the American Civil War, both went out of their way to recruit Catholic chaplains and otherwise treat their Irish soldiers respectfully.

Los invasores

THE UNITED STATES AND MEXICAN cavalries raided back and forth across the river. Finally, a few United States soldiers were killed in May, and the United States declared war. The United States Navy, already stationed off the California coast, occupied the ports and propped up a Republic of California organized by United States citizens already living there. United States troops marched on Santa Fé, taking New Mexico without resistance. U.S. troops, crossing the Rio Bravo, marched on Monterrey.

In Monterrey, seventeen-year-old Samuel Chamberlain had a wonderful time flirting with the local girls and going to dances. Most of the city people didn't mind the U.S. regular army and even welcomed them—the government in Mexico City was an abstraction at best. Chamberlain had joined the army to escape criminal charges for attempted murder. He would be called a juvenile delinquent today, a tough kid from the frontier, but even he was shocked by the volunteer forces. When he wrote his memoirs as an old man (he became a respectable prison warden), he remembered spending most of his time in Monterrey trying to protect innocent civilians from being robbed, raped and murdered by volunteers.

Much of the propaganda used to recruit volunteer soldiers was rabidly anti-Catholic. The chance to attack Catholics and to pillage churches was the attraction for some of these soldiers. As badly as indigenous people had been treated in México, in the English-speaking countries they had been viewed as less than human. There were no English-speaking las Casas or de Zumárragas to defend the people. The volunteer soldiers from the United States never saw anything wrong with indiscriminately killing indigenous people nor with killing mestizos, who they assumed were also indigenous. Chamberlain, with a few regular soldiers, surprised a party of volunteers who had rounded up a group of villagers, raped the women and then stabbed their prisoners. When Chamberlain arrived, they were scalping a man.

Local people defended themselves and turned to guerrilla warfare against the invaders. Bandits and highwaymen became instant heroes when they attacked invading gringo soldiers. While the United States occupied Monterrey and set up a camp in Saltillo, Santa Ana prepared for war. Again, he begged, borrowed and even stole from churches the money he needed for an army. Again, he assembled at San Luis Potosí and lost thousands on the march. Outside Saltillo,[58] on 21 February 1847, Santa Ana didn't beat the gringos...but he didn't lose either. The three-day battle nearly destroyed both armies, but stopped the United States invasion. Santa Ana called it a victory...so did Zachary Taylor, the United States commander.

Taylor had political ambitions (later, he would be elected president of the United States) and belonged to a different party than the president. To keep Taylor from becoming a hero, the president ordered Taylor to maintain his position while a nonpolitical general, Winfield Scott, moved on Mexico City from Veracruz. Scott, who was so fat he had to leave his ship with the aid of block and tackle, landed ten thousand men outside Veracruz on 9 March

---

[58] The United States calls the battle Buena Vista, after the hacienda where they had their headquarters. In México, it's called the Battle of Angostura, where the Mexicans had their headquarters.

1847.[59] All previous assaults on Veracruz had been by sea, but Scott attacked by land, lobbing shells into the city until it surrendered on 27 March—fifteen hundred civilians lay dead in the streets.

Mrs. Calderón de la Barca, when she hadn't been performing her duties as diplomatic hostess or observing high society, had corresponded with a blind Harvard professor, William H. Prescott. Prescott was preparing a history of the Cortés expedition and relied on his friend for descriptions of the Mexican countryside. Scott had no idea of how to get to Mexico City from Veracruz. After the bombardment, the *jarochos* – residents of Veracruz – weren't about to collaborate with the invaders, so Scott relied on the blind man's book to show him the route.

From his front porch outside Veracruz, Santa Ana could practically see the invaders coming. He sent agents to visit Winfield Scott. The agents made the United States Army an offer it couldn't refuse. For a ten thousand–dollar bribe, Santa Ana would put up only a token resistance. Scott turned the money over to the agents, and Santa Ana used the money to pay his soldiers and buy more weapons. He was still the trickster, but perhaps he was a patriot after all.

The United States troops had to pass a narrow gorge near Santa Ana's property if they were to reach Mexico City. He destroyed much of his own farm to prepare a trap in the gorge. The United States troops were pinned down and would have been completely destroyed by the San Patricios' artillery if an army engineer named Robert E. Lee hadn't managed to find a trail around the pass.

The Mexicans were finally forced to retreat and fought their way back to the Capital. Santa Ana was forced to abandon the Capital

---

[59] Despite the humorous aspect of landing General Scott by block and tackle, it was an immense undertaking, especially considering the U.S. Navy did not have any kind of landing craft (Scott designed a suitable craft, but couldn't get enough built in time and used whaleboats), and this was the largest amphibious assault ever attempted anywhere up to that time. The Duke of Wellington, in his own time, and Dwight Eisenhower, a century later, both thought of Scott as a military genius. Eisenhower studied Scott's invasion plans when preparing his own amphibious assault on Normandy in 1944.

while the San Patricios and the military cadets at Chapultepec Castle fought a rear guard action. When the United States flag went up over the San Patricios' last holdout at Churubusco convent, it was the signal to hang fifty of the captured Irish and German soldiers. The cadets were massacred, and according to legend, the last boys wrapped themselves in the Mexican flag and jumped off the castle wall, preferring death to surrender. The United States Marines are taught that the red stripe on their pant legs represents the blood their fellow Marines shed at Chapultepec—a tribute, in a way, to the teenaged marksmen. The Mexicans honor Chapultepec's defenders as *los Niños Héroes* – the Heroic Children. On Saint Patrick's Day (17 March) in Mexico City, the Mexican Army pays tribute to the San Patricios. On Mexican Independence Day (16 September), the Irish National Guard honors them at the County Cork birthplace of the San Patricio leader, John Riley.

The United States occupied Mexico City on 13 September 1847. What remained of the Mexican government finally signed a peace treaty in the small village of Guadalupe Hidalgo on 2 February 1848. The United States "bought" the northern three-eighths of the country, including California, for fifteen million dollars. They also agreed to pay three million dollars in various damage claims against México that United States citizens had accumulated over the years.

Texans chased Santa Ana up and down the country. The former servant, now Governor Juárez of Oaxaca, called out his state militia and refused to let Santa Ana enter the state. His soldiers could come in but not His Most Serene Highness. Santa Ana fled the country once more.

Santa Ana chewed out

I N EXILE, SANTA ANA DID MORE for the Mexican economy than he ever did as president. Typical for him, it was a result of his personal vanity, and he was unable to understand its importance. For a time, he lived on Staten Island, New York, where he rented a room from a candy maker. North Americans had poor dental hygiene and paid no attention to how their teeth looked. Mexicans, including Santa Ana, worried about their teeth, which they kept clean by chewing chicle, a rubbery plant sap. The candy maker thought the ex-general's chicle tasted awful but wasn't bad if it was mixed with mint and dipped in sugar. He sold Santa Ana's candy-coated tooth-cleanser as Chiclets. Mr. Adams, the landlord, became rich and famous as the inventor of chewing gum and created an entirely new agricultural export for Mexican farmers. Santa Ana never received the credit nor any profit from the idea.

Recalled in the early 1850s, when the criollos realized none of them wanted to be president, Santa Ana's final disgrace was in 1855, when he sold another thirty thousand square miles of northern México to the United States for ten million dollars (the Gadsden purchase), and even then the United States cheated México. The U.S. Congress only authorized seven million dollars—and one million of that was stolen before it reached Mexico City. The old general was thrown out once more, supposedly forever. Much of the rest of his life was spent in exile, trying to raise the funds for one more try,[60] but he was never again more than a minor annoyance to the Mexican government.

He was quietly allowed back after Juárez died, since he was no longer a threat…or a hero to anyone. He had outlived Juárez, Sam Houston, de Zavala, Gómez Farías, Zachary Taylor and Winfield Scott. He wouldn't have known that. An old man with Alzheimer's disease, he would wander out on his balcony to give speeches. No one cared what he said or knew if he even noticed that he had an audience. Stories say that out of pity—or because his wife provided tacos and beer—the peons would gather on the front lawn when Santa Ana came out on the balcony of his hacienda to stir the masses one more time. He died forgotten, on 21 June 1876.

---

[60] The Emperor Maximilian dithered over whether to make Santa Ana "Duke of Tampico" or "Marquis of Veracruz" while the wily Santa Ana was raising money in New York to finance his plot to "save" México from another foreign invasion.

Quetzalcóatl and chaos

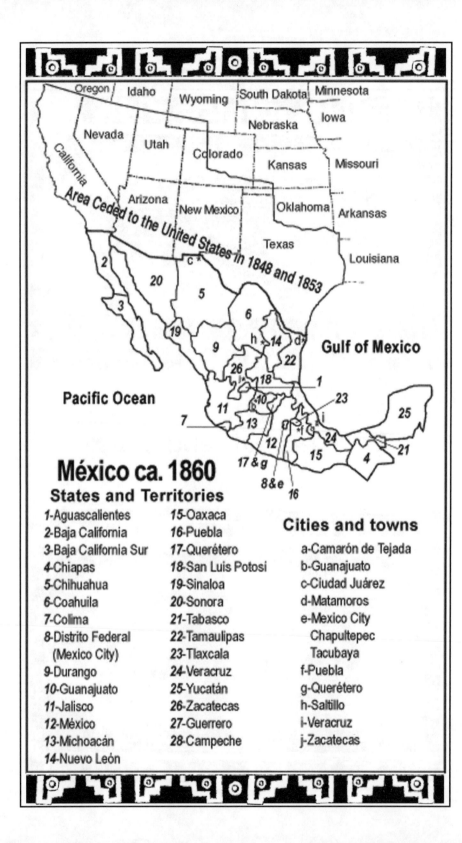

México ca. 1860
States and Territories

1-Aguascalientes
2-Baja California
3-Baja California Sur
4-Chiapas
5-Chihuahua
6-Coahuila
7-Colima
8-Distrito Federal
 (Mexico City)
9-Durango
10-Guanajuato
11-Jalisco
12-México
13-Michoacán
14-Nuevo León

15-Oaxaca
16-Puebla
17-Querétero
18-San Luis Potosi
19-Sinaloa
20-Sonora
21-Tabasco
22-Tamaulipas
23-Tlaxcala
24-Veracruz
25-Yucatán
26-Zacatecas
27-Guerrero
28-Campeche

Cities and towns

a-Camarón de Tejada
b-Guanajuato
c-Ciudad Juárez
d-Matamoros
e-Mexico City
 Chapultepec
 Tacubaya
f-Puebla
g-Querétero
h-Saltillo
i-Veracruz
j-Zacatecas

Need a good lawyer?

"THE WORST INJUSTICE ONE NATION has ever done to another," as Ulysses S. Grant would call the United States war against México, destroyed the criollos as a political force. The country was bankrupt. The money the United States paid for one-third the country's territory would barely cover the outstanding debts. The people had no loyalty to the government, and the government had shown no loyalty to the people. While soldiers had fought well and bravely, their officers had been ineffectual and largely incompetent.

Most people had never really paid much attention to the government anyway. Without enough money in the national budget to even keep the roads maintained, people stayed home—their village and the local town was all they cared about. Who ran Mexico City just wasn't important to most people. Local landlords were the real power; and maybe the state governor.

Even in Mexico City, most people didn't seem much interested in the government, other than as an employer. Fanny Calderón de la Barca had been struck by how calmly most people took the coups. For the civil servants, it didn't matter who was in charge, as long as somebody could pay the salaries. The criollos joked about *la empleomania* – employment mania. The penniless Spaniards who had poured into México during the colonial era, expecting immediate government jobs based on their birth, were replaced by penniless criollos pouring into the city for the same reason.

Even the best leaders, like President de Herrera, thought good laws were enough. They never worked out how to get people to follow the laws, or how to pay for their good ideas.

As a social class, the criollos had been unwilling—or unable—to govern and turned to the military, which seemed to offer professional leadership. Santa Ana and the other generals had been occupied with maintaining their privileges while the country deteriorated. The one president who had tried to reform the government, Valentín Gómez Farías, was a civilian.

While the generals tried to control the national government, and the criollo landowners turned their estates into private kingdoms, civilian leaders were emerging in the countryside. The new leaders were neither criollo landowners nor military men. Santos Degollado was a law professor. Guillermo Prieto, a baker's son and a mestizo, was a newspaper editor. Juan Álvarez Benítez was a small hacienda owner and Afro-Mexican. Melchor Ocampo was a rich landowner, but he wasn't sure if he was criollo or not. He had been left on the hacienda doorstep and raised by the owner, a childless widow, as her own son.[61]

Ocampo had a unusually privileged background, especially for a foundling. His adopted mother sent him to Paris to attend law school and gave him enough money to tour Europe, studying natural history and politics. Returning home to Michoacán, he practiced law, collected plant and animal samples for European scientists, conducted crop experiments, collected books and entered politics.

---

[61] Some historians claim Ocampo was the widow's illegitimate son, others that he was the son of a local priest. The stories that hacienda owners regularly raped their peons may be exaggerated. Responsible hacendados, like Don Jacinto in B. Traven's *La rosa blanca* often claimed parentage when illegitimate children were born, or abandoned children discovered, simply to avoid family feuds among the peons. Most of these children were raised as servants, or put into apprenticeships. Ocampo was rare in being treated as the widow's heir.

In many ways he resembled Thomas Jefferson. Jefferson's unusual religious belief led people to believe that he was an atheist—Ocampo was. Like Jefferson, he wanted to separate the Church from the government. Jefferson had lived in a country with competing religions, but Ocampo faced just one powerful Church and would need a clear reason to eliminate the Church's power. When he became governor of Michoacán, Ocampo's weapon against the Church was a fight over burial fees.

Whether true or not, Ocampo claimed that a peon on his hacienda had been unable to pay for his son's funeral. The priest, according to Ocampo, told the grieving father to just salt the child down and save him for Christmas dinner. The governor paid the burial fees and launched a public relations blitz against the Church. He couldn't get rid of the Church, but he managed to convince the state legislature to regulate fees for church services and to set a sliding scale for them.

In Oaxaca, there was Benito Pablo Juárez García. In the United States, Juárez is usually compared with Lincoln. Both were country boys who overcame poverty, becoming shrewd country lawyers. Both, surprisingly, became president of their country, and both led their country through a civil war, but Juárez has the more amazing personal history.

A Zapotec, he was descended from people who had never been completely conquered by either the Aztecs or the Spanish. The Aztecs were satisfied to control the Zapotec markets and to collect taxes. The Spanish had to be satisfied with indirectly ruling them through Zapotec leaders. After monks converted the Zapotecs, the Spanish were able to gain more control of the area but left these tough mountain people alone for the most part.

An orphan at three, Benito was sent to live with his uncle. He was a shepherd until he was twelve. His uncle realized the boy was too bright to waste his life watching sheep. The nearest schools were in Oaxaca City. Never having been in a city or even worn shoes, and not knowing a word of Spanish, the boy hiked the forty miles through the mountains to the big city, where his sister worked as a maid for a bookbinder. The bookbinder, a religious man, thought the serious little[62] boy might make a decent parish priest. The bookbinder put the twelve-year-old to work in the bindery and paid for his schooling. Earning his keep in the bindery and as a servant and waiter, Juárez graduated with a law degree in 1831. He was not a particularly successful as a lawyer, but he was one of the few who defended poor and indigenous clients. Though he didn't earn a lot as a lawyer (unlike Lincoln, who was an early corporate lawyer), he did, like Lincoln, marry money. Margarita Maza de Juárez, besides being a white woman willing to marry an ambitious "Indian", differed from the unfortunate, mentally unstable Mary Todd Lincoln. Margarita was sensible, thrifty and shrewd; a help, rather than a hindrance, to her husband. With her support, he became a Oaxaca City councilman, then mayor and then congressman by the time the United States invaded.[63]

Returning to Oaxaca at the outbreak of the war, he was elected governor. Although Juárez, like Ocampo, wanted to limit the Church's power, he needed the Church to support his cause: education. He agreed to leave the clergy alone if they would support public education. Schools became an important part of the Oaxaca State budget (the first public girls' schools were opened during his tenure). Puerto Ángel was developed for trade, and amazingly, he cut the bureaucracy and paid down the state debt. When Santa Ana's army collapsed, he had the prestige and power to call out the state militia and keep the fugitive president out of his state. Juárez hadn't forgotten the president's insults when he was a servant, and Santa Ana wouldn't forgive the governor's insults.

When Santa Ana returned to power, Juárez was arrested. Santa Ana never shot his enemies—he was satisfied to exile them. For

---

[62] Literally. Juárez was only four feet seven inches tall as an adult.

[63] The Mexican-American War provides another Lincoln-Juárez comparison. Both were serving as congressmen at the start of the war. Obviously, Juárez was opposed to the U.S. invasion, but Lincoln was one of the few U.S. Congressmen who spoke and voted against the war. As a result, he was targeted for defeat in the next election, and the pundits of the time assumed Lincoln's political career was finished.

Juárez, this meant joining Melchor Ocampo, thrown out to satisfy the Church conservatives, and other exiles in New Orleans. The exiles stuck together, running a small cigarette factory and working out a new constitution for México. Juárez, the dignified ex-governor, had a large family to support, so he took a second job, selling the cigarettes in the saloons.[64] From their contacts in the saloons, the exiles found the gun dealers and smugglers they needed to further their aims in México.

There were always generals looking to overthrow the president, but Juan Álvarez was different. He welcomed advisors like Ignacio Comonfort, who had worked the exiles' plans into a program, explaining what this latest coup hoped to accomplish. Professor Santos Degollado, who had replaced Ocampo as governor of Michoacán, also joined the revolt. Civilian leaders throughout the country joined local army leaders. Santa Ana simply gave up and left the country in August 1855.

Álvarez became president. As promised, he resigned in favor of Comonfort, his civilian vice president. Although Santa Ana had also resigned after staging coups, Álvarez was no Santa Ana. He disliked city life and Mexico City in particular. He was happy to ride out of town and get back to the farm. He said, "I came to the presidency a poor man and am happy to leave the same way."

---

[64] Ulysses S. Grant, Abraham Lincoln and Walt Whitman, all admirers of the little Zapotec, were also in New Orleans at about this time. Tempting as the thought is, there is no evidence that any of them ever met Juárez.

Violating the rules

To THE SHOCK OF THE CONSERVATIVES, the new civilian government started to carry out exactly what they had promised. Justice Minister Juárez pushed through a law limiting Church and military courts to strictly religious and military matters. Bishops with unlicensed butcher shops or soldiers who stole doughnuts would go before civilian courts like anyone else. The reformers then turned their attention to the bloated and ineffective army that had more officers than soldiers.

To the inefficient, disgraced officer corps, this was an open insult. Worse yet, especially in the eyes of the Church, was the law Miguel Lerdo de Tejada Corral y Bustillos wrote. The liberals believed the problem in México was that corporate and Church landowners were unproductive. They felt private enterprise and private ownership would turn the economy around. Also, the government was as always, broke, and taxes on land sales were a welcome addition to the treasury. The *Ley Lerdo* – Lerdo's Law – restricted corporations to properties connected with their business. The Church was really the corporation that Lerdo de Tejada had in mind—specifically the farms, factories and apartment houses the Church owned, but which had nothing to do with religion or charitable work. Unfortunately, the law was used throughout the rest of the century to take land from the indigenous *ejidos* – communal farms.

The Church leaders protested and threatened the new government with religious sanctions. Justice Minister Juárez responded in January 1857 with an even tougher law. Birth, death and adoption records became a government function. The Church couldn't even collect those fees. To top things off, cemeteries were taken over by the Health Department. Ocampo's peon would never have to pay another priest to bury a child.

The Church increased their pressure, threatening that any civil servant who enforced the new laws, or anyone who bought their old properties, would be excommunicated; they would lose their membership in the Church, and believers would be forbidden to help them…or even speak to them. In a nation where everyone was a member of the Church, this was a serious matter. Juárez and the rest of the cabinet pushed back even harder…most of them were Yorkista Masons anyway.[65] Ocampo was an atheist. The *Ley Iglesias* – Iglesias' Law – applied Ocampo's state laws to the entire country. It eliminated fees for most church services and put the rest on a sliding scale. Since most people had little or no money, the practical result was that the Church lost its last sources of income outside of the collection plate.

If the reformers hadn't done enough, they wrote a new constitution in 1857. To help prevent coups, they eliminated the vice president's post. They felt Congress would be stronger if there was only one house, so they also eliminated the Senate. While they added a few things—a Bill of Rights[66]—they left one other thing out. Freedom of religion is never mentioned…but neither is a state religion. For the first time, there was no official religion in México.

---

[65] The main reason Masons are a "secret society" is that Masons were automatically excommunicated by the Catholic Church until the 1990s.

[66] The Bill of Rights included a few unusual rights, ones important to the reformers: the right to an education (something Juárez thought was especially important) and the right to mail service.

For some, this was just too much. The conservatives and the Church officials thought another coup would resolve the issue, but the new government had performed a miracle—the people who appreciated the new Constitution were willing to fight for it. The disastrous invasion from the United States had had one benefit. Average citizens recognized that their bad leaders had been a joke and were only out for themselves. From now on, everyone was a Mexican. A criollo soldier from Saltillo like Ignacio Zaragoza Seguín[67] would loyally serve a Zapotec president; an indigenous general from Nayarit, Tomás Mejía, would die for a Mexican emperor.

President Comonfort tried to keep the conservatives and liberals together, but there was the inevitable military coup. As usual, the president resigned in favor of the winning general. Naturally, there was a catch. The new constitution didn't allow for coups and generals. If the president resigned, the Chief Justice of the Supreme Court (an elected officer) was the temporary president until Congress could select a regular president, and the new Chief Justice was that stubborn Zapotec lawyer, Benito Juárez. If the Aztecs and the Spanish had never been able to conquer his ancestors, they were unlikely to conquer the temporary president.

Congress defied the coup leaders, elected Juárez president and gave him the emergency powers to run the country until they could meet again. The congressmen went home to organize resistance movements. Early Zapotec kings Cosijoeza and Cosojoni had run their country from a cave above Tehuantepec when they were besieged. Their distant descendant, Benito Juárez ran his country out of lighthouses, haciendas, peasant huts, cantinas and horse-drawn buggies.[68] Congress continued to meet now and again, mail

---

[67] Zaragoza was born in Texas but lived in Saltillo.

[68] It sometimes seems that every historical museum in México has Juárez' buggy. French intelligence officers believed the rumor that Juárez didn't know how to ride a horse, and once tried to capture him by carefully destroying every wagon and buggy in the area where he was known to be. Juárez could indeed ride a horse and escaped. Juárez favored buggies because they were fast and were the only vehicles available in the 19th century with shock absorbing suspension. Although primitive, they were stable enough to let the President continue working while fleeing his enemies.

service managed to function now and again, and the Republic survived, even when its territory was reduced to nothing more than the small town below El Paso, Texas (modern Ciudad Juárez).

The Reform War was as much a holy war between the Church and the State, as it was a war over what kind of nation and what kind of rulers the country would have. Even peons on the same hacienda were sometimes fighting each other. The brutality of that war was seen in Tacubaya, a Mexico City suburb, where the students and faculty of the medical school went to set up a field hospital. The hospital was on the reformers' side of the battlefield. The winning conservative general, Leonardo Márquez was universally despised and feared as the Tiger of Tacubaya after he had the patients, doctors and students shot.

For the most part, the conservatives had the same problems the old government had always had; too many generals thought they should run the country, and too many criollos really didn't care. By 1861 the war was over, and the government could begin to implement its reforms. In March, Juárez was elected to a second term. After thirty years of mismanagement, foreign invasion and civil war, México had a bankruptcy lawyer as president. The Church land sales hadn't brought in nearly the funds needed—with the Reform War, the government had been forced to sell land for whatever it could get. Like any lawyer representing an honest debtor, Juárez sought to negotiate with his creditors for more time.

The new government was willing to acknowledge the debts that it inherited from the past governments, but it was going to have to stop payments for the next two years. The United States would wait. They were on the verge of their own civil war and in no position to collect their debts, and they could not afford an unfriendly nation on their border.

Matías Romero, the Mexican ambassador in Washington, did everything possible to maintain friendly relations...and then some. He was the first to note the similarities between his president and Abraham Lincoln. What really made Lincoln receptive to the Mexican diplomat was simple gratitude. Romero escorted the difficult Mrs. Lincoln (she was a shopaholic and mentally unstable) to the Washington fashion stores. Ulysses S. Grant was another close friend. Grant admired the Mexican culture, its people, the Juárez government and Lincoln. When the time came, he was one of the few gringos to assist México without expecting anything in return.

The Phantom Crown

E NGLAND, SPAIN AND FRANCE WERE less forgiving. As it had done in the Pastry War, France proposed taking over Veracruz and collecting customs receipts until the debt was repaid. This was the standard 19th-century way of dealing with debtor nations—creditor nations would simply occupy the debtor country's ports and pay themselves out of tax receipts. The Mexican government offered to negotiate with its European creditors, but the Europeans expected some kind of security while payment terms were worked out. Reluctantly, Mexican forces were withdrawn from Veracruz. The port was basically turned over as collateral on the outstanding loans and a joint force of the creditor nations landed in December 1861.

The English and Spanish negotiators recognized that the Mexicans were negotiating in good faith and doing the best they could under the circumstances. As an offer of good faith, the Mexicans allowed the foreign troops to move out of unhealthy Veracruz and into the mountains before mosquito season. The English and Spanish negotiators realized a functioning Mexican government was in their own interests—Spaniards had been returning to México for several years and had ongoing businesses. The English were running several mines and haciendas. If this honest government collapsed there was no telling when they would be repaid, or if their citizens would be safe. France had less business in México, but claimed much larger debts—mostly due a banker named Monsieur Jecker. Monsieur Jecker was not French, he was Swiss, but Switzerland had no navy, and more importantly, Monsieur Jecker's partner was Napoleón III's half-brother.[69]

The British and the Spanish sailed home when they realized the French had ulterior motives in the invasion. Napoleón III, like his uncle, wanted to expand France, and Europe was out of the question. France had conquered a large part of North Africa and was establishing colonies in Indochina and Africa. México was a tempting target for several reasons. The Pastry War had made France a laughingstock in Europe; Mexican silver mines and farms appeared to be a good investment; the United States, in the middle of its own civil war, was in no position to interfere and the French government listened to the exiles who still believed in a king.

A few elderly, former Spanish colonists and Mexican exiles had never given up the idea of a Mexican emperor. Others, like Juan Almonte, Morelos' son, made the argument that a foreigner—not criollo, not mestizo, not indigenous—owing allegiance to no one was the only way to create social equality.

Finally, there was Napoleón III's wife, the Empress Eugenia. She encouraged the conservative exiles, including Archbishop Labastida. The archbishop (the reform government had warned the Church to stay out of politics, but Labastida continued to meddle in politics and Juárez finally exiled him) and other conservatives painted a picture of Church persecution. Eugenia—with her less

---

[69] Napoleón abdicated in 1815 and his young son, Napoleon II, was emperor (in theory anyway) for the time it took the ink to dry on the father's abdication papers and to sign those for his son. France restored their old Bourbon kings, who were overthrown in 1830 and replaced by a cousin, Louis Philippe d'Orleans. A republican movement overthrew Louis Philippe in 1848. Louis Napoleón, the emperor's nephew, was a French Santa Ana. He had staged a failed coup, came back to be elected President of France in 1852, then overthrew his own government, making himself Emperor Napoleón III. México was not the only unstable country in the early 19th century.

than royal background[70]—was a strange woman for a Bonaparte. She was an *ultra*—aristocratic and Catholic. For her, monarchy was the only proper form of government and the older the Catholic aristocratic family, the better. She knew there was a member of the oldest, most aristocratic and Catholic family in Europe who needed a job. Who better for Emperor of México than Maximilian von Hapsburg?

Maximilian was a distant descendant of the first Carlos. Unlike the second Carlos, he was physically fit and not overwhelmed with the problems associated with inbreeding. He didn't have the energy of Carlos III but wasn't obviously brain damaged or corrupt like Carlos IV. His older brother, Franz Josef, was Emperor of Austria, but no one had found a suitable job for Max. Maximilian was an admiral in the Austrian navy, but the Austrian Empire didn't have much of a coast, and Maximilian's only important naval assignment had been a visit to Brazil. Based on his visit, Maximilian decided he was an expert on the Americas. He'd even written a book about his adventures in Brazil and had no trouble finding a publisher.

Maximilian was viceroy of the Austrian territories in northern Italy, but it wasn't working out. The Austrian-ruled Italians wanted to be part of Italy and had kept up a long-running low-level guerrilla war. He and his wife Charlotte had managed to make themselves personally popular, learning Italian, inviting Italians to join his government and encouraging Italian artists and writers. His brother, Franz Josef, a more military minded ruler, thought these gestures were good but wanted a more military approach to the unending guerrilla war. He couldn't force his brother to quit, but something had to be done about the Italian problem. Moreover, Franz Josef recognized that his brother had "issues". Specifically, he couldn't control money—he was continually overspending

---

[70] Her mother was a Scottish barmaid, who had married an extremely elderly Spanish nobleman. The old husband died, leaving the barmaid a bankrupt noblewoman. She kept the title, but married money when she decided to have children. She did her best to marry her daughters into royalty, but had to settle for a mere Bonaparte for Eugenia.

his extremely generous allowance from the Imperial treasury on building projects or by buying up artwork—and he seemed to have trouble dealing with stress. Charlotte, for her part, was a king's daughter. The daughter of the king of Belgium, granddaughter of the queen of France and Queen Victoria of England's first cousin, was not happy being only the sister-in-law of the Emperor of Austria. She believed she should be at least a queen. An empress would be even better.

There was one more European player: Pope Pius IX. The Pope was fighting his own war against Italian guerrillas, and the once important Papal States were protected only by French soldiers. His entire kingdom would be reduced to a few acres in Rome within a few years. Pius saw monarchy as the Church's best defense against republics. The French revolution had nearly destroyed the Church, and only the first Emperor Napoleón had saved it. France, and another Napoleón had to come to the Pope's rescue when the short-lived Roman Republic ran Pius out of his own kingdom. The Mexican Republic and the reformers had destroyed Pius' understanding of the way the world worked. A republic was bad enough, but these reformers had attacked the Church and even separated it from the State.

The Mexican conservatives wanted a strong central government that would restore them to power. The Pope and Eugenia wanted to strengthen the Church. Charlotte wanted a crown. Franz Josef wanted his younger brother eased out of Italy and out of a possible future as ruler of Austria. Napoleón III wanted to make money out of his occupation of México. Maximilian wanted an election!

The French occupation was much more expensive than Napoleón expected. Winfield Scott had invaded with ten thousand men, and the United States Army of the 1840s was considered one of the world's worst by the standards of the time. The French Army in the 1860s was the world's best, and four thousand soldiers should have been more than enough. The army bogged down attempting to capture Puebla, which Archbishop Labastida had assured Napoleón was overwhelmingly conservative and would welcome the French without a fight. On 5 May 1862, Mexican troops, led by Ignacio Zaragoza surprised themselves and beat the best army in the world.[71] Juárez declared 5 May a national holiday – *Cinco de Mayo*,[72] although he knew, and Zaragoza knew, that this was only a temporary victory. The French replaced their commander and sent thirty thousand reinforcements.

In the village of Camarón de Tejada (in present-day Veracruz State), a French Foreign Legion detachment was annihilated by villagers armed with a mixture of weapons from the previous thirty years of warfare and ordinary farm tools. The Foreign Legion was (and still is) an elite "Special Forces" unit recruited from foreigners who need or want to change their identity and become French citizens. The angry Mexicans cornered sixty-four of the elite fighters in a barn, set fire to it and shot the invaders who refused to surrender. They wiped out all but four of the Legionnaires. The French officer had an artificial hand; the French Foreign Legion preserves the hand as a precious relic. The Legionnaires are probably the only fighting force to celebrate a defeat. Every 30 April, the Legion—with solemn military pomp—displays their fallen leader's artificial hand and holds a parade in honor of the Poles, Italians and other non-Frenchmen who were slaughtered by Mexican villagers while fighting to install an Austrian emperor for the greater glory of France.

With still more troops, the French were finally able to claim control. Only after Zaragoza died of typhoid were they able, in March 1863, to capture the supposedly conservative, pro-Church Puebla, and the city was nearly destroyed in house to house combat. Once

---

[71] Some discount the Mexican victory, giving credit not to Zaragoza, but to either a timely rainstorm or "Montezuma's Revenge". Both sides suffered from dysentery, but Zaragoza's military tactics are still considered a classic defensive strategy.

[72] Contrary to popular belief, Cinco de Mayo never became a major holiday in México, but for some reason (perhaps to do with beer marketing) is widely advertised as THE Mexican holiday abroad. May First (International Workers' Day) is an official holiday and 10 May (Mother's Day) an extremely important unofficial one. México is not, in modern times, much given to celebrating militarism...but Mexicans are passionate about both their labor rights and their mothers.

more, President Juárez had to ask for emergency power, and once more, Congress had fled the Capital. With the foreigners in control of most of the major cities, the French organized Maximilian's election, and not surprisingly, Maximilian was elected Emperor of México.

Maximilian believed he was capable of ruling México, of bringing peace and a "liberal" monarchy to the Americas. After reading a version of the Quetzalcóatl legend forged by a pious monk who had been trying to reconcile Aztec legends with Christianity and Spanish control, Maximilian believed his blonde beard would make him welcome as the returning indigenous god.

In the 19th century, liberalism meant good business practices. Maximilian was no businessman. Napoleón III drove a sharp bargain and apparently Maximilian was too lazy to read the contract. He never understood that he was paying for the French occupation—or that the whole point of the invasion was to collect M. Jecker's notes and give France an American market. Nor did he understand that the conservatives and the Church only wanted him to restore their properties. Nor did he understand that the Mexican people had never wanted him in the first place, that his election was a sham and that he would be seen as nothing but a well-meaning, but hopelessly incompetent, ruler.

The man who would be Quetzalcóatl

FROM THE FIRST, THINGS WENT WRONG. When Maximilian (now called Maximiliano I) and Charlotte, who changed her name to the Spanish form, Carlota, stepped ashore in Veracruz (the boat taking them ashore went slightly off course under Maximiliano's directions and landed in a cemetery), the people went inside and closed their doors. Vultures sitting on the docks far outnumbered the official welcoming party that turned out for the would-be Quetzalcóatl.

The trip to Mexico City wasn't a triumphal march as planned, but a tourist's nightmare. The royal carriage got hopelessly stuck in the mud, and the royal entourage had to flag down a passing stagecoach. When they finally arrived in Mexico City, they found the National Palace staff hadn't even cleaned up yet, and there weren't any clean sheets. Unable to find a bed, Maximiliano ended up spending his first night in his new palace sleeping on a pool table.

Maximiliano was determined to be a modern emperor, despite the drawbacks. He immediately alienated the conservatives and the Church by bringing a few liberals into his cabinet and by refusing to restore the Church lands sold to private owners. He gave the Mexican generals—Leonardo Márquez (the Tiger of Tacubaya), the conservative leader Miguel Gregorio de la Luz Atenógenes Miramón y Tarelo and Tomás Mejía, the indigenous king of Nayarit—equal rank to the French officers. That simply alienated the French officers...who were the real power in México.

Maximiliano had a strange attitude towards the indigenous peoples. He was fascinated with them and had friends like Mejía (as well as an indigenous mistress). He took from the Quetzalcóatl legend the mistaken belief that his "whiteness" made him, and all Europeans, superior in indigenous eyes. What indigenous support the emperor had came from his willingness to restore traditional land holdings (the Reform threatened traditional communal farms) or his support for the Church. Maximiliano treated his indigenous subjects much as the early viceroys did: as children, not as full human beings with their own rights and needs. The French soldiers, along with the Belgian and Austrian volunteers who had joined the expedition, had been led to believe they were superior to the Mexicans and would hold superior ranks to the Mexicans. French soldiers deserted rather than serve under Mejía or Miramón (ironically, considering it was the Mexicans' "Indianness" that bothered their officers, deserters often became "Indians" themselves).

French troops controlled most of the cities, but a guerrilla war continued throughout the countryside.[73] Ex-President Álvarez, the poor farmer who reluctantly led the coup that brought the liberals to power, though in his seventies, took to the hills and led one guerrilla unit. Neither the conservatives nor the liberals were going to support this foreign emperor over the long run.

Napoleón III, despite returning France to a monarchy, was a modern politician. He was the first to use opinion polls. Napoleón saw the polls as a way of heading off popular discontent that might threaten his rule. It was a way of spying on the citizens. Police chiefs throughout France were sent coded telegrams, with a "question of the week". Secret agents throughout France surveyed ordinary French men and women—in markets, on street corners, in cafes.

---

[73] In the 20th century, the French would face the same problem in Algeria and Vietnam (as would the United States in Vietnam).

Then, the chiefs would gather the information, and send coded postcards back to headquarters in Paris. When the question of the week was whether or not France should send more troops to México, the results were clear: the French people were solidly against sending their troops to México.

Napoleón had two other problems as well. The new European power, Prussia, was building an army to challenge France. Prussia and Austria had a short war, which Austria lost. Franz Josef was in no position to help his younger brother militarily or financially, even if he wanted to. Prussia was now looking at France. Napoleón knew a war was coming (he would lose his throne, and Prussia became Germany as a result). A more immediate problem was the end of the civil war in the United States. The French emperor had gambled that either the United States would be broken into two smaller powers, or that the war would last for several years and leave the country too weak to intervene in México. The United States secretary of state, William Seward, had been desperate not to anger European powers during the war and privately sympathized with the French intervention. Even so, the United States tilted towards Juárez. It had never diplomatically recognized the Mexican Empire,[74] and even before the American Civil War ended was openly supporting the Republic.

---

[74] Another matter Maximiliano seemed to not understand. As his empire's territory shrunk, it became harder and harder to send mail. The emperor's personal correspondence was sent in care of his unofficial Embassy but delivered to the official Republican embassy...which, naturally opened the letters, and published the most embarrassing parts.

Dirty laundry

GENERAL GRANT, MATÍAS ROMERO'S old friend and the great admirer of Juárez, funneled troops and weapons to south Texas at the end of the war. While Seward reluctantly applied diplomatic pressure on France to withdraw (someone had to remind him of the Monroe Doctrine), Grant was supplying the republicans with weapons. When U.S. soldiers were surprised unloading wagonloads of rifles in Matamoros, a small battle erupted between the gringos and a group of Austrian volunteers. Not sure what they were supposed to do, the U.S. soldiers captured the Austrians and marched them back across the river into Brownsville.

Matamoros had grown wealthy during the American Civil War (Texas ports were blockaded, and Matamoros was the only place to export cotton) and had a sizable German-speaking community. Brownsville was a dull, dirty little border town.

The Austrians had enjoyed themselves in Matamoros, filling up on German food and going from party to party. Off-duty soldiers from the United States often crossed into Matamoros as well. The captured Austrians weren't at all happy about being marched into Brownsville. They weren't jailed, but they were dumped into a second-rate hotel.

Expected to pay their own hotel bill, the Austrians couldn't afford to send out their laundry. Their leader, Ernst Pitner, sent plaintive letters to his mother complaining about Texas, the Texans and the poor laundry service. His mother complained to Emperor Franz Josef, who called in the United States ambassador. Since the two countries were not at war, and neither officially had soldiers in México, the two sides agreed nothing had happened and there was no battle. Pitner and his men were simply lost tourists, who were escorted back across the border to Matamoros, just in time to be run out again by the republicans.

Most of the Austrians quietly returned home. Pitner stayed with Maximiliano until the end and eventually (with his mother's help) obtained a job with the Austrian diplomatic service. Even as a elderly and respectable consular official, he still complained about laundry.

With the French withdrawal and new arms, the republicans were quickly recovering the country. Maximiliano, as usual, did the wrong thing. Assuming the Mexicans would accept his regime if he had a Mexican born heir, he "adopted" Augustín Iturbide's grandson. There was one little problem. The boy's mother was living (Maximiliano had bought the child from his aunt) and was an American citizen. The story of an American child, kidnapped by European royalty, was a sensation in the U.S. and English press. Secretary of State Seward was besieged with angry telegrams and letters demanding U.S. action. In England, Carlota's older and more respectable cousin, Queen Victoria, was picketed by outraged English mothers. Queen Victoria was the mother of a large family herself and a political realist. When Victoria's letters to Carlota went unanswered, Victoria suggested her government withdraw support from the Mexican Empire.[75]

---

[75] The Iturbide-Hapsburg family is still around, but the child, Augustín de Iturbide Green never had children, becoming a Mexican army officer and later a professor of Romance Languages at Georgetown University. The present head of the family (recognized as such by European royals) is Maximiliano Gustav Richard Albrecht Agustin von Götzen-Iturbide, an Australian businessman.

As the smart one in the family, Carlota was sent to Paris—both to control the damage from the ill-conceived adoption and to lobby for more troops. Napoleón, pleading stomach troubles,[76] refused to meet her, passing her off from one bureaucrat to another. Carlota sent rambling, incoherent advice back to Mexico City, eventually deciding she had to lobby the Pope. Pius, she decided, could shame Napoleón into helping her husband. During a Papal audience, Carlota became delusional, suffered a breakdown and never recovered. She spent the rest of her very long life (she lived until 1927) playing with dolls in a Belgian castle.

With the French leaving, and his much more intelligent wife unable to help him, Maximiliano continued to make disastrous decisions. He signed a decree that classified all rebels against the government as bandits who could be shot without trial. This only meant that republican soldiers wouldn't surrender. It also meant that when he was finally captured, the government had a legal reason to shoot Maximiliano. With his French commander-in-chief leaving, the emperor, who had only his peacetime naval experience behind him, made himself commander of the Mexican army.

The empire lost one stronghold after another. Finally, Maximiliano and what remained of his government abandoned Mexico City for Querétaro City. The emperor had delusions of making a last stand, but in the end, a supposedly loyal Imperial officer simply opened the back door to the convent protecting the remaining Imperial army. Aside from his few remaining Mexican generals, the Imperial government was reduced to a few foreign officers (Ernst Pitner—who supposedly had a supply of clean underwear—among them) and adventurers like Prince Felix von Salm-Salm, a Prussian who had become a United States general during the Civil War.

Born in 1828, Prince Felix, the younger son of a minor German ruler, was a scapegrace. Trained, as a good aristocrat should be, for a military career, he was drummed out of the Austrian army

---

[76] It may not have been an excuse. He died of stomach cancer.

(supposedly for gambling debts), fled to the United States and needing a job, ended up as a volunteer colonel in a New York City unit recruited from German-speaking immigrants. Prince Felix was an exemplary Union officer (eventually being promoted to Brigadier General).

He married a former singer and circus performer, Alice leClerq, who traded on her distant relationship to President Lincoln to become a figure on the Washington social circuit. As Princess Alice, she organized and commanded a battlefield nursing unit during the American Civil War, while her husband ran medical units.

The end of hostilities found the couple bored with Felix' duties overseeing occupation forces in Georgia. Looking around for something to do, they headed for México, arriving in February 1866 just as the French occupation forces were preparing to "cut and run". Prince Felix found himself with the imposing title of Imperial Aide-de-Camp and Head of Household.

Alice—who seemed to be up for almost anything—hung around as a lady-in-waiting to Carlota, but was back in the United States when the Imperial court surrendered at Querétaro in May 1867. Then, the Princess came into her own. She steamed back to Veracruz and made it to Mexico City to badger European consulates for funds to bribe Mexican jailers into freeing the emperor, while pestering government officials for a meeting with President Juárez.

There is a famous painting by Manuel Ocaraza of that meeting. Alice, falling back on her experience as a performer, went down on her knees to beg the president to spare poor Maximiliano in the name of every king and queen in Europe. In the painting, Benito Juárez is sadly telling Alice, "I'm sorry, Madame, to see you on your knees before me; but even if all the queens and kings of Europe were in your place, I still wouldn't be able to save his life. I'm not the one who takes it, it's the people that rule his life and mine."

Juárez did eventually find a loophole to spare Prince Felix' life. He became a Prussian officer, but had his head blown off by a cannonball at the start of the Franco-Prussian War. Alice edited his memoirs and wrote an entertaining tell-all book about her, the

Prince, Maximiliano and Juárez who, she implied, was less than a gentleman.

Juárez received pleas for Maximiliano's life from more than just ex-circus acrobats. Most foreign governments (including the United States); the Pope; the Pope's biggest Italian enemy, Giuseppe Garibaldi; and even Mexican republicans asked Juárez to save the unfortunate emperor. The president refused; he was the same inflexible lawyer that he had always been. Maximiliano himself had signed the law mandating the death penalty for rebels. Besides which, the emperor had been found guilty by a military court, and legally, there was nothing he could do (which didn't stop Juárez from suggesting that other foreigners be given reduced sentences, or merely expelled from the country, as the Salm-Salms were).

Most importantly, Juárez sent a clear message—the days of foreign intervention were over. Maximiliano was executed on 19 June 1867.[77]

---

[77] Max's bad luck continued after his death. The Mexican government would not release the ex-emperor's body despite pleas from the Hapsburgs and several foreign governments. Bureaucratic foot-dragging gave embalmers time to undo the first, hurried and incompetent attempt. After his execution, a local surgeon, using a textbook, did his best to embalm the body, but used too much copper in the fluid. The corpse turned bright green. Before being shipped back to Austria, Mexican embalmers painted the corpse, giving Max a more or less suntanned look. There was nothing they could do about the missing eye. Max had blue eyes, but the several bullets that killed him dislocated one eyeball. The embalmer, not having a blue glass eye in stock, borrowed an eyeball from a taxidermist. The glass eye was noticed—either because the 19th-century Europeans had strange sentimentality towards the dead or because the Hapsburgs were a strange family; at any rate, Max's mother insisted on one last look at her boy's baby blues. Maximilian von Hapsburg was buried in Vienna, under a tombstone written in the Latin Náhuatl script.

Mad Max

MAXIMILIANO AND CARLOTA are the best known for-eigners in Mexican history. They have been the subject of several novels and popular histories (Bettina Harding's *Phantom Crown* is the best), and even a classic Bette Davis film ("Juárez", MGM 1938). Davis played Carlota.[78]

Foreigners often see the Imperial couple as a tragic, romantic pair. Mexicans see them as well-intentioned fools, or worse. By modern standards, they were white supremacists. Like the gachupines of the colonial era, they believed that Europeans were obviously superior to the Mexicans, and the warfare and destruction carried out in their name was justified. Unfortunately, this attitude pervades most foreign writing about the Hapsburgs. The legal concept of

---

[78] I am not the only person whose interest in Mexican history started with this film. It is entertaining, and fairly accurate (though, of course, highly simplified). Some of the casting—Bette Davis as Carlota and Claude Raines as the devious Napoleón III is expected, but there are some oddities. Benito Juárez is played by Paul Muni—an Austrian! Gayle Sondergaard, a major actress of the time, plays the archconservative Eugenia. In "real life", she was anything but and later was "blacklisted" as a Communist sympathizer.

"crimes against humanity"[79] did not exist in their day, but in the 21st century they could be tried and convicted of genocide and terrorism under Mexican, French, Belgian or Austrian laws for the atrocities committed by the soldiers serving in their name.

They were foolish and greedy people, not idealistic, misguided ones. Both were frustrated and unhappy as provincial rulers. Carlota especially resented not being at least a queen, as her mother and grandmother were. When a crown was offered, common sense went out the window. Carlota at least had the sense to bargain for a bigger income than was originally offered, but Maximiliano had never bothered to read the treaty that made him Emperor of México. He prepared for his new job not by studying the economics or the history of México (except for things like the false Quetzalcóatl legend), but by writing a six hundred-page guidebook to court etiquette. The French administrators ignored the emperor. Unlike Maximiliano, they were competent...but brutal. When the French withdrew, Maximiliano generally chose incompetents as replacements, with the possible exception of Prince Salm-Salm, chosen more because he was an aristocrat than for his military or administrative skills.

Maximiliano's foreign policy advisor was German, but no aristocrat. Father Fischer had been defrocked as a Lutheran minister and run out of Texas, somehow ending up as a Jesuit in Italy. The Pope apparently was covering up some scandal involving Fischer, and he was sent to México. Being a native German speaker, he was attached to the Imperial court and at one point, sent to Rome to negotiate with the Pope. The Pope, of course, had a full dossier on Fischer's past and never took him seriously, but he did read the emperor's six hundred pages on etiquette.

---

[79] "Crimes against humanity" was first used by a former volunteer officer in Juárez' army, George Washington Williams. Williams, an African-American, had been a soldier in both the U.S. Union Army and the Mexican Republic, as well as a newspaper editor and lawyer before becoming a Baptist missionary in the Belgian Congo, which was the private property of Carlota's brother, King Leopold II of Belgium. Williams was referring to Leopold's criminal responsibility for human rights abuses of the native people by the Europeans.

Maximiliano's one lasting contribution to México (if you don't count *bolillos* – hard crusted bread rolls – though we should thank French Army cooks for inventing the small Mexican version of the baguette) was to encourage archaeological research, and that needs to be weighed against the emperor's closing of the University. Otherwise, one can only point to laying out Paseo de la Reforma, which was simply the trail the Imperial horse liked to take from Chapultepec to the Alameda—the famous street was laid out later, during Porfirio Díaz' presidency—and rebuilding Chapultepec Castle.

Unfortunately, the Castle bankrupted the government (so much for European superiority over the indigenous bankruptcy lawyer) and was always a sort of white elephant. Juárez lived in the Palacio Nacional, and the old Castle was used as a school. Porfirio Díaz remodeled the place as a presidential palace, but it was too grand for the modest socialist president, Lázaro Cárdenas—besides, the Cárdenas' children had no place to play. It is a popular museum and tourist attraction now; as much for its connections with its earlier history as a fort or later career as Porfirio Díaz' elegant home, as for its Hapsburg exhibits.

The Imperial couple's failure to produce an heir may have a simple reason: Maximiliano built himself a palace in Cuernavaca but somehow "forgot" to build a room for his wife. He did remember to build a small apartment for his indigenous mistress, and—according to legend—father a son. There's serious doubt the fellow was Maximiliano's son, but he was as unlucky, incompetent and romantic as the emperor—he was a Mexican working as a German spy in France during the First World War. If he was Maximiliano's son, perhaps he wanted to avenge his family, but how a Mexican planned to pass himself off as a Frenchman has never been explained. Like putative father, like putative son: both ended up before firing squads.

Or there may be another reason—one that accounts both for the couple's strange behavior and their childlessness—syphilis.

Syphilis was the AIDS of the 19th century. Although it was rampant among central European artistic and aristocratic circles, it was considered a disease of the lower classes or one of marginal people. Treatments were generally ineffective, if they were even available. There is no reason to assume—as most of Maximiliano's biographers do—that he caught the disease from a Brazilian prostitute. He could have just as easily contracted the disease in Europe.

With syphilis then, as with AIDS today, there is a belief in some circles that respectable women are immune. In Maximiliano's day, and to some extent in our own, men who knew they were infected saw no reason to inform their wives (or take any precautions). Untreated syphilis causes sterility and in the later stages attacks the brain, producing psychosis. Maximiliano was delusional and Carlota spectacularly so.

Maximiliano began acting erratically shortly before leaving Italy for México. The voyage had to be delayed when the emperor suddenly lost his temper at breakfast, began throwing dishes around, then was confined to bed with a high fever. Although biographer Joan Haslip speculates that Maximiliano and Carlota slept apart because the emperor wasn't much interested in sex or was impotent (he also drank heavily, which would cause impotence); it may have been that he tried (too late) to protect Carlota from infection.

Carlota began to deteriorate physically and mentally soon after the couple's arrival in México. The French military commander, Marshall Bazaine, wrote that the empire might have had a chance if Carlota, who had a better grasp of financial and political issues, had been in charge. However, she aged rapidly (she was only twenty-four, but looked much older in her portraits) and was having debilitating headaches (again, a symptom of tertiary syphilis). She also started hallucinating, and went spectacularly insane while visiting the Pope. Claiming she was being poisoned by Napoleón (who she decided was Satan), she forced her way into the Vatican while the Pope was eating breakfast, grabbed the Pope's food with her hands and refused to leave.

The pope and a doctor disguised as a priest were finally able to convince Carlota to leave the next day, but only after she and her lady-in-waiting became the sole women in history to spend the night in the Papal library. The Pope spent the night in the Papal telegraph office trying to reach Franz Josef or the King of Belgium.

Sigmund Freud was still a school boy at the time, but Austrian doctors already had a reputation for advanced treatment of the mentally ill. However, they could do nothing. Carlota was eventually put in the care of her brother, the Belgian king. He provided a house and caretakers, but for the next fifty years she was never completely lucid (and usually in no condition to get out of bed); she died in 1927.

Sexually transmitted diseases are no longer seen as something hidden, or as a sign of divine disfavor. It is not syphilis that makes the Imperial couple so repellent. The French occupation of México happened at the same time as the American Civil War. In both, white supremacy was one of the justifications for massive bloodshed and destruction. There is no more reason to defend the selfish, stupid, vain and cold-blooded Hapsburgs any more than there is to defend slaveholders.

Not quite Quetzalcóatl

THE WORLDWIDE OUTRAGE over Maximiliano's execution was short-lived. The strange "Indian" country enjoyed a new respect. Also respected was the Juárez Doctrine, which argued that nonintervention in affairs of other nations is the only way to world peace. This was in direct opposition to the Monroe Doctrine, which the United States used to justify interference in any part of the Americas.

Benito Juárez was the first modern leader of what are now being referred to as "Third World" or "nonaligned" countries. In the 20th century, these leaders have often been respected for similar reasons—fighting off foreign invaders (like Ho Chi Minh of Vietnam), maintaining their independence from the superpowers (like Pandit Nehru of India and Marshall Tito of Yugoslavia), as a symbol of an oppressed people taking control of their own destiny (like Nelson Mandela in South Africa) or proposing common-sense solutions to international problems of war and peace (like Mahatma Gandhi).

The latter half of the 19th century was also a time of nationalist movements, and the "Indian" leader was seen in Europe as a symbol of nationalism triumphing over foreign control. The

Mussolini family in Northern Italy (where Maximilian first ran into a resistance movement) named their son Benito. By a strange twist of fate, the only European leader ever named for an indigenous American (the father of nonintervention in foreign affairs) was the founder of fascism—which promotes imperialist wars and white supremacy.

Respect, no matter how profound, does not pay the bills. México was bankrupt before the French invasion, and the war to drive out Maximiliano as well as the emperor's mismanagement of the economy only made matters worse. Even though France quietly wrote off their sizable debt (they really had no other choice), the country was desperate to finance its development. Juárez was an Oaxaqueño, but he was leading a bankrupt nation that had lost a third of its territory only a few years earlier, and the isthmus, which is the southern part of México, had (and still has) a very different culture than the rest of the country. The United States was interested in buying—or leasing—México south of the Isthmus of Tehuantepec (Chiapas State and parts of Oaxaca and Tabasco States). Before the Panama Canal was thought of, the isthmus was the best and most secure route between the Atlantic and Pacific. Building a railroad here was a good idea, and México was desperate for railroads. The Mexican Congress agreed to lease the entire isthmus for ninety-nine years, in return for needed funding and technical assistance with their own railroads. However, the United States Senate was bogged down in a fight over an unrelated issue and just never got around to approving the treaty.

General Grant, once again, involved himself in Mexican affairs. Other American Civil War generals had found jobs as presidents of railroad companies. Grant had been slow off the mark, and there weren't any railroad companies left in the United States looking for presidents. Matías Romero, still representing his country in Washington, had been trying to raise the money to build a Mexican railway. Who better to assure gringo investors than their most popular general?

The Mexican Railway Company, Ulysses S. Grant, President, started laying tracks. Typical for Grant's business ventures, the company was a failure, but it started México building railways.[80] British companies built most of them: the British had the money to invest. It was a risky financial venture—the Mexican government had no money and paid in land concessions—but immensely profitable. Mexican railroads became a hot investment and like other investments, open to fraud. Anthony Trollope, the English writer, put shady Mexican railway financing at the heart of his 1886 novel, *The Way We Live Now.*

The railways developed the country—but at a cost. They put more and more of México under foreign economic control. The railroad builders weren't interested in tying the country together as much as they were in providing a way to get goods out. Cities only a mountain or two apart were still as isolated from each other as ever—the trains ran north to Texas, or west to Acapulco, or East to Veracruz, but not between, say, Zacatecas and Guanajuato.

Since independence, unemployed ex-soldiers had been a problem. After the Reform War, the French invasion and the guerrilla war against the French, there were more unemployed soldiers than ever. Most simply went back to their old lives, others turned bandit, but there were exceptions. Ignacio Altamirano, an indigenous *norteño* – a Mexican from the northern states bordering the United States, whose culture at this time was similar to that in the U.S. "old west" – had become famous as a guerrilla leader fighter and more famous still when he started publishing his folk tales and short stories. He's one of the outstanding Spanish language writers of the late 19th century—even though he has no Spanish ancestry.

---

[80] It also brought the Chinese to México. Chinese workers had built the railroads in the western United States, but immigration laws in the U.S. favored Europeans. The Chinese could not bring their families to the United States. México had no restrictions on Chinese immigrants, and the Mexican railway was happy to hire the skilled railway workers—and to pay them the higher wages given to experienced workers from the United States.

French soldiers in Oaxaca deserted and "went native". "White Zapotecs"—with their very French features—could still be distinguished from other Zapotecs until after the Second World War. Adding to the problem, this was the "Wild West" era in the United States. Just as in the cowboy movies, bandits in the United States headed for the Mexican border. Often they made it...and were still bandits. Indigenous people, like the Apaches and Comanches, who had been ignored before, suddenly found themselves fighting settlers. Many of these people lived on both sides of the border. The United States saw them as enemies. In México, they were simply citizens. The United States complained that México was harboring enemy forces. The Mexican government complained that the cavalry units chasing indigenous warriors into México were invaders. Ulysses S. Grant was a successful general and unlucky in everything else. For all his pro-Mexican sympathies and deeds (Grant spoke fluent Spanish, always hired Mexican servants and often went out of his way to find jobs for Mexican immigrants he met), he ended up something of a villain—in the standard Mexican history books—because of the cavalry raids during his presidency.

To protect trade, the new railways, the foreign investors and the Mexican borders from the United States cavalry, *los rurales* – the Rural Police – were organized. Porfirio Díaz would later play with the rumor that they were all reformed bandits.

Juárez was no saint. He had become president irregularly the first time. He—and a few friends—had relied on a rather loose interpretation of the constitution to justify his second administration. His third term (1871) started with widespread voter fraud and another attempted military coup led by José de la Cruz Porfirio Díaz Mori. Díaz was one of those ex-guerrillas who had never quite settled back into civilian life. After serving at the defense of Puebla, Díaz became a national leader when he rejected Maximiliano's offer to lead the Imperial army and then escaped from San Juan de Ulúa in Veracruz harbor. He justified his rebellion on the grounds that one term was enough for any president—even Benito Juárez.

That rebellion—along with several others—was put down. Díaz retired to Oaxaca, and the country settled down. As Díaz was to say on another occasion, "Nothing happens in México...until it happens." On 18 July 1872 something happened: Juárez died.

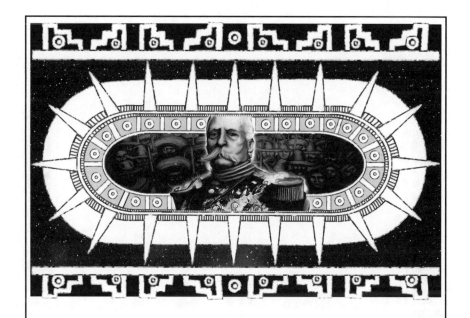

The Good, the Bad
and the Ugly

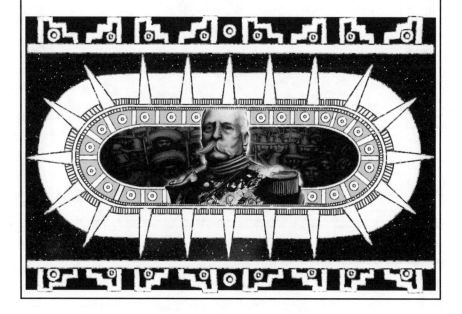

States and Territories

1-Aguascalientes
2-Baja California
3-Campeche
4-Chiapas
5-Chihuahua
6-Coahuila
7-Colima
8-Distrito Federal / México
   (Mexico City)
9-Durango
10-Guanajuato
11-Guerrero
12-Hidalgo
13-Jalisco
14-México
15-Michoacán
16-Morelos
17-Nayarit
18-Nuevo León
19-Oaxaca
20-Puebla
21-Querétaro
22-San Luis Potosí
23-Sinaloa
24-Sonora
25-Tabasco
26-Tamaulipas
27-Tlaxcala
28-Veracruz
29-Yucatán
30-Zacatecas

Places

a- Cananea
b- Cuernavaca
c- Mexico City
   Lecumberri
d- Popocatepetl
e- Tampico
f- Toluca
g- Valle Nacional
h- Veracruz
   San Juan de Ulúa

Gulf of Mexico

Pacific Ocean

México ca. 1900

Quetzalcóatl...or Tezcatlipoca?

THE UNIVERSALLY MOURNED[81] Benito Juárez was no intellectual—the laws, constitution and the Juárez Doctrine are all simple documents—the products of a well-educated country lawyer. He remained in many ways a peasant shepherd. When cabinet meetings ran into the dinner hour, the president thought nothing of yelling out the window of the National Palace to order tacos. Chief Justice Sebastián Lerdo de Tejada, a criollo, an elegant writer and not one to order tacos (let alone yell out a window), became the new president.

Lerdo managed to alienate nearly everyone. He proclaimed amnesty for all past revolutionaries, except for some of Maximiliano's generals and Porfirio Díaz' followers. Immediately, there were several new revolts. Juárez had been anticlerical, but his anticlericalism

---

[81] Almost. The "Indian" Juárez was buried in Panteón San Fernando, the elite Mexico City burial ground of the 19th century. Tomas Mejía and Tomas Miramón—the two generals shot with Maximiliano—were also buried in San Fernando. Mejía was indigenous, but he was a recognized as a king and an acceptable neighbor for the snobby Miramón family; but Juárez wasn't. The Miramóns—not wanting Tomás buried near an Indian—had the general dug up and moved to the pro-clerical stronghold of Puebla. It was natural that the remains of Ignacio Zaragoza, the hero of Cinco de Mayo, who had originally been buried in Puebla, were transferred to San Fernando. The Miramón and Zaragoza families traded graves. Juárez' plot was originally intended for Maximiliano and Carlota.

was more that of the poor peon who couldn't pay the priest's burial fees. Lerdo's anticlericalism was intellectual; Juárez' proudest achievements had been in furthering public education, even if it meant letting the churches run schools. To the more intellectual Lerdo, religion distracted from the educational models outlined in the new national curriculum. Lerdo argued that the people's time would be better spent reading schoolbooks than spent going to Mass or a fiesta. Unlike Juárez, he just didn't understand the people needed entertainment and excitement. When he was excommunicated, Juárez half-seriously suggested importing Protestant missionaries. The Protestants don't have saints (and thus no expensive fiestas in their honor) and have plain services. Poor people would have more money—but duller lives—if they were Protestants.[82] There was a brief religious rebellion against the Lerdo government—this time led by humble farmers who wanted their fiestas, rather than bishops and generals wanting to maintain economic and political control.

By the time Juárez died, the economy was relatively stable. Foreigners realized that there was money to be made in México. Lerdo's government improved the business climate (for the first time foreign businesses could open branch offices in México), but foreign investors complained about the restrictions on taking money out of the country and the lack of special rights for foreigners.

Again, something happened. Lerdo ran for reelection. Foreign financial interests, and popular discontent with Lerdo, opened up new opportunities for Porfirio Díaz. He crossed the border to meet with American bankers in Brownsville, Texas. Having secured the financing and weapons he needed, Díaz crossed back across the border to start his old rebellion—again, the rationale was presidential reelection. The election was a mess—Lerdo and another candidate both claimed they were president. Díaz (commuting between battles and business meetings in New Orleans) eventually

---

[82] Armed warfare has broken out between Evangelical and Catholic indigenous communities in recent years when Evangelicals complained about using tax money for fiestas and other "religious" celebrations.

succeeded in his rebellion, had himself appointed interim president, and called for new elections. Not surprisingly, he won.

Having staged his rebellion on a "no reelection" platform, Díaz served out his 1876–1880 term and stepped aside. He ran again, and won, in 1884, 1888, 1892, 1896, 1900 and 1904 (when he finally got tired of all that electioneering and had the presidential term lengthened to six years). He actually had an opponent in some elections—a Mexico City astrologer who received the best possible treatment in a private mental hospital in nonelection years: his care paid for by none other than Porfirio Díaz.

During the thirty years he presided over México, the country developed both agriculturally and industrially. It was considered a safe place to invest, or to visit; huge engineering projects were completed, and fortunes were made. Unfortunately, very few Mexicans made these fortunes. For the people, life became worse—the new industrial worker made less and less money, and farmers lost more of their land...ending up in a form of slavery. To the outside world, Díaz maintained his image as Quetzalcóatl. By the end of his career, he would look more and more like Huitzilopochtli.

Porfirio the good...

PORFIRIO DÍAZ WAS THE 19TH CENTURY'S favorite dictator. Kaiser Wilhelm of Germany, Teddy Roosevelt, Leo Tolstoy, Mark Twain, Andrew Carnegie and even Karl Marx[83] praised him. Although he looked more and more like a king and acted more and more like one as he grew older, he remained an honest country bumpkin. He didn't learn how to eat with a knife and fork until he was over fifty. His eighteen-year-old second wife finally taught the old soldier some table manners and got him to stop mopping up the gravy with his tortillas at state dinners. Then she got rid of the tortillas, bringing French cuisine to the presidential table.

He was personally honest and set high standards for his advisors. High officials might make money on stock deals during his regime, but open bribery came to an end. He found excellent civil servants like Finance Minister José Ives Limantour Marquet, who

---

[83] As a political theorist, Marx believed that a society had to go through a capitalist phase before it could become a Communist society. Writing political theory didn't put food on the Marx family table, so Karl also wrote for American newspapers. Díaz, by industrializing an agrarian country, was on the side of progress, at least as Marx saw it. In 1846, when Marx was a European correspondent for the *New York Herald,* he enthusiastically supported the U.S. invasion of México for much the same reason.

managed to pay off the Mexican national debt. He was loyal to his friends and to the Republic.

Like Juárez, Porfirio Díaz was from a poor Oaxaca family. Like Juárez, his intelligence was noted, and he was sent to study for the priesthood. Again, like Juárez, he found his real calling elsewhere. For Díaz, it was the army. He was a hero of Cinco de Mayo, when the Mexican army, against all expectations, beat back a French attack on Puebla. During the French occupation, the thirty-two-year-old general became famous as a guerrilla fighter and proved his loyalty when he turned down a personal offer from Maximiliano to join the Imperial government.

His unsuccessful rebellion against Juárez was motivated by the same honorable reason he rebelled successfully against Lerdo: the principle of "no reelection". Díaz would never attack the memory of Benito Juárez, though he might suggest the great leader had held on to the presidency a little too long. After all, Porfirio did give up the presidency...the first time. After Díaz' handpicked successor served out his term, Díaz served again...and again...and again...until he was finally forced to leave.

Despite that slight misunderstanding in the 1860s, the Porfiriate was the era of French influence in Mexico City. José Limantour, the finance minister, lived in Paris more than in Mexico City. French architecture, French cuisine and French philosophy reigned. French "Positivism" influenced more than just dinner-table discussions. It was government policy. Positivists believed that only things that can be seen and verified are important. Feelings, emotions, sentiments or beliefs had no place in the positivist universe. The Aztecs knew that what was seen wasn't necessarily what was real; Tezcatlipoca, the Aztec god of real things, was also a trickster god.

There were no Aztecs in Porfirio's Positivist government. The high government officials were nearly all of European descent, a shrinking minority in México. Furthermore, many of them accepted a form of "social Darwinism" (Darwin's Theory of Evolution applied to race and culture) and believed the indigenous people were a drain on México's development. Some went as far as suggesting that European immigrants be used to drive out the indigenous peoples or at least, to dilute their genetic makeup in México as a whole.

These Positivists (they called themselves *los científicos* – the scientists) were generally well-qualified, honest men. Their philosophy meant Mexicans would pay a very high price in the drive to become a "modern" country.

...the bad...

THE CIENTÍFICOS WANTED foreign immigrants in the countryside. As positivists, it only made sense that people show positive proof that they owned the land they lived on. So, in 1883 a law was passed by Congress that encouraged land companies to survey undeveloped land. The companies received a third of all undeveloped land for resale. Undeveloped meant land with no proof of ownership, but very few indigenous communities could show deeds for their property.[84] Communities that had lived in the same place for eight hundred or more years suddenly discovered they were living on a hacienda. Their crops had to give way to the new owner's crops, and to survive they had to become peons, paying rent on their own homes and on their own fields.

If a peon was too much trouble, he could always be drafted into the army, or the landlord could call the Rurales. Juárez originated the rural police but Díaz made them a strong arm of his government. While in their distinctive gray *charro* outfits – the "Mexican cowboy" costume favored by Mariachi bands today – the Rurales

---

[84] At least some indigenous communities did, and still do, have ancient property records. A boundary dispute between two communities in the State of México was settled in July 2003 in favor of the community that brought into court their title deeds, written in Aztec hieroglyphics and signed by Philip II of Spain.

stood out in places where foreigners might congregate: railroad stations, banks and near foreign-owned haciendas. However, their real job was not to reassure foreign visitors or provide a colorful background,[85] but to evict farmers who couldn't prove land ownership, or to arrest and shoot, "while trying to escape", any enemies of the regime. Díaz and his científico advisors, wanted to give México a good image.

Díaz liked to claim that he'd made México safe for a blonde woman to walk from Laredo to the Guatemalan border in just her underwear without a problem. That was untrue, but México was safer than it had been in years, at least for foreigners. The Rurales were not "reformed bandits", but only the most visible of the unreformed thugs on the government payroll. Fighting for your land or joining a strike could get you drafted or killed. Publishing a labor newspaper might get you thrown out of the country...or worse.

The Flores Magón brothers, three radical journalists, had been put out of business again and again in México. At first, they tried to get around censorship by changing the names of their publications. The authorities no sooner closed down *Ahuizote*, when a new newspaper, *El Hijo de Ahuizote* – Son of Ahuizote – hit the newsstands. When *El Hijo de Ahuizote* was shut down, the brothers started *El Nieto de Ahuizote* – Grandson of Ahuizote. Ahuizote's great-great-grandson was closed down before the brothers got the hint and moved their paper—renamed *Regeneración*—to Texas. Apparently, the Ahuizote dynasty no longer had to grow to maturity every time the brothers started over and could regenerate itself—or perhaps the joke was getting a bit stale.

Díaz sent a hit man who could blend in with the local Mexican-American community to assassinate the most articulate (and dangerous) of the three, Ricardo. The hit man couldn't figure out

---

[85] As part of Mexico City's police reforms in the 2000s, the Federal District Park Police adopted a "charro outfit" uniform, complete with the stereotyped big Mexican sombrero, (though in standard police blue), to give the police a more "user friendly" image. As part of the image, the officers carry six-shooters. However, the guns are actually specially designed 9 mm police standard pistols.

which of the three brothers he was supposed to shoot and missed them all. The Flores Magón brothers moved their operations to St. Louis, Missouri, where a Mexican hit man would be a little more obvious.

Although somewhat safer in the United States, the brothers—as anarchists—were considered dangerous radicals and in constant danger of being deported as "undesirable aliens". What finally ended their career was their militant pacifism. In 1917, when the United States entered the First World War, Ricardo wrote an editorial calling on Mexican-Americans to resist the draft. They were charged with obstructing the war effort and thrown into Leavenworth Federal Penitentiary in Kansas, where Ricardo died under mysterious circumstances in 1922.

Intellectuals like the Flores Magón brothers—who supported the workers' right to fight for better conditions and the right of poor peasants to own their land—had no place in the científicos' plans for the future. To them, landless peasants and no dissent were the price of progress. They were also willing to give away land (usually someone else's land) to railway and telegraph companies, though they did get railroads and telegraph lines built.[86] The railways and telegraph transformed the country, allowing farm and mining products to move to ports. Which meant new ports had to be built, and old ones improved. The port of Veracruz might have rail connections and docks, but no one wanted to do business in such a run down place. So, the city was rebuilt.

One didn't need to be a científico to recognize that Mexico City had a sewage problem, and growth during the Porfiriate was making it worse. Mountains surround the city and there is no natural drainage. Every time it rained, the streets flooded and the sewers backed up. This was not the scientific modern image México

---

[86] The Mexican government wasn't the only government to do this. At more or less the same time (post Civil War) the U.S. government was giving railway companies title to every other square mile of land, on both sides of the completed railway, in order to open up the west. However, in the U.S. and Canada, indigenous people were not considered citizens, and in the west most were nomads.

wanted for their capital. Starting in 1886, the British engineering firm of S. Pearson and Sons began one of the greatest engineering projects of the 19th century, or any century. It took fourteen years to build the thirty-six-mile canal and six-mile tunnel to allow the city to flush its toilets. When the project was finished, Porfirio Díaz, the seventy-year-old leader, with great pride, gave the inaugural flush. Followed by a brass band, the diplomatic corps and other dignitaries, the dictator watched proudly as sewage spewed out the other side of the mountains into the Lerma River. Perhaps Díaz remembered Emperor Ahuízotl when he chose a foreign engineering firm.

Foreigners developed much of México and controlled much of the economy. This was also considered scientific. Besides their low opinion of Mexican people and their obsession with attracting foreign immigrants, the científicos did not want to waste time teaching their own people new skills. The foreign immigrants who came to stay did contribute to the Mexican economy. Although Mexicans had been brewing beer since the 1500s, German immigrants turned brewing into an industry, founding both breweries and bottling plants that made México a major exporter of both beer and glass.

Drinking pulque—the traditional indigenous fermented beverage—lost favor with the middle class and city dwellers. Pulque can be stored in clay pots, but beer comes in glass bottles, and México had almost no glass industry. The German brewers imported entire bottling plants, making Monterrey a major glass-making center.

Europeans weren't the only immigrants during the Porfiriate. The Mormons, followers of a religion originating in western New York in the 1830s, had unusual beliefs and practices that made them a target for persecution in the United States. Under pressure, the new religious group split into various factions, the largest of which emigrated to what was then a part of México, setting up a semi-independent Mormon colony in 1846. The United States gained control of the area that was named Utah in 1848. Most Mormons were either English-speaking, or northern European immigrants who adapted to life in the United States. However, Mormonism allowed a man to have several wives, which was highly illegal in the United States. Under pressure from the United States government and a manifesto by the Utah group's leader, the Mormon church banned the practice.

Some of the multiply-married Mormons went underground, and others fled to México. Their farming skills (Utah and northern México have a similar environment) made them welcome. Other Mormons, looking for cheap farmland, followed the refugees. Ironically, the Mormons believed that the indigenous peoples of the Americas were the "lost tribes of Israel". They either didn't know, or overlooked, the uncomfortable fact that their new farms were stolen from these same indigenous peoples.

African-American slaves had been freeing themselves by running away to México before the American Civil War. After the war, the U.S. army occupied the former slave-holding states until 1876. When the troops withdrew, the former slaves lost most of their economic and civil rights. African-Americans—especially those with farm management skills—were also welcome during the Porfiriate. Langston Hughes, the African-American poet and essayist, was the son of a Toluca factory manager. Hughes later noted ironically that as an African-American he was sometimes forbidden entry to segregated facilities that would admit him when he said he was "Mexican"; and that some places forbade Mexicans, but not African-Americans, and some forbade all "non-whites".[87]

Chinese railway workers had already been immigrating to México, and the Chinese Exclusion Act of 1888 in the United States, which prevented further Chinese immigration including the families of already admitted immigrants, brought in still more non-European immigrants. When haciendas in the Yucatán had trouble finding enough workers, they recruited landless peasants from Korea.

---

[87] In a double irony, Hughes' father was unpopular with the Toluca workers because of his racist attitude towards Mexicans.

In their drive for progress, the científicos wanted immediate results. The positivists had looked at statistics that "proved" foreigners were more productive than Mexicans (the statistics neglected to show that the harder-working foreigners had more to eat, and were healthier). The Mexicans—mestizos and indigenous people—were considered a drain on the economy and were neglected. When oil was discovered (about the same time that oil was first becoming important to the world economy) around Tampico, the giveaways included changing the legal code to meet the foreigner's needs.

México had inherited from the Spanish the idea of the King's Fifth: Cortés owed twenty percent of the Aztec gold to King Carlos, and until the law was changed, the Mexican government had collected twenty percent of any revenue generated from underground sources, including oil wells. If Americans wanted to dig a copper mine, or the British build a railroad across the Isthmus of Tehuantepec, the Mexican government was happy to give the developers whatever they needed.

"Whatever they needed" was fatal to a lot of Mexican people. The Valle Nacional in Oaxaca had foreign-owned tobacco plantations and is a particularly rich agricultural region. The Valle Nacional is also an unhealthy place to live, and there weren't enough willing workers. No problem—it was the Mexican gulag, where prisoners, dissidents and Yaqui and Mayo peoples (both of whom refused to give up their land to developers) could be sent to pick tobacco and die, usually within a few months of arriving.

For industrial workers, "whatever was needed" was usually less than what foreign workers in México received for the same job. When workers went on strike for equal pay at the Cananea copper mine (the largest, richest copper mine in the world at the time), the local militia and the Rurales were called in. The Sonoran governor even allowed Arizona police to enter his state to shoot his countrymen and help put down this affront to foreign business.

By 1910, México looked great to the positivists. It had a positive balance of trade, there were electric lights in most major cities and the Capital was a showplace—the sewers worked and there was even a model prison to display (one científico gushed that Lecumberri Prison offered the "most advanced punishment technology in the world" and held out the new prison as a model for the advanced nations). 1910 also marked the one hundredth anniversary of Father Hidalgo's grito. Coincidentally, Independence Day would be Porfirio Díaz' eightieth birthday, and it was an election year. With great reluctance, the old dictator had decided to mount one last presidential bid. He claimed it would be his last. It was.

...and the ugly

ÍAZ HAS BEEN CALLED the first modern leader for many reasons. One was that the Porfiriate pioneered techniques we know better from later strongman rulers like Adolph Hitler or Joseph Stalin. México had its own death camps, both in the Yucatán and in the Valle Nacional of Oaxaca. The Yucatán haciendas, like Hitler's concentration camps, functioned both as industries and as a way of disposing of an unwanted minority.

The authorities had ignored northern México until the late 19th century. By the time Díaz assumed the presidency, there was interest in the rich farmlands of Sonora. There was a small problem—these prime farmlands had farmers living on them. To the Díaz regime, the Yaqui people were an inconvenience at best. Although they had been recognized by the Spanish crown as an independent country (and had papers signed by the kings of Spain to prove it), they were treated like any other indigenous community. Like other farms owned by indigenous people, the Yaqui farms could be called corporations under the Reforma laws meant to break up the Church estates. In most places, this convenient interpretation of the law forced indigenous farmers to sell their land to a neighboring hacienda or see their land condemned for unpaid taxes and sold to the local hacendado at prices they couldn't afford. Either way, the farmers ended up as peons on their own former lands.

The Yaquis did something unusual. They fought back. Like their nomadic cousins, the Apaches, they were excellent guerrilla fighters. The Yaqui War would continue throughout the Díaz regime and even into the Revolution (only ending when Obregón incorporated the Yaqui guerrillas into his own army with a promise let them keep their remaining lands). The guerrillas weren't deported. Yaquis, most of whom were village-dwelling farmers and not guerrilla fighters, were rounded up and deported to Yucatán haciendas, not only thousands of miles from their home, but in a humid jungle environment, completely different than their arid wheat-growing region.

Bartolomé de las Casas had invented actuary science in the early 16th century by studying what happened when you forced people to move from one environment to another—they died. Which was apparently the intended result in the Yaqui's case. Like Hitler's victims, the Yaquis were forced into overloaded cattle cars, transported across the country (with many dying along the way) and forced to work until they died. As with the Nazi camps, the Yaquis were housed in overcrowded barracks, underfed and worked until they dropped dead. In a final comparison with the Nazis, the bodies were then cremated.

The Yucatán camps were not an efficient death machine. The haciendas were private businesses (several were owned by gringos). Most of the workers were Mayans,[88] supposedly free laborers, though

---

[88] It wasn't intentional, but transporting the Yaquis to Mayan areas further reduced their numbers. Yaqui men died faster than Yaqui women, but the women could not find "adequate" husbands among the Mayans. The Yaqui people are among the tallest people in the world and the Mayans among the shortest. Mayans are unusually strong, but between their short stature, inadequate nutrition and overwork, they were unlikely to have successful sexual intercourse with women twice their size.

in reality they were slaves. They were kept tied to the hacienda through debt. When the hacienda bought up Mayan properties it was paying off the taxes (in theory), and the old owner owed the tax money to the new one. The only way to pay was by working off the debt, but the former Mayan property owner was paid, not a wage, but credit that could only be used at the hacienda store. The store prices were highly inflated, so there was no way to ever pay the debt. The system worked well for the landowner, letting him acquire land for very low prices, if any—often indigenous owners didn't have a title, so the land was simply taken by the government and given in payment for things like railroad building or as rewards for service to the government. The land came with workers who couldn't leave—the laws were changed to treat debtors who ran away with the same treatment runaway slaves had earlier received—they were caught, whipped and then fined—which, of course, increased the debt.

People managed to live long enough to pass on their debts in the Yucatán. The Valle Nacional, in Oaxaca, was the Mexican gulag. People weren't expected to come out alive, and the place functioned as it was intended. Tobacco farmers in the Valle paid fifty dollars a head for workers. It was cheaper to starve them to death than anything else, and that was what was done. Since slavery was illegal—supposedly—the Valle workers were convicted criminals, working off their sentence, but that conviction could be stretched, depending on the need for workers. Felix Díaz, the dictator's nephew and Mexico City's police chief, regularly cleared out the city jail by sending people to the Valle. He got rich on his twenty percent commission for supplying workers. When he didn't have enough workers to meet his quota, Felix simply rounded up vagrants (meaning anyone unlucky enough not to have a room for the night, drunk or just standing on the wrong street corner) and anyone else he decided was undesirable. The world's first gay rights demonstration was held in Mexico City's Alameda Park in

1901. Felix' men invaded the Alameda, rounded everyone up and sent them to the death farms.[89]

Dissident politicians, small town newspaper editors foolish enough to publish unflattering news about pro-Díaz local leaders, striking railroad and mine workers, farmers who resisted takeovers by the local hacendado—all disappeared into the "Valley of Death". Their life expectancy was under one year.

Haciendas were common throughout the country, and gringos were among the largest landowners. People who wrote about them generally praised the system. William Randolph Hearst, the California newspaper owner, owned the largest single piece of private property in México and the world at the time; later, his cattle ranches would become a special target of Pancho Villa (who knew how to get his name in the newspapers), but they were largely unknown outside México.

Under the racist assumptions of the 19th century, even when peonage was acknowledged as a form of slavery, it was justified to people in the United States and Europe as a way of civilizing an inferior people. That these people had a very old civilization, and that they had been independent farmers was either overlooked or swept away with the assurance that the haciendas were modern farms, and that the small farmers had stood in the way of progress.

The haciendas were modern...until a Los Angles reporter visited some of them.

---

[89] Perhaps not everyone. A Mexico City slang term for a homosexual, *cuarenta y uno* – forty-one – probably refers to the fact that any man still a bachelor at forty is presumably gay, but some say there were forty-one men at the Alameda protest, but only forty were sent to the Valle Nacional. The one man released was supposedly Porfirio's son-in-law, Ignacio de la Torre.

Barbarous México

THE EARLY-20TH-CENTURY United States was undergoing its own *Reforma*. In México, Benito Juárez and the reformistas, fifty years earlier, had curbed the power of the big landowners and the Church and changed the laws to reflect middle-class needs. In the United States, Theodore Roosevelt and the "Progressives" curbed the power of the big industrialists and corporations and also changed laws to put more power in the hands of the middle classes. Important to the Progressive movement was a new breed of reporter, the muckraker. So named because they sifted through the dirty secrets of big business, the muckrakers publicized abuses by the powerful and presented eyewitness reports on the effects of these abuses.

John Kenneth Turner had already published reports on the oil industry and was a respected writer of the era. A friend of several Mexican exiles living in his hometown, he became interested in gringo investments in México. His 1908 series of articles in *The American Magazine* destroyed Díaz' benign image in the United States. *Barbarous Mexico*, as both Turner's articles and longer 1910 book were titled, didn't hesitate to call peonage slavery. He condemned not only Díaz and the científicos, but the regime's

U.S. supporters, including President Taft, Standard Oil Company, William Randolph Hearst and the other powerful California media mogul and hacienda owner of the era, Otis Chandler. To Turner, they were all profiting from human misery and from the death camps.

Díaz and his business supporters in the United States fought back. Public relations and advertising agencies (both infant industries then) were hired to restore the dictator's image. Hacienda owners and friendly travel writers were drafted to write anti-Turner letters to their local papers. It was one of the first "spin campaigns" in American politics...and it failed. Before Turner published his articles in book form, he was smart enough to do some more research. He added a chapter on the pro-Díaz publicity campaign and the people behind it.

Turner's book was important for two reasons. It turned attention on the anti-Díaz Mexican liberals, giving them a respectability and legitimacy that they hadn't before enjoyed in the United States. Until Turner's articles appeared, Mexican liberals were often arrested and jailed as potential terrorists or deported back to México (and then to the Valle Nacional). U.S. Federal and State judges were less likely to just look at Mexican liberals as undesirable aliens. Turner reminded them that the United States had always harbored fugitives from dictators, and that Díaz was indeed a dictator.

In the U.S., the Mexican liberals were able to operate openly and raise money for their cause. American citizens, especially labor and church activists, supported the liberals, much as these same groups supported refugees from pro-American Central American dictatorships during the 1980s, despite official government disapproval. As in the antislavery campaigns that preceded the American Civil War, there were a large number of people who felt morally justified in breaking the law. It wasn't only career criminals and sleazy merchants who started smuggling weapons to México, but church groups, polite society ladies and friendly sheriffs in border communities; they all got into the act. A good number of the people involved in smuggling weapons to México did so out of a sense of human equality across the border. In the process, they won a small victory for women's equality in the United States.

Where Mexican women had always accompanied the army and were to serve as soldiers and officers in the Revolution, the United States had always reserved uniformed service for men. In the thinking of the time, women were afforded special protection, and it was improper for a man to touch a woman. Women in those times did not seem to have legs—at least they were never mentioned in polite conversation. Women, both in the United States and in México, wore long skirts. By 1910 the customs service was unable to stop the arms traffic, and they knew that Mexican and Mexican-American women were crossing the border with rifles, pistols and even hand grenades tied to their unmentionable, untouchable legs. President Taft, after some uncomfortable discussions with his advisors, and with great reluctance, authorized training and hiring the first female uniformed service personnel in the United States—female customs agents.

When Turner's articles were published in book format, he wrote in the preface that he expected the United States to send troops into México in support of Díaz (or his successors) when—not if—the revolution broke out. The United States Army was already on alert, and the army wasn't always scrupulous about respecting the civil rights of civilians, especially Mexican-Americans, who were sometimes "deported" from their own country. Turner reasoned that powerful citizens like Hearst and the Standard Oil Company management had too much invested in the Díaz regime to permit a change. Turner hadn't realized what a powerful book he had written. For once, the writer was wrong: too many middle-class voters thought Díaz was a monster and that his government had to go. Who or what would replace the old dictator was something the United States government and the gringo business interests in México hoped to control.

Ghost-writing on the wall

EVERY YEAR PORFIRIO DÍAZ got a little grayer, a few more foreigners bought land, a few thousand people disappeared into the Valle Nacional and...nothing much happened. 1910 was the centennial of Hidalgo's grito. The country appeared strong; Mexico City was modern, with electric lights, flush toilets and a model prison. Behind the scenes were some serious problems: there had been crop failures in 1907, 1908 and 1909, and México was importing corn from as far away as South Africa.

Limantour had balanced the budget by halving the value of the peso. Wages stayed the same, but prices had doubled. Worker's and miner's strikes had only been put down with military intervention. The Yaquis had not given up. Even Popocatépetl was unhappy and in 1910 exploded for the first time since the Spanish invasion. Porfirio's public relations agents were fighting a losing battle against the soon-to-be-published *Barbarous Mexico*, but they could always keep the book out of México.

By 1910, everyone expected some kind of revolution. Or at least they expected Porfirio Díaz to leave the scene. True, he still got up every morning to do calisthenics with the army, but he was eighty years old. No one thought it was going to be easy to replace him—surprisingly, it was. More surprising still was who overthrew

223

the old man: a squeaky-voiced little man, a minor author of books on Hindu philosophy who spent his evenings talking to ghosts.

Francisco Ignacio Madero Gonsález was eccentric and unprepossessing, but he wasn't the mental patient Porfirio paraded out every few years as his official opponent. The Madero family was the second richest in México, for starters, and Francisco was one of the best-educated men in the country. After finishing his education at the Sorbonne in Paris, he studied agronomy at the University of California. He introduced new farming techniques at home, sponsored schools and clinics for the peons and paid his workers a living wage. Until 1910, he seemed a character out of a Tolstoy novel, but was fated to resemble another half-remembered Russian—Alexander Kerensky—the moderate revolutionary who overthrew the Tsar, only to be overthrown by Lenin. The difference was that Kerensky lived to be an old man.[90]

Among Madero's unusual characteristics was a belief in spiritualism. He talked to ghosts. Spiritualists were not necessarily superstitious cranks—it was a respectable movement in the late 19th and early 20th century that had attracted serious thinkers,[91] especially in France and the United States. The spiritualists felt they had scientific proof that the long dead could communicate with the living. Madero's wife would go into a trance and dictate what the ghosts told her. Madero, with his wife taking ghostly dictation, held long conversations about democracy and government reform with his dead brother, Raúl. Raúl had died as an infant, but apparently the dead Raúl had landed a job as ghostly secretary to...Benito Juárez! Juárez had never showed any interest in Hinduism and had been dead for over thirty years. Why he chose Raúl Madero as his secretary in the afterlife (and why he was corresponding with Mrs. Madero) was something best left out of Madero's book, *The Presidential Election of 1910.*

---

[90] After Prime Minister Kerensky was run out of Russia by the Bolsheviks, he taught high school in Brooklyn, New York.

[91] Albert Einstein attended at least one séance in 1933 while working at Caltech.

Díaz had stated in an interview for an American newspaper that he would retire at the end of his 1910 term. Madero was not the only person who read American newspapers, but he was one of the few who recognized what it meant for democratic reformers. Even the científicos (who were elderly men themselves) had begun to consider Díaz' retirement. Madero's book reminded people that Díaz had originally revolted against the government because presidents stayed in office too long. Díaz kept his "no reelection" promise when his first term ended in 1880, but seemed to forget all about it every election year thereafter. You had to be crazy to run against Díaz—his opponent in most elections was. In 1904, Díaz accepted the fact that he was an old man and added a vice president. To balance things out, he made the presidential term six years. Madero did not even call for Díaz to give up the presidency, merely to allow fair elections for vice president.

Turner's book had changed the way Díaz was seen outside México. Madero's book was written for the educated elite (the científicos, for all their progressive thinking, had neglected education, and illiteracy had risen since Juárez' day), but it changed the way the old dictator was seen in México. There hadn't been any change in leadership in thirty years: the country was full of frustrated younger politicians waiting for their chance at power. To intellectuals, the positivist ideas, which seemed so modern thirty years earlier, were outdated and no longer seemed to apply to México. The regime may have gambled that very few people could read anyway, but the Spanish had made the same mistake a hundred years earlier. Larger and larger numbers of people recognized the social inequality in the system. Francisco I. Madero couldn't simply disappear into the Valle Nacional, as the Madero family was rich and powerful.

In 1810, village priests translated radical concepts into something their illiterate neighbors understood. In 1910 village schoolteachers and small town reporters did the same. The intellectual landowner, writing for other intellectuals, suddenly found himself the leader of cowboys, railway workers, miners, small town businessmen, cattle rustlers[92] and indigenous leaders.

When Díaz finally selected a vice-presidential candidate acceptable to himself (another elderly army officer), Madero did the unthinkable. He ran for president. Madero went from speech to speech, gathering support everywhere he spoke. People who had stayed out of politics finally had a candidate to support. Díaz, facing the first real threat to his career, reacted. Madero supporters were attacked, pro-Madero newspapers were closed down and finally, Madero himself was arrested for inciting a riot. It would have looked too much like a tyranny if the little landowner were thrown in prison. So he was locked up in a Mexico City hotel room, and guards were stationed at the front door of the hotel. Madero took the freight elevator, walked out the employees' entrance, got in a waiting car and made for the rail yard. There, he changed into a brakeman's uniform and made his way north to Texas, to direct what would be the first act in the ten-year Mexican Revolution.

Díaz was old and tired, but before he could sail off into exile, he needed a suitable replacement. One who would reassure the foreign business community and—he and the foreign financial interests hoped—keep the radical Madero from taking over. José Ives Limantour, the brilliant finance minister who had balanced the Mexican budget, seemed a likely candidate, but he was old, uninterested in the job and constitutionally ineligible (his father was French[93]). All the other cabinet members were old men too. No one, it seemed, wanted to take over from Díaz.

---

[92] Sometime cattle rustler and bandit José Doroteo Arango Arámbula claimed he learned to read in prison because he wanted to study Madero's ideas. The story is untrue, but the man better known as Pancho Villa did become a champion of adult literacy campaigns.

[93] The constitutional requirement that a president had to be native-born SON of Mexican-born parents was also part of the post-Revolution Constitution of 1917 and remained until the 1990s. Now, the president must be a native-born CHILD with at least one native-born Mexican parent.

Finally, in May 1911, Francisco León de la Barra y Quijano, the Mexican ambassador to Washington was recalled, the vice president resigned, León de la Barra was sworn in as vice president and Díaz resigned. Given the French influence that permeated his long regime, it was only natural that Díaz lived out his last years in Paris. He is buried in Père Lachaise Cemetery.[94]

---

[94] In an odd twist on the story of the switched graves at Panteón San Fernando, one of Porfirio's eternal neighbors at Père Lachaise is the American dancer and radical, Isadora Duncan. There is a mysterious tomb marked with Duncan's name and the year of her death (1929) in San Fernando. If anyone is actually buried in that tomb (there are no records of any burials later than the 1880s), it certainly is not Duncan. Besides Duncan, other foreign "residents" at Père Lachaise include Oscar Wilde, Frederick Chopin, Gertrude Stein and Jim Morrison. Porfirio welcomed foreigners in life, but must find Day of the Dead rather disconcerting!

A not-so-clean break:
The Revolution, part 1

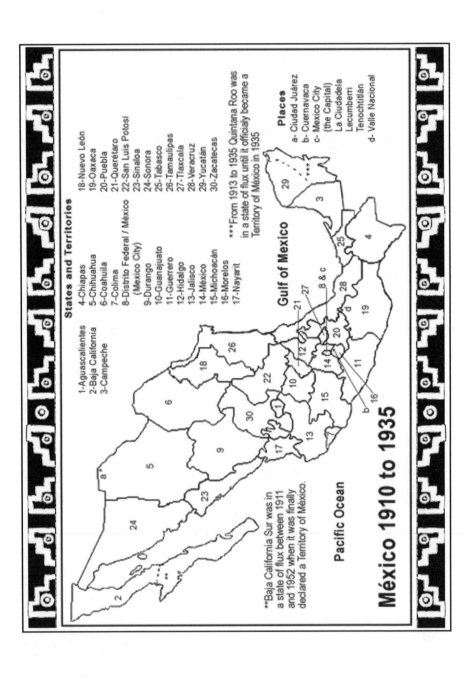

México 1910 to 1935

States and Territories

1-Aguascalientes	18-Nuevo León
2-Baja California	19-Oaxaca
3-Campeche	20-Puebla
4-Chiapas	21-Querétaro
5-Chihuahua	22-San Luis Potosi
6-Coahuila	23-Sinaloa
7-Colima	24-Sonora
8-Distrito Federal / México	25-Tabasco
(Mexico City)	26-Tamaulipas
9-Durango	27-Tlaxcala
10-Guanajuato	28-Veracruz
11-Guerrero	29-Yucatán
12-Hidalgo	30-Zacatecas
13-Jalisco	
14-México	
15-Michoacán	
16-Morelos	
17-Nayarit	

***From 1913 to 1935 Quintana Roo was in a state of flux until it officialy became a Territory of México in 1935

Places

a- Ciudad Juárez
b- Cuernavaca
c- Mexico City
(the Capital)
La Ciudadela
Lecumberri
Tenochtitlán
d- Valle Nacional

Gulf of Mexico

Pacific Ocean

**Baja California Sur was in a state of flux between 1911 and 1952 when it was finally declared a Territory of México.

It pays to advertise

THE RAILROADS HAD BEEN Díaz' most important
contribution to pulling México into the modern
age. While the railroads were designed to take products out of the
country and still left one region isolated from another, most parts of
the country were—for the first time—within a day or two of Mexico
City. The viceroys had been able to "hear, but not obey" the king
of Spain. With trains able to carry soldiers even to isolated state
capitals, governors heard and obeyed Porfirio Díaz. Díaz needed
the railway workers. They were essential to the Mexican economy,
and they knew it. Even if the foreign workers were better paid than
Mexicans, the Mexican railway worker was still better paid than
most other workers. The railways attracted the skilled and ambitious. Most could read. Brakemen, engineers, baggage handlers
and tracklayers knew each other and had contacts throughout
the Republic. Even without a union, they had been able to obtain
some benefits, and they weren't shy about sharing their organizing
skills and insights with other workers.

The railway workers knew Mexico—often a good part of the
United States, as well. Díaz might have an army, but the army
couldn't go anywhere without the railroad. Francisco I. Madero—the
little rich boy with the squeaky voice—had the railroad men.

Díaz canceled the elections and for the first time in many years ignored the democratic façade he had so carefully maintained. Madero, operating from relative safety in the United States, continued writing. The railway workers—helped by the railway unions in the United States—smuggled in Madero's articles along with other revolutionary propaganda and guns. México was set for another rebellion. Madero took out advertisements in Spanish-language newspapers along the border, announcing that the Revolution would start 20 November 1910. The railway workers sent the information south (amazingly, Mexican newspapers reported on this strange advertising campaign—even reprinted the advertisements—as news, of course). And...much as it goes against the Mexican stereotype, the Revolution started on schedule.

You say you want a revolution, well, you know...

O N THE APPOINTED DAY, Madero, who, with his wife, had spent a busy week attending parties in El Paso while arranging for press coverage for the Revolution and telephone service for his "Provisional Capital" (a storage shed sitting on the Mexican side of the border, behind an El Paso smelting plant), crossed the border and posed for the cameras. He'd managed to talk the Bell Telephone Company into running a line across the border in return for hanging up a sign on the "Provisional Capital" that advertised the phone company and would be seen in the news photos. Madero was by no means the first revolutionary to seek corporate sponsors but was probably the first to trade off advertising for technical support. The reporters asked their questions and took their photos, and the Revolution was on.

The reporters did the job Madero expected. Other than a short battle in Ciudad Juárez (there were a few casualties in El Paso, Texas—people don't get to watch a foreign revolution from their rooftops every day—when a few stray bullets crossed the border), Madero didn't have much of a revolution. There were "spontaneous" uprisings throughout México on 20 November, but they went nowhere. However, thanks to advance notice, news photographers had managed to station themselves throughout Juárez (Collier's magazine—at great expense—hired an airplane, hoping to scoop the competition). Whether it was the god of reality and unreality—Tezcatlipoca—at play, or a modern marketing campaign, creating the impression of a mass uprising was more important than an actual uprising would be.

Díaz, seeing the photos, knew his time was up and made arrangements to sail into exile. Interim president Francisco León de la Barra y Quijano's first official act was to schedule new elections. He spent the rest of his six-month term cutting ribbons and dedicating monuments (with the Centennial celebration still under way, there were a lot of new monuments to dedicate) and filling key bureaucratic positions with Díaz die-hards. Naturally, Francisco I. Madero won the election. José Pino Suárez, a newspaper editor, was vice president.

Madero, like Alexander Kerensky, the Russian leader whose moderate revolution a few years later would also rapidly escalate into a violent social upheaval, never really understood how deep the need for change went in México. There were new faces in Congress and state governments, but nothing much changed at the top. His cabinet was mostly made up of the same people who had served Díaz (they were the only experienced people available). The military leaders maintained their posts. The young and ambitious were disappointed, the Díaz holdovers openly contemptuous.

Perhaps Madero really was speaking to Juárez' ghost. He opened the political system, but was unable to cope with the social and economic changes that had occurred since the 1870s. Díaz had been successful in bringing modern industries to México, but not in modernizing working conditions. Except for the railroad workers, the Mexican worker's life was not much better than the peon's. In some ways it was worse. Peons were—at least to some extent—fed, housed and recognized as a community. Industrial workers were either paid piecework (by the unit of production, which meant a machine breakdown or other event cut the worker's already low salary) or a salary that was too low to afford even basic food and shelter. Workers like miners and oil-field hands were often better paid but faced dangerous conditions and lived in polluted, unsanitary work camps (several serious strikes began with protests over health conditions) where they were forced to buy in company stores at inflated prices.

Workers in all industrialized countries had faced similar conditions in the 1870s. Pope Leo XIII (a more forward-thinking man than Maximilian's Pius IX) had given the Catholic Church's approval to workers' organizations in 1883. By 1910, most countries recognized some basic rights for workers, though organized labor movements like Communism, socialism and anarchism were still considered "radical". To the Díaz regime, ANY labor organization—even a Church approved group—was a threat. Labor leaders were assassinated, imprisoned for treason or shipped to the Valle Nacional. During a miner's strike in northern Sonora, the mining company, with the blessings of the state governor, called in sheriff's deputies from Arizona. Unions in the more industrialized countries had already managed to secure minimum wages in their industries and some benefits by 1910. The Anarcho-Syndicalists, the most radical of the worker's movements, promoted the idea that the unions should run the country.

Díaz' government, having brought in foreign companies, also brought in foreign workers. Anarcho-Syndicalism had been especially strong in Spain and Italy, the two countries that sent the most workers. To landless Mexican farmers turned workers their "radical" Italian and Spanish coworkers sounded like traditional Mexicans, as cooperative work and common ownership had a long tradition in México. Even Vasco de Quiroga, the 16th-century judge and bishop who organized the Tarascan cooperatives, was just adapting renaissance Catholic thinking to Mexican traditions. Just as the defenders of Tenochtitlán had adopted European fighting techniques, the Mexican workers adopted the European worker's fighting technique—the strike.

But, like Cortés, Díaz had the more advanced weapons. Strikes during Díaz' day were put down by the army, and the leaders marched off to prison or to the Valle Nacional. In Díaz' México, there was no labor problem. Madero had a difficult situation—the workers had been among the most enthusiastic supporters of his revolution. They began openly organizing anarchist unions (as well as Communist[95] and socialist parties) and striking for better working conditions. This did not sit well with the foreign owners nor with their embassies.

Landowners, especially Mexican landowners, had become fewer and fewer under Díaz. The Reforma had taken land out of Church hands hoping to put it into Mexican ones, but Díaz, in his drive to modernize the country had used the Reforma land laws to take indigenous lands to pay foreign investors. Haciendas and their feudal working conditions had existed since Cortés but grew tremendously under Díaz. Foreign investors owned over three-quarters of the land. The few Mexican hacendados preferred to live in Paris. Madero may have been a model landowner, but he was a rare individual. Simply encouraging his fellow hacendados to adopt more progressive farming methods and maybe some more modern management techniques was not going to help another group that had supported him—the farmers. Land reforms were not going to sit well with the foreign investors nor with their embassies.

Most industrial investors and landowners had the same ambassador—Henry Lane Wilson of the United States of America, ambassador to México.

Huitzilopochtli may not look like a businessman or a college professor, but between Henry Lane Wilson (Mr. Wilson One) and Woodrow Wilson (Mr. Wilson Two) more violence was unleashed in México than by any foreigner since Hernan Cortés.

---

[95] Diego Rivera, a serial liar, claimed to have founded the Mexican Communist Party in 1905. The party was founded in 1905, but its founder was an immigrant worker from India.

Mister Wilson One

ESIDES THE WORKERS' STRIKES, open attacks in newspapers newly freed from censorship (or still pro-Díaz) and cabinet officers who made no secret of hating him, Madero had guerrilla wars to deal with. The most serious was the one in Morelos State led by Emiliano Zapata.

Emiliano Zapata, a traditional village leader, had been attacking haciendas and taking back land seized by foreign landowners even before Madero came to power. Madero, a hacienda owner, was a natural enemy—his mild reforms would do nothing to protect the small farmers who fought with Zapata under the slogan of *tierra y libertad* – Land and Liberty.

Zapata was young, handsome and a natural leader who had received military training courtesy of Porfirio Díaz. Having caused enough trouble for the local hacienda owners even before he inherited his father's job as village leader, he was forcibly drafted into the army. This was supposed to be a simple way to dispose of inconvenient peasants, but Zapata turned out to be a natural soldier and was soon promoted to sergeant. When he finished his army service, ex-Sergeant Zapata's second unusual skill—he tamed wild horses—helped him build a network of supporters and admirers (including some landowners[96]) throughout Morelos State. By the time his rebellion started, he had the complete support of the people of Morelos. President Madero had the shaky support of a Díaz holdover, General Victoriano Huerta Ortega.

Huerta was a drunk. Rosa Eleanor King, an English widow who pioneered the luxury hotel business in Cuernavaca, had the dubious pleasure of housing General Huerta and his foreign advisors: Hennessey and Martel (two brands of French cognac). When he wasn't drinking up Mrs. King's liquor, he was hunting for Zapata. His crude, but sometimes effective, military strategy was to rape, pillage and destroy Zapatista villages and to hang anyone who looked like they might be a Zapatista—meaning any country person unfortunate enough to run across the Federal troops.

The Zapatistas overran Cuernavaca and nearly leveled the city. Mrs. King, along with other foreign residents, evacuated along with Huerta's army. The army never made it the short distance back to Mexico City. Zapatistas had dynamited the train track and slaughtered the retreating army and civilians. Mrs. King survived the retreat, only to find new horrors in Mexico City: her hotel's expensive bathtubs were being sold on the streets in the Capital. Huerta also survived. When sober, he professed loyalty to Madero. When drunk, he nursed resentments against the "weak" president who was letting the country collapse.

Huerta, the foreign investors and Henry Lane Wilson all concluded that Madero had to go. Wilson, like Poinsett nearly a century earlier, never doubted that the United States ambassador had a right to run Mexican affairs. As he saw it, his job was to protect United States interests (meaning the large landowners and U.S.-owned companies) in México. Madero's election had unleashed thirty years of built-up anger and resentment against the foreign control of Mexican resources. Wilson took even mild reforms

---

[96] Horses were the basis of a close personal friendship between Zapata and Porfirio Díaz' gay son-in-law, Ignacio de la Torre. Emiliano's son, Mateo Zapata—who was over eighty at the time—threatened reprisals against a film director who suggested in 2003 that the two Morelianos shared more than equine interests.

(higher taxes on oil exports) as attacks on U.S. rights in México. Madero would have to go.

Unlike Poinsett, Wilson didn't bother with organizing Mexican political parties. He only wanted to find a leader acceptable to himself. To Wilson, what México needed wasn't political reform: quite the opposite. Díaz had created a favorable business climate for American investors, and anything that interfered with business—oil workers' strikes, indigenous communities who refused to move off productive land or cattle thefts from William Randolph Hearst—had to be dealt with immediately. Madero either refused or was unable to stop the strikes, the indigenous uprisings or Pancho Villa. Ambassador Wilson sent frantic telegrams back to the State Department in Washington, claiming México was out of control and Madero had to be replaced: there were anarchists openly organizing and demonstrating and—ominously—the idea of taxing oil production was being raised in the Congress. For Wilson and for his favored advisor, the U.S. oilman, William F. Buckley,[97] a possible oil extraction tax was the final straw.

The "good old days" of Porfirio Díaz were not coming back, but Wilson and Buckley saw no reason they couldn't replace Madero with another strongman president and a tame Congress. For president, Wilson settled on either of two holdovers from the Díaz-era army: Bernardo Reyes and Felix Díaz (the former Mexico City police chief, and the old dictator's favorite nephew). Unfortunately, both men were in prison on treason charges. Unfortunately for Madero, he had commuted their death sentences.

Ambassador Wilson was pressured by Buckley to act quickly. President Taft had been defeated for reelection in November, and the new president, Woodrow Wilson (who was no relation to the ambassador) had campaigned against what he called "Dollar Diplomats" who responded more to big business interests than to the president's goals. In those days, the president of the United States

---

[97] Father of William F. Buckley, Jr., the well-known conservative U.S. writer, and James Buckley, who became a Senator from New York.

took office in March, and Henry Lane Wilson—Dollar Diplomat Numero Uno—was at the top of the list for replacement.

A military rebellion in favor of General Reyes broke out 9 February 1913 and ran into an immediate problem when rebel soldiers sprung the two from prison. Reyes and Felix Díaz insisted on putting on a good show (like Madero's first revolution) of their own. Díaz wasn't about to leave his cell until he finished shaving. But at least he donned his combat uniform. Reyes, in his best dress uniform, made a dramatic appearance when he strutted out of Lecumberri prison. He also made an easy target for machine gunners loyal to President Madero. This left Felix Díaz...and Victoriano Huerta.

Huerta, who was in charge of defending the government and the president, holed up in the National Palace. The rebels captured *la Ciudadela* – the Mexico City military headquarters – and bombarded the National Palace, mostly hitting civilians in between the two. Huerta was crude—a sadist and an alcoholic—but he was no fool. While civilian bodies were piling up in the streets, Huerta, Felix Díaz and Ambassador Wilson struck a bargain. They even signed a contract: Huerta would switch sides and become interim president. Díaz would be the next president.

Ambassador Wilson later justified his "Pact of the Embassy" claiming he wanted to end the appalling civilian casualties. The result was the "Ten Days of Tragedy", as Huerta gave a convincing appearance of loyalty by bombarding not the Ciudadela, but the residential neighborhoods between the fortress and the *Zócalo* – the main city square in Mexico City. Bodies continued to pile up in the streets while Huerta and Díaz met secretly around the Capital and finalized plans for their counterrevolution.

Huerta finally revealed his true intentions when he pulled a gun on Madero (in a cantina, where they were meeting) and took the president prisoner. Pino Suárez and Madero's brother, Gustavo, were also taken prisoner. Setting the tone for his new government, Gustavo was tortured and murdered (he was blind in one eye, and his good eye was gouged out with a bayonet before he was beaten to death). To save his family, Madero resigned, as did Pino Suárez. Congress was called into session to appoint an interim president.

One congressman, Dr. Belisario Domínguez, foolish enough to vote against Huerta, was shot down on the street just outside Congress.

Mrs. Madero talked to ghosts, but she wanted a live husband. She made a frantic round of the foreign embassies, seeking political asylum for her husband. As far as Henry Lane Wilson was concerned, whatever happened to Madero was exactly what he deserved. Wilson later claimed he expected Madero to be locked up in an insane asylum, saying he assumed Madero's rich family and powerful friends would protect him from anything worse. His murder was supposed to look like an accident, and might have, if it wasn't for a teenaged "designated driver".

Automobiles were still rare in 1913, and very few people knew how to drive. Plus, everyone knew that Huerta was a drunk. When the new president's office called the dealer to rent a couple of cars, the dealer wasn't about to trust Huerta with his expensive autos. He sent his teenage son along as chauffeur. The boy found out his job was to take Madero from Lecumberri prison to the Ciudadela. The plan was to have Madero and Pino Suárez (in another car) killed during an "ambush" by Madero supporters. When the shooting started, the boy—no fool he—ran. He hid around the corner and watched as the ex-president and vice-president were dragged out of their cars and executed. The executioners then artfully sprayed the cars with bullets, taking care not to damage the engine or chassis. The boy, not wanting to get into trouble, telephoned his father. Assured that his son was safe, the father called the newspapers.

President Taft was outraged. Ambassador Wilson wrote a short article—revised by Buckley—defending himself but left a disaster for the incoming Woodrow Wilson administration. Ironically, Huerta's government would turn out to be much more radical than Madero's, and the mild reformer's murder led to the first 20th-century cultural and social revolution. With the United States about to enter its first overseas war, its next-door neighbor was in the middle of a full-scale war between several forces, none of which trusted their northern neighbor. Huitzilopochtli and Tezcatlipoca were in control.

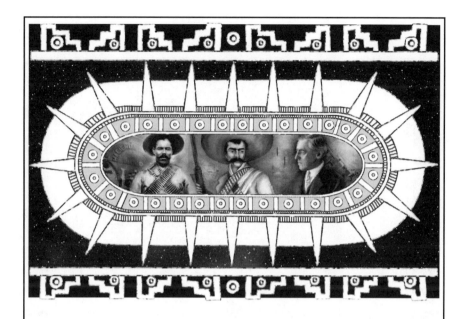

Total War:
The Revolution, part 2

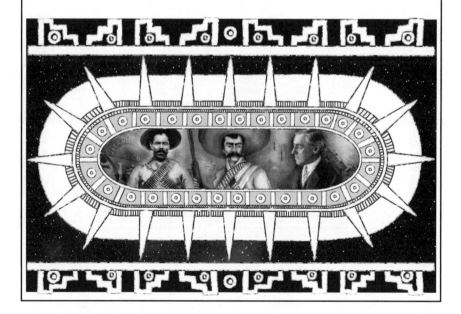

México 1910 to 1935

States and Territories

1-Aguascalientes	18-Nuevo León
2-Baja California	19-Oaxaca
3-Campeche	20-Puebla
4-Chiapas	21-Querétaro
5-Chihuahua	22-San Luis Potosi
6-Coahuila	23-Sinaloa
7-Colima	24-Sonora
8-Distrito Federal / México	25-Tabasco
(Mexico City)	26-Tamaulipas
9-Durango	27-Tlaxcala
10-Guanajuato	28-Veracruz
11-Guerrero	29-Yucatán
12-Hidalgo	30-Zacatecas
13-Jalisco	
14-México	
15-Michoacán	
16-Morelos	
17-Nayarit	

***From 1913 to 1935 Quintana Roo was in a state of flux until it officially became a Territory of México in 1935

Places

a- Ciudad Juárez
b- Cuernavaca
c- Guaymas
d- Huatabampo
e- Mexico City
   (the Capital)
f- Ojinaga
g- Puerto México
h- Tampico
i- Veracruz

Gulf of Mexico

Pacific Ocean

**Baja California Sur was in a state of flux between 1911 and 1952 when it was finally declared a Territory of México.

Back to the future

EVEN BEFORE MADERO HAD first called for revolution, the United States Army had been stationed on the border. The only question at the time was when exactly Porfirio would leave, and how much trouble there would be. President Taft authorized training women customs agents in an attempt to control gunrunning. Henry Lane Wilson, in a particularly hysterical moment, had claimed American citizens were about to be slaughtered in Sonora. A Navy gunship and five hundred marines came to the rescue of a few tourists in Guaymas, Sonora (on the *Mar de Cortés* – Sea of Cortez or Gulf of California), who took advantage of the free trip back to San Diego. Until Madero was overthrown, violence was not aimed at foreigners specifically—unless they were hacienda owners who resisted a takeover—so there was little danger. The Englishwoman, Rosa King, who was attacked by Zapatistas while fleeing Cuernavaca, was not singled out because of her nationality but because she was part of a Huerta-loyalist convoy. Given that the constitutionalists were fighting the foreign-backed Huerta and the landlords and mine owners (who tended to be foreigners), the Revolution did sometimes take an antiforeign appearance.

"We will teach them to elect good men"

H ENRY LANE WILSON AND William F. Buckley claimed they had organized Huerta's coup to keep the country from deteriorating into anarchy—incidentally, to restore the Porfirian peace. As a result, the country descended into anarchy, there was warfare for the next eight years and what emerged was a country very different from the one that existed at the time.

Wilson had been especially worried that Madero would implement radical changes. As it was, Emiliano Zapata—seeking to return haciendas to the farmers—had already rebelled against the failure of the little landowner-president to understand the need for radical reform; the changes Madero sought had been more political than social or economic. Huerta, recognizing his deep unpopularity, holed up in a Mexico City cantina most of the time, and ironically, it was the radicals who benefited from the tyranny.

When Woodrow Wilson took office in March 1913, there was nothing he could do to undo Henry Wilson's major blunder in February. A very different president than the easy-going Taft, the new U.S. president's background was as a Presbyterian minister, historian and university professor.[98]

Taft had come to the presidency more as a skilled administrator than a politician. He saw U.S. foreign policy more in terms of protecting U.S. business interests than anything else and tolerated even the slightly hysterical "dollar diplomats" like Henry Lane Wilson. Woodrow Wilson would, "teach them [Latin Americans] to elect good men," as he once famously said. When the Mexicans refused to listen to his sermons, he resorted to ministering strong lessons, twice attempting to intervene militarily.

Complicating matters for the U.S., the First World War started in August 1914. Anxious to both prop up the British Empire and to keep the United States neutral in the war, the Mexican Revolution would bedevil the preacher-president for both his terms, and leave him a name as one of the greatest villains in Mexican history.

---

[98] The candidates in the 1912 election were probably the most scholarly ever in U.S. history. Taft was a recognized legal scholar, Wilson a professional historian and third-party candidate, ex-President Theodore Roosevelt, among his many other accomplishments, was a well-regarded popular writer on natural history as well as a naval historian.

The Constitutionalist revolution

I N MEXICO CITY, there were anarchists. Huerta was a military man; not one to pay much attention to civilian bureaucracy. The anarcho-syndicalists believed unions should control governments; they and other urban leftists saw Huerta's alcoholism for what it was—an opportunity. Huerta was happy enough in the cantinas, signing papers and giving orders; leaving governance to whomever wanted to do the unglamorous work of drafting bureaucratic regulations and tax codes.

Thanks to the "Embassy Pact", and with leftist intellectuals running the civilian side of a military dictatorship, México under Huerta went—on paper—from having the least favorable laws for organized labor to the country that most favored the workers. Huerta's government implemented educational reforms, strict health and industrial safety codes, progressive labor laws—even the higher mineral taxes that led Buckley and Wilson to plot against the government in the first place.

In Mexico City, Madero's old coalition was organizing to restore what they saw as the legitimate government while the radicals were busily drafting new regulations for Huerta to sign when his hand wasn't wrapped around a brandy glass. Madero's failure had been his inability to bring about social change and the constitutionalists would soon find they were leading a much different movement than the one they started.

The constitutionalists initially had Woodrow Wilson's support. Based on a now forgotten 1912 film "The Life of General Villa",[99] a surprising number of foreigners think Pancho Villa became president of México. That's only in the movies. In real life, it's the cattle barons, not the cattle rustlers, who usually win. In the Mexican Revolution, the cattle baron was Venustiano Carranza Garza.

Unlike his contemporary, fellow cattle rancher and political leader Theodore Roosevelt, who compensated for his poor eyesight and early health problems by becoming an active and adventurous adult, Carranza turned prudent and home loving. Discovering he was too nearsighted to become a surgeon, the young Carranza retreated to his family's Coahuila hacienda, intending to spend the rest of his life reading history books and dabbling in local politics.

As a boy, Carranza had met Juárez, whom he worshiped, but he didn't enter politics until Díaz had already been elected a few times. Porfirio wasn't the only politician who was always reelected. The only way Carranza moved up the political ladder was when the incumbent died of old age. Carranza had nothing else to do particularly, and he was willing to wait. With time to read and study, he made himself an expert on the Mexican constitution, especially the clauses relating to local government and state responsibilities.

As a constitutional scholar and student of Juárez, Carranza welcomed Madero's revolution as a return to constitutional order. Although he dragged his feet when it came to economic reforms, he was the most prominent Coahuila leader to have opposed Díaz. He became governor of Coahuila. His counterpart from Chihuahua, Abraham Gonzales was well-known and well-liked in the United

---

[99] It is claimed that producer Charles Rossher's "location assistant"—the location being the Battle of Ojinaga—places yet another American, later to become famous, at this battle. The "gofer"—a young man trying to learn the film industry from the bottom up—was D. W. Griffith.

States, an active member of the Notre Dame University Alumni Association and a genuine reformer who had implemented labor, financial and educational reforms under Madero.

When Madero was overthrown and subsequently murdered, Gonzales the popular reformer, the scholarly and fussy Carranza and Sonoran governor, José María Maytorena Tapia, agreed to resist the "unconstitutional" Huerta government. Carranza was the "front man" for a simple reason: all three had some concern about Huerta's radical supporters and being relatively conservative reformers they worried that the urban radicals would co-opt their mostly rural revolution. More importantly, all three states bordered the United States. The governors were aware that President Wilson, a constitutional scholar like Carranza, was hoping for a legitimate, legal alternative to Huerta.

The three northern governors held a conference. All of them had the power to call up the state militia and to raise volunteers from elsewhere in México. Their combined strength, they reasoned, would be enough to easily defeat the dictator. They left it to the scholar among them to legitimize a rebellion. Strictly speaking, none of them could just make himself president. If one of them made himself interim president or overthrew the new dictator to make himself president, their government would be as illegitimate as Huerta's. When Díaz overthrew Lerdo de Tejada, he had been appointed interim president until his election, but Madero's revolt had started with the issue of "no reelection". Technically, an interim president cannot be elected president. The governors, of course, all thought they should become president, so none wanted to be interim president, something that would disqualify him from a regular term in office.

Carranza crafted a novel approach. The state forces would be joined under the command of the "Chief of Constitutionalist Forces"—Carranza. The "Chief" was simply an administrator appointed by the governors—he didn't claim to be president, but, so the governors claimed, neither was Huerta. At least the "Chief" could make the argument that his government was the only constitutional one. Foreign governments and businesses could either do business with the Chief, or they could risk having their treaties and business deals canceled when Huerta was overthrown.

To fit with his new title, Carranza invented a persona. His long beard made him look like an old-fashioned prophet (or like John Brown, the radical abolitionist of the 1850s United States). People already looked up to Carranza...they had to: the man stood two meters (six feet, seven inches) tall.[100] As carefully as he had selected his title, he selected his wardrobe. Juárez had always dressed as a respectable lawyer. Díaz wore his uniform. Carranza needed a costume that both advertised the promised return to civilian normalcy and the military authority he assumed. Until he was elected president, he was always photographed wearing cavalry boots, riding pants and a civilian coat cut and designed like a military uniform with a general's gold buttons.

The Constitutionalist army was stitched together out of state militias and volunteer units. Gonzales returned to Chihuahua and called together the guerrilla leaders who had aided Madero— Pascual Orozco Vázquez and Pancho Villa. Villa was never the simple bandit he's sometimes made out to be. Villa had emotional depth, an almost mystical belief in the Revolution and "power to the people". He openly wept when he heard Madero had been murdered and positively adored Gonzales for the latter's commitment to changing the lives of ordinary people and—more importantly—for fostering education in Chihuahua.

Villa would change the way people thought about war. He was an astute businessman—of sorts—who understood the value of good public relations. For good or bad, he was the public face of the Revolution in the United States. He operated closest to the United States border, was willing to cooperate with foreign reporters and

---

[100] Norteños are often much taller than other Mexicans, and people born in the 20th century are much taller than in Carranza's time. Vicente Fox is extremely tall, but is much shorter—under two meters (six feet, four inches). The "giant" of Mexican presidents, Benito Juárez, was slightly under one and a quarter meters (about four feet, seven inches).

looked like a Mexican revolutionary. North Americans expected someone like Zapata, with a sombrero and a big mustache. Villa normally wore a standard army cap or sometimes a British Indian Army-style solar topee…but Zapata and his mustache were far to the south. Pancho Villa was much more available; he grew a big mustache and wore a sombrero for the cameras.

Villa's cooperation with the U.S. press paid off handsomely. Thanks to the media, Woodrow Wilson had seen Pancho Villa in action. There had been battle photographers before 1910, but cameras were too bulky to carry. Most war photos were staged after the battle. Portable cameras and movie cameras were available by the time the Mexican Revolution started. Also, there had been advances in printing, so photographs could now be printed in the newspapers. Finally, people had begun going to the movies and were still amazed to see films of President Wilson taking a walk.

Raoul Walsh, a pioneering Hollywood film director, claimed he only wanted to bring the reality of war to the people. A real battle was something only soldiers and a few adventurous tourists—or unfortunate bystanders like those in El Paso who ended up as casualties of the battle of Juárez without even entering México—ever saw. The closest battlefield to Hollywood was just across the border from Arizona, where Pancho Villa was attacking the (Huerta's) Federal army. Walsh found a cooperative Pancho Villa ready to help. Walsh's "The Life of General Villa" was one of Hollywood's first international hits. Who used who is an open question, but Villa did become the world's first film star.[101]

When the light at dawn wasn't good for Walsh's cameraman, executions would be rescheduled for later in the morning. When Walsh wanted to film a battle scene, Villa was willing to oblige. Furthermore, he added that the Federal army would cooperate,

---

[101] Early films tended to "bleach out" the actors, and dark-haired, dark-skinned men like Villa had an advantage. The first major Hollywood stars were the south Italian, Rudolph Valentino and the Mexican, Ramon Novarro. Valentino died before sound was added to films, and Novarro's thick accent made it hard for him to continue working. He became a civil rights activist, fighting for Mexican-American rights in the 1940s and gay rights in the late 1960s.

so they could stage a battle. Unfortunately, Villa just didn't have enough ammunition to make the thing look real. If Walsh could just buy the ammunition, they would have a great newsreel.

Villa, of course, hadn't told the Federal army a thing about the "staged" battle. With the cameras rolling, the Division of the North overran the Federal positions. It was an unimportant battle—as bloody as any in the Revolution—but it was notable for being the first battle ever captured on film and the first battle most moviegoers ever saw.

Villa's staff showed real creativity on several occasions, not just when the cameras were rolling. They employed a Trojan Horse strategy when they recaptured Ciudad Juárez in 1914. Taking over a telegraph station, they convinced the Federal garrison in the city that they were Federal reinforcements, so it was imperative to keep the tracks clear. The army cleared the tracks, and Villa's forces arrived in record time.

However, exactly what Villa was fighting for was not always clear. "Exterminating justice" was the phrase he used to explain himself to John Reed. Villa and his army would wipe the earth (or at least his corner of it) clean of the villains, but as to who would replace them, he wasn't quite sure. In some places, "exterminating justice" simply meant destroying the debt records in the local hacienda office and lynching unpopular businessmen and priests. Social and economic reforms introduced in Villista-controlled territories were usually successful but did not seem to follow any particular plan or philosophy. The reforms in Villista territory seemed to have as much to do with whether the person in charge read socialist or Communist or capitalist literature as anything—or if they even read.

Pascual Orozco Vázquez was a different sort. Like Villa, Orozco was not just a simple bandit turned revolutionary. He was a middle-class[102] investor in gold mines before joining Madero's revolt. However, beyond insisting that workers be paid in cash, not com-

---

[102] Or possibly of even more exalted background. His father claimed descent from the Hapsburgs.

pany store credits, he had no particular social agenda. His army would eventually go over to the Terrazas family, the wealthiest landowners in México, and at their bidding, murder Gonzales. For the rest of the Revolution, Villa's troops would simply hang Orozco's *Colorados* – Reds[103] – when they ran across them. Like Villa, Orozco was forced to seek "alternative financing" in the United States. Although he was being chased by both the Texas Rangers and the U.S. Calvary (under the command of future General George S. Patton), he was killed in a "Wild West" shootout with a local posse after stealing some horses near Sierra Blanca, Texas in 1915.

---

[103] Orozco originally was supported by the "Liberal Party," which despite its name was an anarchist party and flew a red flag. Orozco changed his political coloration but not the color of his flag.

...More players, a wider stage...

WITH GONZALES DEAD, Governor Maytorena fled the country. Orozco's "counter-counter-counter-revolution" also brought Álvaro Obregón Salido into the field. Like José María Morelos, the insurgent priest, a hundred years earlier, Obregón taught himself how to become a general from reading. Like Morelos, who'd preached for years in the Michoacán back country, Obregón—despite his wealth and gentlemanly ways (a self-made millionaire, he spent his evenings writing poetry)—was a true backwoodsman. Morelos had been a cowboy. Obregón had been raised by older siblings among the Yaqui and Mayo Indians, who accepted him as one of their own and respected his practical gifts. Apparently, he had a photographic memory.[104] Better still, he was able to intuitively grasp how a space could change—by looking at a battlefield (or, as a boy, deer hunting with the Mayos) he knew where to place his troops or hunters based on where his prey would appear. On top of these gifts, Obregón was a successful businessman and inventor.

---

[104] As president, he glanced over the shoulder of a pompous poet, who was scheduled to give a reading of his latest work after the dinner party. Rather than give his own speech at the end of the dinner, Obregón recited the new poem, claiming he'd just made it up.

His early life reads like one of those rags-to-riches stories that were popular in the United States in the late nineteenth century. He was the youngest of a very large family, but orphaned as an infant. Raised first by his two oldest sisters—both village schoolteachers—he was sent to live with an older brother, also a schoolteacher, among the Mayo and Yaqui peoples. As the schoolteacher's assistant, he was already a respected member of the community by the time he was a teenager. He spoke both indigenous languages fluently. His good eyesight made him a welcome addition on long hunting and fishing expeditions.

As a thirteen-year-old boy, he tried his hand at tobacco farming. Inventing a cigarette packaging machine and running a cigarette factory with a few friends seemed like a good idea. The older boys and their relations were sent around to local stores to ask for Álvaro's brand and drum up sales. Storekeepers discovered the packaging was fine, but the tobacco was the worst their customers ever tasted. Obregón's later career was better: in his later teens, he became a professional poker player; good enough that local employers paid him to not play, preferring that their employees didn't lose their paychecks to some kid and have to seek a better paying new job. After that, he'd sold shoes door to door, raising the money to go into garbanzo bean farming.

Garbanzos had to be planted by hand, so the boy genius came up with a workable mechanical planter. After some improvements, the new farm machinery business made the young garbanzo farmer a millionaire.[105]

---

[105] As a result of the devastation during the First World War, Europe faced famines. Obregón, the most prominent garbanzo farmer in México (at the time, temporarily retired from politics), was sent to the United States to negotiate bulk sales of garbanzos to a private relief organization in the U.S. that successfully shipped enough basic food to the Europeans to prevent mass starvation. Obregón and the relief society's organizer had much in common: both were orphans raised by schoolteacher relations among Indians; both became millionaires from early inventions; and both became presidents of their country. While Herbert Hoover's presidency was probably less successful than Obregón's, Hoover would enjoy a very long, productive life after leaving office.

By the time he was twenty-four, in 1910, he was a leading Sonoran businessman; exactly the sort of person Madero's revolutionaries had in mind to run México. Obregón, however, took no part in the 1910 Revolution—his wife had died. He stayed home taking care of his children, writing bad poetry about death and—like Morelos a hundred years earlier—studying military histories and manuals.

As the richest businessman in Huatabampo, Sonora, Obregón was easily elected municipal president. By 1912, with a new wife to care for his children, he could finally put his military studies into practice. He recruited four hundred Mayo and Yaqui soldiers to put down a local anti-Madero revolt, then, putting his 4th Irregular Battalion into the service of Governor Maytorena, joined the Constitutionalist army. Less well known than Villa or Zapata, it was Obregón who would win the revolution on (and off) the battlefield.

Unconnected to the constitutionalists was the other main insurgent force, Emiliano Zapata's Army of the South. Though relatively small, it was a classic guerrilla force made up of local fighters who knew the territory and could count on support from the people. Madero, Huerta and later Carranza would find that Federal reprisals against otherwise peaceable villagers drove more and more neutral farmers into the Zapatista ranks.

The constitutionalists squabbled among themselves, but the two main armies, under Obregón and Pancho Villa, continued to advance south through the country. Villa's media popularity in the United States was only enhanced by his tendency to "liberate" cattle from the largest foreign landowner in México, media mogul William Randolph Hearst. Hearst naturally wanted to protect his investments, and his papers and magazines painted Villa in the most lurid light possible. It didn't help Villa's reputation in the U.S. any when American Civil War veteran and Hearst correspondent Ambrose Bierce disappeared while covering Villa's campaign.[106] But in the competitive newspaper market of the day, Hearst's villains were the heroes to other publishers. Villa had more than a few defenders and admirers north of the border.

Pancho Villa's business interests in the United States—legitimate and otherwise—were mostly conducted from any number of ice cream parlors in El Paso where he met and became friends with fellow ice cream enthusiast[107] General Hugh Scott, who was then stationed at Fort Bliss in the border city. Scott, whose military duties included guarding the border, openly assisted Villa and helped him recruit soldiers in the United States. Even after Villa's incursion into the U.S., when Villa became U.S. Public Enemy Number One, Scott defended Villa as a good soldier and better friend. Even better, George Carrothers, the *New York Times* correspondent assigned to follow Villa's Division of the North, was Woodrow Wilson's first cousin.

Obregón, to some extent, like Villa, cooperated with the foreign press (his Mayo and Yaqui fighters were quite willing to put aside their uniforms and pose in breechclouts and feathers for the cameras), but as a businessman he had long standing ties through groups like the Chambers of Commerce. His media relations were more with the owners than the reporters. During his presidency, when he was lobbying for official diplomatic relations with the U.S., he helped finance the takeover of several Texas newspapers that supported his goals.

---

[106] There are still stories that Bierce was killed by Villa, though we need to remember that the well-known author was over seventy, in poor health and had spoken and written about suicide. He may have just fallen off a horse or had a heart attack, but at any rate, he disappeared on his way to the battle of Ojinaga. John Reed, incidentally, first met up with the Mexican revolutionaries at this same battle.

[107] A man of huge appetites, Villa's sweet tooth was remarkable. According to El Paso historian, David Dorado Roma, Villa spent his afternoons at the Elite Confectionery eating chocolate-covered ice cream "baseballs" and up to a pound of peanut brittle, all washed down with strawberry soda pop.

He was a sophisticated, wealthy exporter with extensive business contacts throughout the border states, and—as time went on—within the military as a highly respected general.[108] Although Villa (and to some extent, Obregón) maintained good relations with the U.S. Army, they still answered to Carranza. Carranza distrusted foreigners in general—the gringos in particular—and he detested Woodrow Wilson.

---

[108] When the U.S. first entered the First World War, Obregón happened to be on a business trip to Texas, which led to rumors that he, not General Pershing, would lead the U.S. Expeditionary Force sent to France.

Woodrow Wilson invades México–
in his pajamas!

WOODROW WILSON HAD MUCH in common with the scholarly Venustiano Carranza, but the two despised each other. Carranza openly distrusted the United States and would go out of his way to personally insult Woodrow Wilson. Pancho Villa was winning battle after battle, controlling large sections of the country and was the best-known Mexican revolutionary in the United States, thanks to both access to the border and his public relations savvy. At the same time, he was also portrayed as a blood-thirsty, semiliterate bandit. Zapata was an unknown, and Obregón had not yet emerged as a revolutionary leader in his own right. The U.S. President was not enthusiastic about any of the potential Mexican leaders, but as a former clergyman and professor, was convinced he had the moral right and intellectual ability to control the Revolution. Besides, a stable México was good for American business. He would never understand that the Mexicans saw him as the worst kind of meddler. Moreover, from the Mexican point-of-view, it was Huerta's coup, at the behest of the United States government, that had touched off the Constitutionalist rebellion.

It was obvious that Henry Lane Wilson's backing of the Huerta coup had been a disaster, but President Wilson—a scholar, after all—was reluctant to act until he had done his research. He dispatched a friend, his campaign biographer, William Bayard Hale, to México in 1914. Hale, a *New York Times* reporter, spoke no Spanish and had never been in México before, but Wilson trusted Hale, and Hale understood Wilson's idealistic belief in constitutional democracy. Working undercover,[109] Hale unsurprisingly reported that Huerta was a tyrant with no popular support. It was only control of the oil fields and the revenues from the oil fields that let him buy the foreign munitions that kept him in power.

Hale was right: Huerta needed ammunition if he was to maintain power. Everyone knew Britain and Germany were about to go to war. The British Navy depended on Mexican oil, and the British—not caring much who controlled the country as long as they could pump oil—kept a mercenary army under their own general, Manuel Peláez, protecting the oil region, but Huerta's forces controlled the ports. The Germans were only willing to supply arms to Huerta in return for blocking oil sales to Britain. Wilson, pro-British but desperate to keep the United States out of the coming war, hoped that if neither the Germans nor the British had the clear advantage, the war could be avoided.

United States intelligence officers learned that the Germans were sending several shiploads of arms to México. Both Carranza and Huerta had, at various times, threatened to cut off oil shipments; effectively knocking the British Navy out of the war and at the same time, seriously crippling the U.S. economy. Although at the time the United States was the largest oil producing country, it was also—then and now—the largest consumer and already dependent on foreign oil imports. Carranza's forces were slowly taking more and more control of the country but were unlikely to capture Veracruz in time to stop the Germans from resupplying Huerta.

On 6 April 1914, six U.S. sailors were arrested in Tampico, which was still controlled by Huerta's administration. The arrests were a mistake, and the sailors were returned to their ship. However,

---

[109] Hale was an undercover agent for more than Wilson. He was also a German agent.

the United States was a new military power in the world, and U.S. officers had not always shown good judgment in México. The United States Navy wanted respect: the ship's captain demanded an apology from the Mexican Navy...and a twenty-one gun salute! The Mexicans, as politely as possible, apologized for the sailors' inconvenience but refused the salute. The "insult to the Navy" received a fair amount of press in the United States. Given the feeling in the United States, this minor incident gave the president a plausible excuse to "avenge the national insult"—and incidentally to cut off Huerta's arms supplies and liberate México from the tyrant. Or so it seemed.

In 1914 the president of the United States was one of the few people in the world with a bedside telephone. He was still asleep at 6 A.M. on 21 April when he received a call confirming that the German ship, *Yripanga*, would be docking in Veracruz later that morning. Wilson had the White House operator set up a conference call between himself, his personal secretary, Secretary of State William Jennings Bryant and Navy Secretary Josephus Daniels. The operator and the president weren't the only ones still in their pajamas that morning.

Daniels was a pacifist, and Bryant had religious objections to warfare. Still, they agreed with Wilson that the only way to stop the *Yripanga* was to take over Veracruz. If the French had once invaded the city over unpaid doughnuts in Mexico City, the United States could take the Customs House in Veracruz to avenge an insult to its navy's honor in Tampico. Daniels had orders sent by radio (a very recent technology at the time) to U.S. Navy ships in the Gulf of Mexico.

Nothing went as planned. As the Spanish found out in 1828, the French in 1838, Winfield Scott in 1847 and Maximilian von Hapsburg in 1863, the jarochas (Veracruz natives) did not welcome foreign invasions. In 1848, army cadets had defended Mexico City from United States marines. In 1914, the Naval Academy defended Veracruz. To protect their Marines, the U.S. Navy bombarded the city. Ordinary Veracruz citizens joined the cadets. There were casualties on both sides. The Marines did complete their mission—occupying the Customs House. The *Yripanga* was an unarmed merchant freighter, and its captain was not about to enter a war zone. He turned his ship around. Mission accomplished.[110]

Although meant to assist Carranza, even that plan went sour. What Wilson forgot was that Carranza was a very prickly nationalist and had never gotten over his boyhood meeting with Benito Juárez, who had struggled to keep all foreign governments out. Wilson, during his pajama conference, had not consulted the "legitimate" Constitutional Chief of México before sending troops into the country. If the United States did not immediately evacuate Veracruz, the Constitutional Chief threatened to invade the United States, even if it meant joining forces with Huerta! He was bluffing, of course. Wilson was furious, but Carranza had made his point. He—not Huerta—was México's legitimate leader, and only he had the right to determine México's foreign policy.

Henry Lane Wilson, who was still in Mexico City, was finally recalled. The United States sent a representative (not an ambassador[111]) to the Constitutionalist government, and other countries withdrew their recognition of Huerta's government. The Marines took their time leaving Veracruz; they didn't withdraw until November, by which time the whole occupation was pointless. Huerta was gone. The Revolution had gone on to a new phase by then.

Worse yet for the Wilson administration, the Latin American nations had all sided with Carranza, and the United States was again seen as the aggressor in México. Veracruz' official name was changed after the invasion to Three Times Heroic Veracruz—its citizens had risen against invaders from Spain once and from the United States twice.

---

[110] Sort of. The *Yripanga* unloaded down the coast in Huerta controlled Puerto México.

[111] To legalists like Wilson and Carranza, the terms used in foreign relations were important. Not being president, the constitutional chief could not receive an "ambassador", but he could receive a "representative".

Harry S. Truman laid a wreath at the memorial to the Heroic Children of Chapultepec in 1948. Truman was applauded at the time, but no one expected an apology for what had been a tragedy of war. The Veracruz invasion was seen differently. México and the United States were not at war, and the intervention was solely for Woodrow Wilson's political benefit. Bill Clinton finally offered an official apology in 1998.

All against all:
The Revolution, part 3

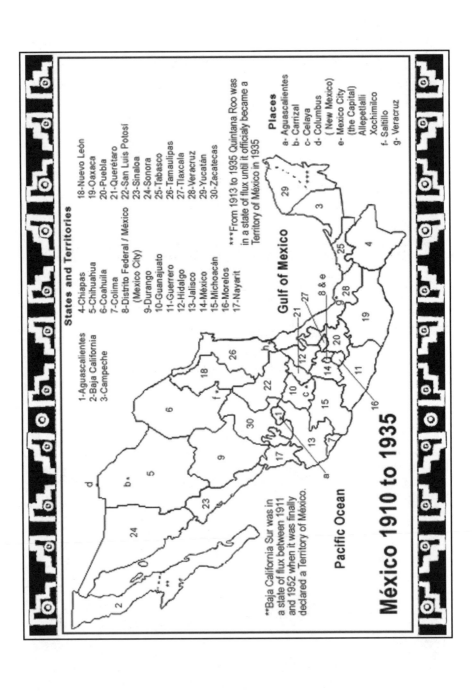

México 1910 to 1935

States and Territories

1-Aguascalientes
2-Baja California
3-Campeche

4-Chiapas
5-Chihuahua
6-Coahuila
7-Colima
8-Distrito Federal / México
(Mexico City)
9-Durango
10-Guanajuato
11-Guerrero
12-Hidalgo
13-Jalisco
14-México
15-Michoacán
16-Morelos
17-Nayarit

18-Nuevo León
19-Oaxaca
20-Puebla
21-Querétaro
22-San Luis Potosí
23-Sinaloa
24-Sonora
25-Tabasco
26-Tamaulipas
27-Tlaxcala
28-Veracruz
29-Yucatán
30-Zacatecas

***From 1913 to 1935 Quintana Roo was
in a state of flux until it officialy became a
Territory of México in 1935

Places

a- Aguascalientes
b- Carrizal
c- Celaya
d- Columbus
(New Mexico)
e- Mexico City
(the Capital)
Allepetlalli
Xochimilco
f- Saltillo
g- Veracruz

Gulf of Mexico

Pacific Ocean

**Baja California Sur was in
a state of flux between 1911
and 1952 when it was finally
declared a Territory of México.

Who's the boss?

WITH TWO BRILLIANT SELF-TAUGHT generals, Álvaro Obregón and Pancho Villa, leading the way, the constitutionalists were the obvious ones to form a new government, but which Constitutionalist leader was in charge?

Carranza's forces were quick to gain control of the country. Carranza, however, was distrusted by both the British and the Americans. Carranza had gambled that his threat to invade the United States if troops weren't withdrawn from Veracruz had forced Wilson to recognize the "Chief" as head of the legitimate government. The British, until much too late, had continued to recognize Huerta as the legitimate president. With no diplomatic representative to the constitutionalists, they asked the United States to look after their interests. When Pancho Villa (by then, openly defying Carranza) had a British subject shot (the Englishman had tried to assassinate Villa), American reporter John Reed made the mistake of asking the Constitutional Chief about the matter. Carranza's secretaries refused to translate exactly whatever words he used to get his point across, but the gist of it was to tell Reed that if the British ambassador recognized the "traitor Huerta", there was nothing he could do about it. Besides, the Mexican Revolution was not Britain's or the United State's problem.

Thems the breaks

THERE PROBABLY WAS NOTHING Carranza could do in any case. Villa was a loose cannon, but as the Revolution went on, so were a lot of other generals. The volunteer generals on the Constitutionalist side often had their own agendas, some much more radical than the Chief's. Civilian groups that backed the constitutionalists had their own demands. To save his rebellion and to undercut support for Villa and Zapata, the Constitutionalist Chief had been forced to make radical social and economic reforms demanded by his allies. Álvaro Obregón, who had recruited indigenous rebel units early in the Revolution, brought in needed allies from the labor unions. Carranza needed the troops and agreed to new labor laws. The old Juárez supporters, still fighting the Church, had their demands. Carranza, devoted to Juárez, at least understood the importance of anticlerical symbolism. He signed the law legalizing divorce on Christmas Day.

When Huerta failed to receive the German weapons he expected to be unloaded in Veracruz, his regime had less than a month to run. Carranza, like Polk during the 1846–1848 American invasion, wanted to prevent political rivals from taking the credit for being the one to reach Mexico City first. While the nonpolitical Winfield

Scott marched inland from Veracruz, Polk had kept the political general, Zachary Taylor, in Saltillo, and all of Carranza's generals had political ambitions, but the most problematic at the time was Pancho Villa. Villa's coal supply mysteriously ran out, and he couldn't get his trains past Torreon. Obregón somehow had all the coal he needed—and more.

Obregón's army advanced on the Capital. Huerta resigned, and his foreign minister became acting president. Congress dissolved itself. The new president didn't even wait for Obregón to show up. The president sent Carranza a message simply admitting his government was completely illegitimate, and Carranza was the legitimate leader of México; then asked the Regent of Mexico City to handle the surrender terms and fled the country himself. Obregón entered the Capital on 15 August 1914.

The upper-class Mexicans and foreigners living in the Capital breathed a sigh of relief when they learned that the educated poet, Obregón, not the semi-educated "Mexican Robin Hood" with his ideas of "exterminating justice", would be their conqueror. After all, Villa had paid Obregón the backhanded compliment of calling him *el perfumado* – the perfumed one – implying his values weren't those of the hard-scrabble northern desert and the people's revolution, but lay closer to those of the hacienda owners and the rich. They must have willfully forgotten the Obregón who recruited Yaqui and Mayo tribesmen and working class "red brigades". He might smell nice, but there was going to be social justice all the same.

Food had run out in the city long before Huerta fled. Essential city services had stopped functioning. The rich had private food sources and could afford to hire someone to cart away their garbage. In the poor and working-class neighborhoods, people were hungry, and the garbage piled up in the streets. Obregón decreed food rationing and the death penalty for hoarding. Emergency taxes were imposed. When foreigners complained, through their chambers of commerce, about the hardship this might cause them, Obregón's response was more subtle, perhaps, but not all that different from what Pancho Villa might have done. The foreigners' organizations were slapped with huge fines on the pretext that they had backed the dictator, and using the same punishment used on all shameful criminals since the Aztecs, the foreigners were put to work carting away the garbage.

Hot water...

EMILIANO ZAPATA AND HIS FOLLOWERS wanted a radical redistribution of the land. In Zapatista-controlled territory, haciendas had been taken over and turned into ejidos. Zapata despised cities and city ways. Carranza's backers were people like himself: norteños, landowners and "modern" businessmen. They wanted the Porfirian reforms and could live with the radical reforms Huerta's cabinet put on the books, but without Porfirio or Huerta. Changing the nature of land ownership was not their first priority. Naturally, the short alliance between Carranza and Zapata wouldn't last.

Then there was Pancho Villa. Villistas controlled most of northern México. Like the Zapatista leadership, they were impatient with legalisms. They wanted "justice", and they wanted it now. Villa personally despised Obregón and felt Carranza had betrayed him when his coal was cut off on the drive to Mexico City.

The Villistas and Zapatistas saw themselves as the revolutionary winners. They wanted to define the new rules under which México would be governed. Between them, they had the most forces in the field.

Originally, Villa had rebelled to avenge Madero. As the Revolution dragged on, he ignored his putative leader, Carranza, and joined

271

forces with Zapata. The Zapatistas had some social programs, and for a while it looked as if either Zapata or Villa would become president. Zapata didn't want the job. There is a famous photograph of the two and their aides gathered around the "throne" Porfirio Díaz used in the Palacio Nacional. Villa is sitting in the chair, laughing at the joke. The unsmiling Zapata was asked to also sit in the chair but suggested instead that they burn it.

For Zapata, justice worked from the bottom up. To Villa, justice came from the man in charge. A few years later, the Russian Revolution ran into the same conflicting visions in the fights between the soviets (village units) and the Communist Party. Foreigners have always expected México to follow European models and forget that Europeans sometimes follow Mexican ones. John Reed, the American Communist, saw the Villa-Zapata forces as Communists. So did a lot of American businessmen. Villa certainly attracted Communist supporters and is still seen as a Communist revolutionary.[112]

While Villistas and Zapatistas had different goals, they had one thing in common: neither accepted Carranza's mild reforms. In October 1914, Villa and Zapata's generals met under truce at Aguascalientes (literally, "hot waters") to form a new government. Voting rules were simple—the generals with the most guns got the most votes. The convention was hopelessly split between the two main forces and chose a series of minor generals to serve as "provisional president" for anywhere from thirty days to six months. Not that these presidents did much—Mexicans can barely remember their names. Mostly they retreated, moving their provisional capitals from one city to another.

Obregón wasn't foolish enough to show up at the convention, but several of his supporters, sympathizers and spies were there. He recognized that the Revolution had gone beyond Carranza, and that the people were mostly on the convention's side. While

---

[112] Communist banners in México often show Marx, Lenin, Stalin and Pancho Villa. Unidad Habitacional Allepetlalli in Xochimilco includes streets named for Marx, Engels, Stalin and Villa.

he helped Carranza retreat from Mexico City to Veracruz, he also started radicalizing the government, undercutting Zapata and Villa's support.

Obregón was playing a three-way game. On the battlefield, he attacked and destroyed one small army after another. Politically, he began pushing the Carranza government to take more radical steps, winning over Zapata and Villa supporters to his (well, Carranza's) side. While developing his own Obregonista organization, he continued acting as a loyal general and cabinet officer for the Carranza government. Obregón was a realist. No foreign government would recognize a country led by an ex-bandit or a peasant leader, and foreign recognition was vital for keeping arms and money coming in.

Carranza seemed to have U.S. support. The gringos evacuated Veracruz, turning it over to the Constitutional Chief. Controlling the main oil export facilities brought the British around eventually. Carranza was viewed as a German puppet when he threatened to simply cut off all oil to all sides in the First World War. The British were the ones who needed Mexican oil (ninety percent of the British Navy's fuel was Mexican oil), but even they eventually gave up on Huerta.

The fatal glass of beer

THE MOST IMPORTANT FOREIGNER to play a role in the Carranza forces never went anywhere near the country. Arthur Zimmerman was quietly drinking a beer in Berlin and thinking about a solution to a business problem, when the answer came to him. Zimmerman was the German Foreign Minister. His problem was to keep the United States out of his country's war with Britain and France. The solution lay in México.

Huerta was gone by July 1914, but the Germans continued to finance his activities (and one supposes, pay his liquor tab), even after the long expected war with England and France had started (on 3 August 1914). While officially neutral in the European war, the Wilson administration tilted towards the British. However, the U.S. had a large German-speaking minority and huge numbers of ethnic Irish. The Irish had been attempting to throw off British colonial rule for centuries and were expected to help the Germans. Both the British and the Germans were busy spreading propaganda in the U.S. while quietly working on plans to use the Mexican Revolution to force the U.S. to intervene—or not intervene—to their own advantage.

German military analysis of the Veracruz invasion and the border situation concluded that the United States military could provide arms and men to the British and French but if there was trouble in México the United States would either have to militarily intervene or they would have to guard their border. Either way, it kept U.S. arms out of British hands and American soldiers out of the European war.

Huerta, with German financing, still hoped to return to México. His downfall was something out of a spy novel. The Hapsburg empire—German allies—was still ruled by Maximilian's older (now very old) brother, Franz Joseph. Nothing much had changed for the Hapsburg family; they were still ruling nations that never asked for them and didn't want them. The Czechs, like the Italians, who had thrown Maximilian out, and the Mexicans, who shot him, had been struggling against Hapsburg control for several years. Their best chance for an independent state would be if the Germans (and the Hapsburgs) lost the war. Czech nationalists had their own spy network and cooperated with the British. A British intelligence agent was following a German intelligence agent in New York City in April 1915. The German agent walked into a hotel and met with...Victoriano Huerta!

Huerta was supposed to be drinking himself to death in Spain. The British agent—not willing to admit his country was spying on the United States (his government wanted to convince the United States that their enemies, the Germans, were the only ones guilty of that)—contacted the Czechs. A part-time Czech spy (and full-time electrician) managed to "bug" the hotel room[113] where financial arrangements were made between the Germans and Huerta. The plan was for Huerta to return to México and stage an uprising—or at least stir up enough trouble to keep the United States Army on alert.

As Huerta made his way south and west, he was trailed by British, German and Czech spies, the United States Secret Service, U.S. Army Intelligence and the New York City Police (how all these

---

[113] Tape recorders hadn't been invented yet. The bug was simply a microphone hidden behind the drapes, that allowed a stenographer in the next room to listen in to the conversations.

various undercover agents kept themselves from tripping over each other has never been explained). Huerta was allowed to get as far as New Mexico before he was arrested as an undesirable alien and thrown in jail. How effective any uprising he might have staged at this point is questionable. He was already dying of cirrhosis of the liver. Despite surprising diplomatic protests from the Carranza government (Huerta was a Mexican citizen, and Carranza was a prickly defender of México's sovereignty), the ex-dictator was locked up at Fort Bliss (El Paso), Texas, where he finally died on 14 January 1916.[114]

---

[114] Huerta is the only Mexican president buried in the United States. On Day of the Dead, perhaps he communes with the spirits in any one of the several bars near El Paso's Evergreen Cemetery.

Zimmerman strikes again

WHILE ZAPATA AND VILLA SOON turned on Carranza, it was obvious that the Constitutionalists were the only real government. The German plan to restore Huerta (undone by an alert British agent and a Czech electrician) was the more serious threat to México, but the "Zimmerman Telegram" is more important in world history, by far.

Zimmerman, probably just to keep the U.S. out of the war, launched a diplomatic effort to both woo the Japanese to the German side and to keep the U.S. Army tied up defending itself from a Japanese-Mexican invasion.[115]

No one is sure how seriously the plan was taken, but Herr Zimmerman did offer the Carranza government German support and—possibly—Japanese troops in return for invading the United States. That alone created an obstacle—Japan and Britain were allies in this war. Assuming Japan changed sides and in the

---

[115] In 1917, William Randolph Hearst produced "Patria", a fifteen-part serial based on a Japanese-Mexican invasion of California. Warner Oland, a Swede who would play Chinese detective Charlie Chan in sixteen films in the 1930s, stars as a villainous samurai fended off by ingénue Irene Castle. Wallace Beery, who achieved critical acclaim for his portrayal of Pancho Villa in the 1934 "Viva Villa!" was a much less likable or sympathetic Villa in the Hearst production.

event of a German victory, Zimmerman held out the possibility that México would recover the territories lost in 1848. Carranza claims he never saw the message, and he probably didn't. Even if he did, he was in the middle of a civil war and couldn't have attacked the United States. Zimmerman probably didn't count on a Mexican invasion either; he just wanted the U.S. to consider the possibility as a reason to keep their army at home. The British, however, took the plan very seriously. At least they used the incident to try to convince Woodrow Wilson and the U.S. public that the Germans had hostile intentions towards the U.S.; forcing the U.S. to enter the First World War on the British side. While the British "won" the First World War, they were bankrupt. The United States replaced Britain as the major world power, thanks in part to Herr Zimmerman.

Carranza was antiforeign and famously rejected the French-influenced artillery expert Felipe Ángeles, and he was more pro-than anti-German, as were Villa and Obregón. The British (and some later historians, like Barbara Tuchman) suggest that the constitutionalists would have accepted the German offer. It's unlikely. The British propagandists and Tuchman,[116] both forget that the rural German-Mexicans, like German-Americans in the same era, were still speaking their own language and often following German customs, but thought of themselves as loyal citizens of their adopted country. A good number of German-Mexicans were also German-Americans. Typical was Joseph Louis Fuchs, a German-speaker from Ohio, who moved to México in the 1890s, "Mexicanizing" his name as José Luis Fox Flach. José Luis' grandson, Vicente Fox y Quesada, would become president

---

[116] In *The Zimmerman Telegram* (1955, 1962), Tuchman accepts without comment a U.S. consul of the time's report that Villa hadn't attacked stores with German names as "proof" of a German conspiracy. She was an expert on European history but made several mistakes in writing about México. Small town shopkeepers, even those with German names, generally were left alone by Villa and tended to support him.

of México.[117] Secondly, since Porfirio, Mexican military training and organization had been based on German models (as, since the American Revolution, was the U.S. military), and many of the better-trained officers (with the exception of Felipe Ángeles) had gone to Germany for advanced studies. Finally, the Carranza government was not even in control of all of México.

---

[117] The gods, gachupines and gringos all seemed to converge in 2005. The trickier god Tezcatlipoca seems to have inspired some historical research. A historian working on a biography of Vicente Fox uncovered a court document in which the president's father, José Luis Fox Pont, claimed he was an American citizen, not a Mexican. This would have been a very serious matter, if—as it appeared—the sitting president had been ineligible for the office in the first place. The Fox administration's official explanation was that one provision of the "Bucarelli Agreement" permitted American citizens to have compensation claims for lands expropriated by the Mexican government heard by a arbitrator rather than the Land Court. Arbitrators were generally much more generous than the courts, and Fox Pont—or his lawyers—had a logical reason to commit perjury. When questions about Fox Pont's citizenship (and by extension, the legitimacy of his son's government), refused to go away, Fox Pont's birth certificate "miraculously" surfaced in Guanajuato. Citizenship requirements were much more fluid at the time, and there is no proof that Fox Pont's father, José Luis Fox Flach ever officially took out Mexican citizenship. George Romney, the American politician, born in Chihuahua of U.S. parents, claimed U.S. citizenship through his parents. But, whether Romney OR Fox Pont was a Mexican or a gringo is still an open question.

The Punitive Expedition:
it seemed like a good idea at the time

G IVEN WOODROW WILSON'S DISAPPOINTMENT with Venustiano Carranza as a potential pupil of his style of democracy, he was easily persuaded to throw support to a more malleable candidate for México's leader—Pancho Villa. Villa had friends in the United States, including Army Chief of Staff Hugh Scott. Villa's army was better disciplined and his advisors more competent than anyone had expected.[118] His Hollywood image and *New York Times* connections (and White House connections through the *New York Times*) made him a popular figure in the United States.

Wilson was also persuaded to support Villa by Secretary of State William Jennings Bryant. Bryant, probably the first U.S. politician to make his personal life a campaign issue (he had run for president in 1896 and was what is called today a "born-again Christian"). Despite having no real foreign policy experience, Bryant had been brought into the cabinet to fulfill Wilson's promise of a moral foreign policy. Pancho Villa (again defying the Hollywood

---

[118] Villa attracted some excellent military and civilian advisors. Felipe Ángeles, a renowned artillery expert, deserted the Federal Army to train the Villistas. The currency issued by the Banco de México lost all value during Huerta's regime, while the currency issued by Villa was accepted by foreign banks and businesses.

stereotype), like Bryant, neither smoked nor drank. More importantly, Villa's army was the strongest in the field and controlled most of the U.S. border.

In February 1914, Wilson had lifted a ban on arms sales to México (meant to bring down Huerta), which had the practical effect of arming Villa and—the U.S. hoped—forcing the disagreeable, but at least well-educated and well-born, Carranza to take a more conciliatory attitude towards the United States.

Obregón eliminated Villa as a contender for México's leader after the two Battles of Celaya (April 1915). Villa was no longer seen as invincible, and with Bryant having been replaced as Secretary of State by Robert Lansing who was less likely to judge foreign leaders based on their personal habits, United States' policy shifted to Carranza. Villa still had his defenders, like Hugh Scott, but the public perception in the United States shifted from a view of Villa as a serious revolutionary, to seeing him solely as a romantic guerrilla leader and bandit chieftain.

America's love-hate affair with Villa ended the night of 9 March 1916 when Villa (or Villistas[119]) attacked the U.S. Army Base at Columbus, New Mexico, burned down most of the town and killed several civilians. This was the first foreign invasion of the United States in over one hundred years, and until 2001, the only foreign "terrorist" attack. As with the World Trade Center attack, the president was politically forced to respond with military force. A five thousand-dollar reward was offered for Villa, dead or alive, and the army was mobilized to hunt the renegade general down.

Although the First World War had started in 1914, and there was open talk of United States intervention in that war, the U.S.

---

[119] There has never been definitive proof that Villa was in New Mexico. Susie Parks, the Columbus telephone operator—a movie fan—telephoned for help when the town was attacked. She looked out the window and thought she saw Villa ride past. Whether she actually saw Villa or not, the attackers could see Ms. Parks. While we often praise telephone operators for maintaining their composure during emergencies today, Susie Parks was truly heroic. The telephone switchboard was in Ms. Parks' living room. Although under fire, she stayed at her switchboard, calmly telephoning for assistance.

Army was unprepared for full-scale military operations. The last invasion of México had been in 1846 and had bogged down when supply lines ran out, and technology had changed dramatically since then, making access to supplies (especially gasoline) a critical problem. The days when an army could seize a village's grain to feed their horses if they needed to were gone.

By 1916, the Revolution was more or less over. Huerta was gone, Carranza and the constitutionalists were in control of the country, and the Wilson administration recognized Carranza as the legitimate leader of the country.

If Wilson thought he was doing Carranza a favor by sending U.S. troops into México to hunt for Villa, he was quickly dissuaded. Carranza had been serious when he'd told John Reed that foreigners should stay out. In the U.S., Hugh Scott, then head of the army, still defended his old friend.

With the U.S. on the brink of entering the First World War and suspicion that Villa's raid was part of a complicated German plot to keep the U.S. Army tied down in México, as well as pleas to protect the oil industry from the Mexican government, there were protracted negotiations.

After Wilson and Carranza finally agreed that the U.S. could pursue "bandits" into México under an old agreement allowing soldiers from either side to cross the border in pursuit of Apache raiders, Scott reluctantly gave the task to the unknown John Pershing.

General Pershing faced a huge task. He was commanding what was still basically an army meant to guard against Indian raids, mostly made up of the famous "Buffalo Soldiers", the all-black frontier cavalry unit, and General Custer's old 7th Cavalry. Under the fiction that this was just a bandit-hunting expedition, Pershing could not count on using the Mexican railroad system nor on any support from the Mexican army. He had to take everything with him—men, horses, mules, artillery, the world's newest and most promising weapon—airplanes—food, cooking equipment and prostitutes.

Sexually transmitted diseases were not easily treated at the time and were a concern for every general. Pershing detailed medical officers to recruit healthy, patriotic prostitutes for the mission, but transportation was the real problem. Pershing commanded the first mobilized invasion, but there was a small problem—the Army didn't own enough trucks and had no auto mechanics. The trains might get Pershing's troops into México, but there was no guarantee that Pancho Villa was anywhere near the tracks.

The General sent young Lt. Dwight D. Eisenhower[120] to every auto dealership in Texas and New Mexico. General Scott risked a prison sentence by simply writing a blank check to Ford Motor Company without congressional approval. For a mobile command center, the general managed to find a good buy on a new Packard eight-seat limousine. Finally, he realized there were no gas stations in rural México (or, at that time, anywhere), and transporting gasoline meant buying still more trucks. The "patriotic ladies" could stay on the train—there weren't that many trucks even after Pershing had asked Ford Motor Company to ship whatever they could from Detroit to New Mexico.

General Pershing, the troops, mules, horses, gasoline, cannons, airplanes and the patriotic ladies finally crossed the border into Chihuahua where they found…nothing. Villagers who were pressured (or beaten) gave the army leads on Villa's whereabouts, but the army found that Pancho had either moved on or had never been where he was said to be. As with de Guzmán's fruitless search for the island city of women after the Conquest, these new conquistadors faced the same Mexican strategy of getting sent on wild-goose chases.

---

[120] Eisenhower's son, General John D. Eisenhower, joked that he owed his life to Pancho Villa. Ike expected to be sent on the expedition and impulsively married his girlfriend at the time, Mamie Dowd. One result of the precipitous marriage was the future general, ambassador and military historian. John Eisenhower's *Intervention: The United States and the Mexican Revolution, 1913–1917* (W.W. Norton, 1993) is the standard reference work on U.S. – Mexican relations during the era.

Once the soldiers left the railroads, the trucks started to break down. Obregón's forces had the only high-altitude airplanes in the world at the time. Obregón and aviation pioneer Alberto Salinas are credited with not only inventing the naval air strike, but with also having the only aircraft anywhere capable of flying over mountains. Pershing's planes couldn't fly over the Sierra Madres; they had to be disassembled and carried over the mountains on mules. One Villista general claimed much later (the general was ninety-five at the time) that he added to the confusion by driving a covered wagon up into the hills, managing to drop hints in every village along the way that a wounded Villa was inside.

Worse, the Mexican Federal Army was attacking the U.S. forces and inflicting casualties (even though there was an agreement between the presidents). The most serious incident was at El Carrizal, Chihuahua, when an arrogant U.S. officer followed up a correctable misunderstanding (his soldiers had taken several lost Mexican soldiers prisoner and abused them) by insisting on free passage though town and firing on the Mexican Army when they refused. The result was a rare Mexican victory, with ten dead U.S. soldiers and twenty-three taken prisoner. A later inquiry was complicated by the fact that the U.S. was using ammunition then prohibited by international treaty.

Like later military operations designed to capture terrorists, the Punitive Expedition was a failure. Carranza, the Constitutional Chief, was the closest thing to a legitimate leader, and the Wilson administration desperately wanted a stable government in their next-door neighbor. Wilson despised Carranza[121] (and vice versa); unfortunately he had no choice but to accept the Constitutional Chief as the only viable government. Carranza (and most later historians) suspected Villa's attack on Columbus was designed to force the United States to openly intervene—which would rally the people to Villa's cause. But, Carranza wanted Pershing out...and

---

[121] It was in reference to Carranza that Wilson said of Latin America: "We will teach them to elect good men".

Pershing's troops wanted to come home (as did the prostitutes)... and President Wilson, expecting that the United States would soon be entering the war in Europe, wanted Pershing home.

For the United States, the Punitive Expedition highlighted the weaknesses in the army—for one thing, they started buying more trucks and transport. The German High Command also was interested in the expedition but, given its failures, concluded that the United States would be an unimportant factor in any military intervention in the War.

Dwight Eisenhower, George Patton and Douglas MacArthur—all important generals in the Second World War—gained early experience with the expedition. Eisenhower did not go to México, but his organizational skills rounding up supplies led to his rapid promotion in the Army. Patton, the famous tank commander, had his first experience with mechanized warfare here. MacArthur, as Allied Commander in the Philippines during the Second World War was the only officer ever to command troops fighting against, and later with, Mexican troops (after the Second World War, MacArthur wrote that the Mexican airmen were his best soldiers[122]).

---

[122] In 1935 the Philippines became a semi-independent commonwealth of the United States, with an independent military force. MacArthur was allowed to simultaneously hold rank as both a United States general and as Field Marshall of the Philippines. México's entry into the Second World War was largely due to support for full independence for the Philippines. By putting Mexican airmen under Filipino command, the Mexican government could not be accused by its critics of selling out to U.S. interests in the war.

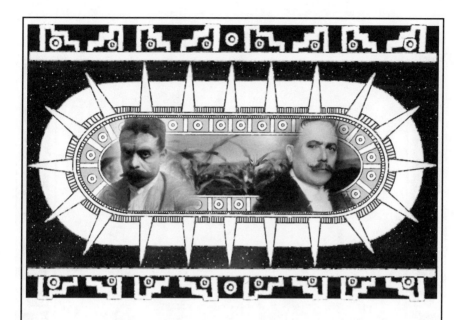

The bloody final act:
The Revolution, part 4

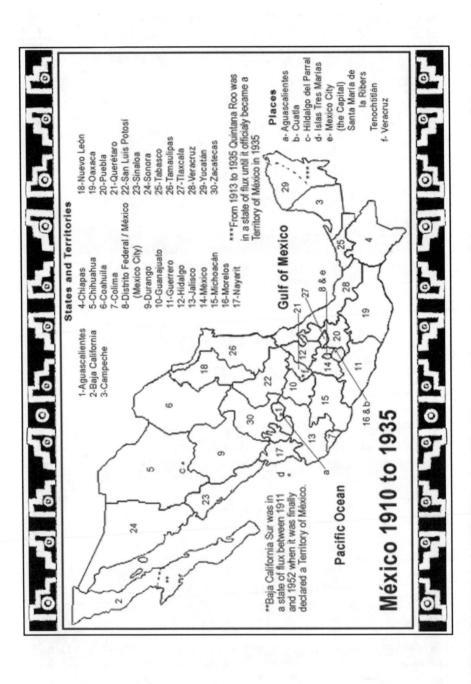

México 1910 to 1935

States and Territories

1-Aguascalientes
2-Baja California
3-Campeche
4-Chiapas
5-Chihuahua
6-Coahuila
7-Colima
8-Distrito Federal / México (Mexico City)
9-Durango
10-Guanajuato
11-Guerrero
12-Hidalgo
13-Jalisco
14-México
15-Michoacán
16-Morelos
17-Nayarit
18-Nuevo León
19-Oaxaca
20-Puebla
21-Querétaro
22-San Luis Potosí
23-Sinaloa
24-Sonora
25-Tabasco
26-Tamaulipas
27-Tlaxcala
28-Veracruz
29-Yucatán
30-Zacatecas

***From 1913 to 1935 Quintana Roo was in a state of flux until it officialy became a Territory of México in 1935

Places

a- Aguascalientes
b- Cuatla
c- Hidalgo del Parral
d- Islas Tres Marías
e- Mexico City (the Capital)
   Santa María de la Ribera
   Tenochtitlán
f- Veracruz

Gulf of Mexico

Pacific Ocean

**Baja California Sur was in a state of flux between 1911 and 1952 when it was finally declared a Territory of México.

Stitching together the revolutionaries

ONCE CORTÉS, WINFIELD SCOTT, Marshall Bazaine (on Maximilian's behalf), Juárez, Porfirio Díaz or Francisco I. Madero entered the Capital, México had had a new leader. Naturally, Carranza became "internal president" soon after Obregón entered the Capital in August 1914. Peace, love and reconciliation did not follow. Mexico City was still a battlefield. Carranza, after gaining recognition for his government at a Washington conference in October 1915, moved his capital to Querétaro and called for a constitutional convention.

In November 1916, with the Revolution seemingly over, Carranza expected some slight modifications to the 1857 constitution that had been written by his boyhood hero Benito Juárez, but nothing more. He seemed not to have understood that HIS México, run by elite landowners, was finished.

Obregón had stayed away from the Aguascalientes convention, but he'd had his feelers there. He had a good idea of what the more radical factions wanted and sensed Carranza's time (and world) had passed. Although a businessman and self-made millionaire, he'd also been influenced by the socialists and labor leaders he'd brought into his coalition.

As a bow to old Juárez supporters and anticlericals, even further restrictions were put on the Church. Obregón's labor allies received a huge benefit. Article 123 of the new Constitution was the first in any constitution anywhere to detail the rights of workers. The piecemeal changes over the course of the Revolution along with the basics of modern labor law—the eight-hour work day with one paid day off per week (the forty-eight-hour workweek was radical at the time), mandatory rest breaks, prohibitions on child labor—were all included. As were slightly odd things like a prohibition on paying employees in poolhalls, cafes or cantinas (unless that's where they worked, of course).

With a bow to Carranza's antiforeign biases, the new Constitution required foreign businesses to take a "Mexican jurisdictional personality", i.e., foreign-owned businesses had to become Mexican businesses and accept the rulings of Mexican courts. The prohibition on reelection (the original issue in the Revolution, when it started six years earlier) was strengthened. The rest of the document shocked Carranza, and at first he refused to accept it.

Most radical of all, and what particularly shocked Carranza, were restrictions on the amount of land any one person could own, destroying the hacendado class at one stroke, and the "new" theory of mineral and water rights. Although packaged as "socialist" it was the old Aztec idea that the waters and natural resources belonged to the king, but now, the king was the people, and the people were represented by the State.

Carranza finally did accept the new constitution but took his time in implementing the changes. Very few haciendas were broken up and he interpreted the clauses on natural resources as only bargaining chips for raising taxes on oil extraction or license fees for new drilling. He constantly worried about the possibility of U.S. intervention in the oil fields and preferred a gradual approach to enforcing the new order.

Even with only mild interpretation, there was armed resistance to various sections of the constitution for the rest of Carranza's tenure and lasting into Obregón's. The oil companies had hired a mercenary general, Manuel Peláez, to keep the Revolution and now the government out of the oil fields. They also financed various rebellions around the country, the most serious being the Cristeros of the mid-1920s who objected to strict interpretation of the anti-religious clauses and turned to terrorism. Ironically, Enrique Gorostieta y Velarde, the mercenary general hired by the religious rebels was that rarest of all Mexicans—an atheist.

Carranza finally became president, where he hoped mainly to prevent the shocking new constitution from coming into effect and more or less running México as he saw fit. This required eliminating the two remaining threats, Pancho Villa and Emiliano Zapata while missing the bigger threat of Obregón.

The world comes to México

WHEN OBREGÓN ENTERED MEXICO CITY in August
1914, it was not worldwide news. The First World
War had broken out two weeks earlier, and the European conflict
dominated the headlines.

Although, thanks to the mysterious coal shortage, Obregón
was the first to reach the Capital, Pancho Villa controlled large
sections of country bordering the United States (where most of
the gringo-owned businesses operated) and had set up his own
government. Zapata, who was not part of the constitutionalists, was
running large parts of the south and attracted some intellectuals,
mostly anarchists, to oversee the administration he reluctantly
felt necessary in his peasant society.

Of course, the winners were attracting new converts. Not all
intellectuals or workers supported Huerta or went over to Zapata.
More and more were coming over to the Constitutionalist side.
Obregón sensed that the Revolution had gone beyond conservatives like Carranza who had found their professional careers
blocked by the octogenarians that filled most positions in the late
Porfiriate. He began recruiting anarchists and socialists both as
advisors and as soldiers. José Clemente Orozco (no relation to

General Pascual Orozco), the one-armed graphic artist, served in the "red brigades". His paintings reflect the bitterness and savagery of the fighting.

Pancho Villa, who was less and less part of Carranza's coalition and more and more an independent force, set up his own revolutionary government in areas under his control without regard for whatever Venustiano Carranza thought was prudent or proper. Villa was, as in the movies, a crude country bumpkin, but then so was Porfirio Díaz. Like Porfirio, he was willing to draw on expert opinion, attracting qualified economists, agronomists and bankers and...military experts.

Both Villa and Obregón were willing to use foreign expertise. Obregón's artillery commander was a German-Mexican, Maximiliano Kloss. Obregón himself was a close student of German military theory and of the latest in military technology and theory when the First World War started.

Obregón was still a Carranza loyalist and kept his foreigners out of sight. Carranza distrusted foreigners, going so far as to reject Felipe Ángeles, who had defected from the Huerta government, as secretary of war. Felipe Ángeles, while still in his early twenties, had written several books on artillery and physics that were standard textbooks in European and U.S. military academies, and was considered one of the world's experts in his field. However, he'd studied in France and was too "French" for the Constitutional Chief. The scholarly, cultivated, "Frenchified" artilleryman had no problem working for Pancho Villa.

Villa, who professed his admiration for the United States to any journalist who would listen, attracted other foreigners as well. Most, like Colonel Giuseppe Garibaldi, the Italian liberator's grandson, or future film star Tom Mix, were adventurers, but he attracted some unusually loyal foreign fighters and supporters.

A footloose New Zealander, Bernard Fryberg, briefly served as a machine gunner in Villa's army. A wandering dentist, Fryberg would become a British hero in the First World War, a general during the Second World War, Governor-General of New Zealand and, as Lord Fryberg, Deputy Constable and Lieutenant Governor of Windsor Castle.

Retired bank robber Oscar Creighton, prized for his expertise with dynamite, joined the Revolution for love...not of Villa, but for a good woman. The story is that Creighton's girlfriend wouldn't marry him unless he proved he could perform good and selfless deeds. The Mexican Revolution (and Pancho Villa) gave him a chance to put his particular skills to use for the betterment of humanity. He died heroically in battle and after the Revolution was buried in the United States with full military honors.[123]

Even General Pershing at one point used foreigners. Only declassified in the 1970s were the details of a Bureau of Investigation (the forerunner of the Federal Bureau of Investigation) plot, which Pershing approved, to suborn Japanese volunteers in Villa's army. Most were machine gunners, but one, Gemichi Tatematsu, usually made breakfast for Villa. Tatematsu was supposed to poison Villa's morning coffee, but for some reason, Pershing's nemesis was late for an appointment that day and only had time for half a cup.

---

[123] Not the subject of Jim Tuck's *Pancho Villa and John Reed, Two faces of Romantic Revolution* (University of Arizona Press, 1984), Fryberg, Tom Mix, Creighton and Garibaldi are diverting sidelight to a "compare and contrast" study of the two early 20th-century revolutionaries.

The bronco buster broken

BY 1916, WITH VILLA MORE OR less out of the picture, the antirevolutionary figures having accepted their defeat, the only real opposition to the Constitutionalists came from the Zapatistas.

Emiliano Zapata, who had been fighting since before Díaz was overthrown, was the most traditional of the four surviving leaders. His fight was to protect his village lands. His family and his village had supported Maximiliano back in the 1860s, when it seemed the Austrian emperor would return village lands to the traditional owners.

The Zapatistas had no radical ideas beyond protecting their land. They were religious. Priests were not persecuted in Zapatista areas and several were active Zapatistas. One priest typed Zapata's correspondence for him; another translated his speeches into Náhuatl (the language spoken by many of his supporters, but not by the leader himself).

A Communist once tried to convert Zapata. Explaining that all profits would be shared among the workers undid the effort. "I'd shoot the man who took my corn!" the horse tamer replied. Zapata had been taught to read by his village storekeeper—an anarchist schoolteacher run out of Mexico City for his beliefs.

Mexican industrial workers had seen anarchism as close to their traditional rural values. Anarchists saw Zapata's traditional rural values as close to their theories. Land was worked in common but every man was his own boss.

It was the Anarchist intellectuals who "created" the radical Zapata. These intellectuals dominated the Aguascalientes convention and influenced the Constitution. Many of the most radical seeming parts of that document are based, not in modern political theory, but on peasant tradition.

Zapata was not about to lay down arms, nor did he think the Revolution was over. There were still large estates, and there were still men in charge of other men. Zapata's revolt would never be over. Carranza resorted to treachery.

Carranza dispatched the ambitious and amoral young Colonel Jesús Guajardo to Zapata. Guajardo claimed he was a defector wanting to join the Zapatistas. Zapata, not trusting Guajardo, asked for proof of his intentions. Guajardo had no qualms about murdering his own officers and presenting their corpses to the village horse tamer as "trophies". On 10 April 1919 Zapata agreed to meet with the alleged Federal turncoat, who greeted General Zapata with a military salute...and then opened fire on him. Zapata would die and fall from his horse, though he is most famous for quoting the Cuban poet José Martí's line, "It is better to die on your feet, than live on your knees." He is buried in Cuatla, Morelos. When Villa's remains were transferred to Mexico City in 1972, the Zapata family refused to allow Emiliano's remains to be transferred to the national monument because of their belief that the government had not lived up to Zapata's ideals and didn't deserve the honor.

Guajardo was promoted to general but was openly despised: not only officers, but ordinary soldiers refused to serve under his command.

Farewell to the Chief

THE CONSTITUTIONAL CHIEF, now President Carranza, would be the next to be eliminated. There were still rebellions, but the Revolution was more or less over. Carranza was president, but his term would be a short one. Under the new Constitution, elections were scheduled for 1919. Juárez had stayed on because of an emergency and had resorted to voter fraud on occasion. Why couldn't his disciple, Venustiano Carranza? When the excuse that the country was still unsettled was rejected, Carranza thought of Porfirio Díaz. Between 1884 and 1888, Díaz still ran the country, although his friend, Manuel Gonzales, wore the presidential sash. Carranza likewise chose a complete unknown, Ignacio Bonillas Fraijo (the Mexican ambassador to the United States) for the honor. Sneered at as "Meester Bonillas" (supposedly, Bonillas had been in the United States so long he didn't speak Spanish), the unknown still overwhelmingly "defeated" the wildly popular Álvaro Obregón.

The Revolution had another short war to go. Carranza had never been seen as anything but a figurehead by even the most committed Constitutionalist. Given his prickly relations with the foreign powers, he couldn't expect much support from the outside world, nor, given his reluctance to enforce the labor and land reform clauses in the new Constitution, from the people who had put him in power. Whether he was stubborn or just greedy, it's hard to say.

Carranza had evacuated his government to temporary locations many times. He loaded a train with soldiers, government documents and the national gold reserve and headed for Veracruz. The train never made it. The railway workers, like the army and most of the population, backed Obregón. As with Cortés' retreat from Tenochtitlán, the gold hindered the retreat. Pulling the extra weight kept the train to a slow crawl, and it was attacked again and again. Carranza was finally forced to flee on horseback and was killed in an ambush in a small village.[124]

Congress annulled Bonillas' election claiming it was fraudulent (which it was) and appointed Carranza's unexpectedly brilliant finance minister (and one of Obregón's brain trusters) Adolfo de la Huerta as interim president until new elections could be held and the popular ex-farmer, ex-schoolteacher, ex-mechanic and ex-general Obregón could assume office on 1 December 1920. The hallmark of the short de la Huerta administration was convincing Pancho Villa to surrender peaceably. Once Obregón was back in power, the flexible de la Huerta, who had been a shopkeeper, a small town banker, a soldier, finance minister and president, returned as finance minister. In 1924, when Obregón backed Plutarco Elías Calles for president, de la Huerta, backed by the oil men and foreign interests, mounted a short rebellion but it never amounted to much. Always flexible, he fled to Los Angeles, California, where he opened a dance studio. He later was allowed to returned to México, living quietly in the Capital until his death in 1955.

---

[124] Apparently, he committed suicide after being wounded several times.

Pancho Villa goes to school...
and maybe Yale

WHEN VILLA MADE HIS PEACE with the new government and agreed to surrender, he was given a full pension and a hacienda, so he settled down...as much as Pancho Villa could ever settle down.

Psychologists have speculated on Villa's mental condition. He could kill people without a second thought, even civilians. How many he personally murdered is still unknown,[125] perhaps hundreds. On the other hand, the man betrayed very real emotional depth. At a memorial service for Madero, he broke down and wept. His admiration and love for the little landowner was genuine.

He loved women...all too much. The stories of him raping rich men's daughters and wives are exaggerated, but he was sexually hyperactive. He married again and again and again. He went to the trouble to obtain marriage certificates for at least twenty-three wives, making him one of the champion bigamists of all times. None of his wives ever spoke of him as anything but loving and

---

[125] One story, possibly exaggerated, has Villa calmly gunning down an off-key singer who interrupted him during a newspaper interview.

gentle. His many children, both by his wives, by several girlfriends and by the one-night stands, all remember a particularly fond and doting father.

Villa loved children. It wasn't unusual for wealthy Mexicans then—and to some extent now—to shelter and educate homeless children. Melchor Ocampo, who was abandoned as a baby on the local hacienda's doorstep, was unusual only in inheriting his foster mother's fortune. Madero had twelve orphans living on his hacienda. Part of Villa's retirement package, when he agreed to surrender to the new Constitutional government, included a hacienda. He brought a trainload of street children from Mexico City—three hundred of them—to the hacienda to be given a decent home and the Villa name, and most important to Villa, an education.

Never having had a chance to go to school, the "Mexican Robin Hood" took to education with a vengeance. Adult literacy was Pancho Villa's last campaign. He had always understood the value of propaganda. Photographs of the ex-guerrilla leader taking classes along with the children or reading to them were used across México to advertise educational programs.

Villa's life is largely a mystery and so is his death. He had made his hacienda a model farm along the lines of Madero's visions. It had the schools, clinics, decent housing, its own electrical plant and telegraph office. Like the old haciendas, it had a company store, but with a twist. The hacienda was too far from Hidalgo del Parral for the workers to go shopping, so the hacienda bought wholesale and sold items below retail to workers and neighboring villages—a sort of revolutionary "Sam's Club".

Obregón's last surviving important rival was regularly featured in the press and was hardly forgotten. When the government, hoping to revive the economy, offered to lease some old haciendas to American companies, Villa's loud and public objections to the antirevolutionary idea forced the government to change its mind. When Obregón's government hoped to reestablish diplomatic relations with the United States there was one minor issue with the United States: the lingering resentment of Pancho Villa. His attack on New Mexico and a few raids into Texas could not be forgiven. After all, he had successfully attacked the gringos and might still cause problems.

So, what happened in Hidalgo del Parral on 20 July 1923 isn't a complete mystery. Villa was driving home from a christening when an unknown group of men—in a house rented the day before, then barricaded—opened fire on the car, killing all eight occupants. The men rode out of town on horseback and were never seen again. A state legislator later claimed to have masterminded the assassination, but there are too many questions about his claim to accept the story. At any rate, it doesn't explain the real mystery of Pancho Villa's death.

Three years after Villa was buried, someone dug up the corpse and stole the head. Who, or why? Woodrow Wilson can be eliminated as a suspect—he died in 1924. General Pershing wasn't known to hold grudges. Obregón's amputated arm (like Santa Ana's leg) had been saved and made the center of a memorial, but there is no evidence he went about collecting other people's body parts. Theories range from probable (old enemies still out for revenge—with their own ideas about justice—or ghoulish souvenir hunters), to implausible—a favorite with American newspapers of the time had Villa's head stolen by California gangsters in the pay of an Oklahoma spinster with an unrequited love for the ex-"movie star". There is another popular gringo suspect: George W. Bush's grandfather.

A story that has taken on popularity since the 1990s is that the head was taken by members of Yale's ultra-secret Skull and Bones society, which uses a human skull in its rituals. The society is connected with the York Rite Masons (Poinsett's "Yorkistas") and both George Bushes are members of the organization. Prescott Bush, father of the first George Bush, also a member, was inducted a few weeks after the head disappeared, and, it is said, was in México at the time Villa's head disappeared.[126] How anyone would have known that the student joining the organization in 1926 would have a son who ran the CIA and later would be president of the United States and a grandson who would also be president, is never quite explained. Or why they wanted the head. Villa's headless body was cremated and interred in the Monumento de la Revolución in Mexico City in 1972.

---

[126] There is also some evidence that Oliver Hardy, the comedian, was in Parral the day Villa was gunned down. Buying alcohol was illegal in the United States at the time and Hardy was a periodic binge drinker who would hole up in Mexican hotels away from the American public and press when he wanted to get drunk. Though Hardy collected Villa memorabilia, neither he nor Stan Laurel are thought to have any connection to the missing head.

Come together, right now

W HERE VILLA CULTIVATED THEM, Carranza despised gringos, and Obregón wasn't out to impress movie-goers but rather the movers and shakers. His main concern was to sell his leadership to the Mexican people and to win over the important businessmen, military officers and diplomats in the United States. He succeeded beyond anyone's expectations. After Huerta's army was destroyed, he turned his attention to the generals who had rebelled against Carranza. When he could, he bought them off (cynically—or realistically—he once observed that no Mexican general could withstand a barrage of gold pesos). Those who couldn't be bought off—like Pancho Villa—he destroyed. Eventually, he was forced to overthrow even Carranza when the older, conservative president tried to control the Revolution he once headed.

It's still Villa and Zapata who loom large in our thinking about México north of the border. Very few gringos have ever heard of Venustiano Carranza or Álvaro Obregón. For better or worse, it was the less romantic leaders—a fussy amateur scholar and a mechanic who wrote bad poetry and not the horse tamer or the bandit—who created modern México.

As president, Obregón showed the same innovative spirit he had shown as a farmer and soldier. Under his leadership, the chaotic forces of the Revolution were brought together. With great skill, soldiers and poets, anarchists and business owners, poor farmers and factory workers, intellectuals and indigenous peoples were united into one "Revolutionary family". Foreign interests—especially the oil industry—were mollified by dealing with a businessman-president. Under the "Bucarelli Agreement" (named for Avenida Bucarelli where the meetings were held) U.S. oil men and agricultural interests agreed to support U.S. and British diplomatic recognition for México and help the new government obtain credit in return for what seemed concessions to their own interests at the time. In reality, it forced the foreign companies to recognize their "Mexican personality" (they became subject to Mexican law), paving the way for their eventual peaceful takeover by the Mexican government. Only the foreign business interests and the Church were officially left outside the Revolutionary family—and that would cost Obregón his life.

In the conservative stronghold of Mexico City's Santa María la Ribera, a former nun, Madre Conchita, led weekly prayer services mixed with antigovernment rhetoric. Madre Conchita wasn't the first terrorist to operate as a religious leader, but she probably was one of the few women to lead a terrorist organization. William F. Buckley, the oilman involved with Henry Lane Wilson, is suspected of having financed the operation. Among her recruits was a part-time journalist and street artist named José de León Toral.

Obregón made the argument that he had never served a full term as president. Despite concern that he would be another Porfirio he was allowed to run and was elected in July 1928. On 17 July, he attended a victory banquet in San Ángel. Toral asked the president-elect if he could draw his picture. Obregón struck a pose and Toral shot him.

Toral was beaten by the police, quickly tried and executed. Madre Conchita was given a life sentence on the Islas Tres Marías—a prison colony off the Nayarit coast. She became a model prisoner, married a fellow convict (in a civil ceremony) and settled into her new life. William F. Buckley was finally deported. Obregón received a hero's funeral, a massive monument was raised in San Ángel to mark the site where he was murdered, and then he was more or less vilified by the historians.

During his presidency, Obregón hadn't made a pact with the devil, but he had made one with the United States and another with the Church. To get the economy moving after the Revolution, he had allowed the oil companies to pretty much continue as they always had under the Bucarelli Pact. He had ignored the Church and even encouraged it to perform social services and provide education where the State could not. Sadly, he ignored his old Yaqui and Mayo allies, encouraging large-scale operations to take their remaining lands. Finally, he had come to power the old-fashioned way—at the head of an army. The other military presidents—Santa Ana and Porfirio Díaz—are villains. Obregón seems to be another one. Having united anarchists, socialists, Communists, fascists, capitalists and traditionalists, he is a heretic to those who take one of those theories as the "true faith". Democrats blame him for México's lack of political parties for most of the 20th century. The one party that governed for most of the century doesn't see him as their founder. He was rich and unscrupulous. Mexicans have always distrusted the very rich. His talents—and his treachery—ran in too many directions to call him either a hero or a villain.

Obregón, the Revolution, and México itself are too complex to neatly classify. Perhaps it was inevitable that what emerged from that ten-year period owes so much to a man who embodied all three of the Aztec gods—Huitzilopochtli, the killer; Quetzalcóatl, the builder; Tezcatlipoca, the trickster.

The New Fire (1920–1946)

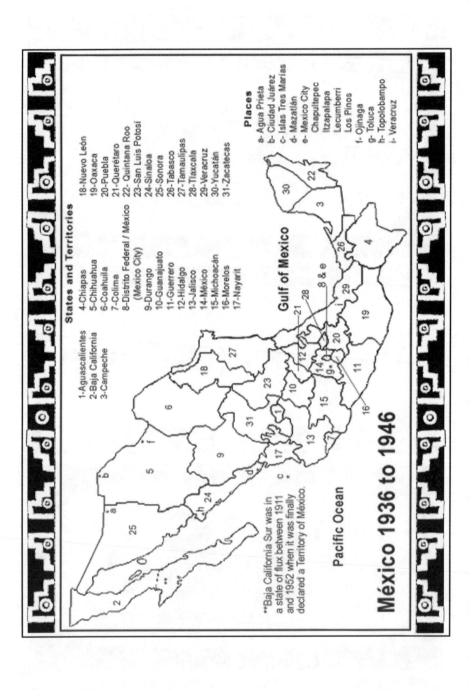

México 1936 to 1946

States and Territories

1-Aguascalientes	18-Nuevo León
2-Baja California	19-Oaxaca
3-Campeche	20-Puebla
4-Chiapas	21-Querétaro
5-Chihuahua	22- Quintana Roo
6-Coahuila	23-San Luis Potosí
7-Colima	24-Sinaloa
8-Distrito Federal / México	25-Sonora
(México City)	26-Tabasco
9-Durango	27-Tamaulipas
10-Guanajuato	28-Tlaxcala
11-Guerrero	29-Veracruz
12-Hidalgo	30-Yucatán
13-Jalisco	31-Zacatecas
14-México	
15-Michoacán	
16-Morelos	
17-Nayarit	

Places

a- Agua Prieta
b- Ciudad Juárez
c- Islas Tres Marías
d- Mazatlán
e- México City
Chapultepec
Itzapalapa
Lecumberri
Los Pinos
f- Ojinaga
g- Toluca
h- Topolobampo
i- Veracruz

Gulf of Mexico

Pacific Ocean

**Baja California Sur was in a state of flux between 1911 and 1952 when it was finally declared a Territory of México.

Stirring the ashes

I T IS ALWAYS TEMPTING TO make post-Conquest Mexican history fit the cyclical nature of the Aztec and Mayan cosmology. Sometimes, it almost works. Huitzilopochtli and Tezcatlipoca were certainly unleashed during the Revolution, but their brother, Quetzalcóatl was awakened. The story of the Revolution is not simply an account of warfare and political intrigue, but one of profound cultural and social changes as well.

The traditional Aztec or Mayan calendars had a fifty-two-year cycle. At the end of a cycle, waiting to see if the gods would keep the cycle turning, or on a whim, end it, the Aztecs held their collective breaths. People scurried to destroy the reminders of the past—for most people, simply throwing out their pots and pans and furniture—while they waited for the first signs that the world would continue, and life would go on. If it did, the Aztecs celebrated with the New Fire Ceremony, sacrificing a victim on top of the pyramid that became *Cerro de la Estrella* – The Star Hill, in the modern Mexico City neighborhood of Itzapalapa where residents now stage a reenactment of Christ's crucifixion on Good Friday – rekindling their fires that had been doused in anticipation of the event and renewing their lives. Had the Aztec calendar been followed, a New

Fire Ceremony would have been held in 1923—about the time Mexico as a whole heaved a sigh of relief that their world would continue, though profoundly changed.

Following the big parade in 1910 commemorating the one hundredth anniversary of the start of the War of Independence, Porfirio Díaz presided over a state banquet. The menu was French. After the 1921 parade, celebrating the one hundredth anniversary of independence, Álvaro Obregón presided over another state banquet. The entrée was *pavo en mole* – turkey smothered with mole sauce (a uniquely Mexican concoction of chocolate, nuts and chiles). After three hundred years of Spanish rule, followed by one hundred years of foreign invasion and financial control and forty years of neocolonialism under Porfirio; Obregón, along with the new leadership, was ready to create a truly Mexican México.

The Revolution was a messy affair that changed…everything. México's population fell by a million during the ten years of revolution (mostly through emigration to the United States, but also because of deaths in battle and disease.[127] Millions more were affected and uprooted by the Revolution. By comparison, the 1915–16 Battle of the Somme killed a million young Englishmen, Frenchmen and Germans and Europe as a whole lost nearly a quarter of its people in the same decade.

While we remember the leaders, most of the actual fighting was done by men and women (women served as not only camp followers but as soldiers and officers) who had never left their home village before. Zapata's troops were old-fashioned farmers, conservative and religious. Most had never been further from home than the next

---

[127] The "Spanish flu" apparently started in the American Midwest, coming to Europe with the U.S. soldiers in the First World War, then spreading around the world. In Europe, the warring countries were hit hardest, but under war-time restrictions, domestic news was censored. Spain, a neutral country, had a free press and thus, the disease became known as the "Spanish" flu. It was particularly virulent in México, killing somewhere between two and a half and four percent of the total population. The Europeans, weakened by the war, were even more devastated.

village. When they occupied Mexico City, the *chilangos* – residents of Mexico City – soon got over their fears of massacre and rape. The invaders were humble, polite, old-fashioned peasant farmers bewildered by the modern world. Many had never seen paper money and couldn't read anyway. Friendly chilangos had to help the invaders negotiate the urban landscape and show them how to use things like indoor plumbing and elevators in bewildering places like hotels, ride streetcars and how to avoid city-slicker con men. More than a few would become city slickers themselves.

Many of the soldiers were young, some very young. Mauricio Ramirez Cerón, who would live until 2005, was a Zapatista spy and scout when he was only fourteen. Future president Lázaro Cárdenas del Río was a sixteen-year-old clerk when he was commissioned as an officer. His only qualifications were that he could read and write, a skill highly in demand in his unit. Josefina Bórquez, a Zapotec woman, later befriended by Elena Poniatowska, was briefly a Constitutionalist colonel when her nineteen-year-old husband was killed…she was fifteen at the time. As with many others, both soldiers and civilians, the Revolution changed her life, taking her far from Oaxaca—including a brief stay (as a refugee) in Texas—to a new life in Mexico City.

Bórquez' time as a refugee was only a matter of a few days, but tens of thousands of others fled the violence, especially in the north, building new lives in the United States. While there had been Mexican-Americans since 1848, the influx of new immigrants created tremendous growth, especially in border regions. Besides a population boom in cities like Houston and Los Angeles, the large number of new Mexican-Americans created other challenges. The Roman Catholic Church created several new dioceses to oversee the new churches required by Mexican Catholics. As the Revolution progressed, and anticlerical measures began to be enforced, Mexican priests and nuns also took refuge in the United States, and the Church had to set up new seminaries throughout the borderlands. Two future Catholic saints, Rafael Guízar y Valencia (the exiled bishop of Veracruz) and Pedro de Jésus Maldonado Lucero (a young Chihuahua priest), worked and studied in Texas.[128]

George Romney, born in México and a very young child at the time, was part of an exodus of Mexican Mormons in 1912 to the United States. The Mormons were the children and grandchildren of Mormons who had settled in Chihuahua in the 1880s, but retained U.S. customs, and often thought—correctly or otherwise—that they were United States citizens. Romney, later president of the American Motors company and governor of Michigan, wanted to run for president of the United States in 1968. Being a "natural born" United States citizen is a requirement for the position, but since Romney did not become his party's candidate (Richard Nixon did), the question of whether or not he was a "natural born" citizen remain hypothetical.

In the insurgency a century before, it was the priests who led the armies. In the Revolution it was the schoolteachers and clerks. The Revolution was often a do-it-yourself affair. As with the insurgentes a century earlier, there were some unlikely leaders. Plutarco Elías Calles, the future president, was a part-time barroom bouncer and grade school teacher in 1911. While Zapata's forces carried banners reading *tierra y libertad*, Calles' troops fought for *tierra y libros* – land and [school]books.

Bureaucrats in Veracruz State, when they joined the Revolution, lacked uniforms: the only ones available were the striped suits from the state prison. In civilian life, these soldiers were mild-mannered accountants and file clerks, but as a fighting unit wearing prison garb, they cultivated their unearned reputation as a bunch of desperate, escaped murderers and thieves. Clothes DO make the man.

---

[128] San (Saint) Pedro de Jésus Maldonado Lucero was a relatively late victim of the violent anticlericalism of the 1920s. Although most clerical restrictions had been lifted by the early 1930s, Pedro was conducting clandestine services when he was arrested in 1936. During his arrest, he was hit in the head with a pistol butt and died of a broken skull. The Church considers him a martyr to the faith.

Military thinking in those years was focused on Europe, but it was in México that there were the real innovations. Wars are barbaric business, and in the days before antibiotics even relatively minor wounds were often fatal. It wasn't unusual for wounded soldiers to commit suicide[129] or have their friends shoot them, rather than leaving them to suffer. Obregón and others drafted the women who followed every Mexican army into a first aid battalion and found qualified nurses to train them. Working with the railroad men and with doctors, Mexican generals invented the Mobile Army Surgical Hospital.

Obregón's inventive mind came up with two completely new concepts—the fox hole (no one in history had apparently considered giving every soldier a shovel to create his own minitrench) and the naval air strike. Alberto Salinas (who started tinkering with his airplanes in 1911, mostly to get the engines to work in the low-oxygen atmosphere over the Sierra Madres, came up with the first prototype turbocharged engine), piloting the "Sonora", attacked a Federal gunboat in the world's first air-naval bombardment, eleven miles off the coast at Topolobampo (in northern Sinaloa State) on 14 April 1914, as Obregón's artillery and infantry attacked the port city. A few weeks later, on 6 May 1914, Obregón's forces did Mazatlán the dubious honor of hosting the Americas' first air-land bombardment.

It was technology that won on the battlefield, but the Revolution's radical changes were social. The Revolution gave social reformers the chance to experiment. *Soldaderas*[130] weren't the only women to gain real power. In the Yucatán, women were given the vote and served in state office. Women took on other tasks as well. Future

---

[129] Obregón had to be restrained from shooting himself when he lost his arm. Ironically, the man who saved his life committed suicide after the Revolution.

[130] The feminine form of the Spanish word for "soldier" may not be perfect Castilian, but the Mexicans needed a word for the women who served as equals in combat positions, long before the Soviet Union put women into combat positions in the Second World War.

president Miguel Alemán Valdés was only a boy when his mother—widowed by the war and needing to support her family—taught herself to drive, bought a dump truck and started a construction company (and later a bus line). Miguel grew up wealthy.

Educational, labor, legal, social and political reforms would come slowly, but were given a jump start by the Revolution. In México, where Porfirio Díaz had said, "nothing happens", everything had happened, and the world took note.

Although much of the country was devastated by the violence of the Revolution, the destruction was not absolute. Food shortages caused by damage to the railroads and the complete collapse of the peso were the worst problems. This mostly affected the cities. Those who lived on their own farms only heard about the fighting or learned about the Revolution when a new official showed up. As the fighting died down, and in areas only marginally affected, it was not unusual for local leaders, who in turn might or might not answer to any one of the bigger factions—the Constitutionalists, the Villistas or the Zapatistas—to stage their own mini-Revolution. Or the *campesinos* – the poor farmers – stopped paying rents to the haciendas and took over the land in the name of one or another revolutionary faction, knowing their oppressors had no way to stop them. As happened after the War of Independence, there were fighters who just never settled down or had nothing to go home to, so turned bandits. Either out of altruistic reasons or because the unsettled times revealed unexpected talents, local leaders often emerged, sometimes half-bandit themselves, who were only marginally under the control of the central government.

Obregón had cynically observed that "no Mexican general can withstand a barrage of gold pesos". He recognized that continuing the Revolution was bleeding the country, and it was better to buy the loyalties of the remaining factions, or where they were too powerful, simply to keep the leaders in place as part of the Revolutionary family. Where the local *cacique* – the old title the conquistadors gave to the local leaders they left in place – was too powerful to oppose, or where he might be useful, he was legitimized as a governor, state senator or given rank within the Federal army. In some places, the caciques were even more thoroughgoing revolutionaries than Obregón's cabinet. In regions like these, the central government more or less let whomever was in control remain, as part of the Revolutionary family. General Emilio Portes Gil thoroughly frightened his Texas neighbors when he became governor of the Socialist State of Tamaulipas.

In Yucatán—which had always been different than the rest of México, more Maya than Náhuatl—colonial racial patterns still existed. By law, *indigenes* – mostly Mayans – still could not walk on the sidewalks in Yucatán. Much of the barbarity in Kenneth Turner's *Barbarous Mexico* had occurred on Yucatán haciendas, which mostly grew henequen – a variety of *agave* – or sisal – yet another variety of *agave* – both raw materials for making rope before nylon was invented. There, a coalition of leftist intellectuals, Mayans and feminists took control under Governor Felipe Carillo Puerto. They collectivized the land and processing plants, and Mayans, for the first time, were brought into the government. Furthermore, Carillo Puerto pushed through voting rights for women, and brought radical feminists into his cabinet.

In the crucial oil state of Tabasco, Tomás Garrido Canabal was left as governor. He used his position to launch a crusade against the old enemies of the people—the rich and the Church. He broke up the large estates, slapped state taxes on the oil companies and persecuted the Church. He rewrote state laws to limit the Catholic priesthood to married men over sixty (since Catholic priests could not be married, this effectively outlawed priests) and decreed the death penalty for nonconforming priests. Garrido's Tabasco is the setting for Graham Greene's *The Power and the Glory*; about a bad priest who redeems himself through persecution.

Garrido's war against the Church took some strange forms. Making fun of clerical celibacy, he named his prizewinning seed bull after the Pope. For the edification and entertainment of the people, he had the cathedral in Villahermosa blown up. He took a more sinister turn with the "Red Shirts". Modeled on political gangs like Mussolini's "blackshirts" and Hitler's "brownshirts", the Red Shirts were a cross between the boy scouts and anticlerical stormtroopers. Though supposedly a youth organization emphasizing sports and education, they were sent to smash up churches, organize antireligious ceremonies (usually featuring desecration of religious objects) and to beat up Garrido's opponents. On the other hand, Garrido—quite advanced for his time—pushed education and gave women the vote.

Although skirmishes with antirevolutionaries would continue through the early 1920s, and there were still outbreaks from time to time—notably during the Cristero Wars in the 1920s; peasant uprisings and terrorist activities fueled by reaction to the government's official anticlericalism—México was relatively safe for foreigners.

There were businessmen looking for opportunities opened up by the social change, adventurous travelers, European immigrants fleeing much worse devastation at home and intellectuals fascinated by this strange, new, revolutionary México. A Lebanese peddler, displaced by the collapse of the Ottoman Empire, started a small business buying the goods and later the homes of wealthy families leaving Mexico City. The Slim family is now the richest in Latin America.[131]

The Hank family, a political and banking dynasty, started with a German soldier, who with no job and no home after his country's loss in the First World War, decided to take his chances in México. His son—who might have been president if not for the constitutional provision requiring presidents have Mexican-born parents—made the cynical observation that, "a politician who is poor is a poor politician". Various Hank family members—none of whom are poor, and some of whom are still politicians—own banks and telecommunications companies in several countries, including the United States.

---

[131] According to Forbes Magazine, the trader's oldest son, Carlos Slim Helú, is the richest man in the world.

The Mennonites, a religious sect of communal farmers, forced out of Germany in the 18th century for their religious beliefs, found refuge in Russia, where Catherine the Great welcomed them for their farming skills. However, the Mennonites are strict pacifists, and Russia instituted a universal draft in the 19th century. The religious farmers found new land in the United States and Canada. Canada was a British territory and automatically England's ally during the First World War. German speaking and opposed to war on religious principles, the Canadian Mennonites were also distrusted for their "Communist" ideas about land ownership. Encouraged by, of all people, Pancho Villa (who had similar ideas about land ownership), the Mennonites founded still-important farming communities in Chihuahua State.

Something to write home about

REVOLUTIONARY MÉXICO ATTRACTED more than just the desperate and dispossessed. Writers with an agenda were the first. To launch his journalistic career, John Reed crossed the border at Presidio, Texas to Ojinaga, Chihuahua during the battle where Ambrose Bierce, a war correspondent since the American Civil War, probably died. Reed helped create the Pancho Villa legend.[132] Just who seduced who is an open question, but Villa's willingness to be interviewed made Reed a star. Villa never bothered with political theory, but he was always agreeable to foreign reporters.

Villa wasn't much for taking his ideas from texts, but 19th-century German economic theories of Karl Marx' *Communist Manifesto*, as explained by John Reed, were close enough to Pancho Villa's own hopes for the future. He had no objection to being labeled a "Communist", which brought him some international

---

[132] Reed was the model for Johnny Sutton, the gringo reporter in the 1932 Hollywood film "Viva Villa". It was Ben Hecht, the screenwriter who wrote several comedies about reporters, who was responsible for Villa's alleged last words: "Tell them I said something important."

support he wouldn't have had otherwise. Reed moved on to greater fame, founding the Communist Labor Party of America and writing about and participating in the Russian Revolution. He died of typhus in Moscow and was buried in the Kremlin wall.

Alma Reed, a radical feminist, and Frank Tannenbaum, an anarchist, came...and stayed.

Alma Reed (no relation to John Reed) was a California freelance writer, a friend of Jack London and a radical feminist for her time. Fascinated by what was going on in the Yucatán, where Carrillo Puerto's socialist administration was bringing in feminist leaders to change the culture of the tradition-bound state, Reed wrangled an assignment to interview the governor and the women's leaders. She got the story and also a fiancé. She would have become Mrs. Carrillo Puerto if the governor had not been assassinated.

The state's main industry was henequen production (henequen was the main source of fiber for cheap rope in the early 20th century). Beyond breaking up the grower's estates, the Carrillo Puerto administration was determined to turn the processing plants over to the workers. The producers and manufacturers naturally turned to "hit men". Reed was out of the country buying wedding clothes when Carrillo Puerto was murdered. Heartbroken, she returned to México, writing on women's issues and politics for the rest of her life.

Frank Tannenbaum and Pancho Villa both had their photos on the front page of the *New York Times* in October 1911. Tannenbaum was leading a student demonstration at Columbia University, and Villa was attacking Ojinaga. Tannenbaum was very much a New Yorker and in common with other student radicals of his era, an anarchist. He gave up on trying to change New York and moved to México to pursue graduate research in 1918. Despite his urban background, he became an expert on Mexican agriculture and rural education, writing sensitive and perceptive books on both over his long career. Despite his political leanings, he was the go-to guy used by both Mexican and U.S. diplomats in the 1930s and 40s.[133]

Other foreigners, attracted by the "new" country were quick to follow. Katherine Anne Porter, a young Texan with left-wing sympathies but no particular political agenda, arrived in 1920. Porter—though her academic reputation has suffered since her death because she had the "misfortune" of writing a popular bestseller (*Ship of Fools*, a 1962 novel dealing with a ship sailing to Germany from Veracruz during the Nazi era) that became a successful Hollywood movie in 1965—along with Tannenbaum and Langston Hughes (who spent much of his adolescence in Toluca) are among the very few English-language writers whom contemporary Mexican literary scholars say understood México and Mexicans.

Porter had grown up in an English-speaking Protestant family, but in rural south Texas most of her friends and neighbors were Mexican-American Catholics. She was familiar with Mexican religious and family customs and—unlike most foreign writers—accepted them as normal human behavior, not colorful local ceremonies to be written about as something exotic. Working as a teacher and journalist, she spent the rest of her life writing fiction, poetry, art criticism and political essays about her adopted country. Unlike most other foreign writers, she knew Mexican writers, artists and political leaders and played an important role in explaining México to outsiders.

Giving a leg up to revolutionary ideas—two legs, actually—while she wrote her stories of Mexicans bewildered by the modern world, Porter supported herself by giving dance lessons, among other things. This brought her to the attention of filmmaker Roberto Turnbull, whose 1927 "Mitad y mitad" pokes fun at the modern world—including the theories of Sigmund Freud. "Mitad y mitad"

---

[133] Tannenbaum lost favor with the Mexican government in the early 1950s when he published his opinion that the Alemán administration's concentration on industrial development—at the expense of agriculture and mining—was a serious mistake.

deals with a young man in a Mexico City basement apartment's growing obsession with a woman's legs exposed by the still new and shocking, "short" skirts then coming into style. The legs were Miss Porter's.

Anita Brenner was born in Aguascalientes (her Lithuanian father had been recruited to manage one of the hot springs in Aguascalientes while he was living in Chicago running a Russian steam room), but her family fled the Revolution in 1911, and she, like Porter, was raised in Texas. Feeling somewhat out of place as the little Mexican girl in Texas schools—and the Jewish girl to her Mexican-American playmates—she considered herself a Mexican, though one with an outsider's perspective that give her the opportunity to look at her native country (which she had left when she was five years old) with scientific detachment. In 1921, she returned to México, where she wrote her first anthropological study, *Idols Behind Altars*. Later, as the *New York Times'* first female correspondent, she was also a secret agent—though whether for the Mexican government or the Communist Party has never been clear—and arranged for Leon Trotsky's escape from Europe to his Mexican asylum.[134] Recognizing México's importance as an ally during the Second World War and conscious that México's Revolution—and México's people—had been negatively presented in the United States for years, Brenner was recruited by the U.S. government to write propaganda that might undo the damage. The result was *The Wind That Swept Mexico*—still one of the best short books on the Mexican Revolution and its aftermath. As a Communist, she was forced out of her job after the war and returned to México. In the post-war period, with tourism becoming increasingly important to the Mexican economy, she became a pioneering editor of Mexican travel magazines.

---

[134] Brenner's exact role in arranging for Trotsky's flight to México is still controversial. Brenner never talked about it, and what little is known was uncovered by her daughter, the art historian Susannah Glusker, who wrote a biography of her radical mother. From the evidence she uncovered, Glusker was unable to determine if her mother worked for the Mexican Communist Party, the Mexican government or Stalin's secret police.

The African-American writer, Langston Hughes, also had Mexican ties. His father, trained as a lawyer, found it impossible to make a decent living under the racial segregation laws then in effect in the United States. The elder Hughes moved to México and became a factory manager in Toluca; then sent for his teenaged son in 1919. Coming to México changed Langston's life. His father had planned to send his son to a racially-tolerant country like France to study engineering. Instead, Langston wrote his first poem on the long train ride from Kansas City to Mexico City. Like many gay teens before and since, Hughes was uncomfortable around his father, preferring the company of the young Mexicans he met while working as an English teacher. Although he lived primarily in the United States the rest of his life, he spent long periods in México (for a time, he and French photographer Henri Cartier-Bresson shared an apartment near the capital's Parque Alameda) and wrote extensively on Mexican folkways and customs. Additionally, he obliquely attacked U.S. racism by way of comparison to México's relative tolerance.

D. H. Lawrence saw a very different México and had very different ideas about race. Unlike the others, the British writer spoke only rudimentary Spanish and had very little contact with even English-speaking Mexicans. With his wealthy wife's money, Lawrence toured the country in a rented limousine, looking at archaeological sites and visiting other English speakers. He then holed up in the Hotel Monte Carlo in Mexico City to write a novel about México that propounded his racist theories.

Lawrence apparently read the same version of the Quetzalcóatl legend that Maximilian had, and he held somewhat similar racial ideas. To Lawrence, the "Indians" were a more natural people and therefore racially superior. Racial mixing was a tragedy that weakened a "race". The result was *The Plumed Serpent*, a confusing story of a Quetzalcóatl cult revival and a destructive love affair between an "Indian" and a "white woman". The best that can be said about Lawrence is that he was a very ill man (he was dying of tuberculosis) who wrote well on ideas that were respectable in his time. Although Lawrence proposed that the "Indians" were the superior race, his novel is still popular among neo-Nazis.

Graham Greene, another clueless Englishman, had better luck with his reputation. Greene was a newspaper reporter who wrote detective fiction. In 1938 he was also a devout Catholic convert. England had broken diplomatic relations with México when Cárdenas expropriated the oil industry, and there was strong anti-Mexican sentiment among the British. While the Cárdenas government and the Church had come to an understanding, the rabidly anticlerical Garrido Canabal was still the cacique running Tabasco. Hired by a Catholic newspaper, Greene went to Tabasco to write an undercover report on religious persecution. He was an incompetent spy and an unhappy tourist—but a brilliant writer. His travels took him though parts of the country that were still extremely unsafe—at one point, a steamship line only agreed to sell him a ticket if he could prove he had life insurance! The result was *The Lawless Roads*,[135] a spirited defense of the Catholic Church and an attack on the Mexican Revolution. It's a useless travel guide but is an extremely amusing book.

From his experience, Greene also gathered the material for his first major novel, *The Power and the Glory*, in which an alcoholic, failed priest discovers his faith through his persecution. A towering figure of 20th-century literature, Greene returned again and again to the problem of holding onto one's beliefs (often Roman Catholic beliefs) under stress. Several of his later novels—even comic ones like *Travels With My Aunt* and *Our Man in Havana*—feature clueless Englishmen adrift in Latin America.

---

[135] Also called *Another México*. Greene's U.S. and British publishers selected different titles.

Bibles for the illiterate

WHILE FOREIGN WRITERS—Tannenbaum and Porter in particular—brought new attention to the creative flowering in México after the Revolution, it was the Mexican visual artists and the relatively obscure (outside of Latin America) academic José Vasconcelos Calderón, who created México's new image. Vasconcelos would have spent his life teaching philosophy courses to upper-crust twits if it hadn't been for the Revolution.

Even though Obregón would favor a more socialist economic system, he had no problem working with conservatives who were experts in their particular field. While still roving the country with his army, he had put together a "think tank" from all political persuasions and charged them with coming up with practical solutions to the country's overwhelming problems. José Vasconcelos was an extremely conservative, elitist philosophy professor but he had a practical turn of mind. He served as Secretary of Education under interim President de la Huerta (between Carranza's death and Obregón's election) and later under Obregón. He and his staff, with full government support, turned to whatever innovative and unorthodox solutions they could find to what was seen as México's single largest problem—illiteracy and the "backwardness" of the countryside.

Vasconcelos—helped immeasurably by the fact that both Obregón and Plutarco Elías Calles had been rural teachers—began recruiting a new kind of teacher. The village *maestros* or *maestras* – teachers – were to be the "vanguard of the Revolution". Official propaganda equated teachers with soldiers: ignorance and poverty were the enemy...books and knowledge the weapons. Although poorly paid, the teachers were dedicated and tough. During the Cristero War, when religious fanatics were likely to assassinate village teachers as representatives of the secular state, sometimes the village "schoolmarm" was armed. In the 1947 propaganda film, "Rio Escondido", the glamorous María Felix played against type as a sickly, recent teaching school graduate sent to clean up "the worst town in México". She does—as María Felix always did—but only by fighting a typhus epidemic and winning a wild shootout with the villains. Somehow, she also manages to teach the children the story of Benito Juárez.

For most rural Mexicans, the arrival of the village schoolteacher was the beginning of the Revolution. The teacher came armed with the blueprints for a schoolhouse. Vasconcelos' staff had designed a standard plan for a building that could be put up by untrained labor using whatever the local building material happened to be—adobe, brick or wood. The schools only had walls halfway to the roof, but in warm climates windows could be added later, before the rainy season...or walls added in cold climates. If there was need for more classrooms, the same plan could be used to add on to the basic model, which originally included a residence for the teacher. Within a month of arrival, a teacher was expected to have their school up and running.

Faced with designing a standard curriculum for both rural and urban students, the former philosophy professor suddenly found himself talking about saddlebags and mules in cabinet meetings. School books were no problem in Mexico City, or on the rail lines. Vasconcelos' team had to consider how to deliver a comparable education to the eighty percent of Mexicans who still lived in communities of less than twenty-five hundred people not served by roads or railroads. Everything from the weight of book covers to the reporting forms the school superintendent needed was considered...and how much a mule could carry. Everything needed to open a primary school, from the texts to the teacher (and his or her personal belongings) was calculated, based on what one mule could carry.

The "mule school" was only the start of a tradition of innovative educational techniques. One of the few benefits given these underpaid agents of the Revolution was a free subscription to one of the national papers' Sunday editions. The teachers, especially those in roadless areas, might get their paper a week or month late, but they did eventually receive it. So, rather than burden the mules with lessons that wouldn't be given for months, texts, especially for adult literacy programs, were inserted as advertisements in the paper. These ongoing lessons were not only literacy lessons but also included other "revolutionary" material—the need for protecting water supplies from contamination, the importance of personal hygiene and the need to eat nutritious food.

One unintended consequence of the revolutionary attitude towards education was a change in traditional women's clothing. The newspapers, for whatever reason, ran the education department advertisements in the fashion section. Women in traditional areas, whose style of clothing hadn't changed in centuries, adapted the latest in Mexico City haute couture to their own needs. What are today considered traditional indigenous Mexican costumes are often partially based on 1920s urban chic.

The innovative spirit of Vasconcelos continued long after he was gone. Radio, television and the Internet have all been pressed into service to provide rural education. In the early 1960s, México was the first country to use satellites to beam basic education into hard-to-reach communities. Vasconcelos himself is credited with inventing the still successful adult literacy program known in English as "Each one teach one". By law, every literate Mexican was supposed to teach one illiterate or pay someone else to give the lessons. Everyone fully expected people to evade the law, but it was successful enough to double the literacy rate within a few years. With innovative primary education, México managed to reduce illiteracy from nearly ninety percent in 1920 to about eight percent today. Most illiterates in México today are older indigenous women who speak a language other than Spanish.

Higher education was only available to the wealthy in 1920. Vasconcelos reformed the University, reinstituting the old University of México as the Autonomous National University of México (UNAM)—constitutionally guaranteeing its operating budget and its self-governance—it became the model for other federal and state universities. UNAM, with three hundred thousand students today, is the largest university in the Americas.

Vasconcelos, for all his brilliant service to the Revolution, went into eclipse, first breaking with Calles and later turning against the Revolution. With mostly conservative and middle-class support, he ran unsuccessfully for president in 1931. As he moved further and further from political power, he became ever more vocal about his racial theories, specifically that *la raza cosmica* – the mixture of European, indigenous and African "races" – was superior to any of the single races. Opposites attract: Vasconcelos became an admirer of—and apologist for—Adolf Hitler. His career ender was becoming the editor of a disreputable pro-Nazi newspaper, funded by the German Embassy until the start of the Second World War, when it was shut down by the government.

Although always acknowledged as the father of UNAM, he was primarily known for his motto *"Todos por mi raza"*[136] – everything for my people. It wasn't until very recently that his accomplishments in other areas of education have been recognized. The new National Library is named in his honor.

---

[136] Given Vasconcelos' association with racist ideology, it's easy to forget that *"raza"* only incidentally means "race" in the sense the word is used in English. The *Diccionario de la Lengua Española* (21st Edition) lists seven definitions. The first refers to nationality and only the last talks about *"raza"* in the sense of ethnicity or bloodlines.

Orozco gets the last word

V ASCONCELOS HAD HIS BLIND SPOTS, even when it came to education. He never liked the movies, so neglected cinema, and despite some pioneering filmmakers like Roberto Turnbull, Mexican films did not become important until the 1940s. One of the few uses his educators made of film was a propaganda newsreel showing Pancho Villa attending classes along with his many adopted children. However, he did understand the importance of the visual arts.

Although his tastes ran to the 19th-century decorative style, he recognized that in a country that was mostly illiterate the only way many could understand the Revolution was through pictures. The problem for Vasconcelos was that the artists he preferred were "politically incorrect"—they had been on the wrong side of the Revolution. The revolutionary artists were—politically and artistically—not his cup of tea, but he had no choice but to employ them to create "Bibles for the illiterate".

A probably untrue story has the big three of the Mexican artists—Diego Rivera, David Alfaro Siqueiros and José Clemente Orozco—sitting at a café discussing their murals. Rivera and Siqueiros maintain the Marxist position that the artist's duty is to educate the masses. Orozco buys some decorated traditional pots from a passing vendor, presents them to his two artistic comrades and says, "The artist is the student of the masses."

Orozco, the oldest of the three, had not let the loss of a hand in a childhood accident prevent him from becoming an established artist and cartoonist even before the Revolution. Of the three, he was the only one to see combat, having served with Obregón's "Red Brigade" of union workers (Orozco belonged to an anarchist typographers' and graphic artists' union.) In his murals and other works, Orozco realistically portrayed the horrors of war and was ambivalent about the results of the Revolution.

An art critic later said that Orozco painted the Revolution that was, and Diego Rivera painted the Revolution that should have been. Rivera, a very big man with an even bigger ego,[137] had been in Paris, making a name for himself as a cubist in the style of Pablo Picasso, during most of the Revolution. An early member of the Mexican Communist Party, Rivera often included identifiable "Communist" icons. In the National Palace, where Rivera painted a huge mural of the history of México, Karl Marx smiles down from heaven like God the Father in Renaissance murals, at a peaceful future of happy peasant farmers, helpful soldiers and schoolchildren.

Rivera's murals and paintings became such a standard of 20th-century mural art that many people just assume the Mexican Revolution was a Communist one. In his later years, Rivera somewhat mellowed, producing portraits of the rich and famous as well as a late, gentle mural featuring nearly everyone who was anyone in

---

[137] Even his biographer, Bertram Wolf, later admitted that he had no idea of how much of Rivera's life story was true. Rivera was one of those people who wanted to be the hero of every story, the bride at every wedding and the corpse at every funeral. He claimed to have been part of pre-Revolutionary activities that happened while he was living in Paris, where the very fat artist claimed he had turned to cannibalism to keep from starving to death. His outrageous lies, however, attracted groupies—especially naïve female ones—long before the term was invented for rock stars. That seems to have been the purpose of those tall tales.

Mexican history enjoying a *Sunday at Alameda Park*, but centered on his artistic mentor, the then almost-forgotten graphic artist José Guadalupe Posadas.[138]

If Orozco painted the revolution that was, and Rivera the revolution that should have been, David Alfaro Siqueiros painted the revolution to come. A committed Communist revolutionary, Siqueiros varied his artistic career with guerrilla warfare. When Leon Trotsky, the military and political genius behind Lenin's successful Communist revolution in Russia was driven into exile by Stalin, he was eventually given political asylum in México. Siqueiros, a loyal follower of Joseph Stalin, led a machine gun assault on Trotsky's home. After his release from prison, he continued to paint, often experimenting with industrial materials, until he was thrown back into prison in 1960 for his part in a railroad strike.

Locked up in Lecumberri, Porfirio's old "model prison", the artist kept himself busy by painting a mural on his cell's walls. When the old prison was remodeled in the 1990s to house the National Archives, special consideration was given to incorporating the former political prisoner's work in the government office.

Upon his release in 1964, he mostly stuck to allegorical works dealing with outer space and the future of humanity and experimenting with new techniques. Siqueiros used industrial grade paint and machine parts for his last major work, *The March of Humanity*, at Mexico City's World Trade Center (criticized by his fellow Communists because it would only be seen by foreign tourists and the few business people working in the building).

---

[138] Foreigners will be surprised that a book about México says little about Rivera's wife, Frieda Kahlo. In her lifetime, Kahlo was better known as Rivera's sometime wife than as an artist in her own right, and her artistic reputation is much higher among foreigners than among Mexicans, who see her as a self-centered artist, endlessly painting herself, in an era and among a culture that valued art for the masses. Kahlo often used Mexican images, but her artistic style is European surrealism.

Lesser known muralists, notably Juan O'Gorman[139] and the U.S. born Pablo O'Higgins, as well as the "big three", covered every wall they could find, inside and outside of México. Orozco painted a history of the Americas on the walls of Dartmouth College in Vermont, and Rivera, despite being a Communist, was happy to work for both the Detroit Public Library (paid for by arch-capitalist Henry Ford) and Rockefeller Center. Because the latter work was destroyed for being "too Communistic", Rivera repainted it on the walls of the Palacio de Bellas Artes in Mexico City. He got his revenge on the Rockefellers, painting in a smug John D. Rockefeller Jr. enjoying a cocktail while workers are attacked by police, and depicting John D. senior as a monkey. Centering the mural, showing a workers' strike in New York, is the founder of the Soviet Union, Vladimir Lenin, shaking hands with a black and a white worker.

Mexican muralism, the "bibles for the illiterate" had a profound impact on art throughout the world. In countries with as different political systems as the United States and Soviet Union, murals glorifying the "common man" were standard throughout the 1930s. Worldwide, revolutionary art followed Mexican models. Even Rivera's mentor, Pablo Picasso, adapted the new mural style to his great antiwar painting, *Guernica*.

Within México itself, murals—often done by anonymous or semi-anonymous folk artists—are still produced and found on or in public buildings throughout the country.

---

[139] Actually, one O'Gorman mural is very well known to visitors to México. His 1939 *La conquista del aire por el hombre,* graces the main lobby of Benito Juarez Airport in Mexico City.

The Schoolmaster

IN THE 1930s, a Mexican diplomat quipped, "My country is the world's largest exporter of oil painters…but only the number two exporter of oil." Artistic recognition was nice, and the intellectuals were concerned about the rural farmers, but it was oil that paid the bills.

During the First World War, the British had discovered just how dependent they were on Mexican oil. Rather than deal with the new government, the Aguila Oil Co., joined by the American and Dutch producers, had hired their own army, commanded by a mercenary general, Manuel Peláez, to keep the Revolution out of their oil fields (and revolutionary ideas away from their workers). Faced with the new constitution that specified that the people of México—not the foreign oil companies—owned the oil, Peláez and his army stayed on the payroll after the fighting stopped. Or rather, Peláez stayed on. Basically, the oil companies paid "protection money" to Peláez, who kept the government and the unions out of his territory. Only slowly did the government regain control.

As the price of diplomatic recognition by the United States, Obregón had let the oil companies more or less have their own way. Rejection of the "Bucarelli Pact" by the army led to a small revolt and gaining control of the oil facilities was a huge factor in Mexican foreign and domestic policy for the next several years.

Plutarco Elías Calles was the illegitimate son of a village drunk and an irresponsible mother. Rejected by good "church going" people, he survived a Dickensian childhood until the Calles family gave him both a home and a name. With enough stability in his life to obtain an education he was able find work as a schoolteacher, though he needed to moonlight to make ends meet as a barroom bouncer in the small, tough border town of Agua Prieta. He maintained a serious resentment towards alcoholism and the Church. When the Revolution came to the border, he—like other small town schoolteachers—was considered the local "educated man" and put in charge of a small unit serving under Obregón.

Although not a particularly gifted military commander, he was ruthless. He destroyed Pancho Villa at Agua Prieta by convincing the U.S. Army to assist in transporting Mexican reinforcements through the United States to Douglas, Arizona on the other side of the border, effectively cutting off any chance for the Villistas to escape north from his trap. Agua Prieta didn't have electricity at the time, so for good measure, Calles "borrowed" floodlights in Douglas and powered them with extension cords run across the border. Villa, attempting a night raid, never stood a chance against overwhelming firepower, floodlights and (unconfirmed) artillery support from Arizona.

Though more conservative than the millionaire turned socialist Obregón, Calles was completely loyal to his leader. Obregón, who had been expected to name former interim president Adolfo de la Huerta as his chosen successor selected Calles instead.

Obregón, desperate for diplomatic recognition from the United States, found disputes with the Americans who lost their haciendas easily settled. Besides, his government could argue that the land seizures weren't aimed at Americans or at foreigners, but at all landowners, and his government was willing to pay compensation. Which they did. The oil companies were different. They were all foreign-owned. The big U.S. companies, backed by the Dutch and British companies pressed the U.S. government to withhold recognition until their rights were guaranteed. Obregón, desperate to restart the economy and needing diplomatic recognition to allow the country to negotiate loans and obtain working capital, finally worked out a treaty with the United States that allowed the oil companies to continue business more or less as usual...though they would at least have to acknowledge that the Mexican Constitution was valid. In short, the oil companies could ignore it for now.

The oil agreement cost Obregón much of his military support. The more radical officers felt that a "gentleman's agreement" with the United States (and the oil companies) mocked what they'd been fighting for. Others, such as Manuel Peláez, the mercenary who had originally been hired by the oil companies to keep the Revolution out of the oil fields and then ran a protection racket keeping the government out, saw advantages for himself in a weak central government. Still others wanted a return to the Porfirian system. Former president and then finance minister, Adolfo de la Huerta was prevailed upon to revolt. It was a short-lived revolt.

The army officers who joined in soon realized that most of the financial backing came from the oil companies, and Obregón had shrewdly responded by calling on the two groups that supported him. Farmer and labor militias quickly put down the rebellion. De la Huerta, luckier than most rebels, escaped to Los Angeles. The ending of the short de la Huerta revolt just left the sore point of national control of oil to Obregón's successor, Plutarco Elías Calles.

Obregón's chosen successor, Calles, cut the military budget and increased aid to rural areas. Having recognized the value of the urban workers, though distrusting the anarchists and Marxists, Calles gained worldwide recognition for naming a union president as Secretary of Labor. Unfortunately, Luis Napoleón Morones—the non-Marxist, non-anarchist Electricians' Union President—was not one of his better personnel decisions.

Power corrupts, it's said: Morones was absolutely corrupt. Fanny Calderón de la Barca was amused in the 1840s by the former tailor turned general who draped his wife in diamonds. No one was amused when Morones began sporting a diamond ring on every finger. He openly solicited bribes, but he kept the unions quiet, mostly by concentrating on noncontroversial "lunch bucket issues". He'd call off strikes (or have the strike leaders killed) in return for a nominal increase in the union workers' wages or benefits. He was hated, especially by the workers, but left Calles free to concentrate on rural reform and deal with the oil industry.

The government continued to chip away at the special rights of the oil companies, winning concessions on taxation and labor rights while Peláez' control weakened. Until he was deported, American wildcat oil man William F. Buckley remained a thorn in everyone's side, forcing one exasperated U.S. negotiator during the period to suggest the oil companies simply hold out until only Buckley was still rejecting the Mexican offer, then assume they had the best deal possible. There would have been slow, but peaceful progress, if Calles hadn't held a grudge.

Cristo Rey

CALLES HATED LIQUOR AND PRIESTS with about equal passion. As revolutionary governor of Sonora, he'd been able to do something about drunks. He made public intoxication a capital offense. No one took him seriously until he had a village drunk marched out and shot in front of his entire community.[140]

A loyal subordinate during the Revolution, Calles was Obregón's choice for his successor to the presidency in 1924. But, where Obregón had overlooked most restrictions on the Church (and to help meet his educational goals, he had encouraged the Catholic Church and Protestant organizations to run schools where there were serious teacher shortages), Calles was inflexible. The Church had quietly recovered since Juárez' round of nationalizations, and Obregón, desperate to provide education, had allowed the Church to run schools where states or the federal government couldn't, or where church schools already existed. In July 1926,

---

[140] Liquor prohibition—which was written into the U.S. Constitution between 1919 and 1933—is usually associated with religious groups in the United States, but prohibition was a common cause for all manner of revolutionaries and social reformers in the early 20th century. Revolutions, after all, seek to remake society and correct its ills. Revolutionaries are serious people and generally puritanical.

Calles ordered that the anticlerical provisions in the Constitution be followed to the letter. All schools, convents, monasteries and other church-run facilities were closed. All church property was nationalized, including the houses of worship. On July 31st, the Catholic Church responded in a way only Mexicans could respond. The new Revolutionary Constitution granted all workers the right to act collectively in their own interests, i.e., strike. The priests had been following Church directives when they refused to follow the new rules, but the government hadn't intended to allow these "special workers" to go on strike.

The "strike" was to last three years. Religious believers, financed by holdovers from the Porfiriate and encouraged by the most reactionary of the clergy, launched a three-year guerilla campaign that would lead to up to eighty thousand deaths, mostly among poor rural people backing the clerical side in the struggle. Soon after the revolt started, an attack on the Guadalajara-Mexico City train, meant to be a robbery, instead became an atrocity in which over one hundred passengers were murdered in the name of religion.

The Pro Suárez brothers, both priests (and later considered saints by the Catholic Church) were executed for their connection to an attack on General Obregón in 1927. The brothers were probably innocent of anything more than giving moral support to the attackers. One brother, facing the firing squad, said, "Lucky me. I win a Christian martyrdom in God's lottery."[141] Ironically, or otherwise, the police station where Father Pro Suárez was executed is now the site of…the National Lottery. If the Pro Suárez brothers were guilty of anything, it was that they were neighbors and associates of the nun turned antigovernment revolutionary, Madre Conchita.

Madre Conchita was ahead of her time; she—like radical Islamic clerics in the 21st century—justified using violence in the name of God and was convicted of that. The convents having been closed by Calles, the independently wealthy former nun held prayer services and gave sermons in the now-priestless churches. Like the radical

---

[141] To die for your faith is one of the means of obtaining sainthood in the Catholic Church.

Islamic clerics of the 21st century, she sought to inflame her follow-ers to violence against the modern, secular state. Her Mexico City home was the center of several plots against the government.

Following Obregón's assassination, she was transported to the Islas Tres Marías, and her property seized. To avoid her house becoming either a political or religious shrine, the building was given to the Evangelical Lutherans. In the 1950s, Madre Conchita, having married a fellow convict and become a model prisoner, was paroled and the remaining property returned to her. Having rejected violence and still a believing Catholic, she deeded the property next to her former home to a Catholic high school. By then, tempers had cooled down. As long as the school's name was not overtly religious, it followed the national curriculum and the nuns who taught there (and still live in the new building on the site) did not wear distinctive clothing, there were no objections to the founder of the _Colegio Hispano Americano._

Unlike Melchor Ocampo, the anticlerical leader of the Reforma, Calles was not an atheist. Like Juárez, he accepted the people's need for religion (Calles sponsored the unsuccessful attempt to start a "Church of México") and apparently had his own idiosyn-cratic beliefs. He put great stock in the norteño faith healer, _Niño Fidencio_ – Child Fidencio – who cured Calles' stomach ulcers. Calles, in turn, protected Fidencio and his followers from persecution by either the government or by more conventional Catholics. The Nuevo Leon faith healer and mystic never went through puberty. He was also a giant. Some believe he was a hermaphrodite, or that he had a hormonal imbalance, but appearing as a gigantic child with adult wisdom added to his mystique. After his death, an entire religion, the Fidenicist Evangelical Church, sprang up among his faithful follow-ers in northern México and Texas. The church combines indigenous rituals with Pentecostal faith-healing practices imported from the United States. It also maintains some Roman Catholic rituals and practices, including the canonization of saints: the church recog-nizes Plutarco Elías Calles as a one of their saints.

The oily ambassador is off-sides

OBREGÓN HAD RISKED HIS presidency to gain U.S. diplomatic recognition. Warren G. Harding sent James Rockwell Sheffield, who tried his best to work in the tradition of Joel Poinsett and Henry Lane Wilson. Poinsett had masterminded Masonic plots; Wilson had sponsored a bloody coup d'etat; Sheffield organized football games.

Convinced "Soviet México" (as he called it, especially after México and the Soviet Union exchanged ambassadors in 1927) was doomed to Catholicism, socialism and what was worse, actually demanding ownership of the oil revenues; a radical remedy was in order. To Sheffield, it was a question of education. Mexicans played European sports like *fútbol* – soccer – not American sports like football. Only people who played an American-style game could produce people who supported American-style (or rather, pro-American) governments. So, with great secrecy, the ambassador contacted universities throughout the United States. College students were recruited as secret agents—their mission (paid for by the United States government): infiltrate Mexican schools and recreation programs and teach the Mexicans the "American Way of Life" and the lateral pass.[142]

More seriously, the ambassador listened to oilmen like William F. Buckley, who were still pushing for United States military intervention to protect their investments. When the United States intervened in a Nicaraguan civil war in 1927 (to protect American investments in that country), Mexican soldiers were sent to assist the Nicaraguan government under the Juárez Doctrine, which called for mutual assistance when asked by a neighbor in need. The two armies spent most of their time avoiding each other while their governments issued inflammatory warnings. President Coolidge (Harding died in office) said that México was on "probation" and could be attacked if it didn't withdraw its troops; President Calles responded that he would order the oil fields torched if American soldiers entered the country. More practically, Calles suggested both countries leave Nicaragua, and that the matter be turned over to the International Court in the Hague. Meanwhile, the luckless Ambassador Sheffield, who had to publicly deny there was any plan to invade, unwisely left papers outlining his suggestions for intervention. The Mexican cleaning staff "expropriated" the ambassador's papers.

President Coolidge had no choice but to cancel the invasion and the football program. Anyone was bound to be an improvement, but Coolidge surprised the Mexicans, and himself, when he chose Wall Street banker Dwight Morrow to replace the disgraced and discredited Sheffield. Morrow's immediate task was to avoid a complete breakdown in relations. Oilmen and other American businessmen would listen to a professional business advisor. Unlike his predecessors, Morrow—who had made his fortune listening to the experts who disagreed with him and then advising wealthy

---

[142] Mexicans have started playing and watching American football in recent years, and several universities and high schools (especially in the north) play the sport. But this has more to do with recent Mexican migration to the United States and cable television than with adopting American values.

investors on how to handle their money—did not arrive with preconceived notions of how México should react. He was quite willing to listen to people like Lázaro Cárdenas and the American radical, Frank Tannenbaum.

Morrow's advice was simple— in México, play México's game by México's rules. The Revolution was a fact—if the Americans wanted to do business, they had to play by the new rules. The United States government could help them learn the rules, but it couldn't change them.

Morrow, being independently wealthy, was able to pursue his personal interests in collecting art. His home in Cuernavaca was filled with contemporary and pre-Columbian Mexican art.[143] At his own expense, the millionaire banker hired the Communist, Diego Rivera, to paint the murals in the old Cortés Palace in that city. He entertained and financially supported artists and intellectuals. Finally, aircraft—and aviators—fascinated Mexicans and everyone else in the early 1930s. It didn't hurt Morrow's popularity at all when his daughter married Charles Lindberg. Several minor diplomatic incidents were avoided when Mexican officials who might have snubbed the foreign power for political reasons were not about to pass up a chance to meet the ambassador's heroic son-in-law.

---

[143] The house is now a restaurant, La Bonita India, on calle Dwight Morrow. Mexican streets are named after almost everyone, but this is the only street ever named for a United States ambassador.

Hail to the *Jefe (Maximo)*

WHEN OBREGÓN WAS ASSASSINATED, it was widely expected that Calles would find some loophole in the Constitution and stay in office (after all, a loophole was found—that Obregón had not served a complete term—that allowed Obregón to run a second time. Instead, Calles surprised everyone, proving he could be a statesman when necessary. He insisted that the Chamber of Deputies follow the Constitution and elect the *Secretario de Gobernación* interim president until elections could be held. Emilio Cándido Portes Gil, though viewed as Calles' puppet (Calles moved from Chapultepec Castle to a house across the road. It was joked that, "The president lives in the castle, but the real leader is across the street watching him."), was a credible stand-in. Like Obregón and Calles, he was a norteño, in his case, from Tamaulipas. His revolutionary Border Socialist Party followed the same path as Obregón, seeking support from the labor unions and supporting agrarian reform.

Prevailing upon Dwight Morrow (a Protestant) to negotiate with the Pope, Portes Gil managed to bring the Cristero Wars to an end. The Church was allowed to function and to maintain control of religious facilities (under license from the state) in return for staying out of politics. The petty restrictions on religious activities could be overcome with a little creativity on both sides. In many places, religious processions—religious activities off church grounds were technically illegal—usually included making arrangements to pay a nominal fine to the local authorities for holding a parade without a permit. Or village fiestas in honor of the local saint, which were often disguised celebrations of an indigenous god to begin with, were rechristened as "folk festivals".

Late in 1929, the worldwide economic meltdown known as the Great Depression started. México was as affected as every other country. Mexican workers in the United States were rounded up and deported, worsening the already critical labor problem. Oil and commodity prices plummeted. Portes Gil kept his nerve, slashed the federal budget (especially the military budget, protecting education and agriculture as much as possible) but mostly worked to guarantee political stability.

José Vasconcelos threw a monkey wrench into Portes Gil's plans for an orderly transition, with a challenge to the official candidate, Pascal Ortiz Rubio, in the 1931 election. Although there was violence and the possibility of another military uprising was in the air, the election went off as planned. Portes Gil, having already cut the military budget, kept the army busy harassing the former educator's supporters. Vasconcelos was rightly convinced that his mostly middle-class constituency had been cheated in the election, though later analysts doubt he would have won anyway. Embittered, he gave up on the Revolutionary family, moving more and more in reactionary political circles.

Ortiz Rubio tried to carve out an independent course, but he was not in good health. Calles also found the new president a little too independent for his tastes. Ortiz Rubio resigned for health reasons, to be replaced by another interim president, Abelardo L. (Luján) Rodríguez. Rodríguez owned a wholesale liquor distributorship in Ciudad Juárez and had become a multimillionaire during the Prohibition era in the United States, and Calles hated liquor and liquor salesmen. Rodríguez had one overwhelmingly positive trait in Calles' eyes—he was a "yes man".

Calles hoped to use Rodríguez' short term—he was only slated to serve the fourteen months until the July 1935 election—as time to find another puppet. Recognizing that Rodríguez was viewed as corrupt and had little interest in rural issues, Calles worried that the short temporary administration was likely to cost the Revolution much of its credibility. Searching for someone with a reputation for honesty and a good record in rural issues, he turned to "the boy scout", Lázaro Cárdenas, the young (and teetotal) governor of Michoacán.

The boy scout's creed

ALTHOUGH CALLES MADE FUN of Cárdenas, calling him "the boy scout" behind his back, the young governor had better revolutionary credentials than most. He was a sixteen-year-old office boy in a backwater city hall when the Revolution started. The only one in his unit who could read and write when the Constitutionalists took over, he was immediately commissioned a lieutenant (according to legend, because he had the sense to free the prisoners in his local jailhouse and bring them along as recruits) and continued moving up the ranks. Armies, even Revolutionary ones, are bureaucracies, and Cárdenas had the virtues of a good bureaucrat. He was polite to everyone, stuck to the task assigned to him and "kissed ass" when he had to. By the end of the Revolution he was a general, despite his age (there were a lot of very young generals in the Revolution), and governor of Michoacán.

Calles genuinely admired some of Cárdenas' political skills. When Michoacán sugar mills closed during the Depression, the governor had a plausible excuse to take them over, both to keep the farmers employed and to provide future revenues for the State. Cárdenas created special "cadres" within the state party for farmers and workers, bringing both groups into the Revolutionary family while strengthening his political base. Calles' only complaint was that Cárdenas was too far to the left. Still, given Cárdenas' enthusiasm for fulfilling whatever task was put before him and his willingness to accept orders from superiors, Calles assumed his unofficial "Maximate" would continue for another six years.

Although Calles organized the various Revolutionary family members into a formal political party in 1929, guaranteeing the Revolutionary Party candidate would automatically win, Cárdenas campaigned vigorously. Calles should have caught on that something was up. Calles had broken with the labor movement (Morones was a crook, and his rival union leader, Vicente Lombardo Toledano, was a Marxist intellectual.) Neither leader appealed to Calles; as a result, neither of the two major unions supported Cárdenas. What Cárdenas was doing was selling himself as a "new, improved revolutionary" and more importantly, he was selling himself to the unions as an anti-Morones, pro-Lombardo (and anti-Calles) candidate.

Cárdenas was indeed not Calles. Where Mexican presidents had always appeared in formal clothing, Cárdenas assumed office in a business suit. He was a young man (only thirty-four) and Chapultepec Castle is no place to raise children. Besides, it really didn't suit the image of a people's president. He moved the presidential compound to Los Pinos, at that time a hunting lodge on the castle grounds, turning over the castle for use as a historical museum (which it remains today). Perhaps most importantly, at Los Pinos, the Cárdenas family could look out their windows without seeing Plutarco Elías Calles watching them.

Meeting with indigenous delegations and farmers' groups in public, Cárdenas was working behind the scenes to ease *el Jefe Maximo* – the top boss – out of power. Calles, worried that small farms were inefficient, was opposed to giving more land to the landless farmers; Cárdenas wanted to expand the program and close the book on the old haciendas once and for all. Where Calles had turned against the unions, Cárdenas began backing them (those that weren't under Morones' control). Noting that real wages had been falling for a number of years, Cárdenas encouraged strikes, especially from the Marxist unions. As he had done in Michoacán, Cárdenas opened the national party to labor and peasant wings, going so far as to appoint Lombardo Toledano as secretary of labor. Calles complained. Cárdenas fired the pro-Calles cabinet members and forced the Jefe Maximo to announce his retirement from politics.

The next year, when Calles made some remarks to the press that could be interpreted as calling for a coup, Cárdenas had the excuse he needed. The old Jefe was roused from his bed, driven to the airport and put on the first plane out of the country. He landed in Dallas still wearing his pajamas.[144]

Having purged the conservative revolutionaries, Cárdenas' administration was pushing labor rights on one hand and redistributing land on the other. With presidential blessings most unions struck for higher wages, beyond the pittances Morones had negotiated during his tenure (most of which the rank and file never saw).

Dissatisfaction with the slow pace of land distribution had kept the old Zapata and Villa supporters out of the Revolutionary family. Nicely meshing Marxism and Zapatismo, Cárdenas "blessed" the creation of new *ejidos* – the traditional native villages where individual farmers "owned" their plots but shared the labor and costs. The new ejidos didn't just include the few traditional communities that had managed to keep titles to their land over the past four centuries, but landless farmers who had been dispossessed by the haciendas over the previous century and villages that just didn't own enough land to begin with. What remained of the large haciendas (including that owned by Secretary of Labor Lombardo

---

[144] The timing of Calles' arrest—when the next plane out of the country was headed for Dallas—may not have been coincidental, but a bit of shrewd, if subtle, propaganda. "*Ir a Dallas Texas*" (to go to Dallas, Texas) is Mexican slang for having totally screwed up, equivalent to the British expression, "to be sent to Coventry". Calles was photographed getting off the plane, still in his pajamas, clutching a book. You can't see the title in the photo, but it is probably not Adolf Hitler's *Mein Kampf*, as Cárdenas insiders leaked to the press. "Media spin" existed, even in México in 1940.

Toledano's family) was broken up and even the new agricultural lands in Sonora that Obregón had made available to commercial cotton growers were distributed to landless farmers.

Threatened more and more by oil worker strikes, Cárdenas was finally able to gain control over Peláez-controlled territory and force the oil companies to accept their "Mexican jurisdictional personality". However, the oil companies were reluctant to honor their contracts. Dragged into court by the union in 1937 (the issue was the oil companies' insistence on hiring foreigners, and their refusal to train Mexican managers and technicians), the oil companies—led by British-owned Aguila Oil—refused to negotiate with government arbitrators as the Supreme Court had ordered.

Cárdenas planned carefully for his next strike, one that would unite all Mexicans…and astound the world. If there was one group that would never be part of the Revolutionary family, it was the Catholic Church, but the Church and the "family" could have common interests.

Cárdenas secretly consulted the archbishop of Mexico City on a delicate religious matter. Was there any moral objection to the State taking over the oil companies outright? Recognizing that this was the first time in almost a century that the government had sought the Church's opinion, the archbishop and his staff carefully researched the question. If the State, on behalf of the people, BOUGHT the oil companies—given that the law already said the State, on behalf of the people, owned the oil—there was no objection in religious law. In fact, Cardinal Pérez was prepared to use the Church's resources to assist the State in what was recognized as a moral action.

Cárdenas announced the takeover on a Saturday night, 18 March 1938. On Sunday morning, every Catholic Church in the country read the archbishop's letter justifying the act…and then took up a collection to help pay off the debt! On Monday morning, there were photographs of Mrs. Cárdenas contributing her wedding ring to the state fund to buy the oil companies. News photos and films soon featured *campesinas* – farm women – contributing chickens or sacks of grain, and priests blessing the offerings. It was a brilliant stroke, popular with everyone from the Catholics to the Communists...though it soon dawned on everyone that, as with Guerrero's expulsion of the Spaniards in 1829, the country had lost critical skilled labor.

Of course, the move was not popular with the foreigners. The British acted badly, breaking off diplomatic relations.[145] Together with the U.S. and the Netherlands, where the other companies were headquartered, the British pushed for an international boycott of Mexican oil. Cárdenas played hardball. Unable to buy supplies, or hire technicians from the old companies, the Mexicans turned to the Soviet Union and to Nazi Germany for assistance. Despite very bad diplomatic relations with the fascist countries (Germany, Italy, Spain and Japan), they were willing to buy oil.

In 1938 everyone knew that the next big war was about to begin. While the British were not nearly as dependent on Mexican oil as they were in 1914, they couldn't hire a mercenary army like they did during the Revolution nor could they do without the oil. Cárdenas told U.S. President Franklin Roosevelt that México was quite willing to pay for the expropriated businesses as soon as a fair price could be worked out. Although the U.S. was the world's largest oil producer at the time, so there was less sense of urgency about the coming war, it still needed Mexican imports and couldn't endanger its supply. Roosevelt agreed to arbitration with the Netherlands quickly joining in. The British were slower to come in, but eventually did. Because of the war (1939–45), when everyone was withholding payments on long-term debts, the repayment was delayed, but the debt and interest were paid off. Britain, the last to join in arbitration, was the last to be paid. The final checks were written in 1962.

Cárdenas left office, not universally beloved of course, but the most universally admired leader since Benito Juárez. Still a young

---

[145] Tensions with the British form the background for Malcolm Lowrey's *Under the Volcano*. The protagonist, Geoffrey Firman, is the British Consul in Cuernavaca. With diplomatic relations broken, Firman has the luxury of dwelling on his personal shortcomings and drinking himself to death.

man, he had a long life ahead of him. He ran rural development projects for many years, oversaw major irrigation developments, befriended and supported a young Cuban lawyer named Fidel Castro and assisted local indigenous groups in their dealings with the outside world. After his death in 1975, he was seen as something of a saint in his native Michoacán—literally. He is probably the only Marxist whose portrait hangs in Catholic churches, and some indigenous people pray to his spirit. Although he privately regretted the path the ruling Revolutionary Party (which became the Institutional Revolutionary Party a few years later) took, he never challenged it, leaving that to his son, Cuauhtémoc. His son and his grandson, another Lázaro, have both been governors of Michoacán and recognized leaders on the Mexican left.

He was as close to a Quetzalcóatl as we'll find in the post-revolutionary period.

Juárez and Peace

IF THE CÁRDENAS ERA was almost a return of Quetzalcóatl, it meant that Huitzilopochtli, the war god, was somewhere in the offing.

When Cárdenas' term expired in 1940, he would have preferred a left-wing candidate to continue his legacy. But the older Mexican conservative movement had been absorbed by a new political movement—fascism—that could not easily be absorbed into the Revolutionary family, so the party leadership chose the much more conservative General Manuel Ávila Camacho to lead the nation and undercut support for the new movement.

A perceptive Mexican author once said that European revolutions followed textbooks—Thomas Paine's *Rights of Man*, Karl Marx' *Communist Manifesto* or Adolf Hitler's *Mein Kampf*—while Mexicans wrote their texts after the fighting was over. Zapata had been seen as an "anarchist", Villa as a "Communist" and Obregón as a "socialist", even though none of them gave much thought to the various differences between the theories. Cárdenas called himself a "Marxist", but his most important accomplishments—the ejidos and the oil nationalization—rested on pre-Conquest Mexican concepts.

In the 1920s, as the Revolution was solidifying in México, the Europeans were trying out a new political theory...fascism. Borrowing from anarchism, socialism and 19th-century Catholic Church teaching,[146] among other things, fascism has a slight debt to México. It was first developed by Italian newspaper editor Benito Mussolini, who had seized control of the Italian government in 1922. He was—and still is—the only European political figure named for an indigenous American or a Mexican. His parents had been active in fighting Austrian domination in northern Italy, and named their son for the hero of anti-Austrian fighters, Benito Juárez. But, where Juárez famously said, "Respect for the rights of others is the way of peace," his namesake said, "War is the health of the state."

While the various national forms of fascism were all slightly different—Hitler's National Socialism made racial purity an obsession and was militantly anticlerical, where Spanish Falangism was pro-clerical and pro-monarchist—all fascists supported a dictatorship of the elite, glorification of the State, violent suppression of dissenters and nonconformists (racial or religious minorities as in Germany, or linguistic ones, as in Spain), a return to traditional sex roles and an economy organized by corporations.

While the three main forms of European fascism had their supporters in México (notably Vasconcelos' support for Hitler), Spanish Falangism had the most influence on the Synarchists, the Mexican fascists.

The Spanish *caudillo* – leader – Generalissimo Francisco Franco, was sort of a fascist Porfirio Díaz (or a more ruthless version of Santa Ana), who'd come to power through a bloody civil war in 1936–38, assisted by Italy and Germany. While Franco's Spain was in no position to threaten war with outsiders as a way of bolstering its

---

[146] Pope Leo XIII's 1891 *Rerum novarum* discussed relationships between business, labor, government and the Church. Labor unions seized upon the Pope's support for unions, business upon the right to private property. The fascists seized upon the Pope's contention that men could not achieve equality in all things.

own economy, it did borrow both Mussolini's corporate state and Hitler's glorification of the race (though in Spain, the discrimination against the Basques, Catalans and Gypsies never included Hitler's "final solution"—murdering all minority people).

Franco had the backing of Spanish monarchists in the Spanish Civil War and won the support of both the elite and the Catholic Church, especially when he turned the Spanish education system over to clerical control. While there were no monarchists in México any more, the elitism, the clericalism and the tendency of ultra-conservatives to still look to Spain as the "mother country", all made Mexican synarchism – Falangism – attractive.

Besides snob appeal, the Synarchists turn toward traditional Catholic values coupled with fears of the Cárdenas government's overtly socialist direction made synarchism attractive to many. It was a modern repackaging of the old Clerical and Conservative movements of the 19th century. The job of the workers and farmers was to obey the elite and educated classes in their working lives and the clergy in their personal ones. Unlike the Cristeros, who were traditional campesinos fighting to maintain their traditions (often with the support of traditional campesino priests), the Synarchists, with support among the wealthy and the upper clergy, had the resources to mount a serious challenge to the Revolutionary state.

Largely a norteño movement, many Synarchists had close ties to conservative Catholics and fascist sympathizers in the United States who attempted to finance one more armed uprising against the "socialist" Mexican government, possibly including William F. Buckley, the oilman who had been deported in the 1920s.

The Revolutionary Party's support for the conservative Ávila Camacho fractured the Synarchist movement. Somewhat based on Obregón's idea that it was better to co-opt the opposition than to fight them, die-hard Synarchists were eventually given settlements in Baja California, which never prospered. The more flexible Synarchists joined with conservative businessmen and the old

Cristeros in starting the *Partido Acción National* (*PAN*) – National Action Party – in 1940, becoming the first organized opposition party.

Although all fascist movements denigrated women, seeing their role as primarily homemakers or baby producers, there is an irony in that the best Synarchist organizers were women. When the time came to consider giving women the vote, it was the left that opposed the idea—their argument was that women would listen to the priests and vote for right-wing antirevolutionary groups.[147]

---

[147] PAN, the political party that most Synarchists eventually joined, has several women leaders. Most *presidenciable* – presidential quality – women have been right-wingers.

México joins the world

Fascism in general, not just the Mexican Synarchists, was a growing concern for the Cárdenas administration and forced the country to take a more active role in world affairs.

When a civil war broke out in 1936 between the Spanish Republican government and the Falangists, the Spanish Republic appealed for help, and under the Juárez Doctrine, the Cárdenas government openly supported them. Led by diplomat Isidro Fabela Alfaro, Mexican foreign service officers modified the Juárez Doctrine. What was new was Fabela's contention that fighting Spanish fascists meant diplomatically challenging Franco's allies and supporters—Mussolini's Italy and Hitler's Germany—as well.

México allowed the antifascist Spaniards to openly recruit soldiers and buy arms, while Britain, France and the United States prevented such activities or looked the other way when Franco's people did the same thing.

Fabela also argued that México, a weak country with no military ambitions and no powerful allies, could be a "moral" force in world affairs. If nothing else, the country could provide a refuge from foreign political intrigues. Famously, Leon Trotsky was admitted as a political refugee, and the Cárdenas administration passed a law (still on the books) that gave automatic refugee status to anyone fleeing a fascist government.[148] With some justification, México claims to have been the first antifascist country, moving to counter not just Franco's rebellion but the countries backing him for ideological reasons.

When the Falangists defeated the Republicans in Spain, México refused to recognize the new government. Antifascist Spaniards found new homes in México. Franco remained dictator of Spain until he died in 1974, but a Spanish Republican government-in-exile continued to exist in Mexico City. When Spain applied for membership in the United Nations in 1946, México's representatives blocked the fascist country's entry. Only in 1964, over México's strong objections, was Spain was allowed to join the UN.

Finally, in the League of Nations and later in the United Nations, Mexican diplomats pioneered the nonaligned nations movement. Diplomats from the smaller and weaker countries were urged to join together in supporting each other's separate interests against the larger countries and their allies.

The antifascist activities had a profound effect on México. Fascism, besides its other unattractive features, is profoundly anti-intellectual.[149] Artists, writers, professors, filmmakers like Luis Buñuel; they all fled to Mexico City, which quickly became the center of Hispanic culture. As the Franco era dragged on, and repression against linguistic minorities increased, Mexico City also became the center of Catalan and Basque literature and arts. In addition, Italian and German political refugees (especially German

---

[148] Saddam Hussein's Ba'athism is the Arab form of fascism. In the short time between the U.S. invasion of Iraq and the fall of the Ba'athist government, several Iraqi citizens were detained crossing into the U.S. at Tijuana. The U.S. wanted México to hold these Iraqis as suspected terrorists, but their lawyers argued successfully that under the 1930s law, they should be given political refugee status. They were. It helped that the Iraqis were Eastern Rite Catholics, as were wealthy Mexicans of Lebanese descent who took an interest in their plight.

[149] Asked by Federico García Lorca's sister why the poet and playwright had been executed, Franco's henchmen told her it was because he wrote poetry, and Spain had no need for poets.

Jews) started what would soon be a major exodus of Europeans to México when war finally broke out in September 1939.

When Ávila Camacho's more conservative, traditional government took office in December 1939, there were genuine concerns about the split in the Revolutionary family between the leftists, who thought Lázaro Cárdenas had not been socialist enough, and those who thought he had gone far enough.

Ávila Camacho took a middle course. México was not immediately affected by the European war, and the administration could continue to focus on agrarian reforms, though at a less frantic pace than under Cárdenas, focusing less on distributing land and more on things like roads, dams and farmers' credit services (which gave very little money to poor farmers, though they financed major rural enterprises in the following years). During the Cárdenas administration, there had been two constitutional changes—one outlawing gambling (Cárdenas was always puritanical) and another redefining "secular education" as "socialist and secular education". Maintaining the ban on casinos and dropping the word "socialist" was a typical compromise with the conservatives.

In the 1940s, México was about to undergo a huge transition that made squabbling about the wording in the constitution, or whether or not gambling was technically legal, seem small.

Unconventional warfare

ALTHOUGH THE CÁRDENAS GOVERNMENT had briefly flirted with the Axis countries (Germany, Italy and Japan) during the oil crisis; even before the Second World War started in 1939, México had agreed to support the Allies (Great Britain, France, the Soviet Union, China and the United States). All recognized the importance of Mexican oil in the coming war and agreed to put aside their disagreements until the fascists were defeated. The Mexican and the United States' governments were both realistic, recognizing neither could afford an enemy for a next door neighbor.

Japan threatened the United States colony of the Philippines. Pro-Filipino sentiment among traditional Catholics in México created anti-Japanese sentiment. Mexican culture is largely a mixture of Spanish and indigenous influence. Filipino culture adds an Asian layer on top. The Filipinos had been converted to Catholicism by Mexican missionaries in the 1500s. The Asian archipelago was part of México – the vice-regency of New Spain – until 1814. After nearly three hundred years of the Acapulco-Manila fleet there were many Mexicans (and Filipinos) with social, family and business connections.

Acquired by the United States in 1898 (during the Spanish-American War), the Spanish-speaking, Roman Catholic majority in the Philippines had their own government and had been promised full independence by 1945. Japan openly planned to invade the Philippines and began a brutal attack in 1941. Germany and Italy, both as allies of Japan (unpopular with traditional Catholics) and of Franco's Spain (unpopular with the leftists) lost still more support among the Mexican people, even among the German and Italian immigrant communities.

After the United States declared war in December 1941, the Axis forces tried to cut off oil shipments. After two Mexican oil tankers were sunk by German submarines, Ávila Camacho declared war, joining the Allies in May 1942.

The United States was providing most of the Allied force's weapons, food and fighting men. Mexico's military forces had never strayed further from home than Nicaragua, when a small army contingent was sent to assist a revolt in 1927. Within México itself, the army was seen more as an internal police force than anything else. At most, the country could only provide token military assistance to the Allies, but, México had resources vital to the Allied cause beyond just oil and minerals. In the end, it would supply forty percent of the raw materials and food the United States needed to fight the war. The United States was only able to turn out weapons by converting factories that normally made consumer products (things like cars, refrigerators, washing machines and radios) to weapons production. Even though there was not much consumer demand in the United States, Mexican industries suddenly found they had a huge new export market. Some U.S. factories simply moved their regular equipment to México, where they could continue to do normal business.

Nelson Rockefeller, the son of Rivera's one-time patron John D. Rockefeller, Jr. and the future New York governor and United States vice president, was at that time a wealthy young man with a serious interest in Latin America. President Roosevelt sent young

Rockefeller on a top-secret mission to research Latin American attitudes toward the United States and the war. Rockefeller's report was worrisome. Nearly every Latin American country, including México, resented the United States, and there was still widespread support for the fascists. However, throughout Latin America, Rockefeller found two gringos were extremely popular. Mickey Mouse and Donald Duck. So Donald Duck learned Spanish. Disney turned out Latin-flavored cartoons, and Donald Duck learned to do the Mexican Hat Dance as part of the war effort.

In return for cooperating with the allies in providing oil, President Franklin Roosevelt had promised technology transfers to México. While Roosevelt was unable to convince Congress to approve these transfers, he was able to convince Walt Disney and Howard Hughes that México needed help in countering fascist propaganda. Both Disney and Hughes' RKO Studios sent film stock and equipment to México along with the technical expertise to set up Churubusco Studios. The early 1940s saw the start of the golden age of Mexican cinema.

Cans of film were useful, but cans of vegetables would win the war. Farming had nearly come to a stop in the countries where there was fighting, which left the United States and México feeding the allies. Vegetable farmers, especially Mexican vegetable farmers, made money during the war.

The huge numbers of soldiers and sailors from the United States also created another problem for the Allies; one that benefited México. The United States was desperately short of workers. The *bracero* – temporary, nonimmigrant worker – program recruited workers willing to go north. Volunteering to work for the gringos was not only profitable for individual Mexicans (then, as now, the U.S. paid significantly higher salaries than a Mexican could earn at home), but it was patriotic as well. If the United States would provide the soldiers, Mexicans could do anything else that was needed. The bracero program was so popular (everyone from poor farmers to teachers and lawyers volunteered to work in U.S. factories and farm fields and to run the railroads), that the Mexican

Republic was itself faced with a new situation: there was more work for everyone but not enough workers.

Women have always worked in México, but now they were asked to do the jobs formerly considered men's work. In the United States, the symbolic woman worker was "Rosie the Riveter", clean-cut, feminine and able to handle heavy equipment. The Mexican "Women Workers' Corps" poster girl was a bit earthier—she carried a baby under one arm and a wrench in the other. Rosie and the Women Workers' Corps poster sent the same message—a female factory worker was still a woman but was a patriot fighting a hard battle at the same time. Veterans of the Women Workers' Corps (with their own distinctive uniforms) led the push for women's voting rights after the war. A few states had allowed women to vote in local elections since the Revolution, but the Women Workers Corps veterans began agitating at the national level for full voting rights nationally. In 1947, women were given the right to vote in municipal elections throughout the country, but could not vote in Federal elections until 1954. However, Argentine women had only gained the same rights in 1952 (mostly because Eva Peron had become an important political figure) and several European nations restricted women's voting rights to local elections as late as the 1970s.

The war and the new enemies sent more refugees, who brought business, agricultural and industrial skills as well as cultural ones. The Spanish Republican government—and the Spanish intellectuals—built flourishing cultural institutions in México, or, like filmmaker Luis Buñuel, made Mexico City, rather than Madrid, the center of the Hispanic avant-garde. Mexican diplomat Gilberto Bosques Saldívar, who rescued somewhere between thirty and forty thousand people from the fascists, saved entire communities of Jews from extermination camps, while keeping an eye on Mexican industry. He convinced his government, for example, to move the Belgian diamond workers of Amberes and their families—along with the equipment, supplies, financial assets and centuries of craftsmanship experience—to México. The diamond workers were mostly Jews, though Bosques also rescued Spaniards fleeing Franco, Germans, Austrians and many others. Technicians, businessmen and engineers were especially welcome, though ordinary farmers and workers also flooded into México.

Even European royalty started new lives in México. The former Tsar of Bulgaria's family started a publishing business, specializing in—of course—high society gossip magazines. Prince von Hohenlohe, who lost his family fortune to Hitler, made a much bigger fortune in México after the war...selling Hitler's "people's car" – the Volkswagen – and eventually building the first Volkswagen factory in the Americas.[150] A Polish diplomat and a scion of that country's former ruling family, Prince Poniatowski, fled with his Mexican wife and young daughter Princess Helene. Princess Helene, who Mexicanized her name as Elena Poniatowska, would become México's most famous journalist.

Most refugees did not have as exalted relatives. More Jews were saved from Hitler by México than in all the major allied countries combined. Plutarco Elías Calles toured Germany shortly after the end of his presidency. Calles admired the Hitler government for rebuilding a strong German economy after the country was defeated during the 1914–18 war and then suffering through a serious depression. Calles also recognized how dangerous the Nazi preoccupation with race could be. When interviewed by the German press, he stressed that México accepted any refugee who was willing to work, and who was in danger from their own government. When the German reporters asked if he didn't mean, "any Christian", Calles—who knew he would be quoted—again stressed he meant any person, "including Jews". While many of the Jews moved to Israel or the United States after the war, those

---

[150] The Volkswagen sedan (known as "*el vocho*" in México, and "the bug" or "beetle" in the U.S.) proved so successful that it stayed in production in México until 2003, long after the model first produced in 1938 had been discontinued everywhere else in the world.

who stayed tended to be small businessmen who created new jobs and industries in the Republic.

México did have a military role in the war: the army guarded the vital oil fields and mines, while the navy patrolled sea lanes as far south as Brazil in the Atlantic and Peru in the Pacific.

Escuadron 201, a Mexican air unit, served in the Pacific and were highly regarded by their commander, U.S. General Douglas MacArthur. MacArthur has the unusual distinction of being the only gringo to have fought against Mexican military units (during the Pershing Expedition) and later command them. Mexican movies sometimes leave the impression that the squadron won the Second World War, which isn't quite true.

Normally, military forces and spending increase dramatically during wartime. Not in México. One tactic Obregón employed to bring the Revolution under control was to openly "buy" potential enemies. Small rebel units were bought off by taking the rebels into the Federal Army and putting the soldiers and officers on the regular Army payroll. Officers maintained the ranks they held in their old armies. This was the same problem México had after independence (and de Iturbide's compromise): México had a huge army and more officers than it needed. Most of these now loyal soldiers had nothing to do, and the retired officers were still receiving pensions.

President Ávila Camacho used the war as an excuse to professionalize the military. The old cowboys, miners, farmers and factory workers with the rank of colonel or general or still enlisted in the armed forces couldn't meet the new requirements and found other jobs. Officer's pensions had often been based on how much of a threat the old officer had been. Wartime, and the need to watch the military budget, was the excuse for reorganizing these pensions. Some of the old rebels settled for a single payment (often taking the form of a concession to open gas stations carrying the new PEMEX brand name), and fortunately, some died of old age. The Mexican military budget actually dropped during the war and has continued to decline ever since.[151] For the size of its population, México now has one of the smallest armies in the world, and it even turns a profit. The military forces have their own bank (supposedly to handle soldier's and sailor's paychecks and pensions, but the bank is also a successful home mortgage lender). The military bank, Banjercito, processes tourist visa fees, so naturally has been a major investor in resorts and hotels. Military factories produce more uniforms and equipment than the country's forces can use. The excess production is exported. Because the military is supposed to guard natural resources, and México's watersheds and forests are an endangered natural resource, one of the army's main tasks is planting trees. By planting fruit trees, the Army has also become an important agricultural enterprise.

---

[151] In December 2006, the new Calderón administration proposed raising the military budget and cutting funding for education. This has led to massive protests, and a few schoolteachers formed a guerrilla unit to fight against militarism!

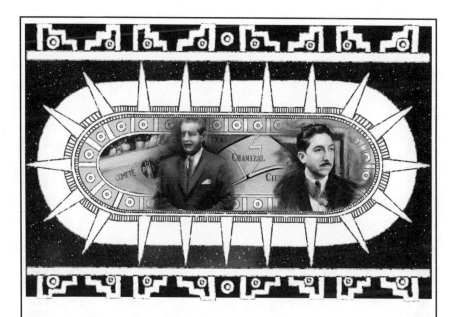

The PRI: I'm not sure I'm ready for an institution

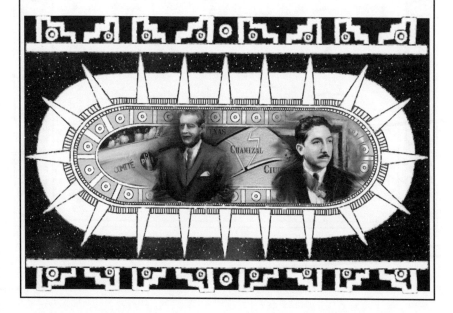

México ca. 1968

States and Territories

1-Aguascalientes
2-Baja California
3-Baja California Sur
4-Campeche
5-Chiapas
6-Chihuahua
7-Coahuila
8-Colima
9-Distrito Federal / México (Mexico City)
10-Durango
11-Guanajuato
12-Guerrero
13-Hidalgo
14-Jalisco
15-México
16-Michoacán
17-Morelos
18-Nayarit
19-Nuevo León
20-Oaxaca
21-Puebla
22-Querétaro
23-Quintana Roo
24-San Luis Potosí
25-Sinaloa
26-Sonora
27-Tabasco
28-Tamaulipas
29-Tlaxcala
30-Veracruz
31-Yucatán
32-Zacatecas

Places

a- El Paso (Texas)
b- Mexico City
Ciudad Universitaria
Coyoacán
Los Pinos
c- Ojinaga
d- Tijuana

Gulf of Mexico

Pacific Ocean

We're living in a material world

A T THE END OF THE SECOND WORLD WAR México was
still poor and agrarian, but more prosperous than
it had ever been. The Revolution had eliminated the worst abuses
of Porfirismo: haciendas and peonage were horror stories told by
aging relatives, and farmers had at least some land of their own.
There were jobs, if not at home, then in the United States. There
were competing unions, new schools, new roads and new products.
The military was reduced and lost all political importance. The
Church pretended to be deaf to government propaganda and the
State pretended to be blind to the Church activities. As a nation
that had actually fought on the winning side in the World War,
México had a voice in the new United Nations. It had developed
better diplomatic and economic relations with the United States.
In the post-war period, the government would shift to the left or
the right, but the Party would bring it back to the middle. If it didn't
quite look like the return of Quetzalcóatl, at least Huitzilopochtli
and Tezcatlipoca were nowhere to be seen.

If the Revolution was over, or so the thinking went, it was
time to preserve the accomplishments and move on. A joke going
around the United States in the late 1990s said that "Institution"
and "Revolution" were a contradiction in terms, but when Ávila

Camacho's replacement, Miguel Alemán Valdés founded the *Partido Revolucionario Institucional (PRI)* – Institutional Revolutionary Party – in 1949, the meaning was closer to something like "the party that instituted the Revolution" or "the party based on what the Revolution instituted".

Alemán, the first civilian president since Madero,[152] ended the military's role in the Party, creating a purely civilian institution. The Communists were no longer welcome as part of the revolutionary family and socialists were marginalized, though some of Cárdenas' political innovations—farmers and workers organizations—were maintained, along with what were called Popular Sectors – official PRI groups representing both the fast growing middle class and civil servants like teachers, policemen, garbagemen and local and Federal government clerks.

The middle class itself was one indication of how successful the revolution had been. Statistician and historian James Wilkie estimated that less than eight percent of the Mexican population would qualify as middle class under the Porfiriate, based on census data and other records from the Porfiriate up through 1960. By 1940, about one-fifth of Mexicans fit the definition, but by 1960, a full third of the population was middle class.

Sociologist Oscar Lewis, who somehow convinced people to let him and his researchers listen in on and follow their every activity and then to produce a series of classic studies on Mexican family life, studied mostly the poor. No small detail was overlooked—Lewis and his team would count the number of eating utensils a family had, note whether there was an alarm clock in the apartment and note every other item a family owned. Comparing the goods a family owned against their neighbors is how Lewis classified the poor.

---

[152] Not counting the somewhere between forty-five minutes and three hours that Pedro Lascuráin Paredes served. When Madero and Pino Suárez were forced to resign at gunpoint, foreign minister Lascuráin was sworn in as interim president and named Huerta as his acting foreign minister. Then resigned, giving Huerta a fig leaf of legitimacy as interim president, as per Ambassador Henry Lane Wilson's "Pact of the Embassy". Lascuráin himself could never remember exactly how long he was president, though he thought it was under an hour.

When he started his research in the 1940s, owning a wristwatch was an indication of slightly better status than one's neighbors. In the 40s, the family with the radio was the best off family in the apartment block. By the 50s, he'd stopped counting watches and soon stopped paying attention to radios. By the late 1950s, one of Lewis' subject families supplemented their income by charging the neighbors a fee to sit in their front room and watch TV!

With the PRI focused on industrialization, consumer goods previously unavailable in México started appearing. The Party had decided that goods available elsewhere would be available domestically, so the government steered development funds towards Mexican businesses that made equivalent goods. While there might not be ten brands of canned tomato soup in the super-market, there would be at least one Mexican brand (there would be a supermarket, too).

México was still overwhelmingly an agricultural nation. Alemán and his successors still paid attention to agricultural development; irrigation projects and market roads were particularly large state investments in the post-war era. While half the country still lived in small villages of under twenty-five hundred people in 1960, by then those villages were more likely to have a road and a school. Many took the road out. Cities doubled...and doubled again...and again. Less than one in twenty Mexicans lived in the Federal District (Mexico City) when Madero was president (1911–13). By 1960, one in seven Mexicans was a chilango,[153] while by 2000, it was nearly one in five, and the Greater Mexico City area (which by then sprawled into parts of the States of México, Morelos and Hidalgo) was home to a quarter of all Mexicans.

The successes of the Mexican Revolution—in improving health care, education and opportunity—began to have a negative effect. No country at the time considered that a growing population was a particular danger to their future, but México's was growing much

---

[153] Originally something of a term of abuse, meaning anyone born in Mexico City, now Mexico City's residents proudly call themselves "chilangos". Chilango is also the title of a hip magazine.

faster than most others. Between the end of revolutionary violence in 1920 and 1950, the number of Mexicans doubled—from fourteen million to over twenty-eight million. By 1960, there were over thirty-eight million people and the numbers continued to rise. The assumption among all planners in the early and mid-twentieth century was that agricultural production would continue to expand, but with about the same (or fewer) workers, as mechanization and better seed varieties increased crop yields. One reason the government began emphasizing industrial development after the Second World War was the recognition that there were was a limit to the farm land available, and the growing population was going to need work. Ruiz Cortines, the bland agricultural economist, who served as president in the 1950s, recognized the need for better nutrition and a healthy diet among the masses, and by his success, created conditions where even more young Mexicans were growing up and having families of their own.

There was a growing sense that the numbers could not continually rise without consequences. People had faith in technology to resolve basic problems with food, but providing jobs, schooling and housing for growing numbers of people would be challenge. Huasteca women from Veracruz State, had an answer—and one that completely changed western civilization.

For centuries the Huasteca had lived in harmony with their environment—having only the number of children that they were able to adequately care for. Unlike other indigenous societies that limit their numbers, the Huasteca did not resort to infanticide, abortion or sexual abstinence. Fascinated scientists wanted to know the secret, which the Huasteca women were quite happy to share—wild yams. *Dioscorea villosa*, which grows throughout eastern North America, is a source of diosgenin, a chemical which causes the body to produce progesterone, a female hormone which inhibits fertility.

Unable to interest pharmaceutical companies in the United States in pursuing the research, Dr. Russell Marker moved to Mexico City and began producing diosgenin. Once the chemical composition was known, and with additional research by a Roman Catholic doctor, John Rock, who was searching for a way to prevent pregnancies among his mostly lower-middle-class patients in Boston while satisfying religious objections to artificial birth control, oral contraceptives first became available in the late 1950s.

Because the effects of "the Pill" were indirect (it did not kill the sperm or directly interfere with fertilization), Pope Pius XII gave his approval of the drug for use by Catholics in 1958. This was one of those rare times the Pope and the PRI were in agreement: for the PRI (perhaps cynically) it meant they could encourage poor Mexicans to have smaller families and concentrate more of the state's resources on the "productive" middle class. Even after a later pope, Paul VI, decided in 1968 that the Pill was not acceptable for use by Catholics, Mexicans had come to expect the State to offer birth control pills and other family-planning services. Family planning became so popular that the right to control family size was added to the constitution. Today México remains at the forefront of the nations that brought a new problem—the population explosion—under control. Although México's population continued to grow (estimated at about one hundred twenty million in 2007), the rate of growth is among the lowest in the world and the number of Mexicans will slightly decline over the next several decades.

Freed from the worries about unwanted pregnancies and with fewer children requiring care at home, Mexican women moved into other pursuits more and more (as did women elsewhere in the world). With less worries about their daughters "getting in trouble" when out of the home, conservative parents were also more likely to let their daughters move in wider circles or even leave home. For the first time, girls like Xóchitl Gálvez Ruiz, from a traditional Mayan family, could go to Mexico City to pursue a university degree. Gálvez, together with other Mayan students, squatted for several years in abandoned buildings and begged on the streets. Unable to afford textbooks and supplies, the Mayans would buy a single text for all of them to use. Gálvez emerged from her squatters' camp *cum* study group with an advanced degree in accounting.

She went on to have a distinguished career as a businesswoman and politician, later serving in Vicente Fox's (2000–2006) cabinet as México's first secretary for indigenous affairs.

Gálvez was studying at UNAM during its greatest period of expansion. The huge number of younger, better-educated Mexicans—who no longer needed to be kept under strict parental control—created a huge demand for more university education.

UNAM, the Autonomous National University of México, had far outgrown the facilities Vasconcelos had used when he refounded the 16th-century institution in 1920. In the 1950s, an entirely new suburb, *Ciudad Universitaría* – University City – was laid out south of Coyoacán to house what was by then—and still is—one of the world's largest universities. Other universities sprang up all over the country or were greatly expanded.

The students were not just from the elite families but included poor students like Gálvez and former shoe-shine boy and son of an auto mechanic, Ernesto Zedillo Ponce de León, who came from Tijuana to Mexico City to study at the other major national university (IPN, the National Polytechnic Institute) when he was sixteen. Zedillo would later earn a PhD at Yale University, become president of México and after his term in office, return to Yale as a professor.

By the numbers

ALEMÁN WAS FOLLOWED IN OFFICE by Adolfo Ruíz Cortines. Using statistics to relate the accomplishments of the Revolution and the Institutional Revolution has a lot to do with Ruíz Cortines.

Ruíz Cortines was the last of the old leadership, and the first of the new bureaucratic and academic leaders. Sixty-two when he assumed the presidency in 1952, he was the last president to have served in the Revolution. An agricultural economist, his military career had been as an army bureaucrat in the quartermaster corps.

The PRI leadership depended less and less on revolutionary ties, and more and more on institutional ones—academics and bureaucrats became the party leaders. If Ruíz Cortines stands out in any way, it's because he was so colorless, but he was one of the best of the bureaucratic presidents. One Mexican wit said, "He is the only man with boring mistresses." The 1950s was an era for grumpy old men in high office.[154] Ruíz Cortines, who preferred

---

[154] Before Ruíz Cortines, Carranza, who was fifty-eight when he became president, was the oldest man to serve as president of México (not counting one or two viceroys who were over eighty). The early 1950s was an era of "old" leaders. U.S. President Harry Truman, German Chancellor Konrad Adenauer and Indian Prime Minister Jawaharlal Nehru were in their sixties when they took office. British Prime Minister Winston Churchill was seventy-one.

playing dominoes with his cronies to being photographed with movie starlets or driving around the Capital in flashy convertibles like Alemán, was one of them.

Alemán was always being photographed at the opening of something: new bridges, dams, highways, office buildings, supermarkets, even the new UNAM campus. Ruíz Cortines also poured government money into roads and dams (and the pockets of politicians who suddenly went into the road and dam building business), but he could do without the publicity. He was happier analyzing things like the 1950 census data, which had asked Mexicans how often they ate fish, meat or eggs in any week. With his background in agricultural economics and concerned about reports of protein deficiencies in México, Ruíz Cortines spent six years pushing egg and chicken production, making them staples of the Mexican diet...and giving away turkeys.

These were live turkeys, hopefully, a source of more turkeys, meat and eggs for poor families.[155] In the U.S., while it was not uncommon for politicians to distribute turkeys (dead and plucked) to poor constituents with an expectation of their support at the next election, this small, mostly rural, Mexican assistance program is a good example of how the government programs became Party programs. Until the 2000s, there was no suggestion that the birds, seeds or building materials given to needy people were anything other than payment for party support at the next election.

After election law reforms in the late 1990s, the government had to run television commercials to spread the message that anyone—regardless of political party—could have a free turkey. Using government funds to spread party propaganda is now a serious criminal offense, but in every election, candidates still try it. In 2006, one creative PRI candidate spent municipal funds to give

---

[155] Although meant primarily as a rural assistance program, very few colonias anywhere in México have restrictions on raising livestock. "City folks" often keep chickens, ducks, turkeys or even pigs and goats in the backyard. Elena Poniatowska's *Here's to You, Jesusa!* was based on conversations with Josefina Bórquez, as the two tended the chickens the cantankerous eighty year old was raising in her one-room Mexico City apartment.

away women's underwear…with the candidate's face and campaign slogan printed on the front. The candidate lost, by the way.

Ruíz Cortines was not a stupid man. He hated politics (he said he'd rather eat toads than be president), but accepted the way the system worked, even though he was an honest man himself.

Alemán had been flashy, but the low-profile Ruíz Cortines had a gift for public relations as well. Alemán had tolerated—even encouraged—bribery and corruption as the price of speedy development. Shortly after taking office, Ruíz Cortines' chauffeur made an illegal U-turn in front of Los Pinos and received a traffic ticket from a city traffic cop. The cop was given a medal for his honesty. Naturally, all this was filmed for the newsreels (TV wasn't widely available until later, and most people still watched their news at the movie theater or heard it on the radio.) More seriously, he released an audit of his holdings when he became president and offered to release one when he left…which he did.

Alemán, who had gone on to serve as the new secretary of tourism (he liked public relations), never explained his huge wealth, much of which came from timely investments in suburban real estate just as Mexico City was growing and the middle-class housing market was hot (thanks to his government policies and the roads he had built to his suburban tracts).

New Frontiers — the 1960s

If Ruíz Cortines resembled Harry Truman or Dwight
Eisenhower, his successor, Adolfo López Mateos, is
sometimes compared to John F. Kennedy. Young, handsome and
with a playboy reputation (Kennedy kept his affairs with movie stars
away from the public. López Mateos was regularly photographed with
glamorous actresses, and never denied gossip about his supposed
affairs[156]), and, like Kennedy, he had a reputation as an intellectual.

Kennedy and López Mateos were often shown surrounded by
intellectuals, and López Mateos came by his reputation honestly.
The president's mother was a rare woman for her time. She was an
educational pioneer, a writer and the administrator of a Mexico
City orphanage.[157] It was an unusual orphanage, also serving as
a literary and cultural "salon". Adolfo's sister was a well-known

---

[156] México—as with other Latin American and "Catholic" countries—have a
relaxed attitude towards sex. While it may be considered sexist now, a politician's
reputation was enhanced, rather than damaged by allegations that he kept mistresses. The "Monica Lewinski scandal" that so bedeviled Bill Clinton, increased
the U.S. president's popular standing among Mexicans.

[157] A surprising number of Mexican leaders have been teachers, raised by teachers,
or orphans. Some, like Obregón, have been all three. Besides Obregón, Juárez and
Calles were orphans. All three, as well as Porfirio Díaz were schoolteachers at one
time or another…and interim president de la Huerta became a dance teacher.

editor and translator. Among her clients was the reclusive German refugee author who called himself "B. Traven". The author, despite having been born an illegitimate member of the German Imperial family (some have speculated that Kaiser Wilhelm II was his father) was an anarchist who had fled to México to escape Hitler and had built a reputation, despite writing in German under a false name, as one of México's greatest novelists.

The president's literary abilities were such that when the recluse claimed he was only the German translator of Adolfo López Mateos, writing under the name "B. Traven", it sounded almost plausible. Obviously, it was a joke. *The Treasure of the Sierra Madre*—Traven's first Mexican novel—was published in 1927, when López Mateos was only an eighteen-year-old student. More important was López Mateos' appointment of future Nobel Prize for Literature winner, Octavio Paz, as Ambassador to India and making room in the civil service for artists and intellectuals.

López Mateos had been Secretary of Labor in Ruíz Cortines' cabinet, and there were hopes that given his pro-labor and pro-agrarian stance, he'd be another Cárdenas. While he continued land distribution into the early 1960s and nationalized the electrical companies, his labor record is spotty at best.

Faced with a serious railway strike and rural unrest—conditions were not improving as well in the countryside as the statistics indicated; some areas did very well, while others lagged behind—López Mateos saw the strikers as "outside the Constitution". Or rather his *Secretario de Gobernación*,[158] Gustavo Díaz Ordaz Bolaños Cacho,

---

[158] I have left *Secretario de Gobernación* in Spanish because the usual translation, "Interior Secretary" (the title in most European countries for the cabinet officer responsible for domestic security) is likely to mislead U.S. readers. *Secretario de Gobernación* is roughly equivalent to the British Home Secretary or the U.S. Secretary of Homeland Security. Because México has no vice president, the *Secretario de Gobernación* assumes executive authority should the president die or resign until Congress names an interim president. When Obregón was assassinated, Emilio Portes Gil, his *Secretario de Gobernación*, was selected by Congress to serve as interim president until the 1929 Congressional elections, when Pascual Ortiz Rubio was elected to serve the remaining four years of what should have been Obregón's six-year term.

did. Díaz Ordaz was more than willing to use repressive measures and used the army to break the railway strike and then, claiming rural dissidents were "Communist guerrillas", he had them hunted down and killed.

Despite this, López Mateos managed to avoid being blamed by the public for the crackdown and—because of his rural programs and nationalization of the electrical industry—remained personally popular.

There is one other comparison between López Mateos and John Kennedy. Despite their youth and seeming energy, both men were very ill. Kennedy had Addison's disease, López Mateos uncontrollable high blood pressure. He suffered blinding migraines throughout his presidency (soon after leaving office, he suffered a massive cerebral hemorrhage and never recovered), which could account for his passivity and dependence on Díaz Ordaz.

The Mexican government took on a "good cop, bad cop" personality over the next several years. On the one hand, the country had a liberal social climate and robust intellectual life. Two future Nobel Prize winning writers, Octavio Paz and Carlos Fuentes were active in the period, and a third, Colombian author Gabriel García Márquez, would make Mexico City his home. García Márquez would be the most prominent of the large number of leftist artists and writers who fled repressive regimes throughout Latin America for the intellectual and artistic freedom of México.

By the late 1960s, under López Mateos' successors, domestic dissent was repressed, and opposition leaders were marginalized. Starting with the 1958 railway strike, dissident union leaders—and dissidents in general—were either branded as "radicals" and denied jobs, or branded as "Communist guerrillas"—especially rural dissidents—hunted down by the army and killed.

News was controlled. Newspapers were not overtly censored—rather, the government controlled access to paper (newsprint requires a steady supply of pine trees and water for production; México being mostly desert, a government agency imported paper from Russia, Norway and Canada), and government advertising—Party controlled—made up the bulk of most "independent" newspapers' revenue. Control of advertising revenue also allowed the Party or government to control what was broadcast on radio. The only television network was government owned. TV news anchor Jacobo Zabludovsky later said he considered it his job to promote the PRI.

For the masses, life was relatively placid. The peso was stable, and the growing middle class could afford Prince von Hohenlohe's Volkswagens. A successful rural electrification program extended the "good life" to the campesinos, who could finally listen to the radio and see how city folks lived by watching *telenovelas*.

The brainchild of actor-turned-producer Ernesto Alonzo, the telenovela was not inspired by American soap operas (with their open ended scripts that allowed the storyline to develop over several years—or even decades) but by the novels of Honoré de Balzac whose stories of rich and poor in 19th-century Paris were written as serialized chapters in French newspapers. The original telenovelas focused on the foibles and misadventures of Mexico City's upper class much as Balzac had written about his own native city's "movers and shakers". As in the French novels, often a poor but deserving heroine—after various tribulations—would triumph in the end, capturing the heart of a rich and deserving hero. Telenovelas provided ordinary people a glimpse of the lifestyles of the rich (and often devious), giving newly minted and upwardly mobile middle-class people a sense of what material goods signified wealth and modern life.

The simple plot line (poor girl overcomes obstacles to get rich boy) could obliquely criticize society and the government, for example: the villain is a corrupt politician in one. Or it might highlight social problems: a housing shortage in Mexico City in the late 1990s had one telenovela heroine searching not just for love but for an affordable apartment for her mother.

Wildly successful since their debut in 1957, the Mexican telenovela formula was copied throughout the world, and the Mexican originals were dubbed into other languages and proved popular in such disparate countries as Ivory Coast and the Soviet Union, where one telenovela—by showing a relatively functional "social-ist" state —is sometimes credited with the demise of that country's Communist government. By 2007, Televisa (which produces most telenovelas) was earning more in foreign rights from this one genre than the British Broadcasting Corporation earned from all their foreign sales.

México's new relationship with the United States, its traditional neutrality, its leadership in Hispanic and Latin American culture and López Mateos' desire to move México to the political left all came crashing together during the 1962 "Cuban Missile Crisis". Cuba and México were more than just geographical neighbors. They had shared cultural ties since Cortés first sailed from the island to conquer *Nueva España* – New Spain. "Spaniards" who emigrated to México during the 19th century were usually Cubans, not gachupines, who easily integrated into Mexican society.

In the late 1950s Cuba, like México under Porfirio, was politi-cally controlled by a military strongman, Fulgencio Batista, and under the economic control of foreign interests—including shady ones. Only ninety miles from Florida, American gangsters oper-ated openly in Havana.

A young Cuban labor lawyer, Fidel Castro, finally succeeded in overthrowing the gangsters and Batista with private, covert Mexican assistance. While locked up as an undesirable alien in the Mexican oil port of Pozo Rico, the friendly police chief loaded an abandoned American-owned yacht, Granma, with weapons and supplies for an invasion and freed Castro and his associates. Obviously succeeding, Castro took over Havana on New Year's Day 1959.

Castro's government, being Communist, was unacceptable to the United States, which attempted to force other American states to cut political and economic ties with Cuba. México led the opposition to the U.S. boycott, based on the Juárez Doctrine's policy of noninterference in other nation's internal affairs.

When it was discovered that the Soviets were setting up missile bases on Cuba, the U.S. threatened nuclear war. López Mateos, who was on his way to a Hawaiian vacation (and some relief from his blinding headaches), returned immediately to Mexico City. López Mateos, despite his illness, worked with both the U.S. and Soviet leaders to diffuse the situation on a global level. At the same time, the Mexican ambassador in Havana, the tough Second World War diplomat, Gilberto Bosques, who had saved tens of thousands from the Nazis, negotiated a face-saving agreement with the Cuban leadership.

The Mexican role in preventing nuclear annihilation is seldom noted, but México did receive a small reward. In 1848, the mid-point of the Rio Bravo (the Rio Grande River in the United States) became the border. However, a few years later the river changed course, leaving a few hectares (one hectare being about two and one-half acres) of México stranded in El Paso, Texas. The few residents of Chamizal were Mexicans, but their land was claimed by the United States (which occasionally deported the people from their own homes). It isn't a particularly valuable piece of real estate, and it took a few years to work out the details, but the river's 1848 course was officially recognized as the border—returning the small El Paso neighborhood to Mexican control.[159] President Lyndon Baines Johnson got wildly enthusiastic press coverage in México when Chamizal was ceded back to the Republic. López Mateos was hailed as a second Juárez.

He wasn't. Nor was he Quetzalcóatl, nor even Lázaro Cárdenas. Huitzilopochtli and Tezcatlipoca were waiting in the wings for his successors.

---

[159] As a result of new surveys, it was discovered that a small piece of the United States was in Ojinaga, Chihuahua, and a larger piece of México was in Presidio, Texas. The two uninhabited parcels changed nationality with almost no publicity in 1970.

We all want to change
the world....

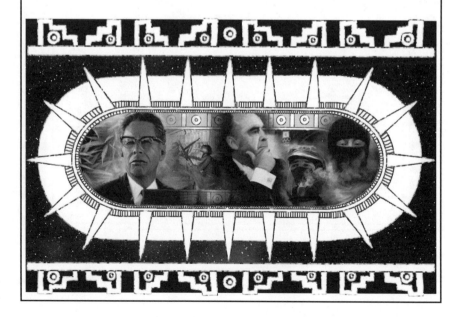

México ca. 1988

Everybody, let's rock!

When Gustavo Díaz Ordaz took the oath of office as president of México on December 1, 1964 he could look back over the past forty years with pride and satisfaction, and he could look forward with hope and confidence.... Peace and stability came as a result of a general consensus, within a gradually developing democratic framework.

Charles C. Cumberland. *Mexico: The Struggle for Modernity.* Oxford University Press, 1968

THE REVOLUTION HAD BEEN A SUCCESS. México was a modern country, with a growing middle class, who could afford to buy Mexican-made autos and consumer goods, who could expect their children to receive a decent education and with some work, a university degree and a decent career. Even blue-collar workers could look forward to a few weeks vacation a year, and poor campesinos received at least enough to get them through the year...or they could emigrate to the cities (or the United States) and improve their lot.

Miguel Alemán had institutionalized the revolutionary family, eliminating the need for military presidents. While Ruíz Cortines had served in the Revolution, since Alemán, Mexican presidents have come from civilian careers.

A Mexican, Jaime Torres Bodet, was selected to lead the new United Nations Educational Scientific and Cultural Organization (UNESCO). Mexican diplomats, including future Nobel Prize winning poet, Octavio Paz, distinguished themselves as representatives of an important, nonaligned nation that enjoyed good relations with both of the two superpowers—the United States and the Soviet Union.

Mexican students in the 1960s did what previous generations of students have always done (though for the first time, they probably could enjoy sex without worrying about pregnancy): talk to each other and experiment with new ideas...and demand change.

In 1958, UNAM students had staged noisy street protests over a canceled showing of the new Elvis Presley film, "Jailhouse Rock". It was a minor incident and quickly settled (the Party and the theaters arranged for extra showings and student discount tickets), but it was the start of something bigger. Elvis' role as the nonconformist, lower-class Vince Everett had resonated with the students, even the middle and upper-class students, the beneficiaries of the Institutional Revolution. Ironically, because of the successes of the Institutional Revolution the students had access to the wider world and as Mexicans, saw themselves as active participants in that world.

While rock 'n' roll would not be forbidden over the next twenty-five years, the government's attitude was, at best, ambivalent. "People are strange," as Jim Morrison of the Doors sang. With many radio stations unwilling to play the disturbingly new (and potentially revolutionary) music in the U.S., Mexican stations just across the border set up powerful transmitters that broadcast their signals as far north as Iowa and North Carolina.[160] On the other hand, the PRI used the excuse that they were protecting Mexican culture by attempting to limit Mexican access to the new music. The authorities didn't seem to realize that radio waves do not travel only in one direction, but in all directions. What could be heard going north to Iowa could be heard going south to Mexico City.

Several Mexican rock 'n' roll bands developed, and listening to—or copying—foreign rock 'n' roll was seen as somewhat more subversive than it really was. In the left-wing press, where a previous generation of writers might have made reference to Karl Marx or Antonio Gramsci, writers like Carlos Monsiváis Aceves peppered their essays with rock lyrics. The Beatles, who never appeared in México, had a tremendous influence on literature and culture (one Mexican radio station played nothing but the Beatles, twenty-four hours a day, three hundred sixty-five days a year for over twenty years) and Jim Morrison's lyrics would—by 2000—be considered an essential part of world literary culture and widely studied in universities.

---

[160] U.S. AM radio stations were and still are legally limited to fifty-thousand watts. XREF, in Ciudad Acuña broadcast at two-hundred-fifty-thousand watts. Originally featuring religious programming, the station became a huge success in the United States when Del Rio, Texas disc jockey, Robert Smith, began playing the new music, using the pseudonym, "Wolfman Jack". A central figure in the 1973 George Lucas film, "American Graffiti", Wolfman Jack later worked for a similar "border blaster" station in Tijuana.

The tourist invasion

IN 1946 MÉXICO WAS UNDAMAGED by the war, and the Revolutionary violence had ended. Tourists, who normally went to Europe, discovered México also had beaches, ruins and colorful local celebrations to be seen. Furthermore, prices were much lower than in Europe, and it was easier to drive across the border than to fly to Europe. Tourism would quickly become a major industry. Even before the war ended, Tennessee Williams holed up in what was then the small seaside town of Puerto Vallarta, the setting for *Night of the Iguana*. A successful 1962 film adaptation—directed by John Huston, starring Richard Burton as a failed priest turned tour guide and Ava Gardner as an expat hotel operator, helped turn the sleepy seaside resort into a major tourist destination. In recognition of the film's importance, Puerto Vallarta later erected a statue of Huston.

Despite jokes about Montezuma's Revenge,[161] tourists continued to give glowing reports of their Mexican vacations, and catering to foreign visitors became an increasingly important economic activity. For residents of Mexico City and the growing resort towns like Acapulco, this also meant going to nightclubs. In the 1950s, nightclubs featuring dancing girls in exotic costumes and "exotic" drinks were popular throughout Europe and the United States. Attending one was considered part of any vacation. So, México had to have nightclubs, and the government underwrote their development... and, so that tourists would see that they were popular, sometimes arranged for civil servants to spend their evenings in them.

At the end of the war, U.S. veterans could take advantage of the "G.I. Bill", allowing them to attend the college of their choice. Entrepreneurial educators set up the Community College of Mexico City, which had a terrible academic reputation but gave rootless U.S. veterans a rationale for living in Mexico City. Their best-known student was William S. Burroughs, who suddenly had a hankering to study in México after he was arrested in Texas for marijuana possession. Burroughs, with a modest independent income that allowed him to write, was a heroin addict and homosexual. He wrote about both, turning out *Junkie* and *Queer* during his time in the city. Burroughs seemed to be under the impression that he was living as an outlaw, but neither possession of small amounts of heroin for personal use, nor homosexuality were—or are—crimes in México. Shooting one's wife—which Burroughs did in 1949—was. He claimed it was an accident, but fled the country before standing trial.

---

[161] Originally, "Montezuma's Revenge" was the name given by U.S. troops during the 1846–48 war to a much more serious—and often fatal—ailment, dysentery. Dysentery is spread by fecal contamination. It was the leading cause of death in military campaigns at the time, spread by poor hygiene and the cavalier attitude towards latrine placement by 19th-century armies. In modern times, "Montezuma's Revenge" means the minor diarrhea caused by eating unfamiliar foods and upsetting one's routine—a normal occurrence for vacationers. Mexicans, with good humor, name the same ailment *turista*.

While Burroughs was living in the city, Jack Kerouac and Alan Ginsburg were regular visitors. Kerouac's *On the Road*—although written in 1949—is still believed by many to be an accurate portrait of Mexican culture. Kerouac was stoned most of the time, and his observations made nearly sixty years ago are unlikely to still hold true, if they ever were. Still, the book's popularity led to a flood of younger tourists—less well-heeled or fussy than the busload from the East Texas Baptist Women's College who so bedeviled the Reverend T. Lawrence Shannon in *Night of the Iguana*—looking for adventure, sex and cheap drugs. In the 1960s these tourists would include the hippies, who made traditional Mexican clothing and styles fashionable throughout the Western world.

A host of books, throughout the 1960s and 70s, presented México as an escape from bourgeois conventionality. Not only the hippies, but thrill seekers and those in search of enlightenment began traveling the country along with the well-heeled tourists looking for sun and sand or ruins and colorful local customs. By 2000, tourism would be the third most important economic activity in México (after oil production and remittances), accounting for about nine percent of the Gross Domestic Product. Over twenty million tourists visit México every year.

Joint efforts

MÉXICO'S INDIGENOUS CULTURE HAD ALWAYS accepted the use of certain "mind-altering drugs"—peyote, hallucinogenic mushrooms and marijuana. Peyote and the mushrooms were generally used medicinally or ritually and marijuana smoking, while considered somewhat *naco* – lower class – was never frowned upon.[162]

After the Second World War, drug use became a growing concern, especially in the United States. While there was an argument to be made that the drugs that were considered dangerous were those outside the control of pharmaceutical companies (like naturally growing substances found in México), or that marijuana was considered dangerous in the United States because it was mostly used by poor Mexicans and African-Americans, the result was that the U.S. government considered Mexican drugs a threat and a law enforcement concern.

México's more tolerant attitude towards drugs attracted a new kind of tourist. William S. Burroughs and Jack Kerouac both came

---

[162] Pancho Villa—who did not tolerate foul language or alcohol use among his subordinates—expected them to smoke marijuana. His troops, with his full support, regularly sang their "theme song"—"la Cucaracha"—a silly song about smoking marijuana with the Virgin of Guadalupe and shaving Venustiano Carranza.

to México in part because of it. Even nonnatural drugs were generally available. In México, Burroughs, a heroin addict, could obtain the refined opiate, heroin (opium poppies grow well in some parts of México, and Acapulco was a center of opium distribution in the 19th century), since México treated heroin addiction as a medical problem at the time, and heroin addicts were given prescriptions. Most illegal Mexican heroin was smuggled into the United States: the mastermind of the operation in the late 1940s and 1950s was Lola la Chata, an illiterate indigenous woman living in Tepito (conveniently married to a Mexico City policeman).

The new breed of American tourists who began coming to México in the 1960s were less interested in bullfights or colorful nightclub acts—or in glamorous venues like Acapulco and Mexico City. Cheap, quasi-legal drugs and freedom from what was seen as a puritanical culture in the United States spurred their visits.

The new tourists, generally young and with less cash than the older generation of visitors, had a profound impact on both México and the U.S. Small seaports and fishing towns—especially on the Pacific Coast—turned into resort communities. Whether the Mexicans were simply following Juárez' advice to stay out of other people's affairs, or traditional good manners towards guests was behind it, word got out that México accepted unconventional lifestyles. Hippies, artists and ordinary people seeking a short break from their routine lives came in ever increasing numbers.

In the United States and elsewhere, "going to Mexico" meant rejecting middle-class propriety and living a more colorful, less stressful existence than people believed they experienced at home. Hippies and would-be hippies began wearing typical indigenous Mexican clothing, making the sometimes despised "indio" a cultural norm in the wealthy countries. By 2000, a long-haired man in the U.S. wearing what Mexican indigenous people have always worn—baggy cotton trousers and shirt, an earring and a necklace—was unremarkable. So was marijuana use.

Though the U.S. and other countries would continually pressure Mexican authorities to control the trade and eventually make it illegal in México, marijuana cultivation became an increasingly important cash crop. Explosive demand in the U.S. (by 2000, the United States consumed a quarter of the world's narcotics supply) made México a logical supplier. As tastes changed, Mexican smugglers changed their products but improved their supply capabilities. When cocaine (made from coca, an Andean plant that does not grow in México) became popular, Mexican smugglers worked with South American suppliers to handle distribution.

The drug trade is, of course, a criminal enterprise. The result was that criminals had a lot of money to spend and invest. This created two problems. First, any Mexican investment in the late 20th century was assumed by outsiders to involve criminals, making it difficult for Mexican businesses to attract investors. Secondly, because criminals cannot use the courts or legal system to resolve business issues, they turned to "alternative dispute resolution methods". They bribed officials, poured funding into political parties and resorted to violence to enforce contracts. In the early 21st century, México is portrayed as a violent society, largely because the criminals—satisfying demand in the United States—use weapons bought in the United States to kill each other and to kill those who interfere with their activities.

The growing number of sophisticated, educated young people, changing social attitudes and the government's attempts to maintain the institutional benefits of the Revolution all tragically collided in October 1968.

The Ghosts of Tlaltelolco

I N 1910, THE CENTENNIAL CELEBRATION would mark the end of the Porfiriate. In 1968, the Summer Olympic Games would be the beginning of the end of the Institutional Revolution.

In the 1960s, as it was under Porfirio, México was held up to other nations as a "model" of economic and social progress. Unlike the other Latin American nations, it enjoyed political and economic stability and had a developed, modern infrastructure. Mexico City was chosen for the first Summer Olympic Games to be held outside what was then called a "First World" country.[163]

As in 1910, when Porfirio had planned to show México to the world in the best possible light, in 1968, López Mateos' successor,

---

[163] Even today, México is sometimes called a "third world country", which originally meant a nation that was not a rich capitalist one, like France or the United States (the "First World"), nor one with a Communist government. However, "third world" began to mean countries with abject poverty and a virtually nonexistent middle class. The phrase "developing country" was coined to mean less wealthy nations with some industry, but México "developed" into an industrial nation in the 19th century, so that term, too, is misleading. While there are parts of México where abject poverty is all too common, the modern definition, used by the Organization for Economic Cooperation and Development (OECD), uses per capita income and general economic and social conditions to classify nations. The OECD calls México a "middle-class" country.

Gustavo Díaz Ordaz and the PRI wanted to show a modern, progressive México. New sports and housing facilities were built, the streets expanded, and the new Metro (Mexico City's subway system) was rushed into operation. At the same time, they—like Porfirio—were haunted by the thought that something could go wrong.

In 1910, Porfirio had underestimated middle- and lower-class resistance to his rule. In 1968, the middle class was a much larger proportion of the people (thanks to the Revolution) and the lower classes had expectations and abilities (again, thanks to the Revolution) that their grandparents did not enjoy.

There were a lot more young people on the streets in Mexico City; 1968 was a year when youth all over the world had rebelled. In the United States, protests against the Vietnam War had started attracting large numbers of students...and turned violent. In Czechoslovakia, where a reform Communist government had briefly taken control, the Soviet Union intervened militarily and the student protests turned into guerrilla warfare. Even in London, where political violence is very rare, students and police clashed during a demonstration against British involvement in Vietnam. Growing unrest forced both Presidents Lyndon Johnson in the United States and Charles de Gaulle in France to announce their retirement. In France, the issues involved labor rights and the educational system, uniting students and workers.

Díaz Ordaz, when López Mateos' *Secretario de Gobernación*, had been responsible for cracking down on union unrest. When Miguel Alemán founded the Institutional Revolutionary Party he had excluded the far-left, and under his successors the unions had gradually been made part of the Party structure. The leadership was chosen (often through fraudulent elections or violence against dissenters) more for their party loyalty than for their willingness to fight for their workers. For ordinary rank-and-file workers, voting against the Party or just refusing to show up at pro-Party demonstrations could cost them their jobs...or, in some cases, their lives.

After the Second World War, the ideological Cold War between the United States and the Soviet Union was responsible for both superpowers' attempts to intervene in other nations' internal affairs. In México—geographically and economically tied to the United States—U.S. fears of "Communists" coupled with the PRI's own interest in isolating dissident unions, led to the contradictory situation where a left-wing, theoretically socialist country was tacitly supported when it cracked down on dissenters and dissident unions that were labeled "Communist".

The PRI leaders were also being practical. The United States government was not shy about using its power to stop radical reforms in Latin America. In 1954, Jacobo Árbenz, the Lázaro Cárdenas of Guatemala, attempted to nationalize banana farms owned by United Fruit Company. Allen Dulles,[164] director of the U.S. Central Intelligence Agency, was on the United Fruit board of directors. To Dulles, Árbenz was not a reformer, he was a Communist: the CIA openly organized a brief but bloody coup. After the 1959 Cuban Revolution, the United States backed increasingly reactionary and even fascist regimes in Central America, leading to civil wars that lasted well into the 1980s.

Officially, the Mexican government maintained neutrality and eventually sponsored peace negotiations among factions in these wars. Unlike the 1930s, when the government either ignored or actively abetted Mexican support for the Spanish Republic, Mexican supporters of the rebel groups in Central America were often harassed, although only half heartedly.

Threats to Mexican industry that might affect U.S. interests (including strikes) were also seen as "Communist". Although the CIA was not going to attempt to overthrow the Mexican government, the agency was not above subverting Mexican officials

---

[164] The Dulles family has a "Mexican connection". Alan and his brother, U.S. Secretary of State John Foster Dulles owed their considerable personal fortune and political connections to their grandfather, who had been the United States ambassador to México in the 1890s. John Foster Dulles' son, John W. F. Dulles, eschewed politics, wrote Mexican history and later taught Latin American Studies at the University of Texas.

or "suggesting" that specific social movements or leaders were "Communists". If nothing else, the danger of refugees flooding into the United States or a repeat of Henry Lane Wilson's blunder in 1911 stayed the hand of the spies in Washington.

With the Olympics scheduled to open in mid-October 1968, the Díaz Ordaz government was desperate to preserve an atmosphere of peace and stability. Changing social attitudes, the international student protests, fear of Communism and even Díaz Ordaz' personal ugliness all collided in what is called Tlaltelolco—the beginning of the end of the Institutional Revolution.

A few high school boys, playing soccer, touched off the explosion. The boys started a fight over a disputed goal, and the police responded in force. The police had been quietly removing troublemakers from the streets for weeks, but a fight within a few blocks of the National Palace seemed more serious than it really was. Even in the pre-Internet, pre-text messaging era, word of the police crackdown got around. High school students throughout Mexico City started protesting and were joined by the University students. The Army was sent to raid the University and arrest student leaders. This was seen as an attack on the University's proud sense of autonomy (achieved by Vasconcelos in 1920). UNAM's *rector* – elected president – Javier Barrios Sierra, resigned in protest. The administrators and faculty joined the students in protesting. Universities and high schools throughout the country went on strike.

During one mega-march on the National Palace, the students started chanting, *"¡Sal al balcón, chango hocicón!"* – "Come out on the balcony, you ugly monkey face!" Always sensitive about his physical appearance, Díaz Ordaz lost control of himself. He snapped, "These bastards aren't youths. They're blood-sucking parasites who don't have the balls to fight." He had no intention of addressing the students. Instead he ordered his *Secretario de Gobernación*, Luis Echeverría Álvarez, to restore order. Incidentally, Echeverría is believed to have been receiving bribes from the Central Intelligence Agency at the time.

The most visible sign of the crackdown were the armed soldiers and tanks in the streets. Echeverría also had underground military units [165] set up that answered directly to him. Their mission was to infiltrate student groups as agitators and escalate protests to give the government a rationale to crack down even further.

Unable to march on the National Palace, a peaceful demonstration was planned for Tlaltelolco Plaza on 2 October 1968. Tlaltelolco, the former business suburb of Tenoctitlán, was the site of Cuauhtémoc's final surrender to Cortés. A monument there reads, "Neither a tragedy nor a triumph, here the painful history of México began." High-rise apartments—mostly occupied by the new middle class—surround the plaza. The middle-class residents joined the student protests, as did many union workers. Although the government at the time claimed someone in the crowd started shooting with a rifle, survivors of that night claim an organized group of young men with military haircuts opened fire and set off a flare. Immediately, military helicopters hovered over the demonstrators and opened fire on the crowd. Armed troops surrounded the area, preventing ambulances and journalists from entering. Later reports tell of military trucks seen leaving the area carrying dead bodies.

At the time, based on government information, news headlines read, "Four dead, twenty wounded." The actual number of dead and wounded is unknown—estimates range up to over a thousand, though between two hundred and three hundred deaths is usually considered the correct number. No one knows how many were arrested that night. Many were never seen again.

In México and, over the next several years, throughout Latin America, a new verb entered the Spanish language...*desaparecer* – to make someone disappear. In the rest of Latin America, pro-American governments came to power (often with CIA assistance) and dissenters became *desaparecidos* – the disappeared

---

[165] Literally. To keep the groups' existence secret, their paychecks were passed through the Mexico City subway maintenance department and the cemetery budgets.

ones. While more subtle than the overt "dirty wars" in other Latin American nations—which made no secret of using concentration camps and mass murder in the name of "stability"—dissents were repressed. For the most part though, México remained relatively free, and Mexicans lived relatively peaceful lives.

Political repression in México was never as violent nor as overt as in the rest of Latin America. In Chile (a very small country) for example, tens of thousands of people were tortured and at least three thousand murdered during the military regime. Luis Echeverría was never accused of complicity in more than twenty-five murders.

Though they were likely to be marginalized by being frozen out of good-paying jobs, dissidents were relatively free to do and say what they wanted. One joke at the time had a gringo and Mexican discussing free speech. The American said, "I can yell, 'Down with Richard Nixon', in front of the White House and nothing will happen to me." The Mexican replies, "That's nothing, I can yell, 'Down with Richard Nixon AND Leonid Brezhnev!' in front of Los Pinos!" But yelling, "Down with Díaz Ordaz, or Luis Echeverría," (who was overwhelmingly elected president in 1970) would have been more problematic.

The crackdown continued for many years. Jesús Piedra Ibarra, a young medical student involved with attempts to organize an independent medical workers union, was snatched off a Mexico City street by government agents in 1975 and never seen again. His mother, Rosario Ibarra de Piedra, a Monterrey housewife, would be a thorn in the side of the PRI for the next thirty years. Getting no satisfactory answers to her son's disappearance from Luis Echeverría, she organized family members of other victims of state disappearances to press for answers and to seek to bring Echeverría to justice. In 1988, she ran for president to press for answers. An unusual candidate, she asked voters to support another party's leader, Lázaro Cárdenas' son, Cuauhtémoc. By then, the Party had alienated even the children of the Revolutionary leadership.

When he heard of what happened in Tlaltelolco, México's Ambassador to India, Octavio Paz, immediately resigned in protest and spent the next several years in self-imposed exile. Intellectuals, like the students, the workers and a good part of the middle class, were withdrawing their support from the Institutional Revolution and joining smaller leftist parties.

Trying to balance the Institutional Revolution with the new conservative tone of the times, Echeverría and his successors created an almost schizophrenic political culture. While there was repression at home (small rural dissident groups were branded as Communist revolutionaries and were disappeared...or murdered), the country was more open to political refugees than at any time since the Second World War—generally from other Latin American nations where repression was much more overt. Echeverría, partially to win over rural voters and partially to project a more populist image, began appearing in traditional peasant clothing and expected his cabinet officials to do likewise. He wanted people to forget Díaz Ordaz (who had died of stomach cancer soon after leaving office) and his English suits. Following his term in office, Echeverría campaigned openly for the position of Secretary General of the United Nations and even tried to convince Mother Theresa to recommend him for a Nobel Peace Prize. Mother Theresa didn't bite. By then, the shallowness of his reforms had become clear.

Echeverría, somewhat in the spirit of Obregón who bombarded his enemies with gold pesos, attempted to win over opponents with jobs and government contracts. He was fortunate that huge new oil fields had been discovered in the early 1970s, just as oil prices worldwide were at an all-time high. With the prospect of huge payoffs, the Echeverría government borrowed massive amounts of money, which was poured into new jobs for intellectuals, cultural centers, film production, the arts and sciences as well as rural development, housing and highways.

Oil prices dropped a few years later, leaving Echeverría's successor, José López Portillo y Pacheco, in an especially embarrassing position. The Echeverría administration had created what had been called "the Mexican miracle" on borrowed money. The assumption—both in México and in the United States—had been that oil prices would continue to rise, and that México was about to become a very wealthy country. U.S. banks wanted to loan money to México and even paid a "commission" to Mexican bureaucrats who managed to convince their department heads to take on a development project. A tiny village on the Yucatán peninsula, Cancún, was selected for a new resort community, and between 1970 and 2005, it went from a settlement of a few dozen fishermen to a city of a half million people and is now one of the world's major tourist destinations. Cancún was an exception. Most development projects were either ill-conceived or unnecessary. To keep farmers in the country, huge supermarkets were built in rural areas, but no plans were made to keep the stores stocked— and the rural residents didn't have the money to buy more than essentials. Somewhat on the theory "if you build it they will vote for the Party", four-lane highways and bridges between small rural communities were built where a paved two-lane road would have more than met demand.

The PRI was not the first nor the last political party in the world to use infrastructure development as a way to build political cal support (nor the only party to push wasteful spending), but by expecting oil prices to continue to rise, the money spent was on an unprecedented scale. When he came into office in 1976, López Portillo could afford to be arrogant. "In the economic world, there are only two kinds of countries: those that have oil and those that don't have it…and we have it!" he bragged.

México skids on an oil slick

THEN, BEGINNING IN 1981, the price of oil on the world market fell—and continued to fall. The country was all but bankrupt, and most of the cash within the country was in U.S. dollars (or owed to U.S. banks). López Portillo, the scion of an old criollo family and a poet as well as an athlete (as president, he would toss his javelin around the yard at Los Pinos every day after his morning swim), was seen as something of a joke by Mexican opinion makers. As the peso continued to lose value, he said he would defend the peso as fiercely as a dog defends a bone. For the rest of his life, he couldn't go out in public without people barking at him. There wasn't much on the bone to defend. The peso itself was a joke.

Shortly before leaving office, López Portillo upset world financial markets (and nearly caused the collapse of several U.S. banks) when he nationalized all banks in México. What had been a stable currency (used as a benchmark for other currencies), with a value of eight to the U.S. dollar since the 1930s, was essentially worthless. By 1993, when it was revalued (one new peso=one thousand old pesos), it took more than three-thousand pesos to equal one dollar. By then, the nationalized banks had been reprivatized and sold to the highest bidders, mostly foreign banking companies. Throughout the 1980s and 90s business-oriented people also became disenchanted with the Party, but not willing to join the left, they drifted into the old Synarchist, Falangist, proclerical PAN.

Shocks to the system...

IF SHRINKING PAYCHECKS, rising prices and the political repression wasn't enough, things were about to get much worse. On 19 September 1985, at 7:39 in the morning, an earthquake, measured at 8.1 on the Richter Scale, killed at least nine thousand people in Mexico City and destroyed many of the shoddy new buildings dating from the Echeverría era.

While there was devastation throughout the country (the aftershocks were felt as far away as Houston, Texas), it was in Mexico City that people most clearly saw the PRI as a failure. Unable to provide even minimal relief, and with the army sent out not to assist but apparently to guard wealthy foreign businesses (or to loot), ordinary people discovered extraordinary talents. According to legend, a fourteen-year-old Boy Scout, identified only as *el chamaco* – the kid – took charge of his neighborhood and directed relief operations—at least someone in uniform was competent.

When several of the Tlaltelolco high rises collapsed, survivors quickly organized digging operations, calling on the services of their own residents—not just doctors, nurses and bulldozer operators, but unusual specialists like sewer workers as well—to mount a search and rescue operation. They were so successful that the group, *los Topos de Tlaltelolco* – the Mole Men of Tlaltelolco, officially

404

Brigada de Rescate Topos Tlaltelolco – has since become a world-renowned search and rescue volunteer service. When a tsunami devastated Indonesia and south Asia in 2004, the German airline, Lufthansa, immediately sent the Mole Men and their equipment to Indonesia where Australian Air Force crews and planes were put at their disposal.

While there were some heroes, there were many more obvious scoundrels. Foreign assistance—at first refused by the government—was slow in reaching people in need…if it ever made it. Mexicans were too busy (or shocked) to take to the streets in protest (too many of them were living on the streets), but that didn't mean they weren't capable of a response. Leftists who had abandoned the PRI earlier had joined any number of smaller political parties. The failure to meet basic needs after the 1985 earthquake convinced many more within the PRI that it was time for a change.

...and aftershocks

THE POLITICAL EARTHQUAKE CAME when Cuauhtémoc
Cárdenas, son of the great 1930s leader, joined the
Partido Auténtico de la Revolución Mexicana (*PARM*) – Authentic
Party of the Mexican Revolution. Until then, PARM had been a
small party allied with PRI that always backed the PRI presidential
candidate as their own. With built-in name recognition, Cárdenas
was an ideal presidential candidate when PARM broke with tradition and joined other small parties interested in changing the
system. He ran as a coalition candidate for president against the
PRI in 1988. Rosario Ibarra had already agreed to run on a small
Trotskyite ticket. She used the campaign to press for an investigation into the disappearance of her son and others, but asked the
voters to cast their ballot for Cárdenas.

PAN, breaking with their tradition of not running a candidate
or only running a figurehead to push their clerical and elitist
ideas, also decided to mount a serious campaign as a democratic
conservative alternative. A respected conservative, Manuel de
Jesús Clouthier del Rincon, looking to the future and not expecting to win, named his cabinet in advance. If—or when—he lost,
he would set up an "alternative presidency" to push his program.

His "Secretary of Agriculture" was a wealthy rancher and former Coca-Cola executive from Guanajuato, Vicente Fox y Quesada.

By election day, it was obvious that the crowd-pleasing Cárdenas would beat the designated PRI candidate, a dull Harvard-educated economist, Secretary of Budgetary Affairs, Carlos Salinas de Gortari. With everything else that had happened over the past few years in México, there were real fears in Washington that a leftist revival would destabilize México, just as the economy was starting to recover.

Initial results showed Cárdenas had over half the votes. Then—mysteriously—the computer counting the votes crashed. Even more mysteriously, the computer room caught fire. The outgoing Congress declared Salinas the winner. The president at the time, Miguel de la Madrid Hurtado later claimed—then denied—that his party had lost the election but that he was told by the Americans that a non-PRI victory was unthinkable.

Cárdenas could have—like Obregón or Madero—conceivably mounted armed resistance. PARM was founded by politically active military men when Alemán "institutionalized" the Revolutionary Party and eliminated the military cadres Lázaro Cárdenas had included in the Party structure. PARM still enjoyed strong support from the officers.

Cárdenas—and the left—extracted a price for maintaining stability. The PRI could not undo election results for legislative candidates, and for the first time, there was a credible opposition in Congress. The government agreed to radical changes in the political system that would guarantee free and secret ballots, oversight by an Electoral Commission and—most importantly—a new proportional representation system that assured no party in Congress would have more than two-thirds of the seats. In addition, the Federal District was, for the first time,[166] given self-government. The new *Partido de la Revolución Democrática* (*PRD*) – the Democratic

---

[166] The Cabildo, the council which governed Mexico City since the viceroys, was appointed by the national government.

Revolution Party – which was formed by uniting the anti-PRI left-wing parties, has been overwhelmingly in control of the Federal District since first electing Cárdenas as *Jefe de Gobierno* – Mayor or Governor of the District – in 1997.

The biggest beneficiary of the political and social reforms was—oddly enough—not the PRD, but PAN. PRD leaders were assassinated or died in mysterious car accidents (as did PAN candidate Manuel Clouthier, soon after the 1988 elections), and party workers were continually harassed. PAN—with its mixture of religious conservatives and business-oriented leaders and most active in the northern states bordering the United States—appealed to the similar Republican Party in the United States, which provided much more than just advice. In 1994, Republican North Carolina Senator Jesse Helms became Chairman of the Foreign Relations Committee. Helms attacked the PRI as a dictatorship in Senate hearings, claiming again and again that PRI victories over PAN in state and local elections were due to fraud (which they often were). Abuses against PRD were ignored.

The Republican Party provided political advisors to PAN and helped the party raise money for the 2000 presidential election—the first U.S. style campaign, featuring slick television advertising, bumper stickers and competing attempts by the various candidates' staffs to "spin" their message, held in México. The PAN candidate, Vicente Fox, did become the first non-PRI candidate and first opposition candidate to win the presidency, but he did not—as his campaign continually said (and U.S. media repeated)—"end seventy-one years of one-party rule in México". The reforms forced on the political system by the threat of a revolt by Cárdenas backers had made Congress an equal branch of government. No one party controlled Congress after 1992.

If PAN benefited the most from the 1990s reforms, the second biggest beneficiary was also not a member of the old revolutionary family: the Catholic Church.

Body (politic) and soul

WHAT REMAINED OF THE OLD Revolutionary platform was anticlericalism. Even there, the Salinas administration broke with tradition. Partly to counter the growing strength of PAN, partly under pressure from groups in the United States that saw anticlericalism as reactionary and a human rights abuse and partly because radical changes within the Roman Catholic Church in the 1960s made some anticlericalism seem obsolete, the Salinas administration took the radical step of establishing diplomatic relations with the Vatican and changing the Constitution to ease religious restrictions: priests, nuns and ministers could now vote, wear religious clothing in public and churches could now own houses of worship[167] and even openly run religious schools.

The PRI and most Mexican political leaders since the days of Juárez had been officially anticlerical, but México had remained a Catholic country with close to ninety percent of the population claiming to be Catholics. Manuel Ávila Camacho had broken the

---

[167] Since 1857, when Juárez seized the Church's property, the government had given concessions to denominations to hold worship services in state-owned buildings. In new towns and developments, churches were built for public use, but in theory the state could decide to use the buildings for something else.

taboo on religious belief, openly proclaiming himself a Catholic, though as president, he never attended services publicly. (A priest would come to Los Pinos on Sunday mornings to say a private mass for the president's family.) Religious nonbelief was no longer an unofficial requirement for public office.

The Catholic Church itself had radically changed its social orientation. The Second Vatican Council (1962–65), among other things, gave approval and support to incorporating local customs within religious services (which in the early colonial period had been responsible for the spectacular success of the Catholic Church in Latin America) and gave local bishops and leaders more autonomy within their own countries. In many ways, Vatican II applied the unique traditions of Mexican Catholicism to the entire world.

More importantly perhaps, the Church sought to adapt to changing social, economic and political conditions and urged the faithful to take part in their national affairs. In other words, the Church was no longer an alien, outside entity, but a Mexican one, and the faithful were encouraged to take a proactive, rather than reactive, role in Mexican affairs.

Finally, "liberation theology", beginning in the 1950s in Brazil, became important after the Vatican Council's reforms approved of the Church's activism, particularly in Latin America. Seeking to redefine Christian salvation in terms of helping the poor and oppressed, liberation theologians and their followers sought social justice and redistribution of wealth throughout Latin America. In a way, they wanted an "Institutional Revolution" of their own (in some cases, they openly supported armed ones). On the one hand, the Church had become less alien and more Mexican. On the other, it was a competitor with the PRI for the leadership for social equality in México.

With competition for the hearts and minds of the Mexican believers from traditional Catholics, those who accepted the changes in the Church and the liberation theologians, there were three competing visions of the role of religion within Mexican life. Four, if you count the growing popularity of other religions: Evangelical Protestantism grew tremendously after the 1960s, spurred by U.S. missionaries (operating somewhat clandestinely) and U.S. trained Mexican pastors, especially among indigenous peoples. Seventh-day Adventists, who had been a presence in the Mexican south, Mormons and Jehovah's Witnesses also gained new converts. Per capita, México has more Jehovah's Witnesses than any other country. The Mexican census does not ask religious belief but where the country was once considered to be ninety to ninety-five percent Roman Catholic, the number of Catholics (including those who only consider themselves Catholics because their family follows some Catholic traditions) is now only about eighty percent of the entire population.

Roman Catholicism, the traditional religion in México, had always spoken of a community of believers. Evangelicals and other faiths talked more in terms of personal religious salvation, which made sense to poor people seeking their own individual economic or social betterment. Juárez himself had pointed out that "Protestant virtues"—economic betterment through individual effort, sobriety and thrift—could benefit Mexicans, and Juárez had been the one person responsible for permitting Protestants to openly practice their religion in México. Juárez thought better of the idea, when he said that the people's lives would be drab without fiestas to honor their favorite (Catholic) saint. Mexican Protestants do have a semi-saint of their own—they celebrate Juárez' birthday with their own fiesta in Mexico City.

To the Catholic Church, the Evangelicals were a larger threat than the PRI. To the PRI, the liberation theologians were a force to be co-opted by the official Revolutionary Party before they joined the upstart PRD or one of the other new parties on the left...or joined guerrilla movements, as some did, though more commonly in the Central American republics.[168] Church and State had a mutual interest in better relations.

---

[168] Or more than joined. In Nicaragua, Cardinal Miguel Obando y Bravo, the Archbishop of Managua, sided with the Marxist Sandinista Liberation Movement, and several priests—as in the 1810–20 Mexican War of Independence—became guerrilla fighters.

Beginning in the mid-1970s, Catholic leaders in the United States acted as go-betweens in discussions between the Vatican and the United Mexican States. Beginning with a low-key official visit by Pope John-Paul II in 1979, the thaw in Church-State relations eventually led to an end to official anticlericalism.

John-Paul II had been a leader in modernizing the Church in the 1960s. A Polish cardinal at the time, taking an activist role in his own society meant confronting Communists. John-Paul's importance in bringing down Communist governments in Europe and in the collapse of the Soviet Union is well known. Usually overlooked is that his anticommunism made him a foe of the liberation theologians, who, in seeking to end economic inequality and injustice, often allied themselves with Marxist or Communist movements.

Liberation theologians were frozen out of higher church offices or removed from decision making within the Church. Within México this benefited the traditional pro-Church party, PAN. Encouraged since Vatican II to take a proactive role in public affairs, both the modernists and the traditionalists within the Church overtly supported PAN's candidates and programs.

With PAN's growth (especially after Vicente Fox won the presidency in 2000), the Church took an even more active role in Mexican affairs. Marta Sahagún, Fox's second wife, like Napoleon III's wife, Empress Eugenia, attempted to influence her husband's government in favor of the most conservative elements within the Catholic Church. An influential group of businessmen who were members of Opus Dei,[169] known as *el Yunque* – the Anvil, a symbol of the Spanish Falangists that was adopted by the Mexican Synarchists – were rewarded with government contracts. During the Fox administration, it was noticeable that public university graduates were passed over for appointment to decision-making government posts in favor of the

---

[169] The Spanish-based "Opus Dei" includes both clerics and laity. Religiously and politically conservative, it actively encourages its members to take political and economic leadership positions within their nations.

graduates of the Opus Dei controlled universities, like *Universidad Anáhuac* and the Autonomous University of Guadalajara.

The *Legionarios de Cristo* – Legionnaires of Christ, a Catholic youth movement founded by a synarchist priest in the 1930s and modeled on fascist and Nazi youth movements – obtained some respectability in PAN controlled communities. In Aguascalientes, a long-time Synarchist and PAN stronghold, Legionnaires formed gangs that attacked gays, Protestants, Mormons and indigenous people.[170]

Religion, a taboo subject in Mexican politics for most of the 20th century, was again important. In 2004 a small political party openly campaigned as the party of feminists, indigenous people, gays, the handicapped and Protestants.[171] In Veracruz State, a Mormon church-supported party was active in local elections and the mainstream parties, especially on the local level, began pitching their campaigns to religious voters, or religious minorities. During the 2006 Presidential election, rumors that Andrés Manuel López Obrador was a Protestant (he wasn't, but as a young social worker, he lived and worked in a Protestant community) probably gained the candidate as many votes as it cost him. In troubled areas like Chiapas and Oaxaca, religious differences between communities have led to violence in the 21st century.[172]

---

[170] The Legionnaires may be losing influence. In May 2006, the then eighty-six-year-old founder, Marcial Maciel was censured by Pope Benedict XIV and ordered to retire to a monastery to perform penance for the rest of his life, following investigations into allegations of pedophilia by Father Maciel and into sexual and physical abuse of students by Legionnaire priests in México, Chile and Spain.

[171] In Oaxaca State, a one-armed, Baptist, Zapotec, transgender candidate for Federal Deputy was given respectable coverage by the country's media, though she had no chance of winning the election.

[172] Statistically, the fastest growing religion in México is, surprisingly, Buddhism. However, that is due to an increase in Asian immigration more than conversion, and Buddhists still are less than one-half of one percent of Mexicans. Buddhists, so far, have not run into conflicts with other Mexican religious communities.

The Party's over

As the PRI moved away from its revolutionary roots and adopted "institutional" values, the leadership had less and less in common with the voters. PRI leaders were generally among the best educated people in the country (both Salinas and his successor, Ernesto Zedillo, had earned PhDs at Ivy League universities; Salinas at Harvard, Zedillo at Yale) and spent years working in administrative jobs within the government. That was part of the problem. The PRD and PAN leaders, by contrast, came from backgrounds more suited to competitive political campaigns—Vicente Fox had been a businessman and farm manager; Andrés Manuel López Obrador (the PRD and PRD-led coalition candidate in 2006) had been a social worker and union organizer before entering politics.

PRI—representing a broad coalition of interests—had always worked out their differences privately, eventually agreeing on a course of action. After the 1985 earthquake, when ordinary people, rather than the government, first took an active role in determining what services they would receive, the PRI's internal consensus approach seemed sinister to many or at least alien to the voters.

What the PRI had decided was to forge a closer economic and social relationship with the United States (which may have been a factor in the stolen 1988 elections). The best economic thinking of the time (Salinas was an economist) was that the so-called "Washington Consensus" offered the best plan for better economic conditions in Latin America.

The Washington Consensus was that large international money-lenders (the International Monetary Fund, the Inter-American Development Bank and the U.S. Treasury Department) should lend money to Latin American countries in return for them opening their markets to foreign businesses. As a corollary, it was suggested that governments dispose of government-owned industries and businesses like health services and schools, as well as more obviously income-generating businesses like airlines or telephone companies. The belief was that private businesses—in quest of a profit—would be more efficient and provide better services than government operations, providing a benefit to ordinary people.

What was overlooked was that established foreign businesses—multinational corporations—and already wealthy individuals would be the only ones with the capital to buy government businesses...and that these companies would then seek to maximize their own profits, returning them to their own countries.

That sounded much like the plans Porfirio's científicos had for the Mexican economy in the late 19th century. Then, it was called "liberalism", so the new economically-based political theory became known as "neo-liberalism". Salinas, an enthusiastic neo-liberal, was also pushing for another popular economic and political idea of the time—integrated trading blocs.

The Europeans, after the Second World War, had realized that doing business with each other made more sense than killing each other and had, over fifty years, created a strong economic and political union. Based on their success at dropping trade restrictions between their own countries and doing away with protections for internal markets (like agriculture), other groups of nations had copied the idea in one form or another. Salinas' variation was the North American Free Trade Association (NAFTA) which envisioned "open markets" between the United States, Canada and México. In theory, businesses and workers in any of the three countries could earn income and do business in any of the others within the Free Trade Association. For México, NAFTA was meant to provide more jobs. Manufacturing plants were supposed to migrate from high-labor-cost Canada and the U.S. to México, and Mexican farmers were to be free to sell their lower-cost produce on the open market. For the United States and Canada, the benefit was lower consumer prices and the opportunity to move capital into newer industries like information technology and genetic engineering.

To "sweeten the deal" and sell it to the U.S. and Canada—and in line with neo-liberal thinking—the Salinas administration sold off several government businesses (like the banks, airlines and telephone company) and made changes that seemed to end the revolution. The *ejidos* – the cooperative farms that Lázaro Cárdenas and Adolfo López Mateos had expanded to give land to the land-less – were allowed to be broken up into individually owned farms over the next several years. Many of these farms were too small to survive except in cooperatives (if the ejido owned a tractor, it meant ten or twenty small farmers could plow and harvest each others' crops at one time. As private landowners, none of them could afford a tractor on their own.) Where developers saw a potential for nonagricultural projects—in areas attracting foreigners looking for Mexican property (like in the Baja and other beachfront locations), or near cities, where suburban communities and shopping malls were sprouting up—farmers who didn't see the advantage of selling out were often pressured, or cheated, into selling their land. Even worse for the farmers, the Salinas administration began withdraw-ing subsidies to agricultural producers. The understanding was that NAFTA meant farmers in all three countries would no longer receive government subsidies, but it was politically impossible for the U.S. and Canada to take this step.

Mexican agriculture, which had been sufficient to support the population, declined. The poorest farmers simply gave up, moving either to the Mexican cities, or crossing the border into the U.S. to work as laborers on the larger corporate-owned farms in the U.S.

While, on the whole, there was more money available in México, NAFTA meant an unequal distribution of the results—those who could invest in foreign companies or work for them got richer. Middle-class wages fell and many—especially in rural areas—were economically destroyed by the changes.

Cárdenas and the PRD may not have taken up arms, but a Mayan woman did. Wearing a ski mask to hide her identity, *Comandanta* [sic] Esther led a small contingent of similarly disguised Mayan farmers into San Cristóbal de las Casas, Chiapas on New Year's Day 1994. Armed only with toy AK-47s, the uprising was a protest against the new NAFTA treaty that went into effect that day. Poor farmers like Esther saw themselves as losers in a "new" Mexican state and in a new economic system where their farms would have to compete against mechanized, fertilized and government-sub-sidized corporate-owned agribusinesses in the United States and Canada. Mayan traditionalists, who rejected the constitutional reforms that gave individuals rights over communal rights, joined the rebels, who exchanged their toy guns for real ones.

The army, having eschewed firing on its own people in the years following Tlaltelolco, only halfheartedly took on the rebels. A temporary peace agreement was worked out by the Bishop of Chiapas, and the Zapatista Army of National Liberation – EZLN – was largely left alone. However, Rafael Sebastián Guillén Vicente, though the son of Spanish immigrants and not a Mayan, sym-pathized with some of the goals of the original group and—as a professor with access to the latest technology—recognized that the rebellion could have a wider impact over the Internet than it could back in the Chiapas highlands. As *Subcomandante* Marcos, Guillén crafted an image of the rebels as simple peasants who had mastered modern communications. Marcos mixed jokes and pop culture references (he once sent a taunting public mes-sage to police chiefs signed, "Speedy Gonzales, ¡Arriba! ¡Arriba! ¡Ándale! ¡Ándale!") with his serious critiques of the effects of global commerce on peasant economies in his public statements. What was new in all this was that Marcos and the Zapatistas spread their message worldwide by the Internet. Marcos became an international star, cultivating an image as a ski-masked, post-modern guerrilla mounted on a burro, armed with an AK-47 and a laptop computer. Though the Zapatistas received international support, there were clashes with the military from time to time. Most clashes involved Zapatista communes' land disputes (as part of the settlement, the Zapatistas were given control of their own communities[173]) or religious and political differences with neighboring communities and individuals.

While the political reforms prevented open rebellion, there was low-level violence for several years. PRD and anti-PRI union leaders were assassinated and the untimely death of PAN leader Manuel Clouthier in a car accident seemed suspiciously convenient to the conspiracy minded. Within the PRI, there was open dissention between various factions, as well as serious problems within the administration and the Salinas family itself. Carlos Salinas, who had come into office as a pro-U.S. president, was seen more often as the sinister kingpin of a crime family in the U.S. and México than as a world leader.

With agriculture in rapid decline, one of the few export crops in demand was marijuana. Exporters were becoming exceedingly wealthy, and the suspicion was that Salinas was personally profiting from the business. At the request of the United States, he appointed an army general to oversee narcotics control efforts, only to have the General later exposed as being in the pay of the *narcotraficantes* – drug traffickers. Salinas' personal fortune continued to grow and questions about the family's wealth forced the president to appoint a special prosecutor (his ex-brother-in-law) to look into

---

[173] Traditionally, and constitutionally, communities can become *municipios libres* – free municipalities. Municipios libres have not seceded from the government but they don't recognize its authority within their territory and don't expect any basic government services, like roads, electricity or police protection. Venustiano Carranza used the time-honored right of the communes to create *municipios libres* when he crafted his rationale for the Constitutionalist Army at the beginning of the Revolution.

the matter. The special prosecutor was found dead in his car with his throat slashed and an obviously fake suicide note.

Raúl Salinas, the president's brother, unable to account for the billion dollars he'd spirited out of México to Switzerland, was accused of masterminding the murder. Raúl's guilt was never proven, but no one was ever able to account for the money either. Salinas' sister was later arrested in Switzerland using false papers to recover the funds, and his youngest brother would be murdered in 2004. Salinas himself, at the end of his term, moved first to Cuba and then to Ireland to avoid prosecution. He visits México privately and is believed to still wield power behind the scenes or through protégées like Elba Esther Gordillo Morales.

Gordillo, a former grade school teacher from the Mexico City suburb of Nezahuacóyotl, as head of the party-controlled teachers' union (her rivals tended to fall off buildings or mysteriously shoot themselves), became leader of the *dinosaurios* – dinosaurs – who attempted to maintain PRI control at any cost. PRI reformers, who were pushing for a more democratic PRI that was willing to separate the party from the bureaucracy and unions (similar to reforms proposed for the Communist Party by Mikhail Gorbachev in the Soviet Union) found their leader in Luis Donaldo Colosio Murrieta.

Since Obregón had selected Calles over de la Huerta as his successor, the outgoing president had always chosen his party's next presidential candidate—in effect, the new president. However, reformers had succeeded in forcing the Party to accept a system under which candidates were selected in open committee meetings. Colosio—expected to win easily in 1994—who, like Lázaro Cárdenas, campaigned widely as the "new" face of the Party. The dinosaurios and Salinas were both suspects when Colosio was assassinated at a campaign appearance in Tijuana. His campaign manager, the shoe-shine boy turned economics professor, Ernesto Zedillo, was chosen as the substitute candidate. PAN and PRD had forced the government to agree to international observers and a new election law, but there was no hint of fraud, nor any surprise when Zedillo won easily.

The morning after...

Z EDILLO'S PRIMARY TASK was to clean up the mess left by the Salinas administration. Salinas had a PhD in economics from Harvard, but the economy was a mess, and the peso collapsed three weeks after Zedillo took office. The Salinas administration had imposed temporary, secret currency manipulations and restrictions to prop up the peso and had not informed the incoming Zedillo administration.[174] When the true state of the peso became known after Zedillo's inauguration, the collapse was inevitable. Mexican businesses, earning their income in pesos but owing debts denominated in U.S. dollars, were in serious trouble. Other Latin American countries, especially Brazil, which depended on Mexican markets at the time, also felt the "tequila effect". The Clinton administration in the United States worked out an emergency fifty billion-dollar loan package that allowed the Zedillo administration to stabilize the peso (and, incidentally, to repay the loan early). Zedillo, the accidental president, is mostly

---

[174] The Salinas administration had secretly sold bonds, denominated in dollars, with a value of more than double the foreign reserves of the country. Salinas, in the briefing books for the incoming Zedillo administration had "neglected" to expose this practice. Although the new president, himself an economist, scrambled mightily to try to save the peso, nothing could be done. The peso was finally "floated" the night of December 21, 1994.

remembered for staying out of the way of the reforms and for not contesting the results of the 2000 election, which was very narrowly won by Vicente Fox. Following the end of his term in office, Zedillo returned to Yale University as a professor.

It might also be noted that PAN, as a party, did not win the 2000 election: Vicente Fox ran as the leader of the Alliance for Change coalition. While clerical support for PAN did not hurt any, Fox was presenting his party as a capitalist (as opposed to socialist), democratic alternative to PRI. By including the Green Party and a few smaller left-wing parties in the Alliance, Fox's supporters argued that voting for the PRD or a smaller left-wing party was a wasted vote—that the only way to bring change was to back a single non-PRI candidate—theirs, of course.

In that election, the PRD did poorly, and subsequently faced internal dissension as its various factions fought among themselves. However, it went on to become the party of the left, commanding anywhere from a quarter to more than a third of the national vote, though it remains strongest in Mexico City and a few states. The PRI also faced serious dissent and continued to lose voters and leaders to other parties, but remained the largest single party in the country.

Growing out of the bloodshed of the Revolution, when Huitzilopochtli seemed to stalk the nation, and producing a fair share of Quetzalcóatls along the way, the Mexican system collapsed under the new realities of the post-modern economy and the trickery of Tezcatlipoca-wannabes like Carlos Salinas.

Gods, Gachupines
and Gringos

Modern México

States

1-Aguascalientes
2-Baja California
3-Baja California Sur
4-Campeche

5-Chiapas
6-Chihuahua
7-Coahuila
8-Colima
9-Distrito Federal / México (Mexico City)
10-Durango
11-Guanajuato
12-Guerrero
13-Hidalgo
14-Jalisco
15-México
16-Michoacán
17-Morelos
18-Nayarit

19-Nuevo León
20-Oaxaca
21-Puebla
22-Querétaro
23-Quintana Roo
24-San Luis Potosí
25-Sinaloa
26-Sonora
27-Tabasco
28-Tamaulipas
29-Tlaxcala
30-Veracruz
31-Yucatán
32-Zacatecas

Places

a- Candelaria (Texas)
b- Ciudad Juárez
c- Guadalajara
d- Guanajuato
e- Mexico City (The Capital) Los Pinos
f- Oaxaca
g- San Miguel de Allende

Gulf of Mexico

Pacific Ocean

Sometimes a not-so-great notion...

NAFTA WOULD—OVERALL—MAKE MÉXICO wealthier, but there was serious dislocation in the economy. Even before the trade agreement was finalized, U.S. and Canadian manufacturers, taking advantage of lower labor costs in México, had been moving plants "south of the border" – called *maquiladoras*. A pre-NAFTA agreement, meant partially to avoid Mexican emigration to the United States, allowed the maquiladoras to export their goods to the U.S. as if they were made in the U.S.A. Specifically, the goods were not taxed as imports by the U.S. government.

Creating a huge demand for workers in border communities, several cities like Juárez and Tijuana mushroomed. Public services were strained. In normal communities, business owners and managers spearhead demands for public improvements like expanded sewers and school systems. In the border towns, these leaders were absent, living in communities on the U.S. side and only commuting to México to work. A good number of the residents did not have a stake in the community either, seeing themselves as simply living in these towns for the sake of their job or planning to move elsewhere after earning some money.

As in other boom towns, the floating population included more than its share of social deviants. Mexican border towns had functioned for years as an outlet for activities not tolerated in the United States (liquor consumption during Prohibition and prostitution always) and as a low-cost source of goods and services, legal and otherwise, for people on the U.S. side. Mexican border residents, for their part, bought products, especially agricultural equipment, in border towns in the United States.

Smuggling had always existed (as along any border) and was an important part of the local economy on both sides. Smuggling of local products like cheese, cigarettes and candelilla was often tolerated, or simply ignored by authorities on both sides of the border. Candelilla—the plant used, among other things, for the wax in religious candles—was vital to the economy of the small community of Candelaria, Texas. As the small border community's name indicates, candle making was its only industry. With candelilla sometimes forbidden and sometimes taxed, local authorities looked the other way as rowboats of candelilla crossed the Rio Grande.

Displaced farmers, workers and narcotics traders made some of those small-time smugglers fabulously rich. Carrying narcotics to the U.S. was a natural extension of the smugglers' trade, as was carrying the firearms and currency required by the Mexican criminals from the United States to México. Smuggling people rather than goods was more difficult, but that business also boomed.

One of the assumptions behind the NAFTA agreement was that Mexican wage earners would earn an income more in line with those paid in the United States and would have no reason to emigrate. Along the border, the higher salaries paid in the United States had created a regular pool of workers who "commuted" to the United States, for periods as short as a day to regular career positions. Though a high percentage of the Mexican workers on the U.S. side were not registered aliens, the practice was widely tolerated. In Texas, Arizona and New Mexico, businesses often made informal agreements with families or villages to keep them supplied with workers. One Mexican worker would have the legal document allowing him to work in the U.S., which would be used to pay the worker. The worker listed as "José Gonzales" on the company payroll might be José's nephew or neighbor, but both the workers and the employers benefited.

The social dislocation caused by the Salinas administration's changes in agricultural policy and NAFTA in general fueled the growth of the border communities on the Mexican side, just as social changes in the United States were creating huge growth on their side of the border. U.S. cities near the border, like Phoenix and Houston, were also expanding throughout the late 20th century. Construction workers were in particularly high demand, and Mexican workers were the nearest handy labor source. The growth along the southern U.S. border occurred at the same time that there was a decline in available laborers in the United States, mostly due to a lower birth rate and increased education (college graduates were unlikely to take jobs as farm workers or general laborers). Businesses that depended on low-skilled or low-paid labor throughout the United States came to depend on Mexican (and later, Central American) workers.

Under NAFTA, the assumption that the industries depending on lower-wage workers would naturally move to México proved untrue. By hiring Mexican workers in the United States, some industries (like meat packing) did the opposite of what the experts thought they would. Instead of exporting production, they imported labor. "José Gonzales", who worked for a year or two building houses in Houston before sending his nephew "José Gonzales" to take his place on the construction crew, was replaced by a new kind of Mexican worker.

Desperate to support their families, Mexican workers took any job they could find anywhere in the United States. U.S. industries might import workers, but these workers exported their paychecks. The remittances sent home by workers quickly mounted, becoming an important source of income for families at home. Especially in rural areas, the prosperity of neighbors who received funds from their relations who were working north of the border encouraged young men without prospects of supporting their own families at home to also emigrate north. By 2000, it was not unusual to find entire communities with no adult men under sixty-five residing permanently at home.[175]

While many of those who remained behind in México benefited from remittances (by 2007, remittances became the second largest source of foreign currency in México, after direct business investments), spousal abandonment was becoming a social issue at home, and Mexican men who missed their families, or who saw more opportunity for their families in their new home, asked for their relations to join them in the United States.

The flood of Mexican immigrants into the United States, especially into places that had not traditionally attracted Mexican immigrants, like the Midwest and South, upset existing social patterns. The United States traditionally had distinguished between racial communities, and these communities were either separate or had long-established ways of relating to each other. Communities that were "black" and "white" suddenly found they had to deal with three communities: "black", "white" and "brown".

While many gringos discovered the joys of Mexican cuisine, or began to learn Spanish, others were less likely to welcome the newcomers. Even before the World Trade Center attacks of 11 September 2001, antiforeign prejudices, English-only movements and a general ignorance of México and Mexicans led to anti-Mexican actions and rhetoric not seen or heard since the Mexican-American War of 1846–48. After the 9/11 attacks, antiforeign activities took a sinister turn when fear of terrorists led to greater border security, aimed, it seemed, more at stopping Mexican immigrants than preventing terrorists from entering the country.

The need for workers in the United States, the relatively lax immigration procedures and poverty in México all contributed to what became known as the "illegal alien crisis". Technically, enter-

---

[175] Because so many Tzotzil Mayan men started spending years away from home, working in North Carolina and Georgia, Tzotzil women's traditional *huipile* – blouse (actually the fabric that the blouse is made of) – recently changed for the first time in centuries. To keep in touch with the husbands, married women added a pocket to hold their cell phones.

ing and working in the United States without proper documentation had always been illegal, but until 2002, these technicalities
were generally overlooked by Mexican workers, U.S. employers
and the U.S. Immigration and Naturalization Service. National
security concerns, coupled with the new political popularity of
anti-Mexican (and antiforeign) sentiments, created demands to
make immigration even more difficult. The result was "human
trafficking". Smugglers – called *coyotes* – who before had carried
loads of marijuana or cigarettes or candelilla, found assisting people
crossing into the United States a more profitable industry.

Although conservatives have controlled the presidency since
2000, the Mexican left—and the revolutionary spirit—is by no
means dead. The accomplishments of the Revolution that Díaz
Ordaz could look back on in 1968 with "pride and satisfaction" was
one of the great stories of the 20th century and the changes that
turned a semifeudal backwater into a middle-class nation were
very real. The Revolution had not reached everyone, and there were
still massive numbers of poor. Emigration—to the cities or to the
United States—was only a short-term solution for them. For many
in the middle class, the economic changes resulting from NAFTA
left them angry and frustrated. Their actual earnings dropped as
Mexican businesses faced even cheaper foreign competitors, and
middle class people saw less and less future for their children. The
rich got very rich, and the middle class and poor had more goods
available, but less money to spend.

The growing demand for narcotics in the United States also
created new "entrepreneurs" who did not operate by the normal
rules of commerce or by any rules except those they could enforce
by bribery, intimidation or violence. The social changes—feminism,
gay rights, a growing awareness of environmental concerns—all
fueled a continuing interest in "revolutionary" change. How much
of the call for social change was due to increased interaction with
foreigners and how much to the continual desire for modernity
within México was an open question.

Small change(s)

THE PRD, THE COALITION of the left that Cuauhtémoc Cárdenas put together, became the loudest voice for reforms augmenting social changes, benefiting the poor and the insecure middle class. While the PRD was not (and still is not) nearly as large a party as the PRI or PAN, it did (and does) control Mexico City. Under PRD leadership, the Capital became something of a laboratory for social change. Strict air pollution laws, anti-discrimination ordinances to protect gays and indigenous people, old-age pensions and legal abortions came into Latin America through Mexico City local ordinances.

Under Cuauhtémoc Cárdenas, the city faced serious problems, mostly because the PRI-controlled Federal legislature cut funding for the Federal District government. Statistically, crime did not skyrocket, but media attention and continued complaints (from the PRI) about crime in Mexico City gave the metropolis a bad reputation and injured its tourism industry. Cárdenas often stuck to symbolic gestures, naming a lesbian to an appointed seat in the Federal Chamber of Deputies and convincing the local assembly to appoint a woman, Rosario Robles, as interim "mayor" when he stepped down to run for president (for the third time) in 1999.

In 2000, Cárdenas—hoping to expand his party's appeal to the poor and those who opposed NAFTA—had unwisely tried to appeal to the Zapatistas. The Zapatistas, being mostly traditionalists, wanted little to do with a party that represented modernity, and Mexican voters, who saw the Zapatistas as reactionaries or as dangerous armed guerrillas, overwhelmingly voted for other candidates. Cárdenas stayed on as moral leader of the party, but the new leader was Robles' replacement as "mayor", a former Tabasco-state social worker and union organizer, Andrés Manuel López Obrador.

Having served as head of his home state's Indigenous Institute and as head of the state's Consumer Protection agency, López Obrador was being groomed for higher office within the PRI when he became one of the early dissidents to join Cuauhtémoc Cárdenas in 1988. In 1994, he had been the candidate for governor of Tabasco, losing to Roberto Madrazo, who spent more on his campaign than Bill Clinton did running for President of the United States two years earlier![176] López Obrador became a national figure when, while leading a protest march by indigenous workers in Tabasco, he appeared on television in a blood-splattered shirt following a confrontation with the police. Appointed PRD party president, he moved to Mexico City and in 2000 was elected *Jefe de Gobierno*—effectively governor of México's largest single community and mayor of the largest city in the Americas.

Wildly popular (at one point polling nearly eighty percent as the choice for president among potential voters throughout México), his administration embarked on an ambitious campaign within the

---

[176] Following the election, President Ernesto Zedillo was forced to send a special investigator to look into the campaign irregularities. Santiago Creel Miranda (later the Fox administration's *Secretario de Gobernación*) discovered numerous irregularities, including excessive spending on the campaign. Madrazo's campaign spent approximately seventy million dollars, compared to the Clinton-Gore campaign's reported expenditures of sixty-two and a half million dollars. Creel was not a prosecutor and turned the matter over to the Tabasco State Prosecutor's office, which—being controlled by Madrazo—declined to take any action. Creel was later PAN's candidate for *Jefe de Gobierno* of the Federal District, losing to López Obrador in 2000.

Capital that included everything from new universities and more highways to old-age pensions, youth employment programs and even free circuses and rock concerts. The city formed a partnership with billionaire Carlos Slim Helú to restore historic buildings in the central city and began ambitious programs to improve air and water quality.

Although he was derided by conservatives for some of his administration's initiatives (to improve the lot of prostitutes, the city helped found an old-age home for retired "working girls"), it was assumed he would be elected president on his reputation for honesty and efficient management in 2006.

Mexico City police were notoriously corrupt. When the President still appointed Mexico City's police chief, López Portillo named a childhood friend, Arturo Durazo Moreno to the post. Maybe López Portillo was thinking of the old adage, "it takes a thief to catch a thief." Durazo was a thief. As long as he kept criminals out of the rich neighborhoods, Durazo and his fellow gangsters on the police payroll (including hitmen hired as homicide detectives and fences as theft investigators!), were free to terrorize and rob the poor...and the city coffers.

López Obrador decided to make changes from the bottom up. Instead of a police official or army officer, he appointed a professional in public administration, Marcelo Luis Ebrard Casaubón, to overhaul public security. The administration put more resources into police training and, radically, moved police resources from wealthy neighborhoods to lower-class ones. The Televisa television network mounted a campaign against him, painting him as soft on crime and building support for a mega protest march by middle- and upper-class residents against insecurity in the city. First attacking it as a right-wing plot, López Obrador turned the march to his advantage by turning it into one protesting the Fox administration's lack of assistance in crime prevention.

A minor legal case involving the city's use of a piece of disputed land for an access road to a private hospital was used by both PAN and PRI to move for López Obrador's removal from office on criminal charges. The case eventually collapsed into farce (at one point, three or four "owners"—all connected to PAN—surfaced to claim the disputed access road land, none having any proof to back their claims and all accusing the others of lying for political motives). López Obrador turned himself in—on television—to the authorities, and the judge had no choice but to look at the charges, then threw the case out for lack of merit. Unfortunately for López Obrador, media and political attempts to paint him as corrupt or as a dangerous radical began to stick.

In 2006, López Obrador was the obvious choice to be his own party's candidate. The PRD, being too small to run a credible national campaign, formed a fusion ticket with other small left-wing and centrist parties. Vicente Fox, more in the tradition of PRI than his democratic PAN, attempted to force his party to select a candidate of his own choice, but PAN held primaries similar to those held by U.S. parties. The winning candidate was someone like Salinas or Zedillo, Felipe de Jesús Calderón Hinojosa—a bland, relatively unknown, Ivy league trained economist. Calderón's father had been an early PAN leader who quit the party over its too close adherence to fascism, and Felipe campaigned as a law and order candidate. The PRI candidate was López Obrador's Tabasco nemesis, Roberto Madrazo Pintado. Elba Esther Gordillo, the leader of the national teachers' union who had been expelled from PRI, organized her own party and put up an unknown candidate. A small party formed by uniting the failed feminist-gay-Protestant-indigenous coalition and a few small regional socialist and social-democratic parties, also ran a candidate.

The United States, which after the 11 September 2001 attacks attributed to the Al Qaeda terrorist organization had gone to war against Iraq and Afghanistan, made border security a political issue. When the United States was attacked, México was a member of the United Nations Security Council. Although the Fox administration faced serious economic and political pressure to support the U.S. invasion, over ninety percent of Mexicans opposed Mexican involvement in the war, and México's Ambassador to the United

Nations refused to break his country's tradition of nonintervention in other nation's disputes. The PRD and PRD-controlled groups had been the loudest opponents of Mexican involvement, and the George W. Bush administration began to worry about the effects of a leftist México, especially when other Latin American countries were electing left-wing or socialist leaders unfriendly to the United States or hostile to U.S.-based business interests.

After the attacks, many in the U.S. saw all foreigners as a threat. Mexican nationals and the growing number of Mexicans emigrating to the United States had been a sore point for the extreme right for years. Until the attacks, however, anti-Mexican prejudices were motivated by the same factors that had always existed in the United States—anti-Catholicism, racism or the simple dislike of non-English speakers. However, the attacks made anti-Mexican—and anti-immigrant—rhetoric and political positions respectable. Although the people who attacked New York in 2001 entered the United States through Canada or Great Britain, there were calls to seal the Mexican border on the assumption that a terrorist COULD enter the country. Added to the already anti-immigrant rhetoric were stories—by mostly unknown fascist and white supremacist groups—of a plot by the Mexican government to take back lands ceded in 1848 and claims that drug smugglers would make common cause with Middle-Eastern terrorists.

The term *Reconquista* (originally referring to the Castilian conquest of Moorish—Muslim—Spain) had been discussed by Mexican and Mexican-American intellectuals. They were talking about the Mexicanization of border culture—Tex-Mex food, Spanglish (the border creole of English and Spanish regularly used in the region) and Mexican architectural styles being reinterpreted in the United States and naturalized in the region. However, even otherwise reputable news organizations used ALL references to reconquista as evidence of the "plot".

With even reputable politicians calling for stricter immigration policies and armed guards and fences along the border, immigrants protested. Mexican consulates in the United States (like other foreign consulates) provided services and documentation to their citizens and had no reason to distinguish between those who had entered the United States legally and those who didn't. The "illegal aliens" had committed no crime in México, and there was no reason for their consulates not to help these immigrants. However, the assistance given their compatriots, coupled with the immigrant protests, fueled anti-Mexican sentiment in the United States. Relations between the Fox administration and the Bush administration deteriorated. There was genuine fear in Washington of how the Mexican government would respond if a less friendly administration came to power.

López Obrador was not campaigning on a simple antigringo platform, but he was looking to renegotiate NAFTA to correct imbalances in agricultural and industrial policy, for continued Mexican government ownership of PEMEX and for loosening economic ties to the United States in favor of closer ties to Latin America, the European Union and the Asian countries. In U.S. media, he was described as a "fiery leftist" or a "populist". "Populism"—in mass media publications and even in military manuals—was described as a threat to the United States second only to foreign terrorism. Whether dispatched by the Bush administration or hired on their own, U.S. political consultants working for Calderón used every opportunity to describe López Obrador as a dangerous radical, a megalomaniac or simply a person wasteful of public resources. The charges stuck, and as election day neared, López Obrador's polling numbers fell. His own political missteps—blaming a "plot" by Carlos Salinas for every attack on his administration[177]—and his open disdain for rivals (at one point refusing to show up for a televised presidential debate)—cost him further support.

---

[177] Which turned out in one case to be true. Salinas provided funds for an Argentine businessman—who was incidentally Rosario Robles' boyfriend—to bribe some members of the López Obrador administration, which the businessman filmed. When an arrest warrant was issued, he fled to Cuba, where he stayed in a house owned by Salinas. The Federal government would not press for his extradition, but the Cubans arrested him on a warrant from Mexico City's local prosecutor.

With five candidates, no one expected any one candidate to receive a huge majority, but it appeared that López Obrador would be elected president on 6 July 2006. However, as vote counting progressed, a statistically improbable number of votes for Calderón came in, putting the PAN candidate only .58 percent ahead of his rival.

Many of the disputed election results came from the State of Oaxaca, where a long-running dispute between a dissident local and the national teacher's union had escalated into street violence. The dissident teachers, trying to dislodge Elba Esther Gordillo and push other reforms, had regularly gone on strike every May. A Gordillo ally, Ulises Ernesto Ruiz Ortiz, was the PRI governor, having been elected the previous year in a election marked by open fraud, voter intimidation and...high comedy—the outgoing governor, to bolster claims that the opposition was resorting to violence, tried to claim he was the victim of an assassination attempt but was forced to admit the glass fragments that hit him were self-inflicted wounds when his own bodyguards had shot into his car.

Ruiz, in addition to breaking with tradition by confronting the striking teachers, sent in police to dislodge them from the center of Oaxaca City, where he had made himself even more unpopular by "refurbishing the center" and removing traditional small business and sidewalk vendors in favor of foreign chains and businesses catering to tourists and foreigners. Anti-NAFTA protesters, peasants ruined by new agricultural policies and even some foreign residents joined the growing protests. Ruiz, Gordillo and Calderón all blamed López Obrador. When a freelance American photographer was killed during one protest, the international outcry gave the Fox administration a rationale for sending in the military and the paramilitary national police to put down the disturbances.

As in 1988, there were suspicions of fraud and of clandestine U.S. involvement in the outcome of the presidential election. The PRD and its allies initially refused to accept the results, blocking Calderón from taking the oath of office in the Congressional Chambers (he was sworn in hastily at Los Pinos, the presidential residence) and blockading streets in Mexico City. The left only recognized Calderón as "de facto president" with many maintaining López Obrador—who, like Manuel Clothier, set up an alternative presidency—was the "legitimate president".

Huitzilopochtli, Tezcatlipoca and Quetzalcóatl—if they are still around—have not clearly revealed themselves...yet.

Now, back to the future...

THE UNITED STATES AND MÉXICO share a common border, but have hugely different histories and cultures. More Mexicans are moving to the United States, and more people from the United States move to México every year (English is now the second most widely spoken language in México, edging out Náhuatl, Mayan and German.[178])

The rest of the world is also more aware of México and the Mexicans. A recent television commercial featured a young, unhappy Mexican searching and finding happiness and home-cooking (and the bouillon cubes being advertised) in a Mexican restaurant...in Beijing! In a Corona Beer commercial, the Red Army performs the Mexican Hat Dance in Moscow's Red Square. Israeli high school students, and not just the offspring of those Jews who found refuge in Latin America, are eager to learn Spanish. Why? Because they want to watch Mexican telenovelas without having to read subtitles! Unionized Mexico City prostitutes and "exotic"

---

[178] It's a question for linguists to resolve whether the various mutually unintelligible words used by different Mayan groups are separate languages or dialects of the same language. The number of German speakers has declined over the last several decades, though it is still widely spoken in Chihuahua and Coahuila, especially by Mennonites.

dancers complain to the authorities about South American, Polish and Russian "illegal aliens" cutting into their business. Mexican election officials helped set up elections around the world, for countries as different as East Timor, South Africa and Iraq. In Baghdad, voters in Iraq's 2005 legislative election used Mexico City ballot boxes and voting stations. An Indian computer firm recently "offshored" software development to Guadalajara.

In the short-term, the López Obrador alternative presidency appears to be nothing more threatening than a "think tank" and training school for future leaders. Calderón's administration, having begun with a military operation against drug dealers, appears to be fostering better relations with the United States. Domestically, the administration has been supporting—or not blocking—leftist programs, possibly hoping, like previous administrations, to co-opt the opposition. Although PAN is still proclerical, gay marriages were legalized in both the State of Coahuila and the Federal District in 2007. Abortion laws were liberalized in the Federal District. Election laws were changed to meet objections raised by PRD and PRI politicians after the 2006 elections.

While the United States continues to identify Mexican immigrants as a threat and pushes ahead with border security measures, some measures have already been scaled back, and there is growing opposition in U.S. border communities to new security measures which interfere with normal commerce and social intercourse.

México—the world's tenth largest economy—is focusing on new challenges like global warming and environmental depredation. Clandestine logging is seen by many Mexicans to be a more serious national security threat than drug dealing, and the Calderón administration has launched an ambitious project to plant a billion trees over the next six years. Mexico City's latest Jefe de Gobierno, the former police chief Marcelo Ebrard, made worldwide news when he ordered all city employees to ride bicycles to work at least one morning a month.

Mexican radio stations—even Zapatista stations—play foreign rock 'n' roll...and the foreigners keep coming. Already in the top five tourist destinations in the world, increasing numbers of foreigners are moving to México.

Foreigners, particularly retirees from the United States and Canada, learning that México is a relatively inexpensive, stable place to live, flood into the country (unlike most countries, México offers renewable, nonimmigrant visas). English became almost as common as Spanish in a few communities, notably the area around Lake Chapala in Jalisco State and San Miguel de Allende in Guanajuato State (which has attracted foreigners since the odd couple of popular historical novelist James Michener and antiestablishment cult figure Neil Cassady popularized the small town).

While a few gringos come to México to pursue careers or business opportunities or to find a wife, still others come in search of a less stressful and "traditional" Mexican society. Most are retirees, satisfied to live out their lives someplace with a lower cost of living and a slower pace than they knew in their own wealthier countries. Some bitterly complain that México is too modern, but a number have followed in Vasco de Quiroga's footsteps, finding a new career fomenting social change.

Besides retirees from the United States and Canada, large numbers of Koreans, Chinese, Russians, Ukrainians, Congolese, Ethiopians and Middle Easterners have come as economic or political refugees. Even the gachupines are back.* Spanish-owned banks, construction companies, power plants and oilfield service providers are only the most visible sign that the former colonial power again recognizes México's potential wealth.

The Mexicans will interpret whatever happens in terms of their own history. When Felipe Calderón sent the army after narcotics dealers, some commentators thought of both colonial-era Inspector de Gálvez and Don Porfirio's Rurales. López Obrador and Vicente Fox both made use of Madero in calling for resistance to entrenched

---

* Editor's note: 15 January 2008 President Calderón appointed Juan Camilo Mouriño Terrazo *Secretario de Goberación*, the second most powerful post in the Mexican government. Mouriño Terrazo, scion of a wealthy Spanish family, is a citizen of Spain and only a naturalized citizen of México—a real gachupín.

power. Is Subcomandante Marcos' post-modern, Internet, revolutionary propaganda all that different from Morelos' printing press, or Madero's press conferences, or Pancho Villa's movies? Are *Empanadas Ruso*—sold by Russian immigrants—a new cuisine, or just another variation on the traditional foods?

Is the world more Mexican, or México more like the rest of the world? Mexicans continue to incorporate new ideas and new peoples into their own culture. The Gringos and Gachupines are not going away...nor for that matter are the Mexicans. And the Gods are eternal.

Aztec and Mayan calendars were circular for a reason—they did not believe in the "march of time". To the ancient peoples, things might not happen exactly the same way when we return to the same point on the calendar, but what happened in the past could happen in the present and in the future.

"Alas, poor México...too far from God, too close to the United States!" Porfirio Díaz once joked. Perhaps Don Porfirio had things backwards. Poor México...not far enough from Huitzilopochtli, Tezcatlipoca or Quetzalcóatl...and too much a part of this world.

Bibliography

Because this book is for English speakers, I've cited the standard English translation or reprint wherever possible, even if I read the work in Spanish. H. G. Ward's *Journal of a Residence and Tour in the Republic of México in 1826* is the exception. I doubt Ward's book is available anywhere outside of a few libraries, but the Spanish translation listed here is more accessible. With novels, I haven't been consistent: if I read a book in Spanish, I give the Spanish-language edition. If I read it in translation, I give that citation. B. Traven wrote in German, but was his own English translator. Most of his books are still in print, in German, English and Spanish.

I can't count the number of websites I consulted, mostly to double-check dates and spelling. Especially useful were the Internet Movie Database (imdb.com); *Borderlands*, an online magazine published by the El Paso Community College (http://www.epcc. edu/nwlibrary/borderlands/index.htm); and the Latin American Network Information Center of the University of Texas (http:// lanic.utexas.edu/). Where a website is the standard reference, or the source for specific data, I have included the link in the bibliographical listing.

For recent events (after about 2000), I relied heavily on news-papers, especially *el Universal, la Jornada* and *Milenio de Hoy*, all Mexico City dailies. To a lesser extent, I also consulted *Cronica de Hoy, Desde de Fé, Nuevo Excelsior* and *El Financiero*, also Mexico City newspapers, as well at the national news publications *Siempre, Proceso, Mexico Business* and *Narco News Bulletin*. Online U.S. pub-lications, especially the *Los Angeles Times*, the *Houston Chronicle* and the *Arizona Republic*, as well as the *New York Times*, the *Nation, Counterpunch* and *Raw Story* were also combed for contemporary information.

Kelly Arthur Garrett, of the former *Mexico City Herald*, is THE "guru" on contemporary Mexican politics, and his columns and articles were consulted religiously.

_____*Black/Brown: Shared Lineage in México*. 2001 (http://www. angelfire.com/journal/issues/mex.html)

_____*Calles de México*. México: García Hnos., 1924

_____*Costumbres y tradiciones del istmo de Tehuantepec*. (http:// www.itistmo.edu.mx/www2/cronologia.html)

_____*Historias y leyendas*. México: García Hnos., 1924

_____*El Niño Fidencio Curandismo Research Project*. Brownsville: The University of Texas at Brownsville & Texas Southmost College (http://vpea.utb.edu/elnino/fidencio.html)

Altamirano, Ignacio M. *La Navidad en las montañas*. México: Editorial Jus, 1998

Arthur, Anthony. *Radical Innocent: Upton Sinclair*. New York: Random House, 2006

Azuela, Mariano. *Los al abajo*. México: Fundo de cultura económica, 1960

Becker, Marjorie. *Setting the Virgin on Fire: Lázaro Cárdenas, Michoacán Peasants, and the Redemption of the Mexican Revolution*. Berkeley and Los Angeles: University of California Press, 1995

Brandenburg, Frank Ralph. *The Making of Modern Mexico.* Englewood Cliffs, NJ: Prentice Hall, 1964

Breeden, Francis F. *The Essential Codex Mendoza.* Berkeley: University of California Press, 1997

Brenner, Anita. *The Wind that Swept Mexico.* Austin: University of Texas Press, 1971 (reprint of 1944 edition)

Brenner, Anita (Photos by Edward Weston and Tina Modetti). *Idols Behind Altars.* Cheshire, CT: Biblo & Tannen, 1929 (reprint)

Brown, Jonathan C. *Oil and Revolution in México.* Berkeley: University of California Press, 1993

Burroughs, William S. *Junky.* Hammondsworth: Penguin Books, 1971

Burroughs, William S. *Queer: A Novel.* Hammondsworth: Penguin Books, 1986

Cabeza de Vaca, Álvar Nuñez (Roleno Adrono and Patrick Charles Pautz, trans. and eds.). *The Narrative of Cabeza de Vaca.* Lincoln and London: University of Nebraska Press, 2003

Calderón de la Barca, Francis Erskine (Fanny) (Howard T. and Marian Hall Fisher, eds.). *Life in Mexico.* Boston: Doubleday and Company, 1966 (reprinted many, many times since 1841)

Carrasco, David and Scott Sessions. *Daily Life of the Aztecs.* Westport, CT: Greenwood Press, 1998

Chamberlain, Samuel E. *My Confessions.* New York: Harper and Brothers, 1956

Clendennon, Inga. *Aztecs: An Interpretation.* Cambridge: Cambridge University Press, 1993

Coe, Michael D. *The Maya: Fifth edition, fully revised and expanded.* London: Thames and Hudson, 1993

Cortés, Hernán (Anthony Padgett, trans.). *Letters From Mexico.* New Haven, CT: Yale University Press, 1986

Cumberland, Charles C. *México: The Struggle for Modernity.* New York: Oxford University Press, 1968

Díaz del Castillo, Bernal (Genaro García, eds; A. P. Maudslay, trans.) *The Discovery and Conquest of México 1517–1521.* New York: Da Capo Press, 1996

Diaz, Gisele and Alan Rodgers. *Codex Borgia: A Full-Color Restoration of the Ancient Mexican Manuscript.* Mineola, NY: Dover Publications, 1993

Directorate for Science, Technology and Industry. *National tourism policy review: tourism policy and trends in Mexico.* Organization for Economic Cooperation and Development, October 2001 (http://www.oecd.org/dataoecd/43/54/33650486.pdf)

Dulles, John W. F. *Yesterday in Mexico: A Chronicle of the Revolution.* Austin: University of Texas Press, 1961

Eisenhower, John S. D. *Intervention! The United States and the Mexican Revolution, 1913–1917.* New York and London: W. W. Norton, 1993

Eisenhower, John S. D. *So Far from God: The U.S. War with Mexico, 1846–1848.* Norman: University of Oklahoma Press, 2000

Fehrenbach, T. R. *Fire and Blood: A History of México.* New York: Collier Books, 1973

Fuentes, Carlos (Alfred Macadam, trans). *The Years With Laura Díaz.* New York: Farrar, Straus & Giroux, 1998

Fuentes, Carlos. *La Muerte de Artemio Cruz.* México: Fundo de cultura económica, 1962

Fuentes, Carlos. *La región mas transparente.* México: Fundo de cultura económica, 1958

Fuentes, Carlos. *Gringo Viejo.* México: Fundo de cultura económica, 1985

Fuentes Mares, José. *Poinsett, historia de una gran intriga.* México: Ediciones Océano, 1982

Glusker, Susan Joel. *Anita Brenner: A Mind of Her Own.* Austin: University of Texas Press, 1998

Grabman, Richard. *Life in the Fast Lane (Doesn't Have to Make You Lose Your Mind).* México: Gordon Jardine y Asoc, S.C., 2004

Grabman, Richard. *Bosques' War: How a Mexican diplomat saved 40,000 from the Nazis (and maybe prevented World War III)*. Mazatlán, Sinaloa: Editorial Mazatlán, 2007

Grant, Ulysses Simpson. *Personal Memoirs of U.S. Grant*. New York: Charles A. Webster & Co., 1885 (several modern reprints available).

Grayson, George W. *Mexican Messiah: Andrés Manuel López Obrador*. University Park: Pennsylvania State University Press, 2007

Greene, Graham. *Lawless Roads*. London: Penguin, 1947

Greene, Graham. *Another Mexico*. New York: Viking Press, 1982

Greene, Graham. *The Power and the Glory*. New York: Viking, 1962

Guzmán, Martín Luis. *The Eagle and the Serpent*. New York: Knopf, 1930

Guzmán, Martín Luis. *The Memoirs of Pancho Villa*. Austin: University of Texas Press, 1965

Hall, Linda B. *Alvaro Obregón: Power and Revolution in México, 1911–1920*. College Station: Texas A & M University Press, 1981

Hall, Linda B. *Oil, Banks and Politics: The United States and Postrevolutionary México 1917–1924*. Austin: University of Texas Press, 1995

Harding, Bettina. *Phantom Crown: The Story of Maximiliano and Carlota of Mexico*. New York: Halcyon House, 1934 (reprinted by Ediciones Tolteca, 1967 and later).

Haring, C. H. *Empire in Brazil: A New World Experiment with Monarchy*. New York: W. W. Norton & Company, Inc., 1968

Harris, Charles H. III and Louis R. Sadler. *The Texas Rangers and the Mexican Revolution: The Bloodiest Decade, 1910–1920*. Albuquerque: University of New Mexico Press, 2004.

Hart, John. *Revolutionary Mexico*. Berkeley: University of California Press, 1987

Hawley, Chris. "New Battleground". *Arizona Republic,* August 27, 2005 (on campaign spending by Roberto Madrazo in the 1994 Tabasco governor's race).

Haslip, Joan. *The Crown of Mexico*. New York: Holt Reinhart & Winston, 1971

Henderson, John S. *The World of the Ancient Maya: Second Edition*. Ithaca, NY and London: Cornell University Press, 1997

Henríquez Escobar, Graciela and Armando Hitzelin Egido Villarreal. *Santa María la Ribera y sus historias*. México: Consejo Nacional para la Cultura y las Artes and Universidad Nacional Autónoma de México, 1995

Hochschild, Adam. *King Leopold's Ghost*. Boston: Houghton Mifflin, 1998

Hogan, Michael. *The Irish Soldiers of México*. Guadalajara, Jalisco: Fondo Editorial Universitario, 1997.

Hughes, Langston. *The Collected Poems of Langston Hughes*. New York, Vintage Classics, 1995

Hughes, Langston. *The Ways of White Folks*. New York: Vintage Classics, 1990

Hughes, Sallie. *Newsrooms in Conflict: Journalism and the Democratization of Mexico*. Pittsburg, PA: University of Pittsburg Press, 2006

Jones, Terry. *Patron Saints Index*. Catholic Community Forum (http://www.catholic-forum.com/saints/indexsnt.htm)

Kandell, Jonathan. *La Capital: The Biography of Mexico City*. New York: Random House, 1988

Katz, Friedrich. *The Secret War in Mexico: Europe, the United States and the Mexican Revolution*. Chicago and London: University of Chicago Press, 1981

Katz, Friedrich. *The Life and Times of Pancho Villa*. Stanford, CA: Stanford University Press, 1988

Kerouac, Jack. *On the Road*. New York: Viking Press, 1957

King, Rosa E. *Tempest Over Mexico: A Personal Chronicle*. Boston: Little Brown, Company, 1935 (available as a download from: http://tempestoverMéxico.com).

Krauze, Enrique. *Álvaro Obregón: El vértigo de la victoria*. México: Fondo de cultura económica, 1987

Krauze, Enrique (Hank Heifetz, trans). *Mexico: Biography of Power – a History of Modern Mexico 1810–1996.* New York: Harper Perennial, 1997

Krauze, Enrique. *Emiliano Zapata: El amor a la tierra.* México: Fondo de cultura económica, 1994

Krauze, Enrique. *General misionero: Lázaro Cárdenas.* México: Fondo de cultura económica, 1987

De las Casas, Bartolomé. (Nigel Griffin, trans.). *A Short Account of the Destruction of the Indies.* London: Penguin Books, 1995 (originally published 1552 as *Brevisima Relación de La Destrucción de Las Indias* and in English since about 1560, there are too many translations and editions to chose from. The Penguin edition is the most accessible.)

Lawrence, D(avid) H(erbert). *The Plumed Serpent.* Ware, Herfordshire: Wordsworth Editions, 1995 (first printed in 1926)

Lenchek, Shep. *Jews in Mexico: A Struggle for Survival.* MexConnect, 2000 (http://www.mexconnect.com/mex_/travel/slenchek/sljewsinMexico1.htm)

Leo XIII (Pope). *Rerum novarum: Encyclical of Pope Leo XIII On Capital and Labor (15 May 1891).* Vatican City: Libreria Editrice Vaticana (http://www.vatican.va/holy_father/leo_xiii/encyclicals/documents/hf_l-xiii_enc_15051891_rerum-novarum_en.html)

Lewis, Oscar. *Five Families.* New York: Basic Books, 1959

Lewis, Oscar. *The Children of Sanchez: Autobiography of a Mexican Family.* New York: Random House, 1961

López Obrador, Andrés Manuel. *La mafias nos roba la Presidencia.* México: Grijalbo, 2007

Lowery, Malcolm. *Under the Volcano.* New York: Vintage Books, 1958

Marine Corps Heritage Foundation. *Lore of the Corps.* Triangle, Virginia: National Museum of the Marine Corps, 2006 (http://www.usmcmuseum.org/Museum_LoreCorps.asp)

Matthews, Matt, C. *The U.S. Army on the Mexican Border: A Historical Perspective*. Combat Studies Institute Press, Fort Leavenworth, Kansas. 2007 (http://usacac.army.mil/CAC/csi/RandP/OP22.pdf)

Meyer, Michael C. and William H. Beezley (eds.). *The Oxford History of Mexico*. Oxford: Oxford University Press, 2000

Morris, Walter E., Jr. and Jeffrey J. Foxx. *Living Maya*. New York: Harry N. Abrams, Inc., 1987

Niemeyer, E. V. *Revolution at Querétaro: The Mexican Constitutional Convention of 1916–1917*. Austin: University of Texas Press, 1974

Obregón, Álvaro. *Ocho mil kilómetros en campaña*. México: Fondo de cultura económica, 1959

Parks, Henry Bamford. *A History of Mexico*. Boston: Houghton Mifflin Co., 1960 (long out of date)

Paz, Octavio. *El laberinto de la soledad*. México: Fundo de cultura económica, 1970 (As *The Labyrinth of Solitude*, also available in English in several different editions).

Peña, José Enrique de la (Carmen Perry, trans. and ed.). *With Santa Anna in Texas: A Personal Narrative of the Revolution*. College Station: Texas A & M University Press, 1975

Pitner, Ernst (Gordon Etherington-Smith, trans.). *Maximillian's Lieutenant: A Personal History of the Mexican Campaign, 1864–7*. Albuquerque: University of New Mexico Press, 1993

Poniatowska, Elena (Helen R. Lane, trans). *Massacre in Mexico*. New York: Viking, 1975

Poniatowska, Elena (Deanna Heikkinen, trans.). *Here's to You, Jesusa!* New York: Farrar, Straus and Giroux, 2001

Porter, Katherine Anne. *The Collected Stories of Katherine Anne Porter*. np: New American Library, 1970

Prescott, William Hickling. *A History of the Conquest of Mexico & A History of the Conquest of Peru*. np: Modern Library, nd (originally published in 1843 and 1847 respectively)

Quinonesk, Eloise and Eloise Quinones Keber (eds.). *Codex Telleriano-Remensis: Ritual, Divination and History in a*

Pictorial Aztec Manuscript. Austin: University of Texas Press, 1995

Real Academia Española. *Diccionario de la lengua española, vigésima primera edición*. Madrid: Editorial Espasa Calpe, 1992.

Reed, John. *Insurgent Mexico*. New York: International Publishers, 1969 (reprint of the 1914 book)

República de México, Constitución Federal de 1917 con reformas hasta 2004. *Constitución Política de los Estados Unidos Mexicanos*. Base de datos políticos de las Américas, 2007 (http://pdba.georgetown.edu/Constitutions/Mexico/Mexico2004.html)

Riding, Alan. *Distant Neighbors: A Portrait of the Mexicans*. New York: Vintage Books, 1985

Ridley, Jasper. *Maximilian and Juarez*. New York: Tichnor and Fields, 1992

Ross, John. *Zapatistas: Making Another World Possible: Chronicles of Resistance 2000–2006*. New York: Nationbooks, 2006

Ruiz, Ramón Eduardo. *Triumphs and Tragedy: A History of the Mexican People*. New York: W. W. Norton & Company, 1992

Schwartz, Stuart B. (ed.). *Victor and Vanquished: Spanish and Nahua Views of the Conquest of Mexico*. New York: Bedford/St. Martins, 1999

Simpson, Leslie Beard. *Many Mexicos*. Berkeley: University of California Press, 1961

Soares, Andre. *Beyond Paradise: The Life of Ramon Novarro*. New York: St. Martins Press, 2002

Soustelle, Jacques (Patricia O'Brien, trans.). *Daily Life of the Aztecs*. New York: Macmillan, 1962 (originally published in French, 1911)

Stevens, Peter F. *The Rogue's March: John Riley and the St. Patrick's Battalion, 1846–48*. Sterling, VA: Potomac Press, 2005

Taibo II, Paco Ignacio (William I. Neuman, trans.). *No Happy Ending*. Scottsdale, AZ: Poisoned Pen Press, 2003

Taibo II, Paco Ignacio (Laura Dali, trans.). *Return to the Same City*. New York: Mysterious Press, 1996

Tannenbaum, Frank. *Mexico: The Struggle for Peace and Bread*. New York: Alfred A. Knopf, 1950

Tannenbaum, Frank. *Peace by Revolution: An Interpretation of Mexico*. New York: Columbia University Press, 1933

Thomas, Hugh. *Conquest: Cortés, Montezuma and the Fall of Old Mexico*. New York: Simon and Schuster, 1993

Timmons, Wilbert H. *Morelos of México: Priest, Soldier, Statesman*. El Paso: Texas Western Press, 1963

Tolliver, Ruby C. *Santa Anna: Patriot or Scoundrel*. Houston: Hendrick-Long Publishing Co., 1993 (A juvenile history, but a relatively decent introduction to Santa Ana.)

Traven, B. *La Rosa Blanca*. México: Cia. General de ediciones, S.A., 1971

Traven, B. *The Treasure of the Sierra Madre*. np: Hill and Wang, 1984

Traven, Bruno (Alfredo Cahn, trans.). *Un puente en la selva*. México, D F: Ediciones populares, nd

Trollope, Anthony. *The Way We Live Now*. Ware, Herfordshire: Wordsworth Editions, 2001

Tuchman, Barbara W. *The Zimmerman Telegram*. New York: Macmillan, 1966

Tuck, Jim. *Pancho Villa and John Reed*. Tucson: University of Arizona Press, 1984

Tuck, Jim. *Sexenios in a Changing World: López Mateos and Diaz Ordaz (1909–1970) – (1911–1970)*. MexConnect, 1999 (http://www.mexconnect.com/mex_/history/jtuck/jtmateosyordaz.html)

Tuck, Jim. *High Hopes, Baffling Uncertainty: Mexico Nears the Millennium Carlos Salinas de Gortari – President 1988–1994*. MexConnect, 1999 (http://www.mexconnect.com/mex_/history/jtuck/jtsalinas.html)

Turner, John Kenneth. *Barbarous Mexico*. Austin: University of Texas Press, 1982 (reprint of 1912 edition). Available widely in México (where it is required reading in most history courses) as *"México Bárbaro"*.

Vincent, Ted. *Black Indian Mexico*. (http://members.aol.com/_ ht_a/fsln)

Ward, H. G. *México en 1826*. México: Fondo de cultura económica, 1986 (Excerpts from Ward's two-volume *Journal of a Residence and Tour in the Republic of México in 1826*.)

Wilkie, James W. *The Mexican Revolution: Federal Expenditure and Social Change since 1910*. Berkeley and Los Angeles: University of California Press, 1970.

Wilson, Henry Lane. *Diplomatic Days in Mexico, Belgium and Chile*. Garden City, NY: Doubleday Page and Company, 1927

Womack, John. *Zapata and the Mexican Revolution*. New York: Knopf, 1969

Zapata, Luis (E. A. Lacey, trans.). *Adonis García: A Picaresque Novel*. San Francisco: Gay Sunshine Press, 1981

Zavala y Alonso, Manuel. *Artes y historia México*. (http://www. arts-history.mx/)

Index
places and people...mostly